YOT A&! 8

KIYOHIKO AZUMA

CONTENTS

YOTSUBA&!
KIYOHIKO AZUMA

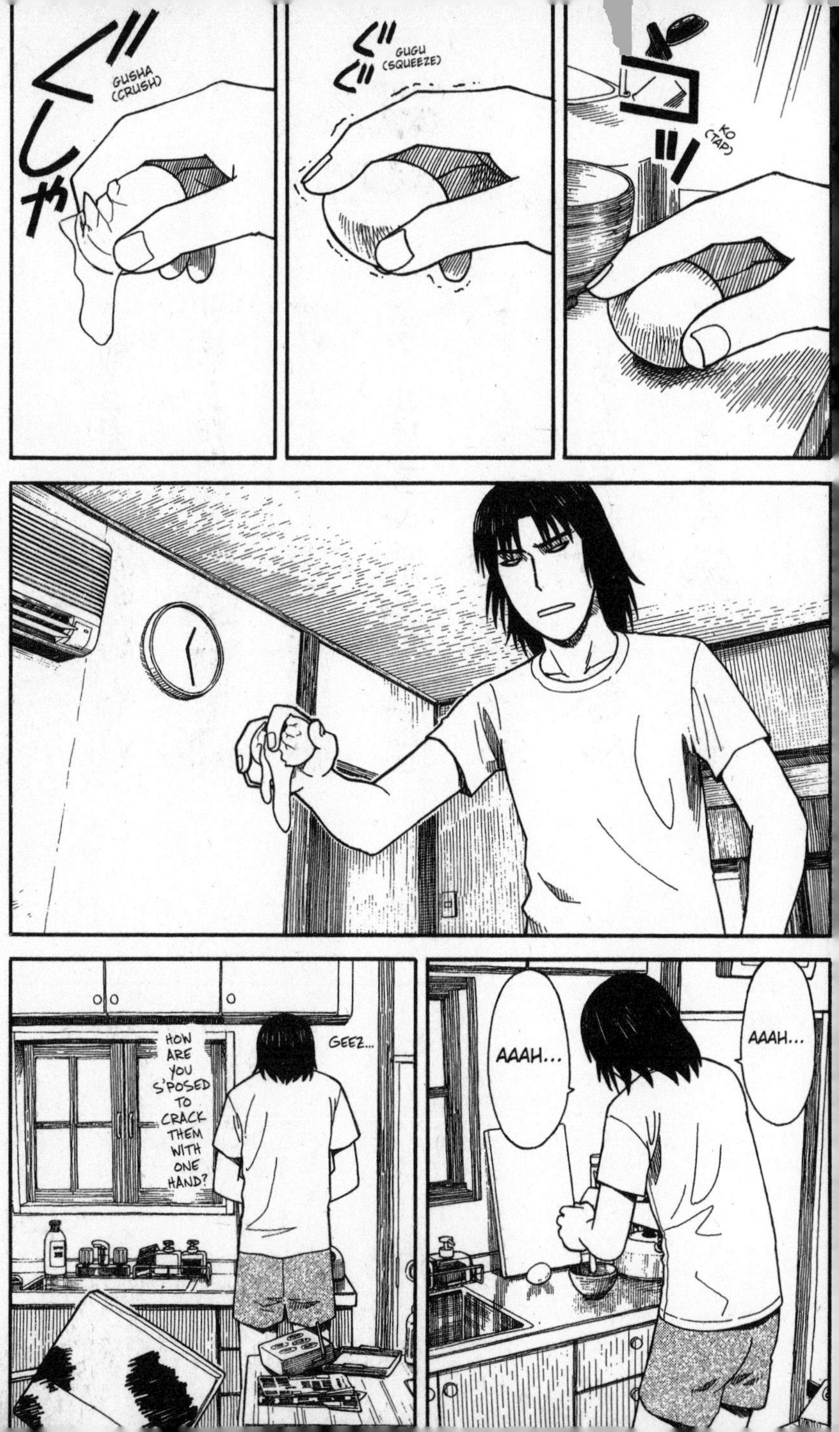
KO (TAP)
GUGU (SQUEEZE)
GUSHA (CRUSH)
AAAH...
AAAH...
GEEZ...
HOW ARE YOU S'POSED TO CRACK THEM WITH ONE HAND?

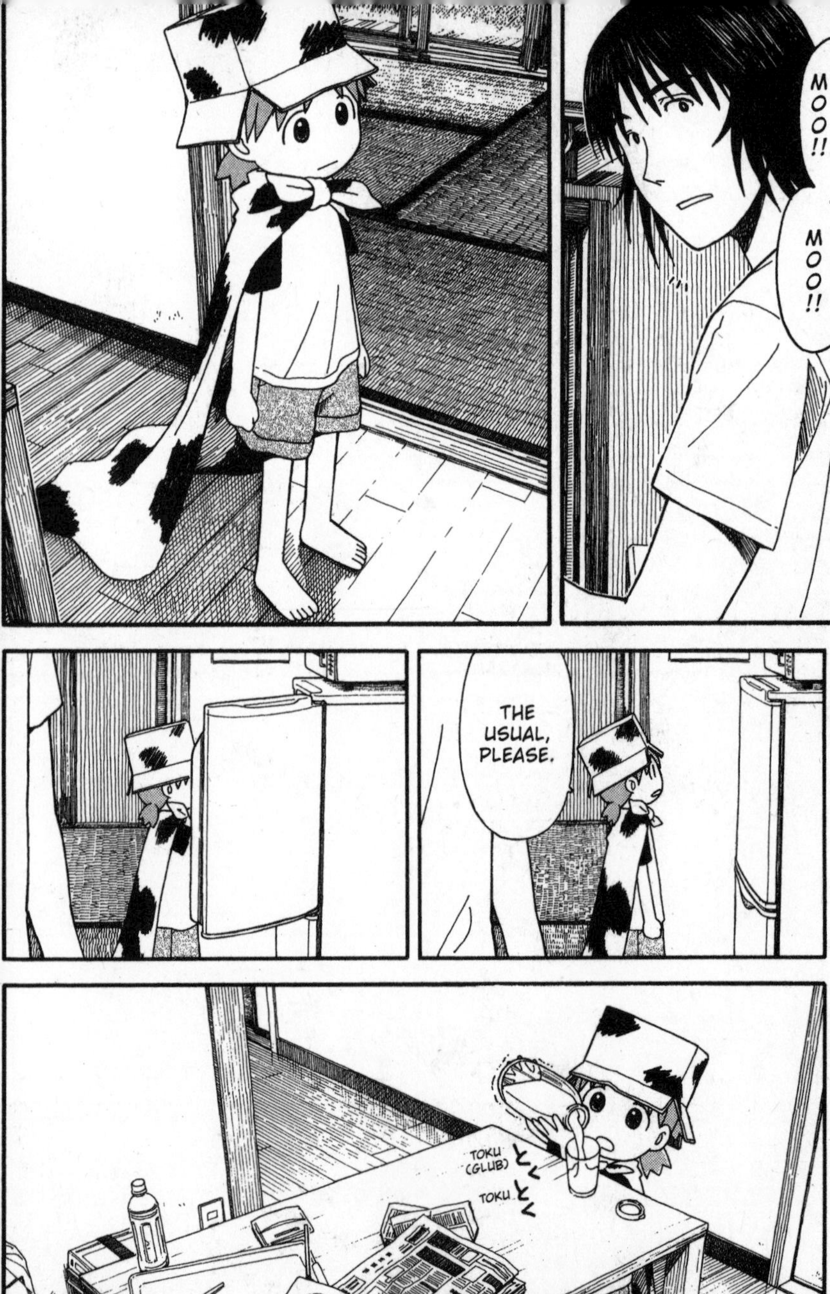
MOO!!
MOO!!
THE USUAL, PLEASE.
TOKU (GLUB) とく
TOKU とく

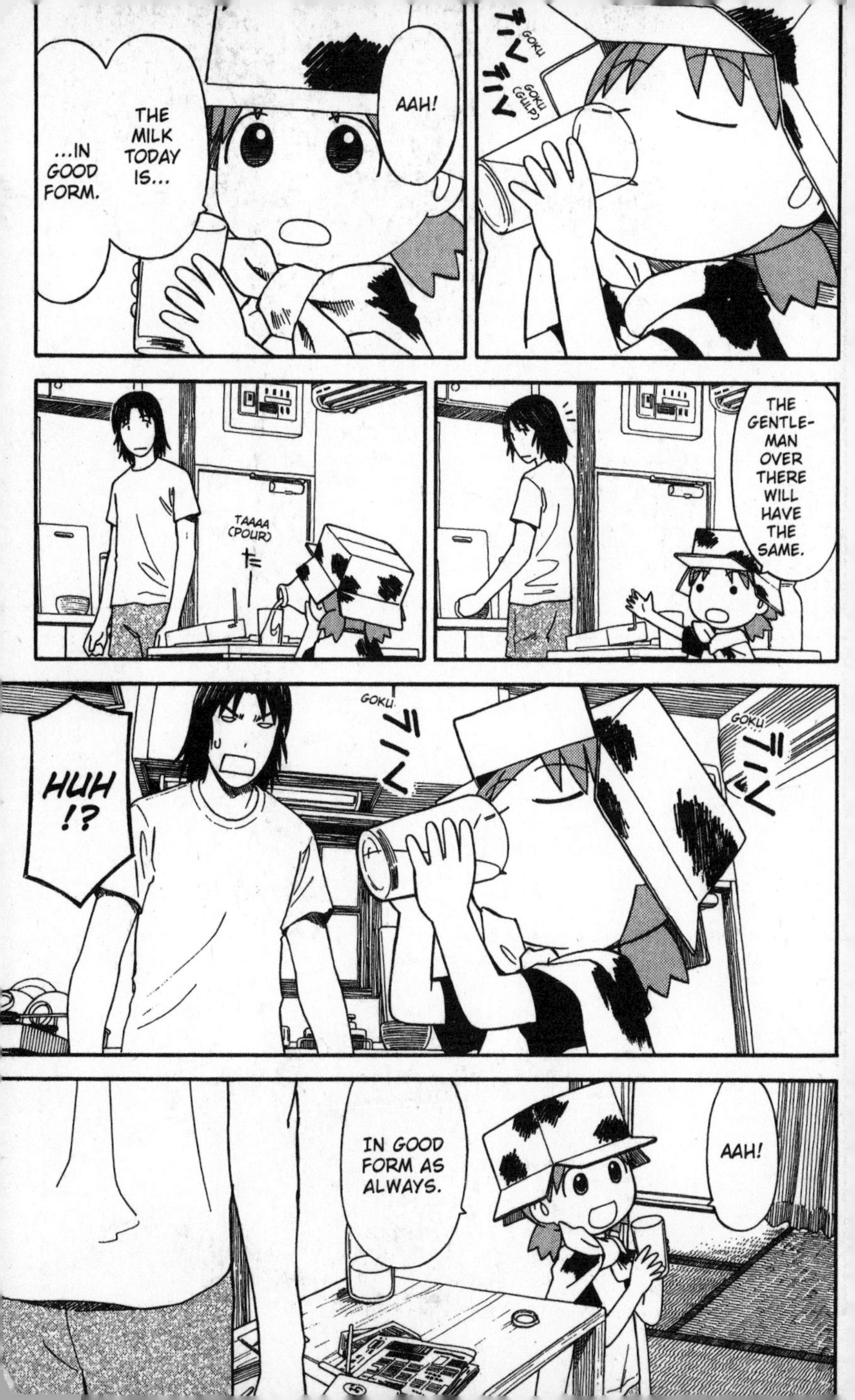
GOKU
GOKU (GULP)
AAH!
THE MILK TODAY IS...
...IN GOOD FORM.
THE GENTLE-MAN OVER THERE WILL HAVE THE SAME.
TAAAA (POUR)
GOKU
GOKU
HUH!?
AAH!
IN GOOD FORM AS ALWAYS.

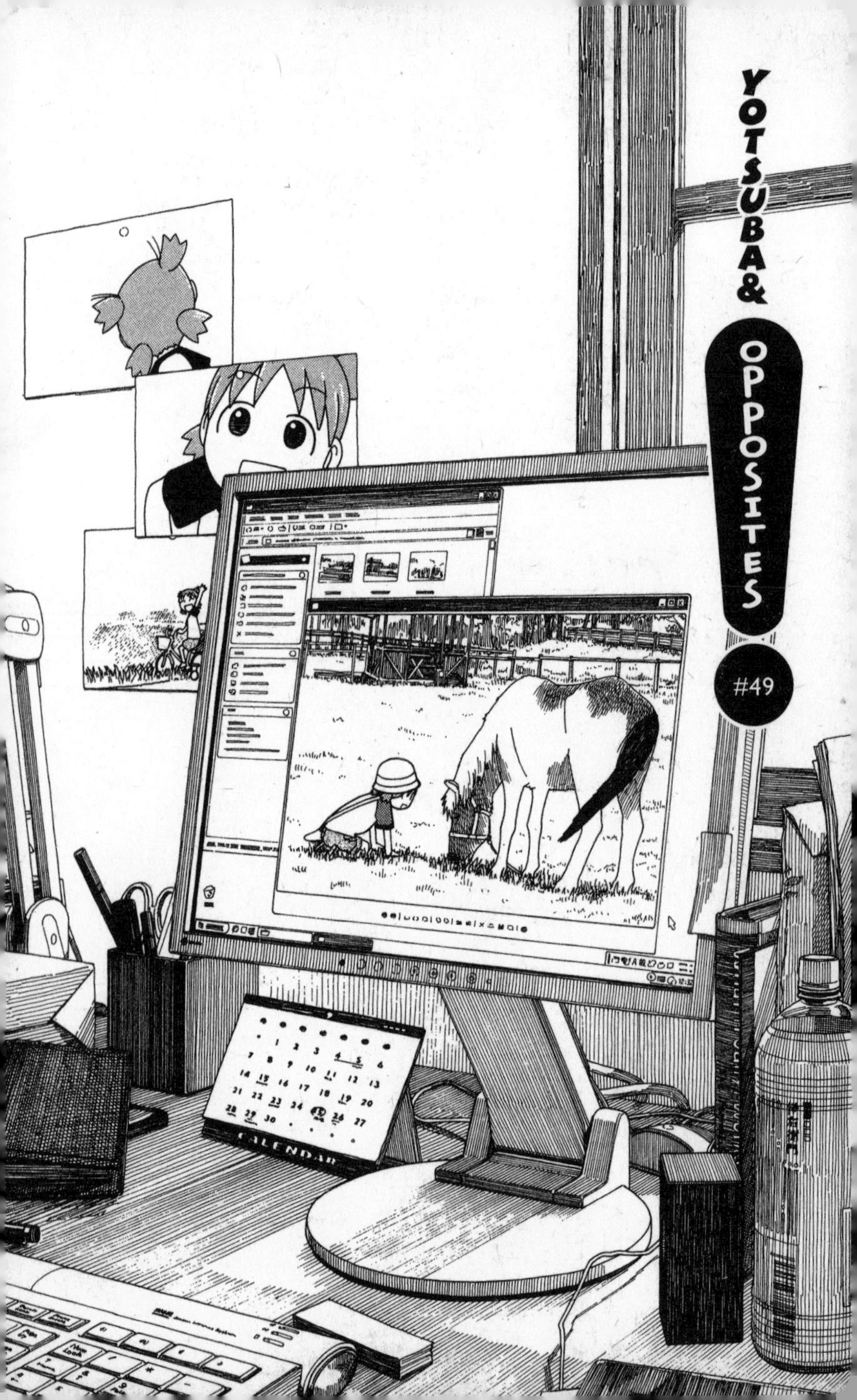
YOTSUBA&
OPPOSITES!
#49
CALENDAR

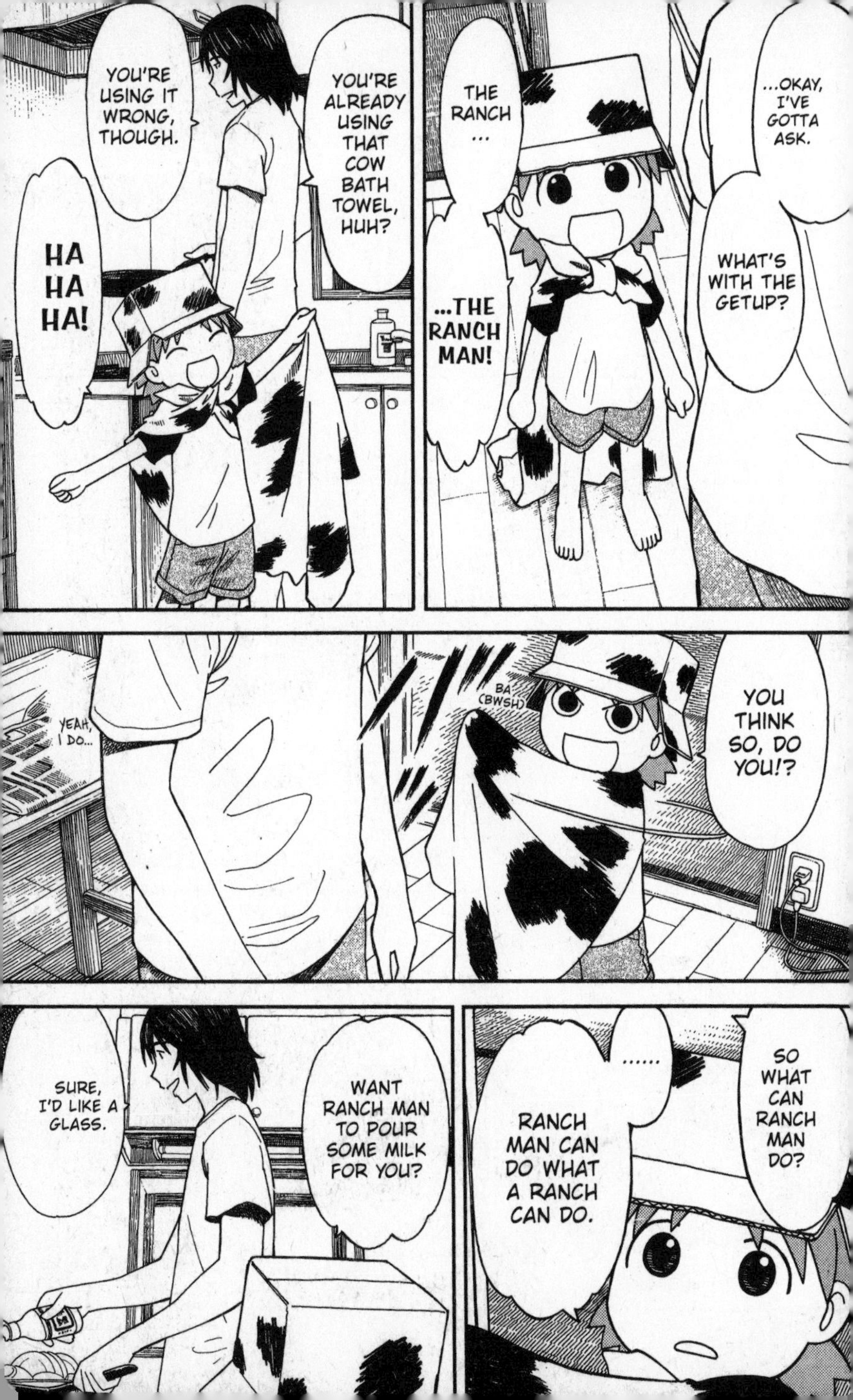
...OKAY, I'VE GOTTA ASK.
WHAT'S WITH THE GETUP?
THE RANCH...
...THE RANCH MAN!
YOU'RE ALREADY USING THAT COW BATH TOWEL, HUH?
YOU'RE USING IT WRONG, THOUGH.
HA HA HA!
YOU THINK SO, DO YOU!?
BA (BWSH)
YEAH, I DO...
SO WHAT CAN RANCH MAN DO?
......
RANCH MAN CAN DO WHAT A RANCH CAN DO.
WANT RANCH MAN TO POUR SOME MILK FOR YOU?
SURE, I'D LIKE A GLASS.

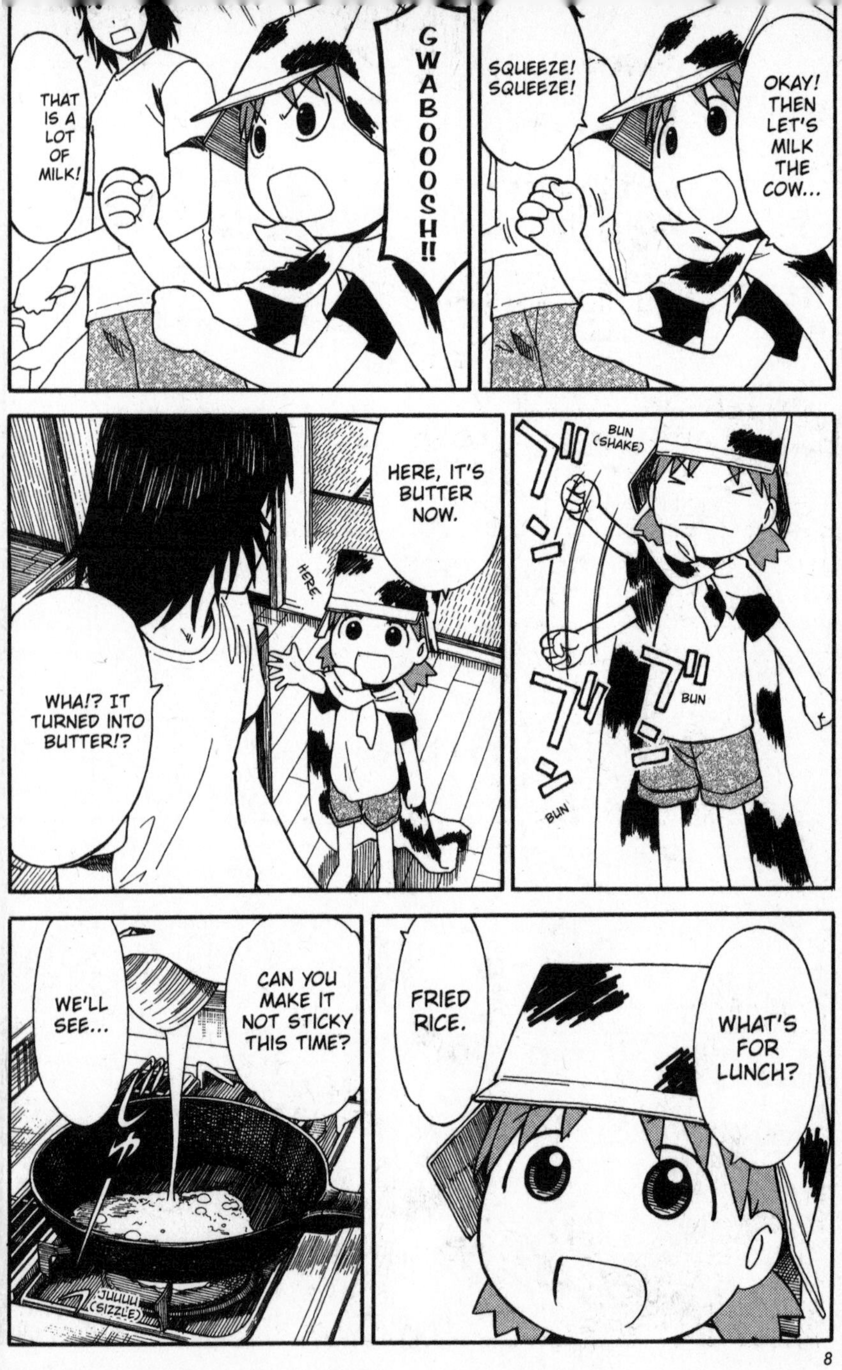
OKAY! THEN LET'S MILK THE COW...
SQUEEZE! SQUEEZE!
GWABOOOOSH!!
THAT IS A LOT OF MILK!
BUN (SHAKE)
BUN
BUN
HERE, IT'S BUTTER NOW.
HERE.
WHA!? IT TURNED INTO BUTTER!?
WHAT'S FOR LUNCH?
FRIED RICE.
CAN YOU MAKE IT NOT STICKY THIS TIME?
WE'LL SEE...
JUUUU (SIZZLE)

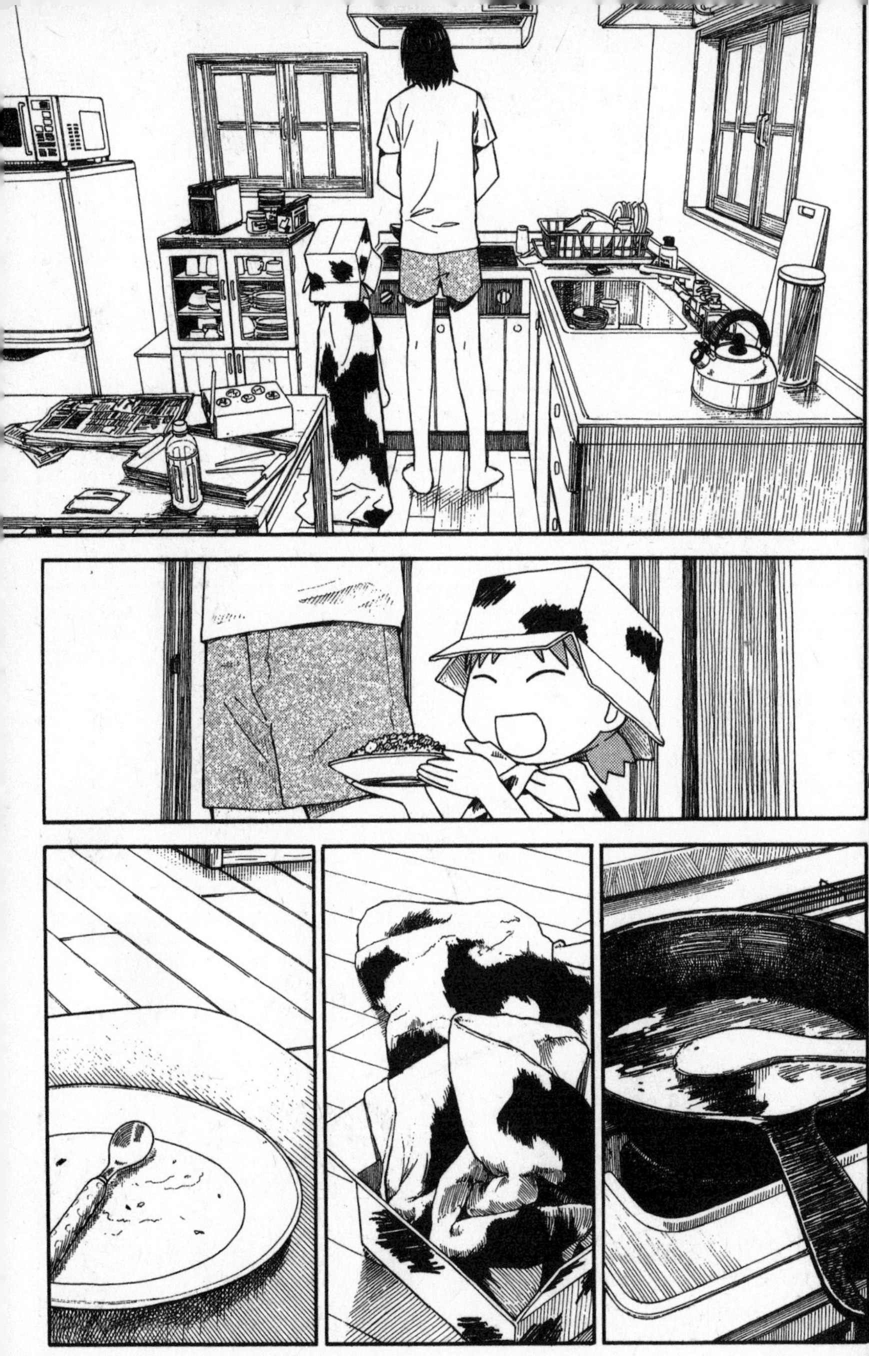

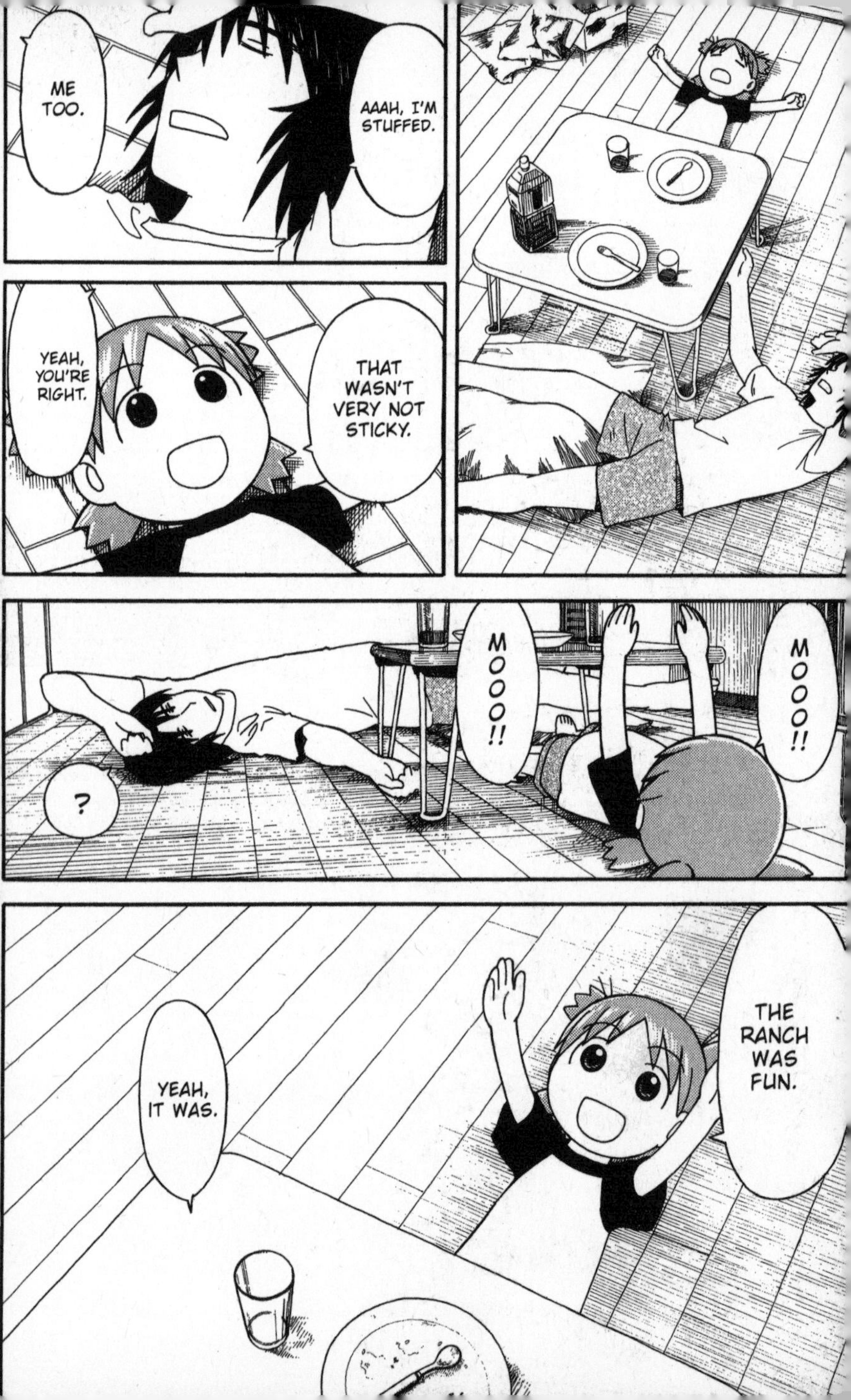
AAAH, I'M STUFFED.
ME TOO.
THAT WASN'T VERY NOT STICKY.
YEAH, YOU'RE RIGHT.
MOOOO!!
MOOOO!!
?
THE RANCH WAS FUN.
YEAH, IT WAS.

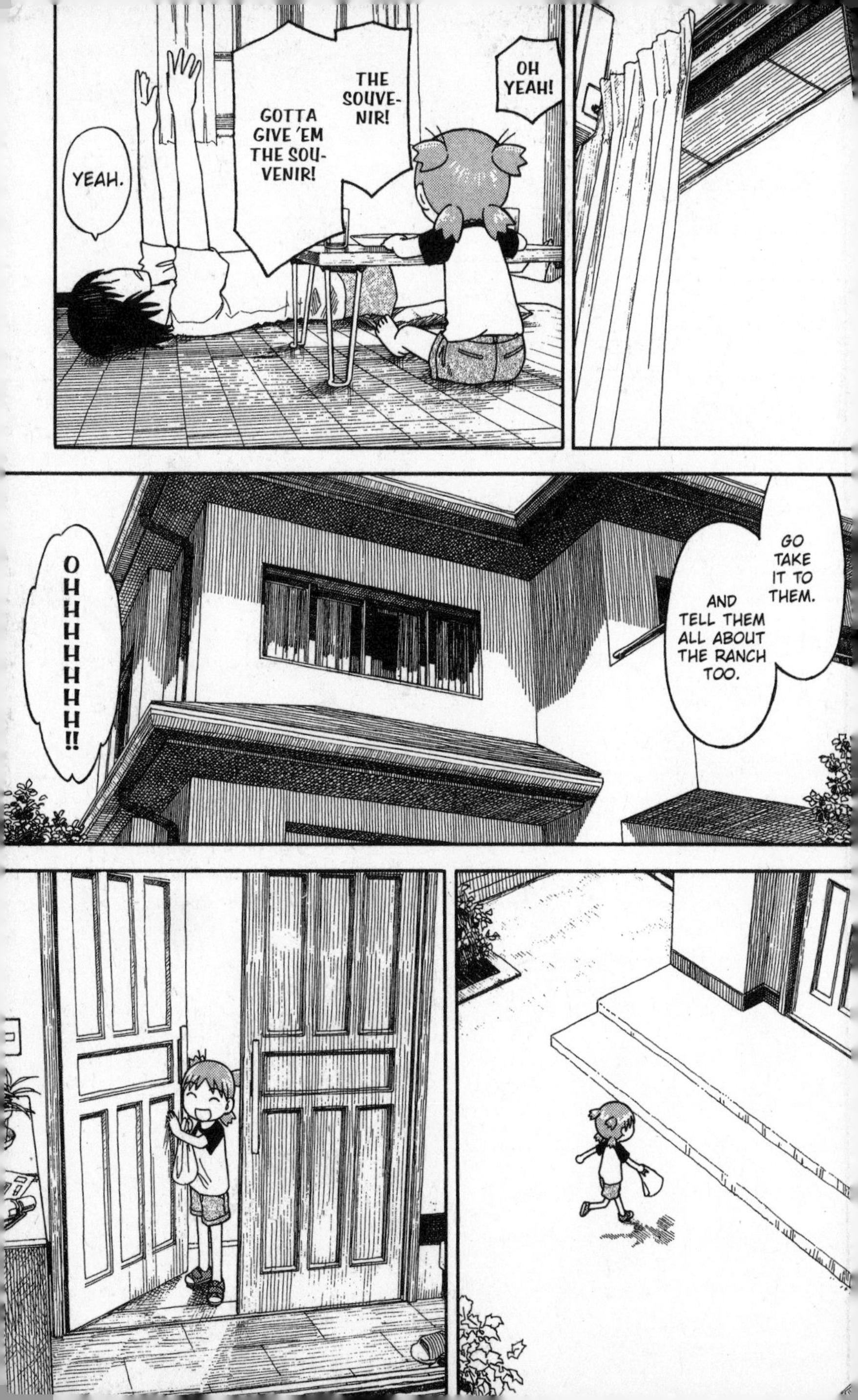
OH YEAH!
THE SOUVENIR! GOTTA GIVE 'EM THE SOUVENIR!
YEAH.
GO TAKE IT TO THEM.
AND TELL THEM ALL ABOUT THE RANCH TOO.
OHHHHHHH!!

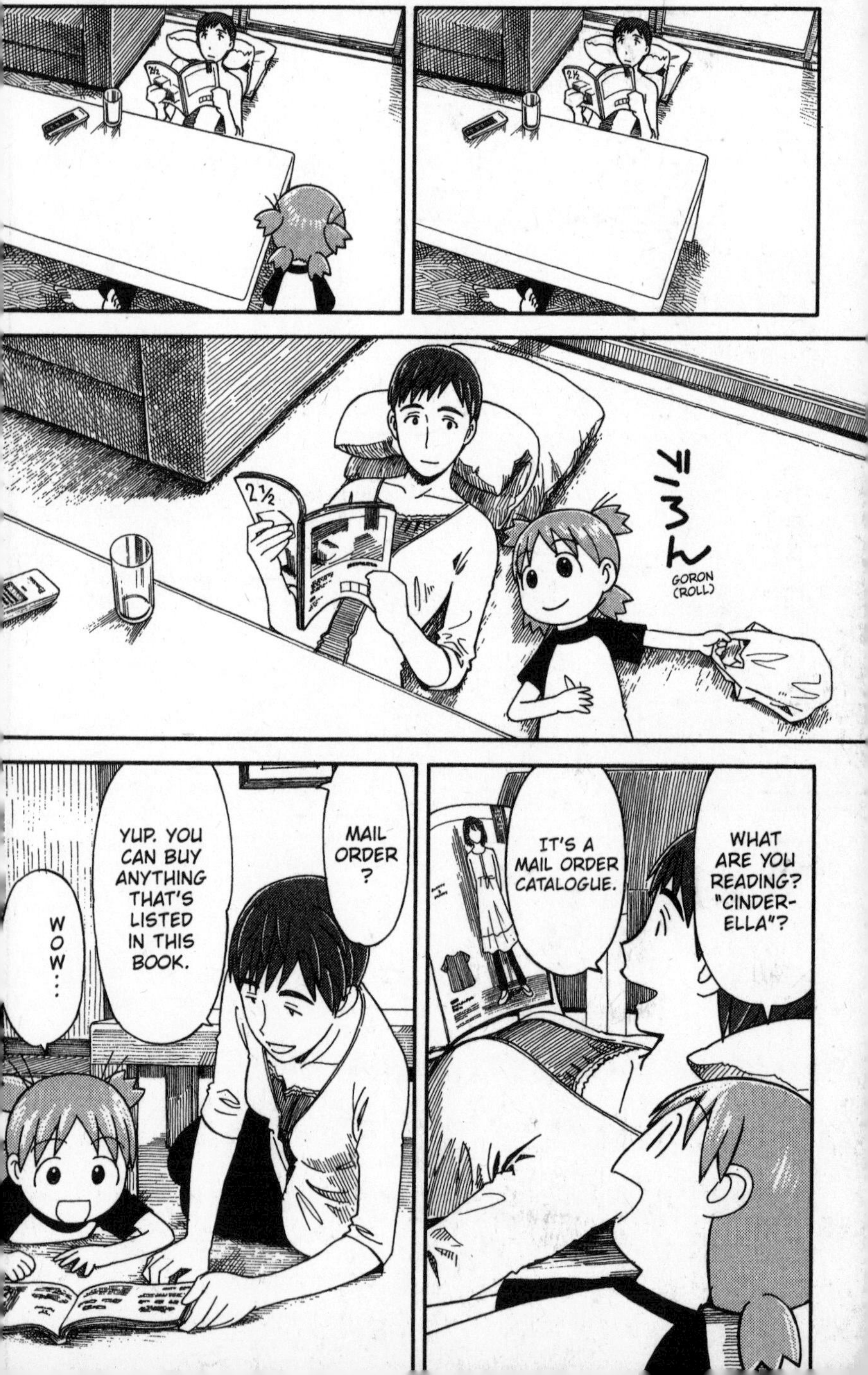
ごろん
GORON (ROLL)
WHAT ARE YOU READING? "CINDERELLA"?
IT'S A MAIL ORDER CATALOGUE.
MAIL ORDER?
YUP. YOU CAN BUY ANYTHING THAT'S LISTED IN THIS BOOK.
WOW...

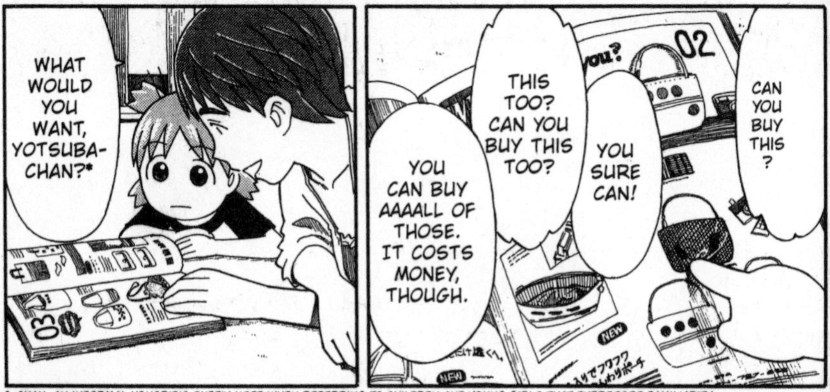
CAN YOU BUY THIS?
YOU SURE CAN!
THIS TOO? CAN YOU BUY THIS TOO?
YOU CAN BUY AAAALL OF THOSE. IT COSTS MONEY, THOUGH.
WHAT WOULD YOU WANT, YOTSUBA-CHAN?*

*-CHAN: AN INFORMAL HONORIFIC SUFFIX USED WHEN REFERRING TO CHILDREN AND YOUNG GIRLS THAT EXPRESSES FAMILIARITY.

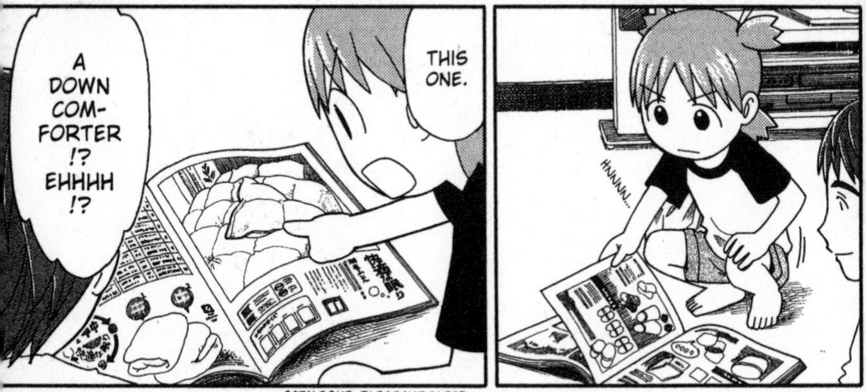
HNNNN...
THIS ONE.
A DOWN COMFORTER!? EHHHH!?

CATALOGUE: PLEASANT SLEEP

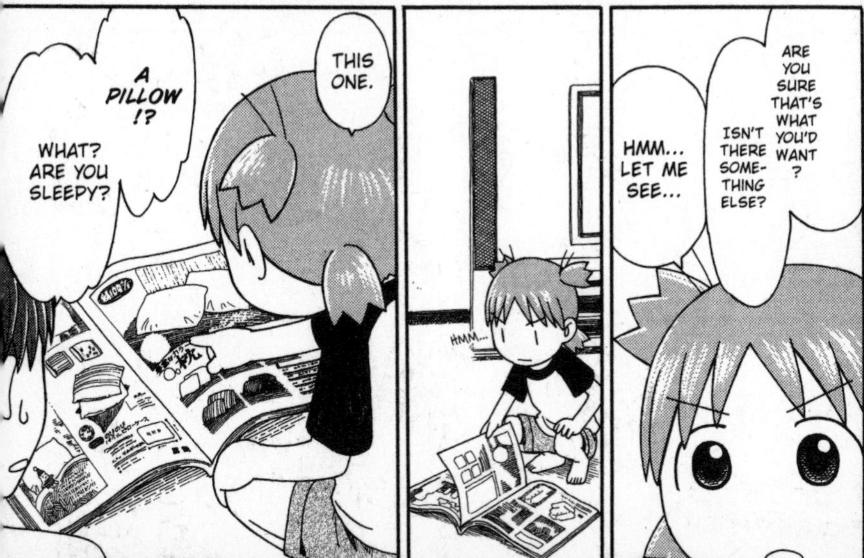
ARE YOU SURE THAT'S WHAT YOU'D WANT?
ISN'T THERE SOMETHING ELSE?
HMM... LET ME SEE...
HMM...
THIS ONE.
A PILLOW!?
WHAT? ARE YOU SLEEPY?

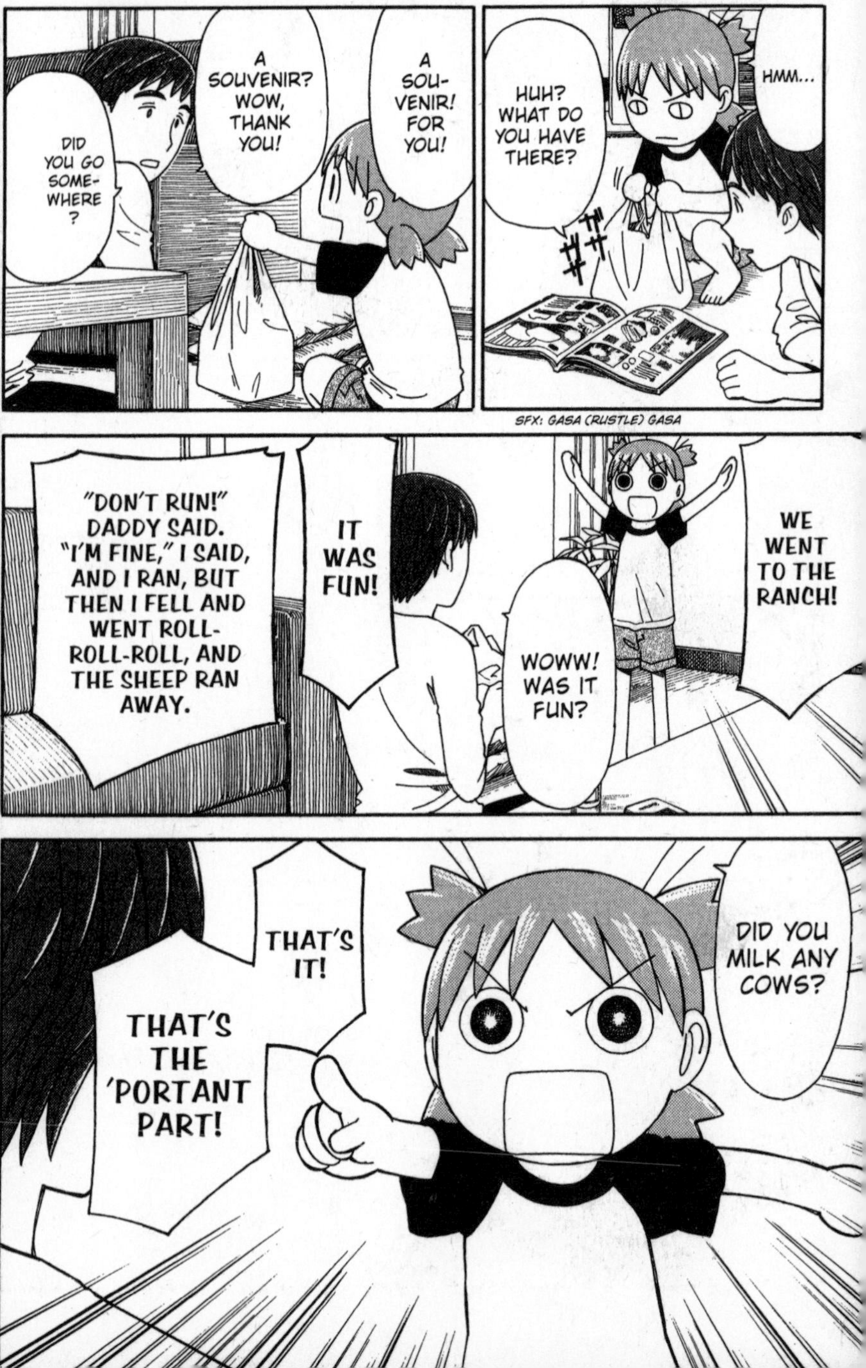
HMM...
HUH? WHAT DO YOU HAVE THERE?
SFX: GASA (RUSTLE) GASA
A SOU-VENIR! FOR YOU!
A SOUVENIR? WOW, THANK YOU!
DID YOU GO SOME-WHERE?
WE WENT TO THE RANCH!
WOWW! WAS IT FUN?
IT WAS FUN!
"DON'T RUN!" DADDY SAID. "I'M FINE," I SAID, AND I RAN, BUT THEN I FELL AND WENT ROLL-ROLL-ROLL, AND THE SHEEP RAN AWAY.
DID YOU MILK ANY COWS?
THAT'S IT!
THAT'S THE 'PORTANT PART!

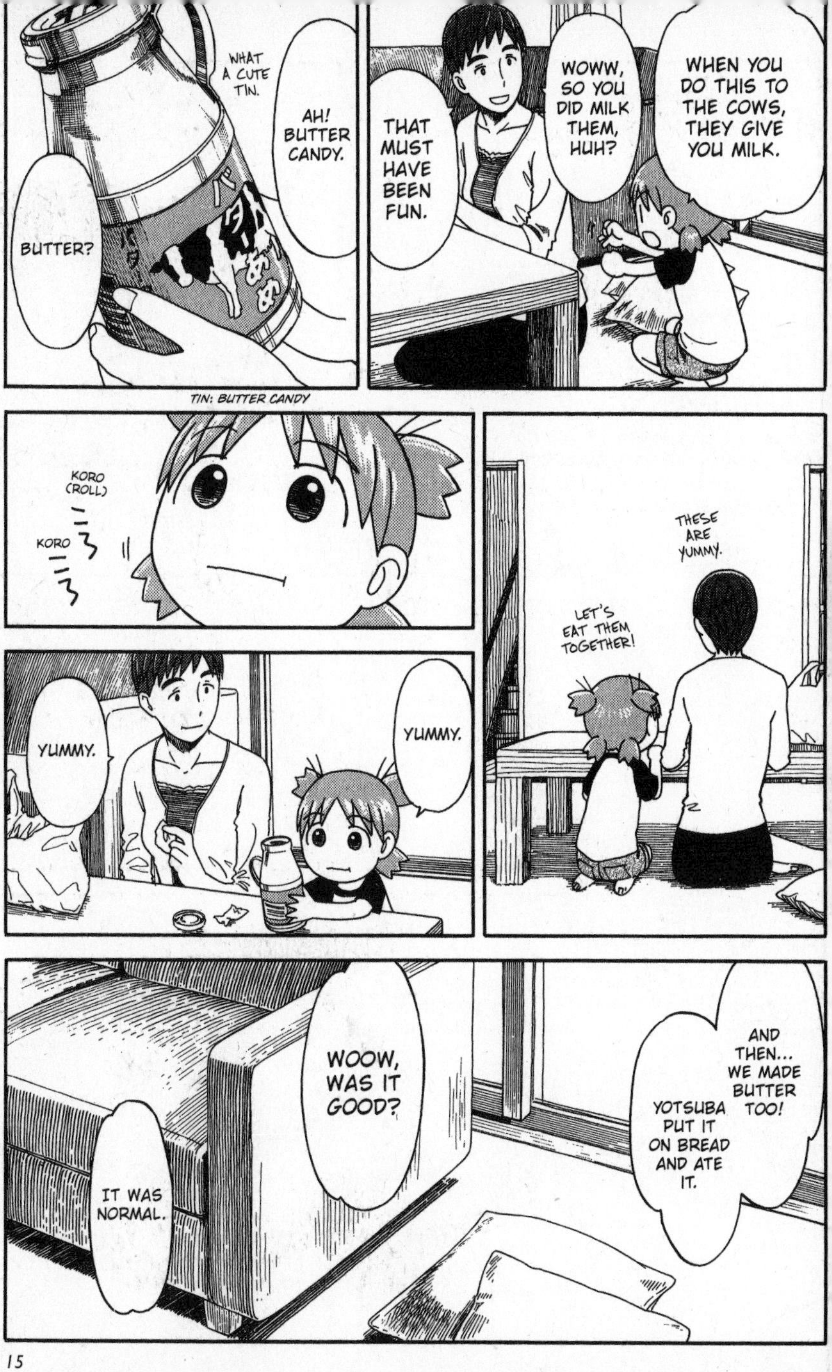
WHEN YOU DO THIS TO THE COWS, THEY GIVE YOU MILK.
WOWW, SO YOU DID MILK THEM, HUH?
THAT MUST HAVE BEEN FUN.
AH! BUTTER CANDY.
WHAT A CUTE TIN.
BUTTER?
TIN: BUTTER CANDY
THESE ARE YUMMY.
LET'S EAT THEM TOGETHER!
KORO (ROLL)
KORO
YUMMY.
YUMMY.
AND THEN... WE MADE BUTTER TOO!
YOTSUBA PUT IT ON BREAD AND ATE IT.
WOOW, WAS IT GOOD?
IT WAS NORMAL.

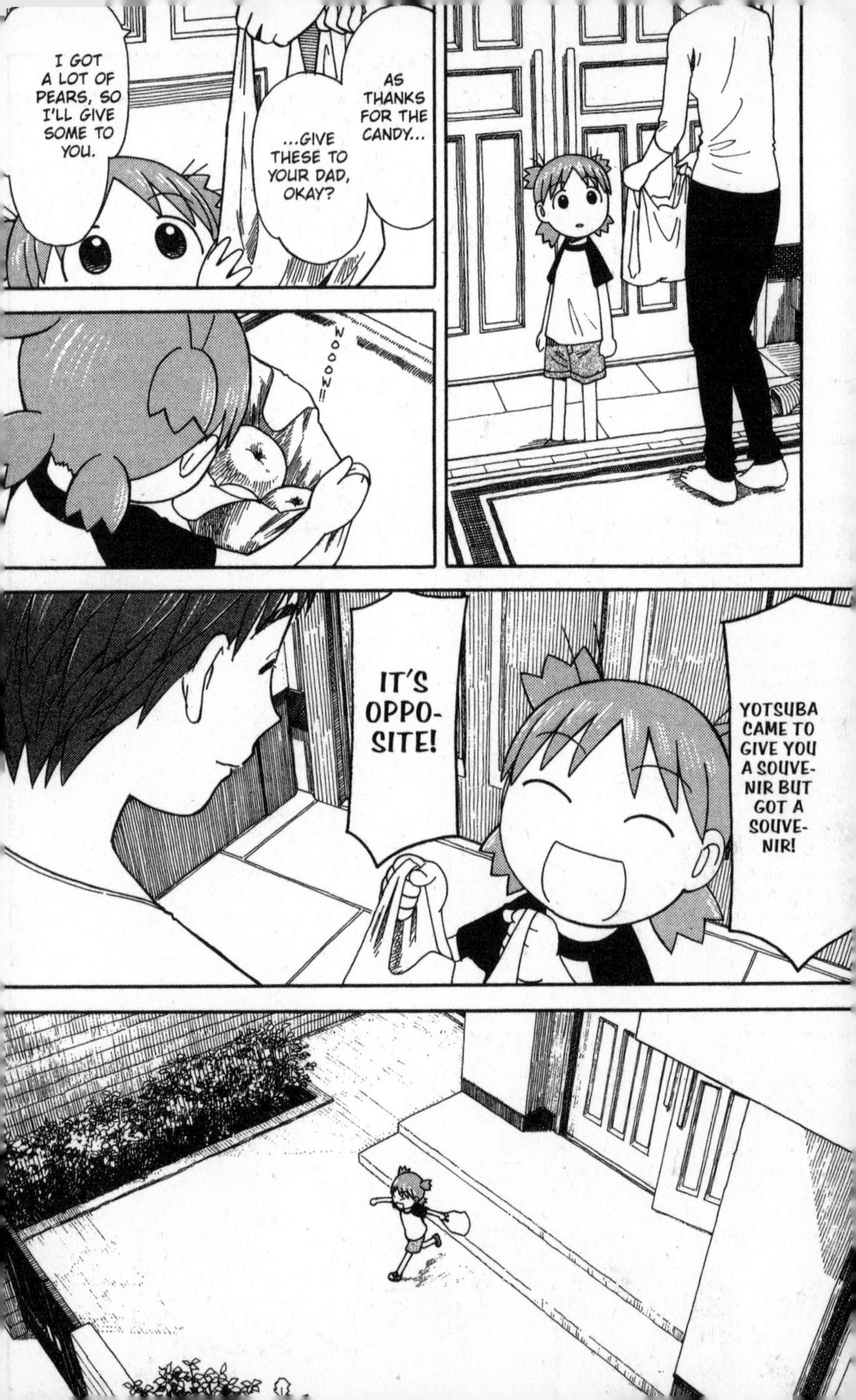
AS THANKS FOR THE CANDY...
...GIVE THESE TO YOUR DAD, OKAY?
I GOT A LOT OF PEARS, SO I'LL GIVE SOME TO YOU.
WOOOOW!!
YOTSUBA CAME TO GIVE YOU A SOUVE-NIR BUT GOT A SOUVE-NIR!
IT'S OPPO-SITE!

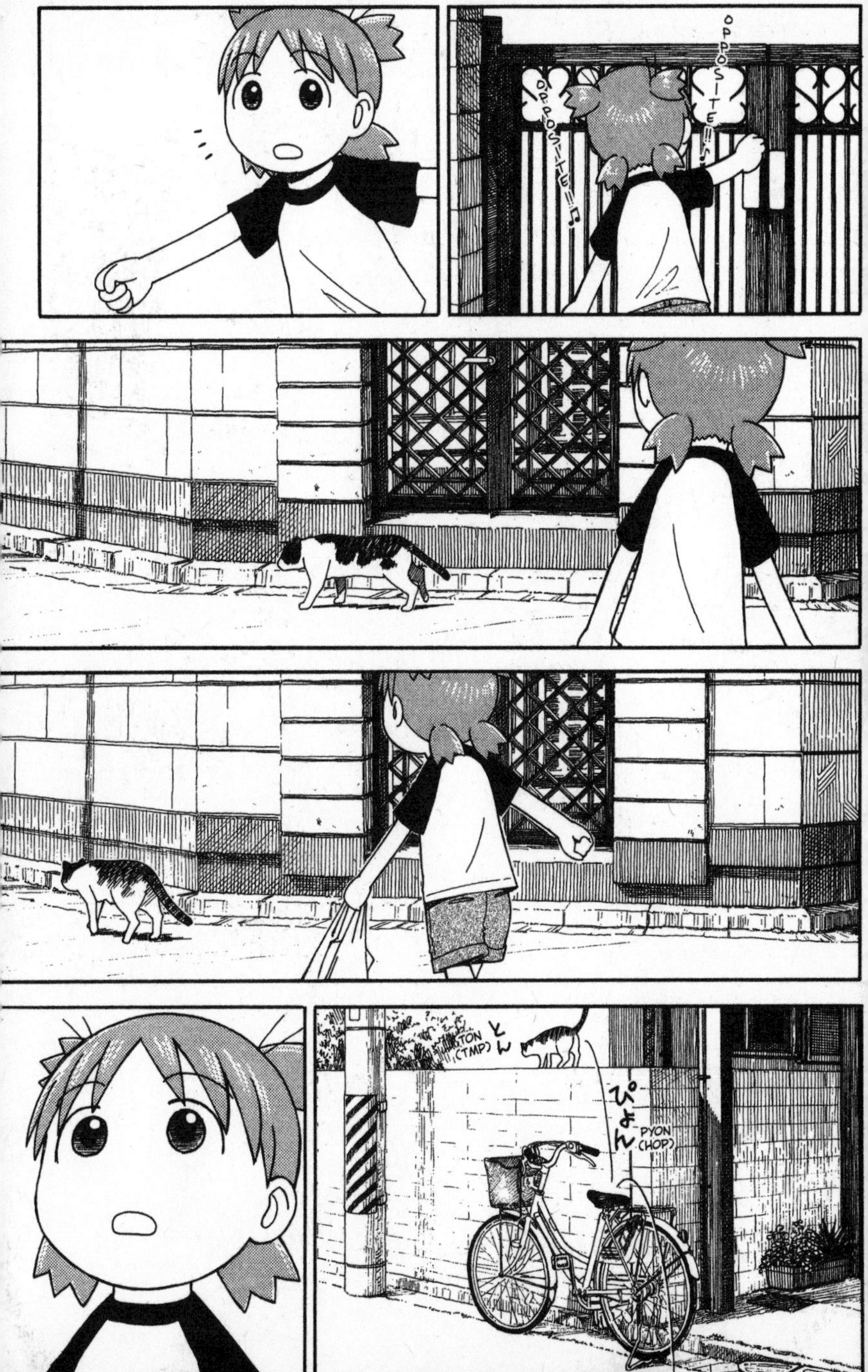
OPPOSITE!!♪
OPPOSITE!!♪
とん
TON (TMP)
ぴょん
PYON (HOP)

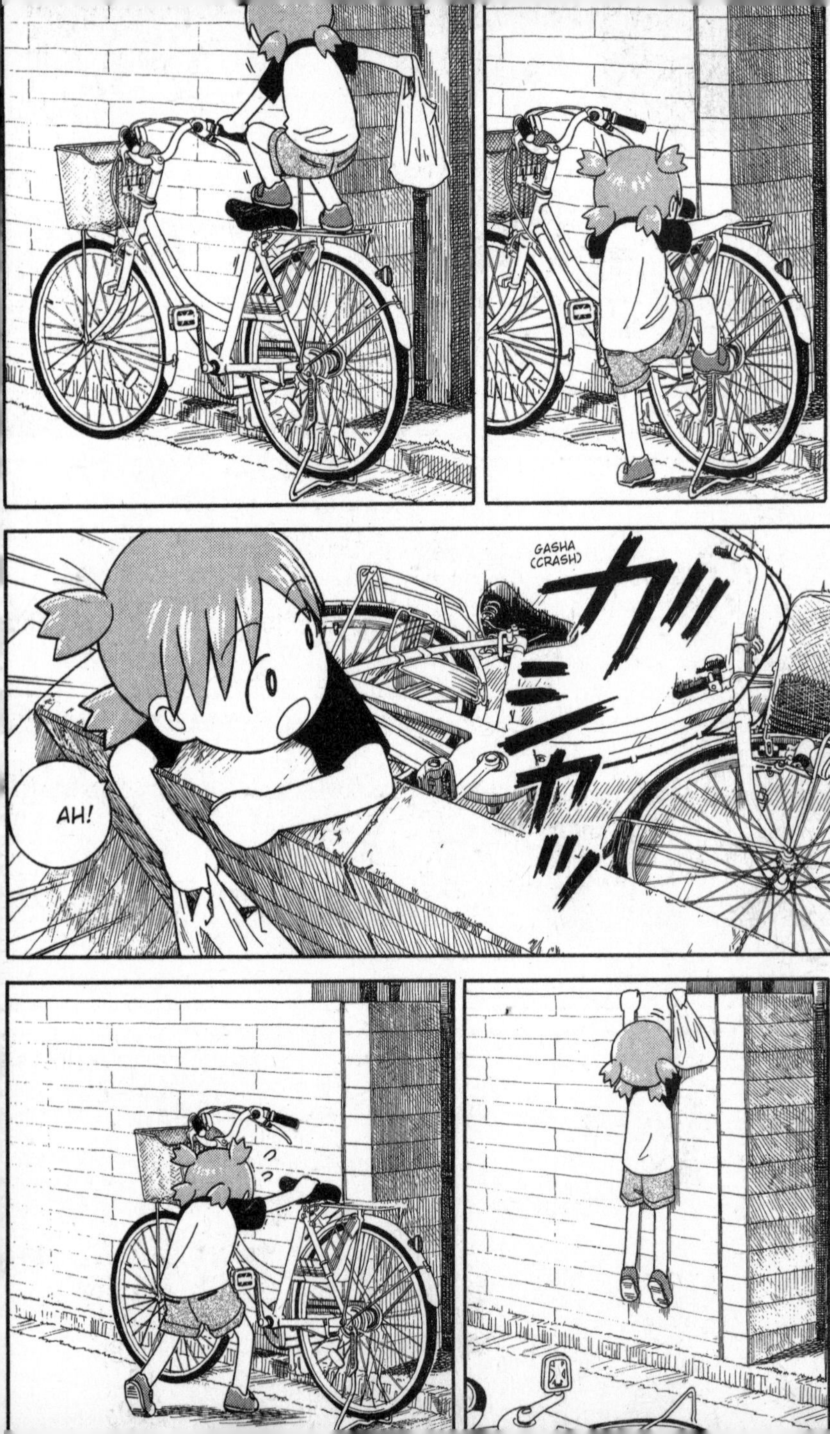
GASHA (CRASH)
AH!

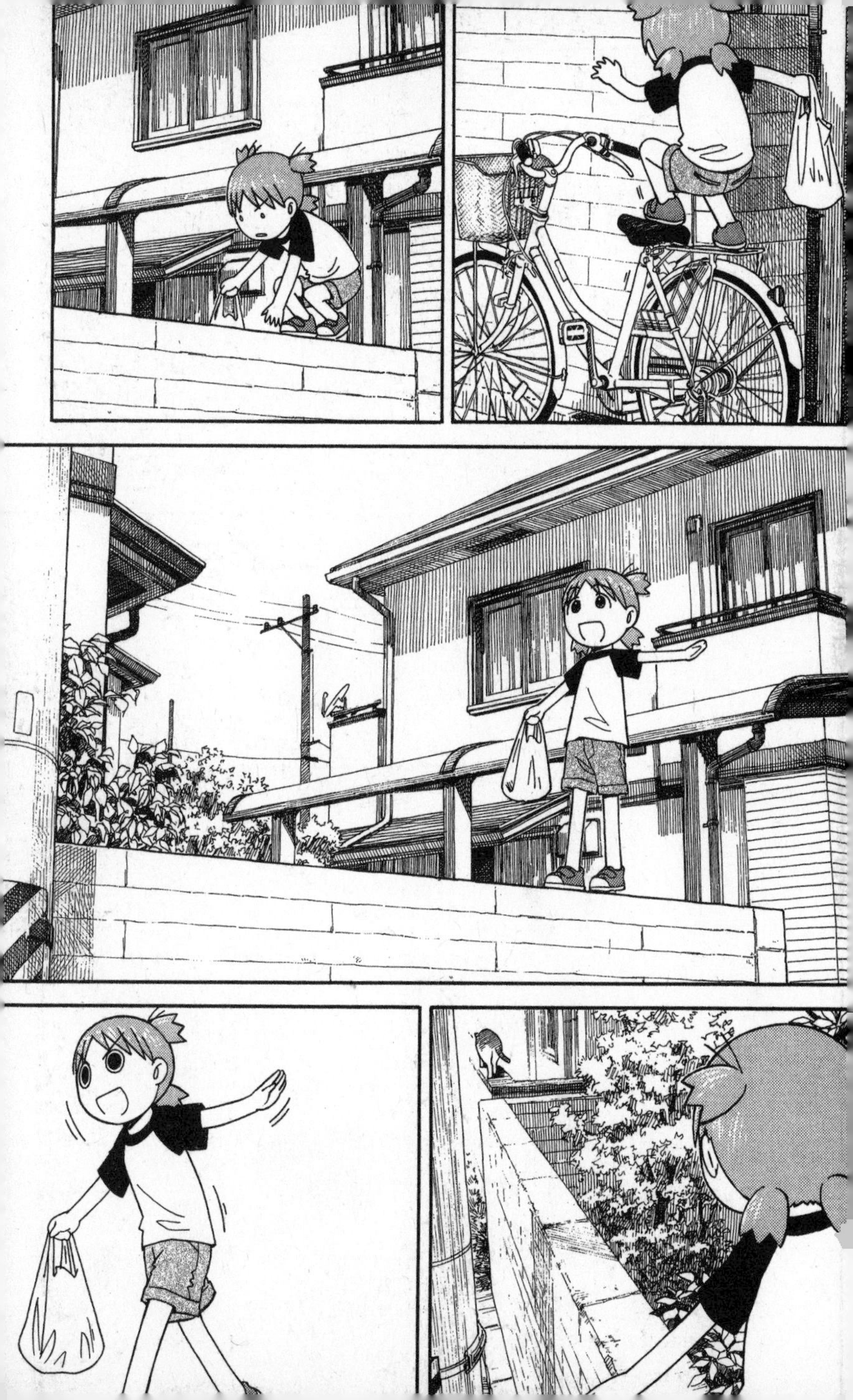

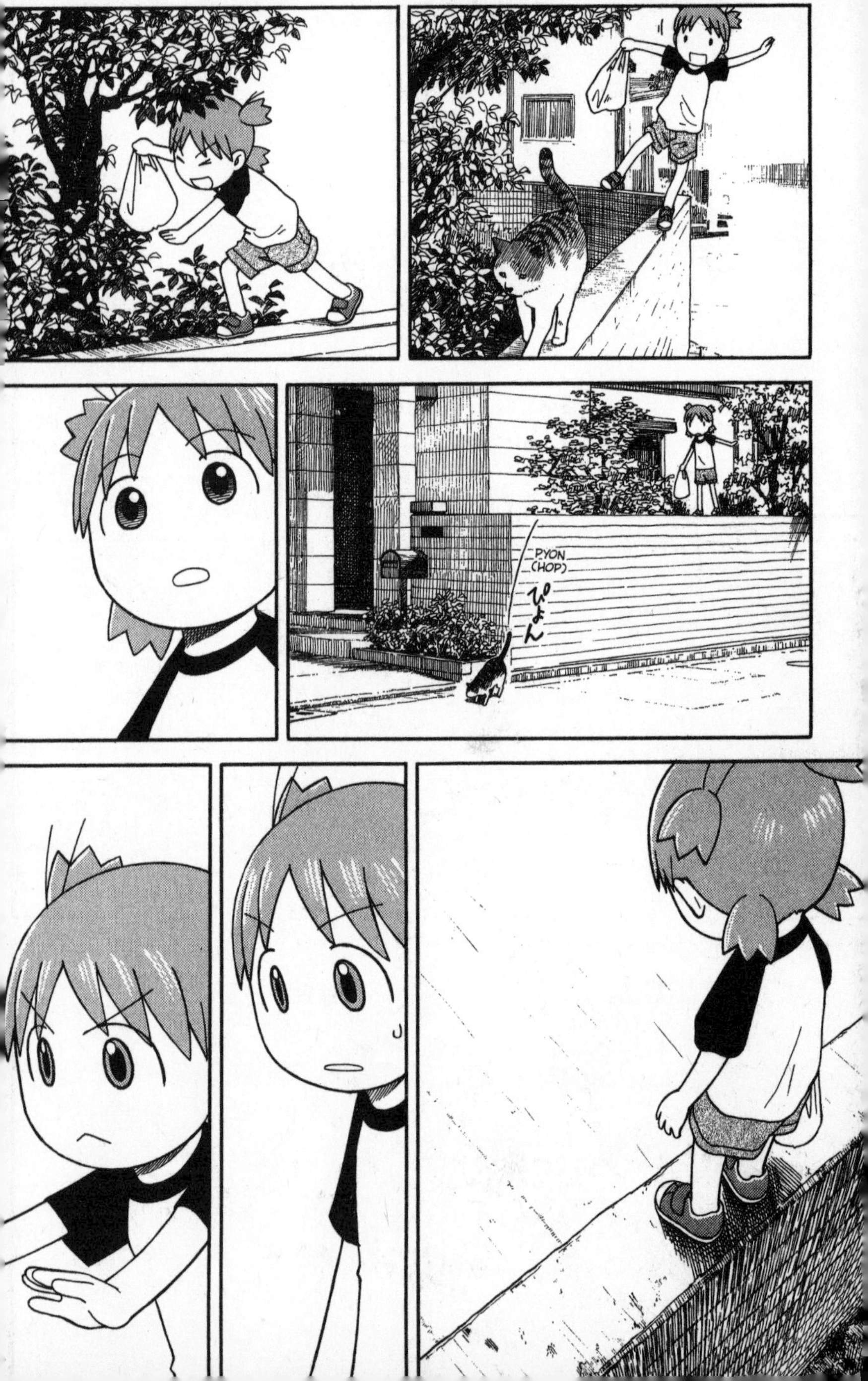
PYON (HOP)
ぴょん

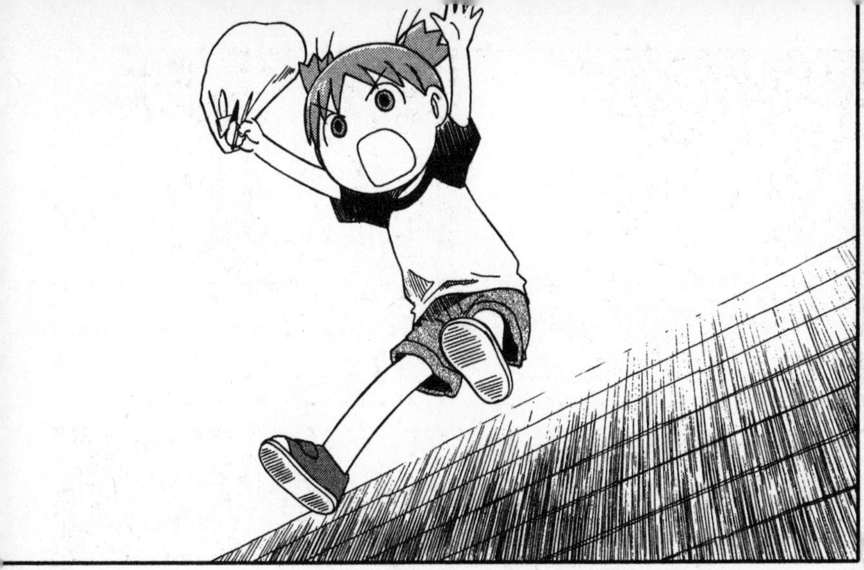

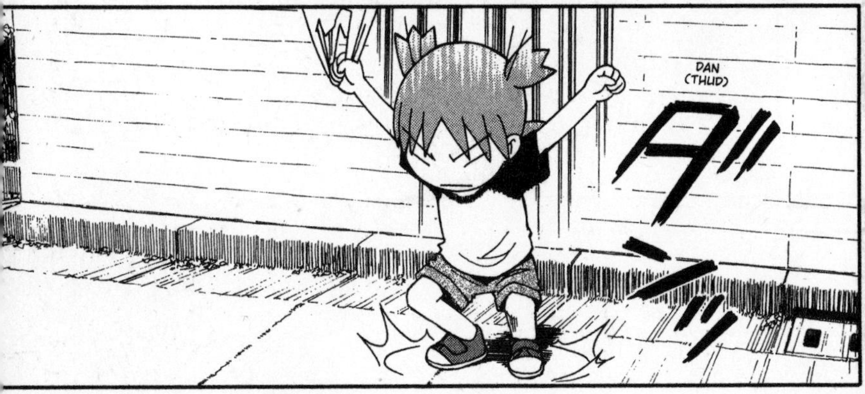
DAN
(THUD)
ダンッ

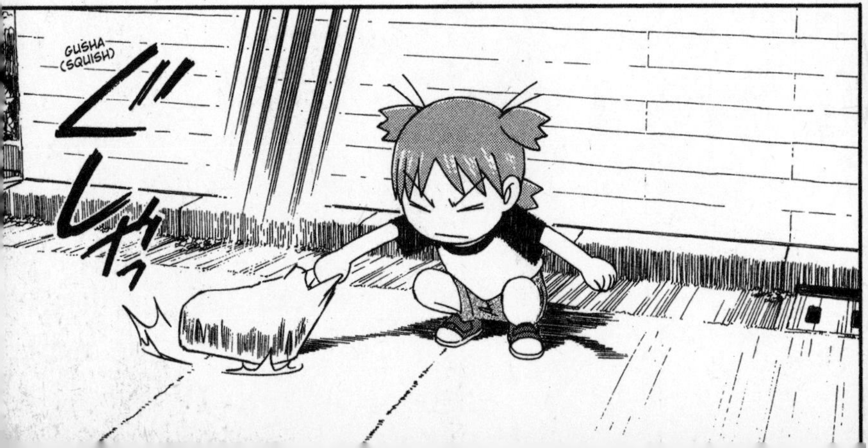
GUSHA
(SQUISH)
ぐしゃっ

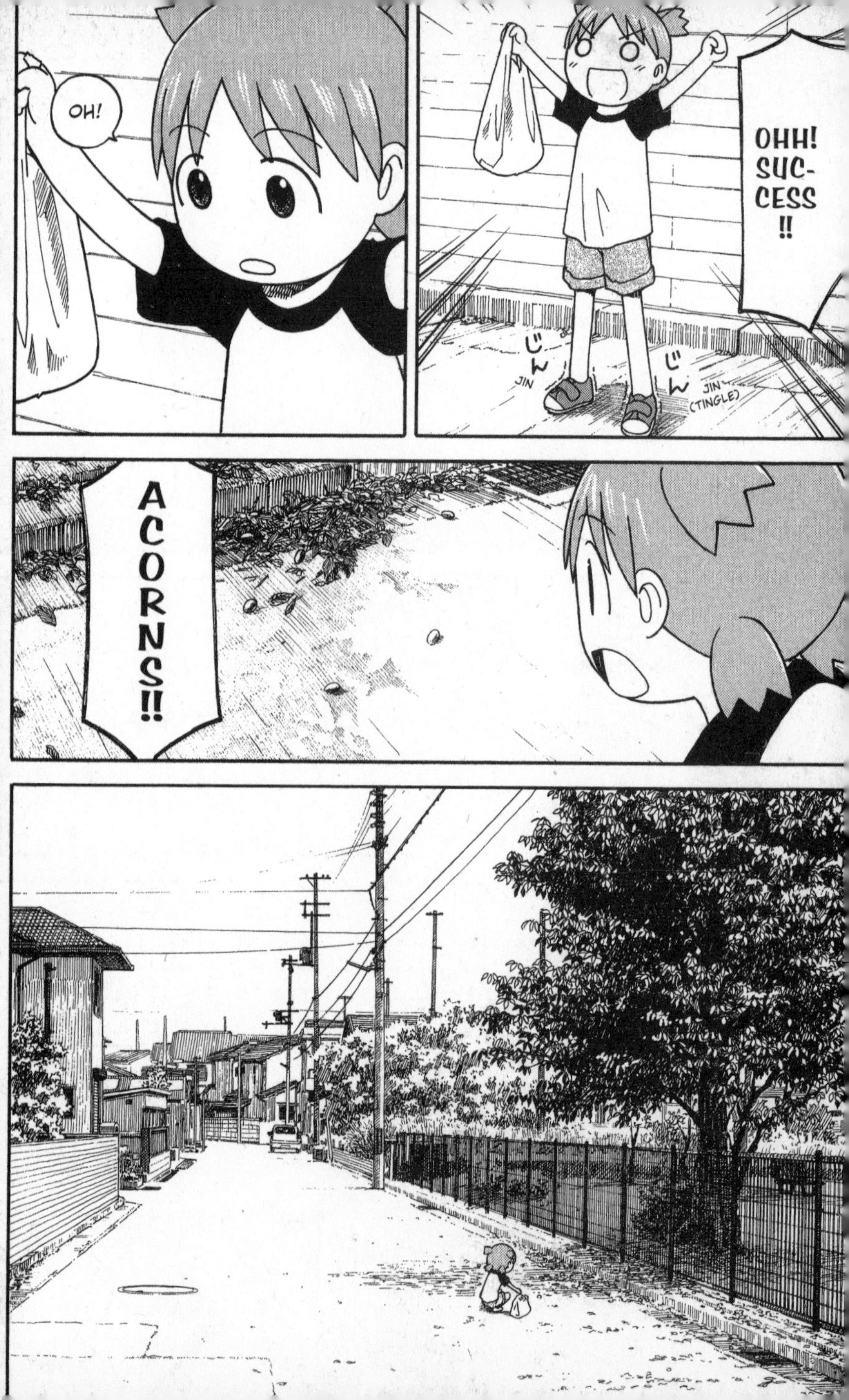
OHH! SUC-CESS!!
じん
JIN
じん
JIN (TINGLE)
OH!
ACORNS!!

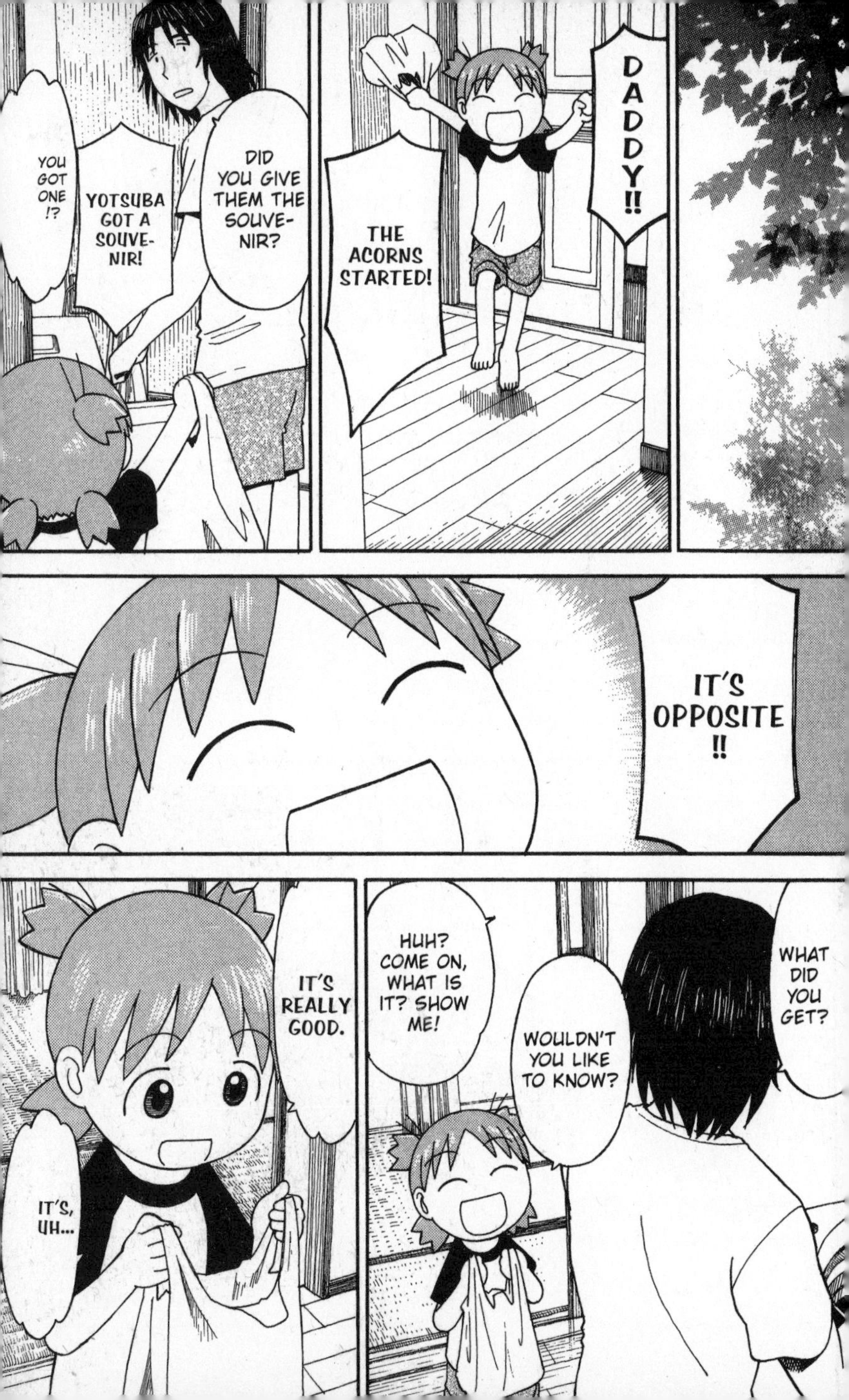
DADDY!!
THE ACORNS STARTED!
DID YOU GIVE THEM THE SOUVE-NIR?
YOTSUBA GOT A SOUVE-NIR!
YOU GOT ONE!?
IT'S OPPOSITE!!
WHAT DID YOU GET?
WOULDN'T YOU LIKE TO KNOW?
HUH? COME ON, WHAT IS IT? SHOW ME!
IT'S REALLY GOOD.
IT'S, UH...

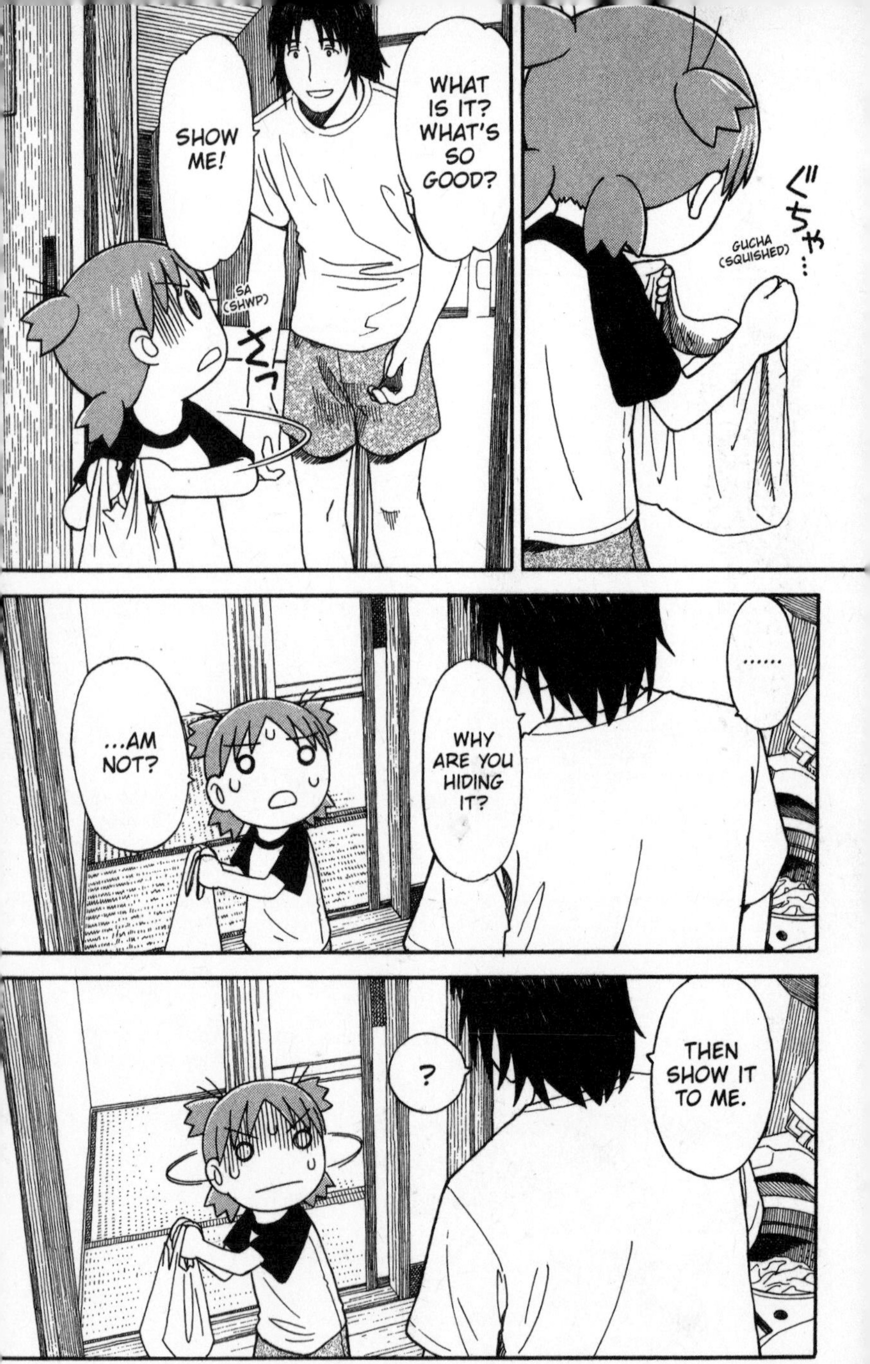
ぐちゃ…
GUCHA (SQUISHED)
WHAT IS IT? WHAT'S SO GOOD?
SHOW ME!
SA (SHWP)
さっ
......
WHY ARE YOU HIDING IT?
...AM NOT?
THEN SHOW IT TO ME.
?

YOTSUBA& THE RESTAURANT

#50

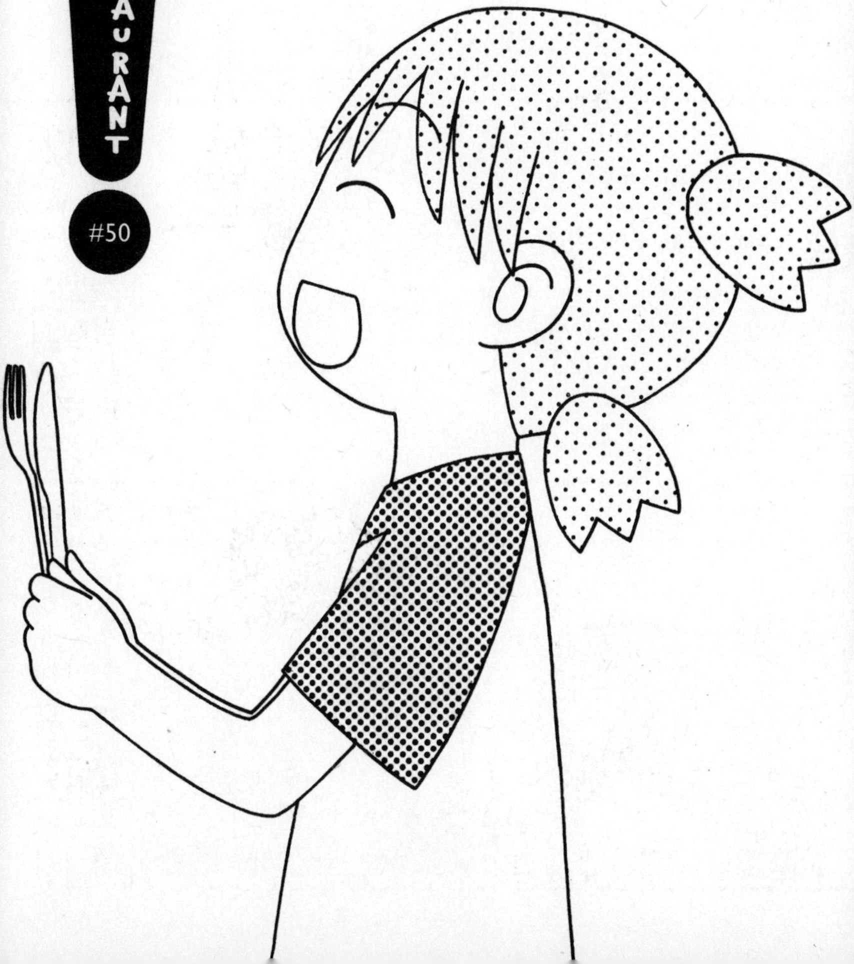

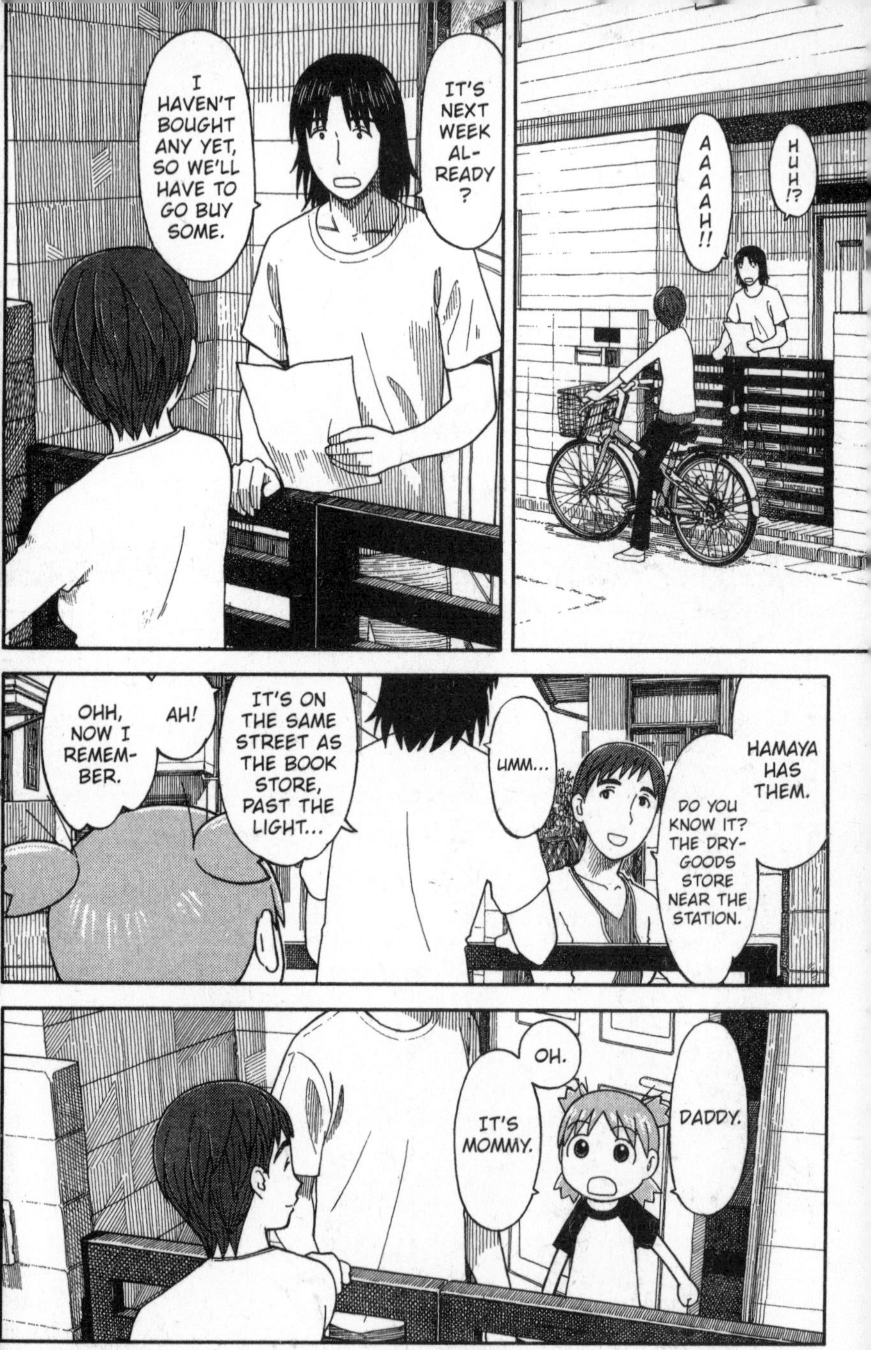
HUH!?
AAAAAH!!
IT'S NEXT WEEK AL-READY?
I HAVEN'T BOUGHT ANY YET, SO WE'LL HAVE TO GO BUY SOME.
HAMAYA HAS THEM.
DO YOU KNOW IT? THE DRY-GOODS STORE NEAR THE STATION.
UMM...
IT'S ON THE SAME STREET AS THE BOOK STORE, PAST THE LIGHT...
AH!
OHH, NOW I REMEM-BER.
DADDY.
OH.
IT'S MOMMY.

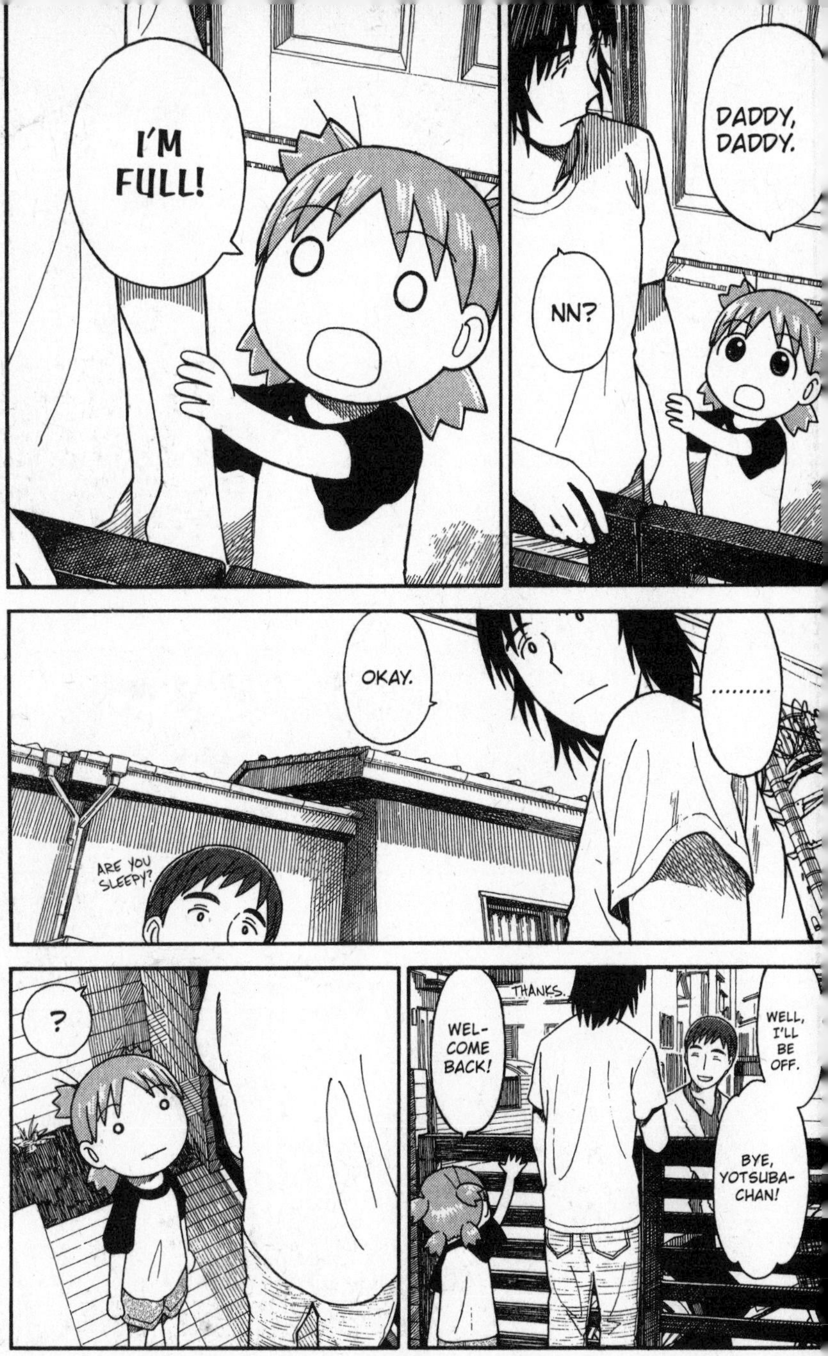
DADDY, DADDY.
NN?
I'M FULL!
....
OKAY.
ARE YOU SLEEPY?
WELL, I'LL BE OFF.
THANKS.
WEL-COME BACK!
BYE, YOTSUBA-CHAN!
?

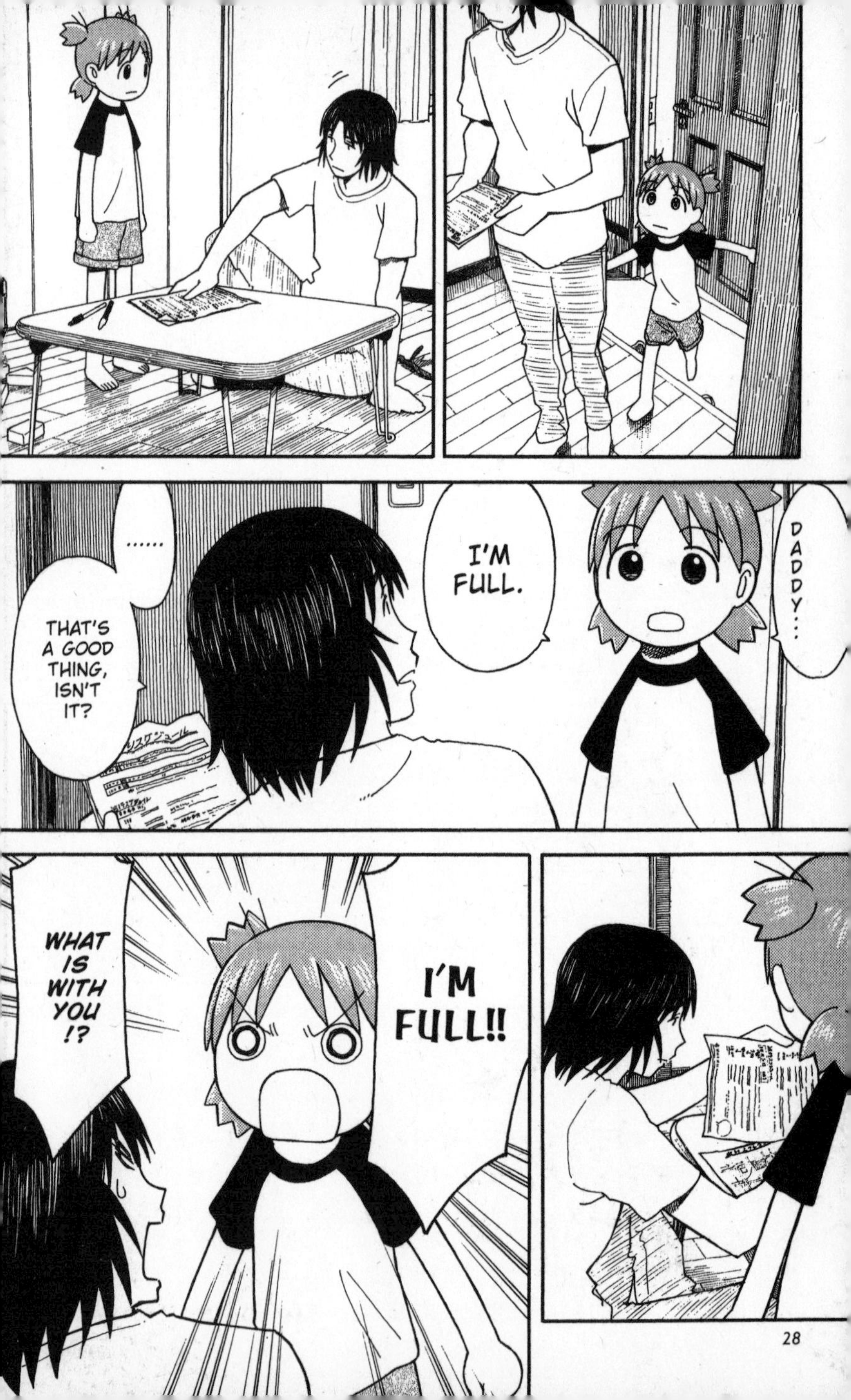
DADDY...
I'M FULL.
......
THAT'S A GOOD THING, ISN'T IT?
I'M FULL!!
WHAT IS WITH YOU!?

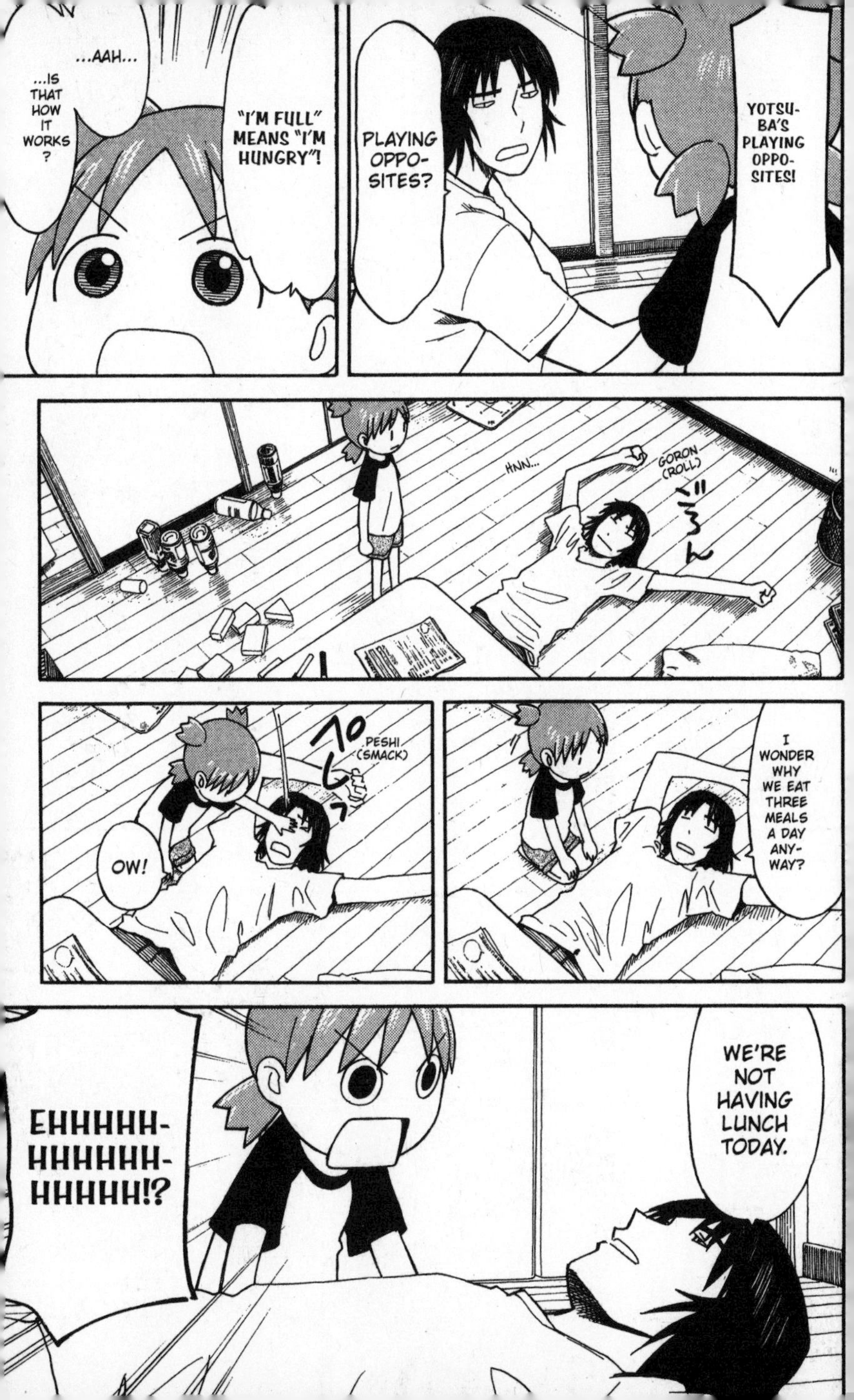
YOTSUBA'S PLAYING OPPOSITES!
PLAYING OPPOSITES?
"I'M FULL" MEANS "I'M HUNGRY"!
...AAH...
...IS THAT HOW IT WORKS?
HNN...
GORON (ROLL)
I WONDER WHY WE EAT THREE MEALS A DAY ANYWAY?
PESHI (SMACK)
OW!
WE'RE NOT HAVING LUNCH TODAY.
EHHHHH-HHHHHH-HHHHH!?

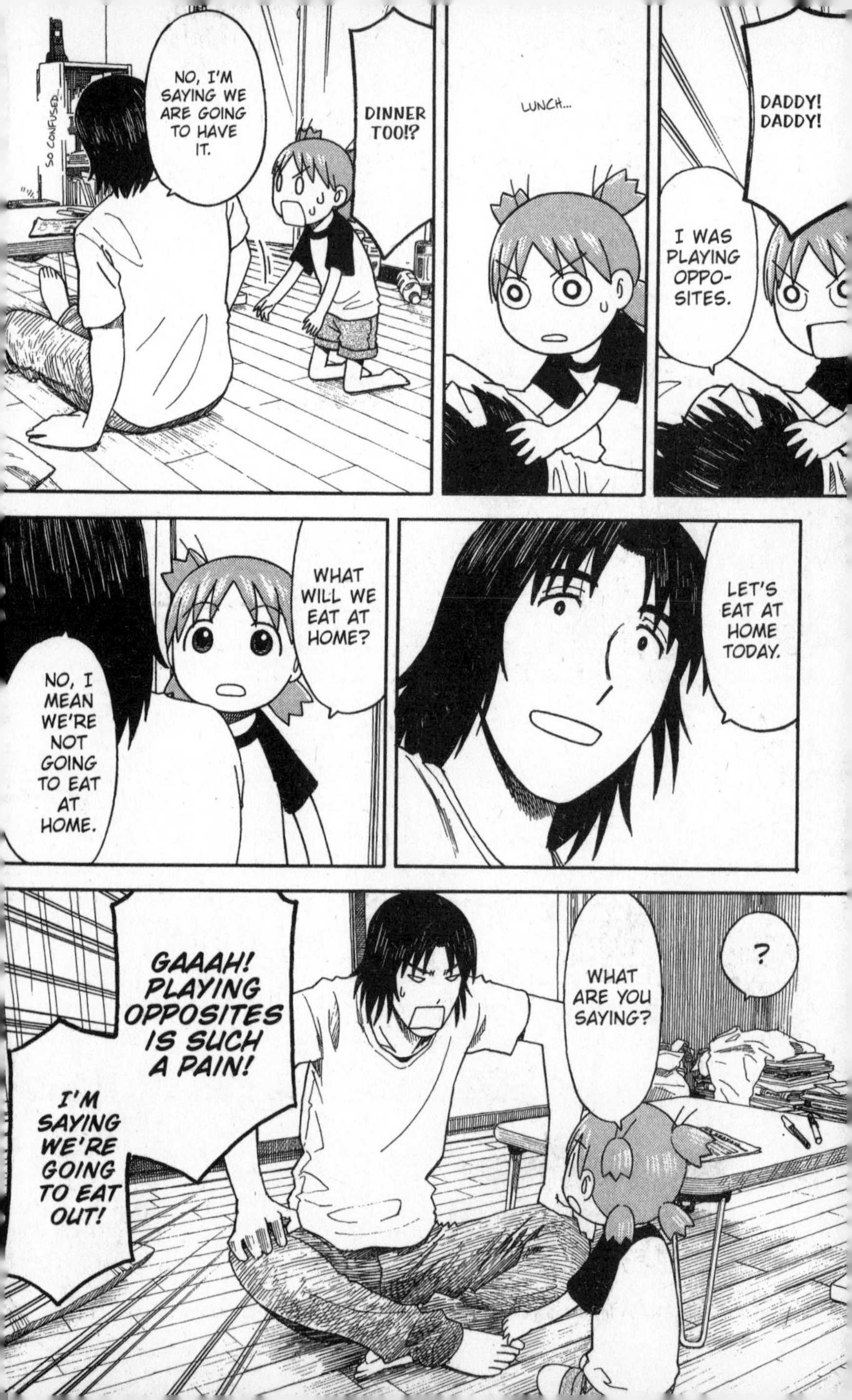
DADDY! DADDY!
I WAS PLAYING OPPO-SITES.
LUNCH...
DINNER TOO!?
NO, I'M SAYING WE ARE GOING TO HAVE IT.
SO CONFUSED...
LET'S EAT AT HOME TODAY.
WHAT WILL WE EAT AT HOME?
NO, I MEAN WE'RE NOT GOING TO EAT AT HOME.
?
WHAT ARE YOU SAYING?
GAAAH! PLAYING OPPOSITES IS SUCH A PAIN!
I'M SAYING WE'RE GOING TO EAT OUT!

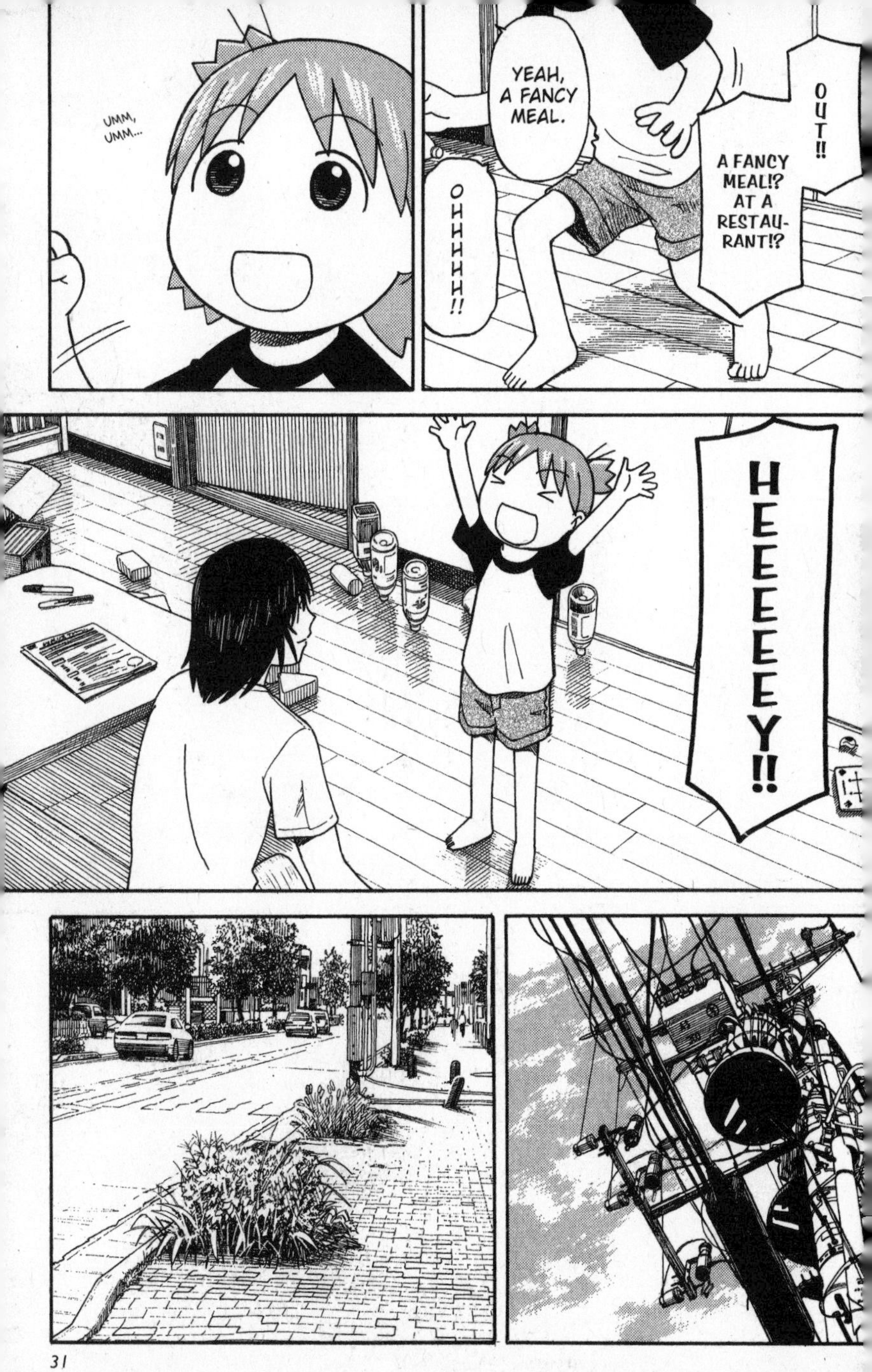
OUT!!
A FANCY MEAL!? AT A RESTAURANT!?
YEAH, A FANCY MEAL.
OHHHHHH!!
UMM, UMM...
HEEEEEEY!!

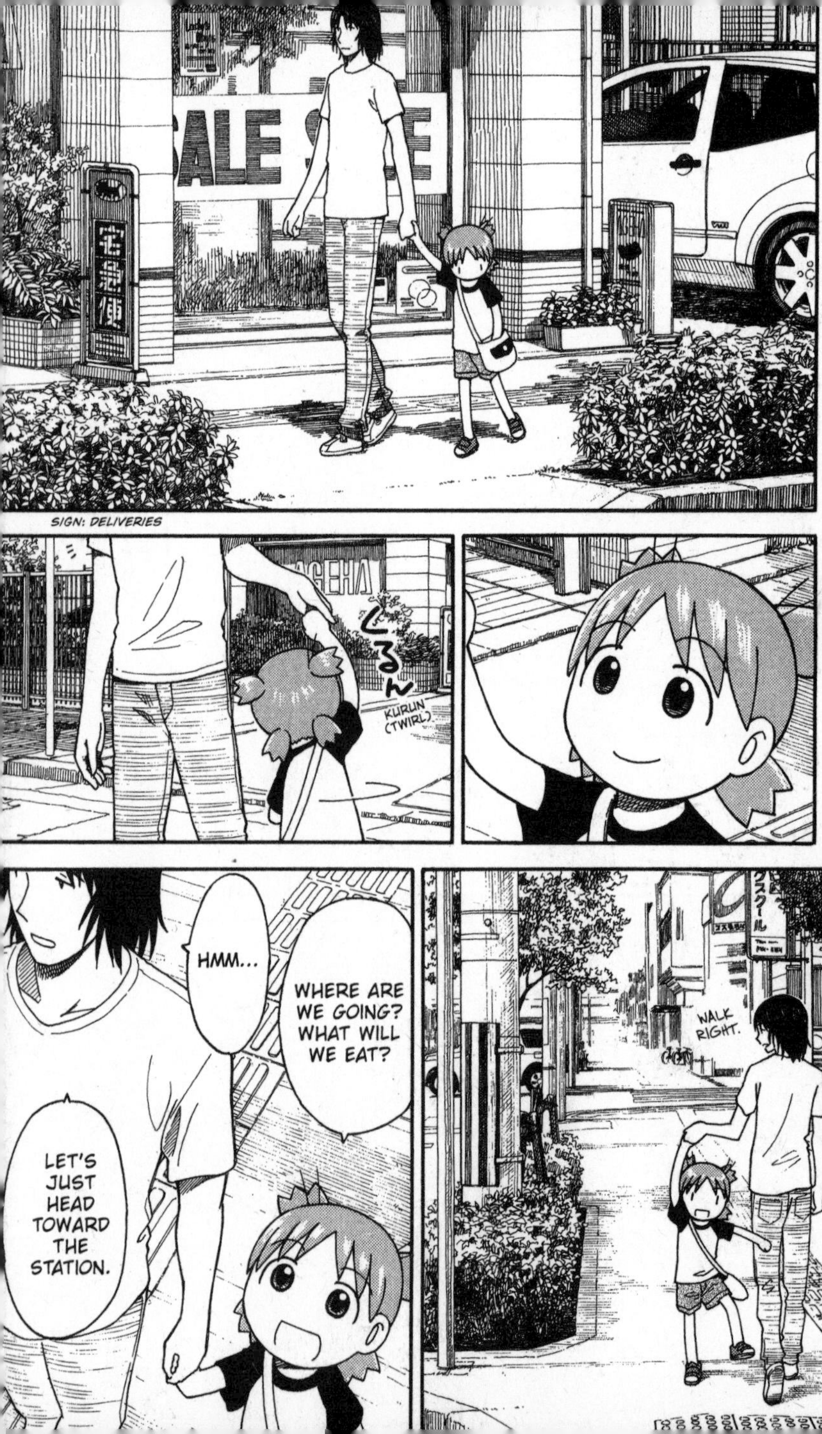
SALE
宅急便
SIGN: DELIVERIES
くるん
KURUN (TWIRL)
WALK RIGHT.
WHERE ARE WE GOING? WHAT WILL WE EAT?
HMM...
LET'S JUST HEAD TOWARD THE STATION.

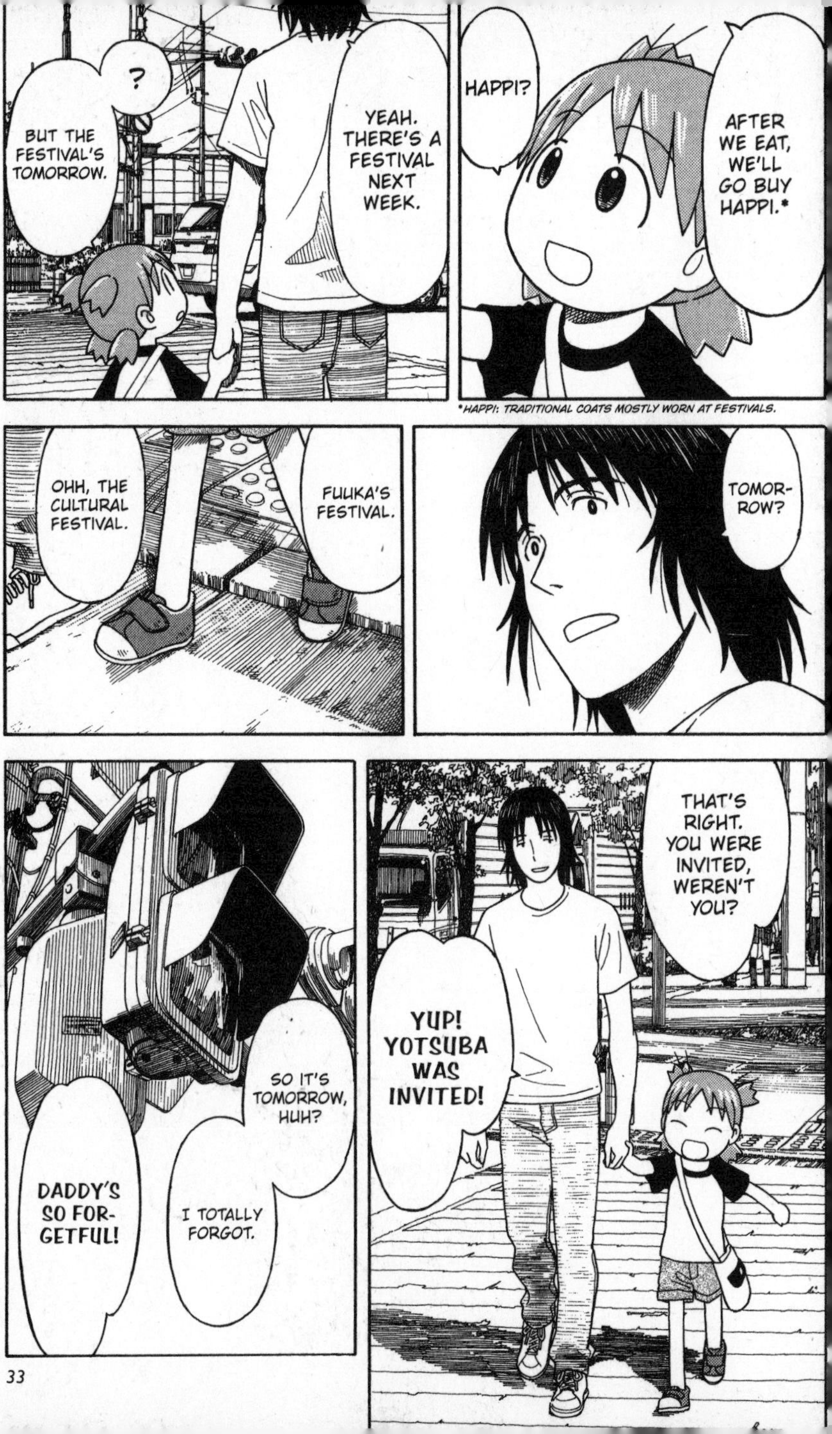
AFTER WE EAT, WE'LL GO BUY HAPPI.*
HAPPI?
YEAH. THERE'S A FESTIVAL NEXT WEEK.
?
BUT THE FESTIVAL'S TOMORROW.
TOMOR-ROW?
FUUKA'S FESTIVAL.
OHH, THE CULTURAL FESTIVAL.
THAT'S RIGHT. YOU WERE INVITED, WEREN'T YOU?
YUP! YOTSUBA WAS INVITED!
SO IT'S TOMORROW, HUH?
I TOTALLY FORGOT.
DADDY'S SO FOR-GETFUL!

*HAPPI: TRADITIONAL COATS MOSTLY WORN AT FESTIVALS.

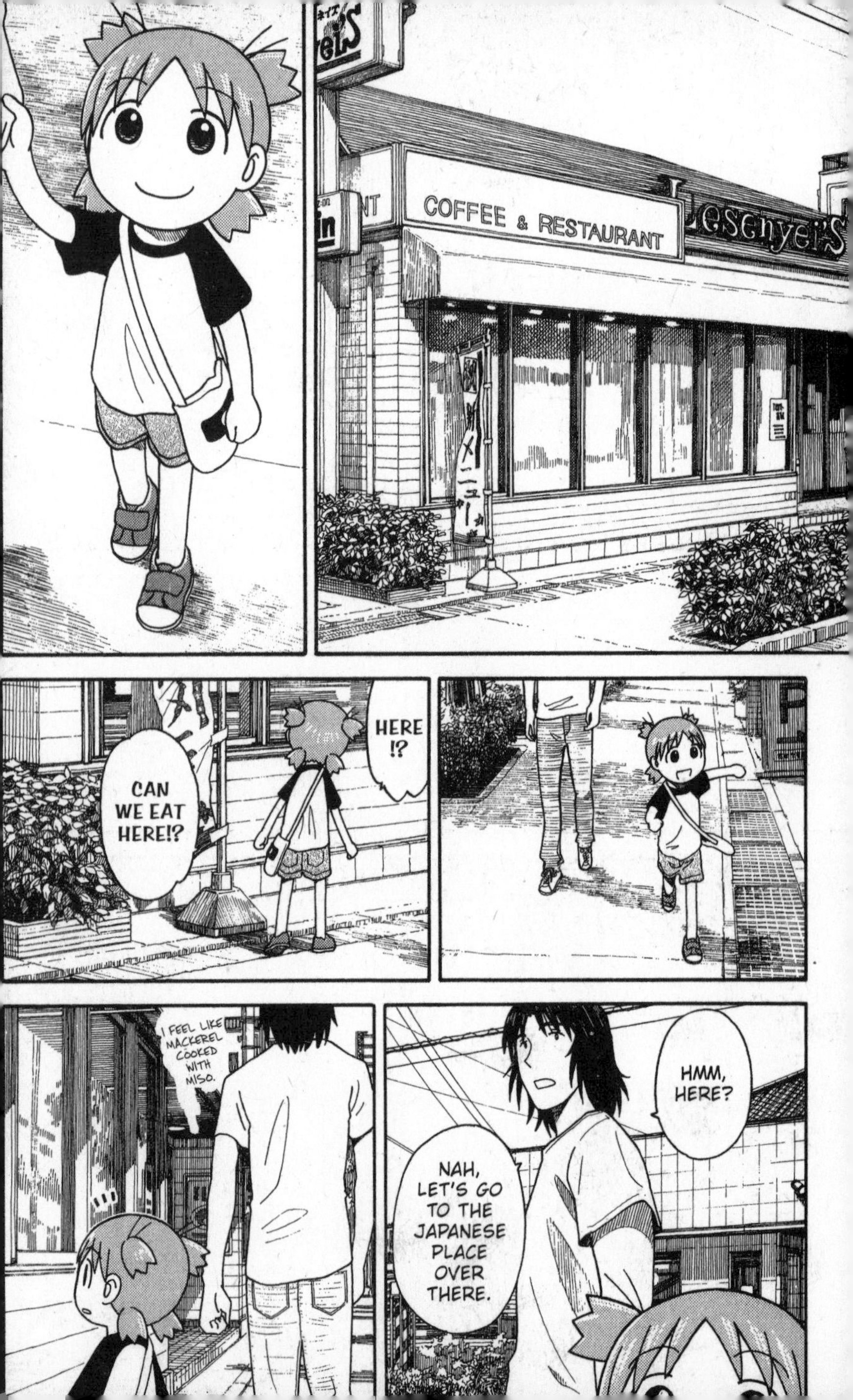
COFFEE & RESTAURANT
HERE!?
CAN WE EAT HERE!?
HMM, HERE?
NAH, LET'S GO TO THE JAPANESE PLACE OVER THERE.
I FEEL LIKE MACKEREL COOKED WITH MISO.

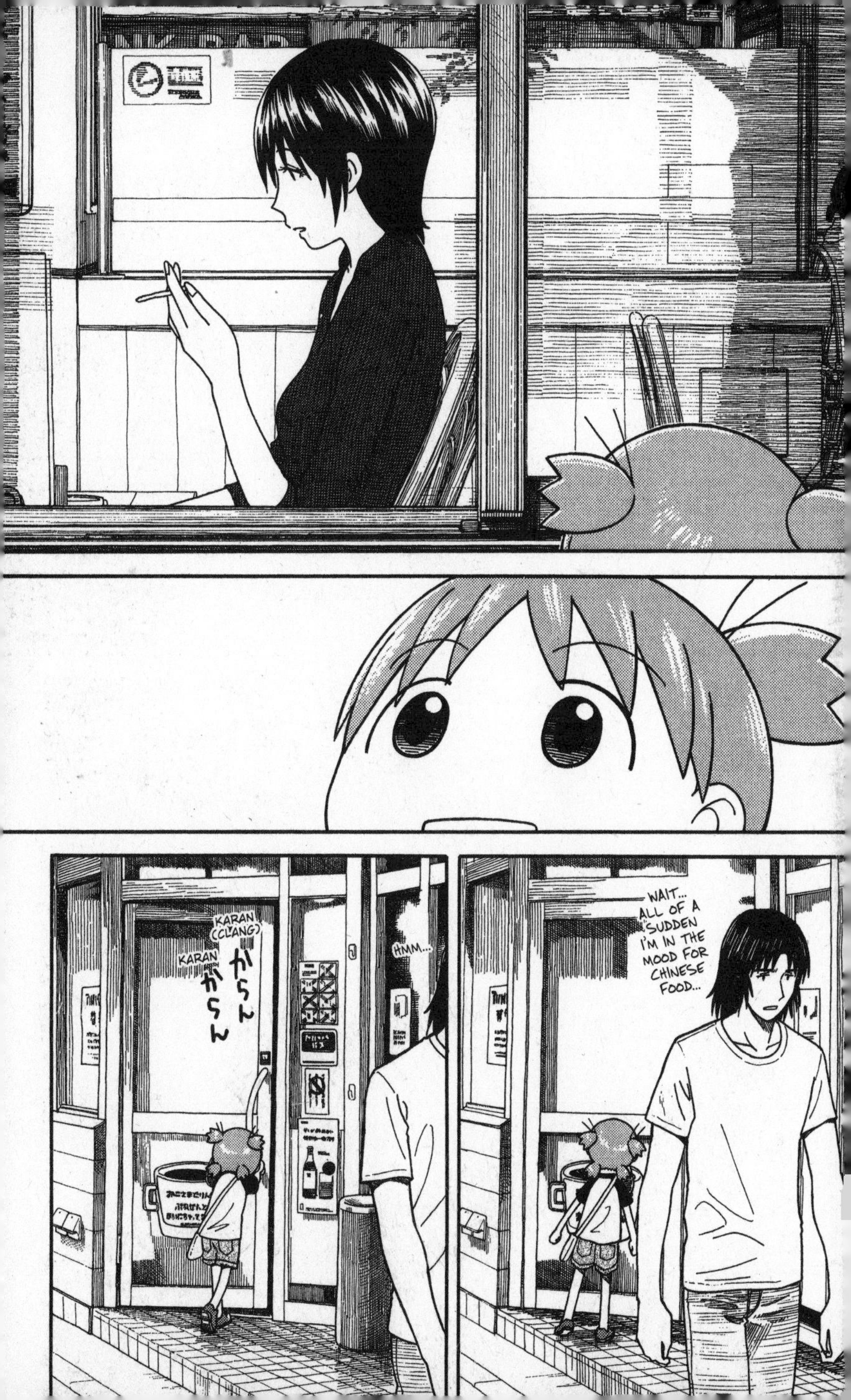
WAIT... ALL OF A SUDDEN I'M IN THE MOOD FOR CHINESE FOOD...
HMM...
KARAN (CLANG)
がらん
KARAN
がらん

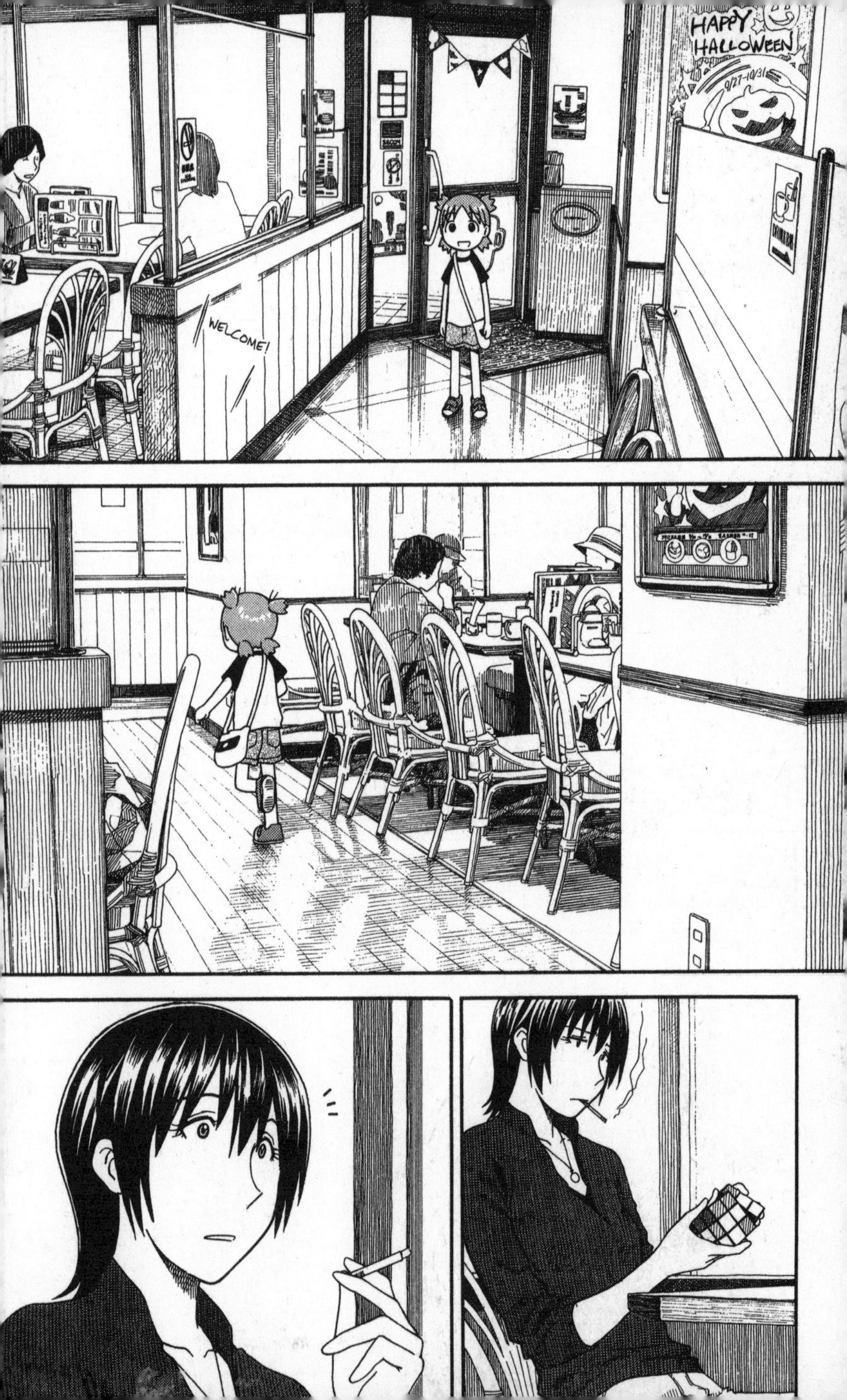
HAPPY HALLOWEEN
9/27-10/31
WELCOME!

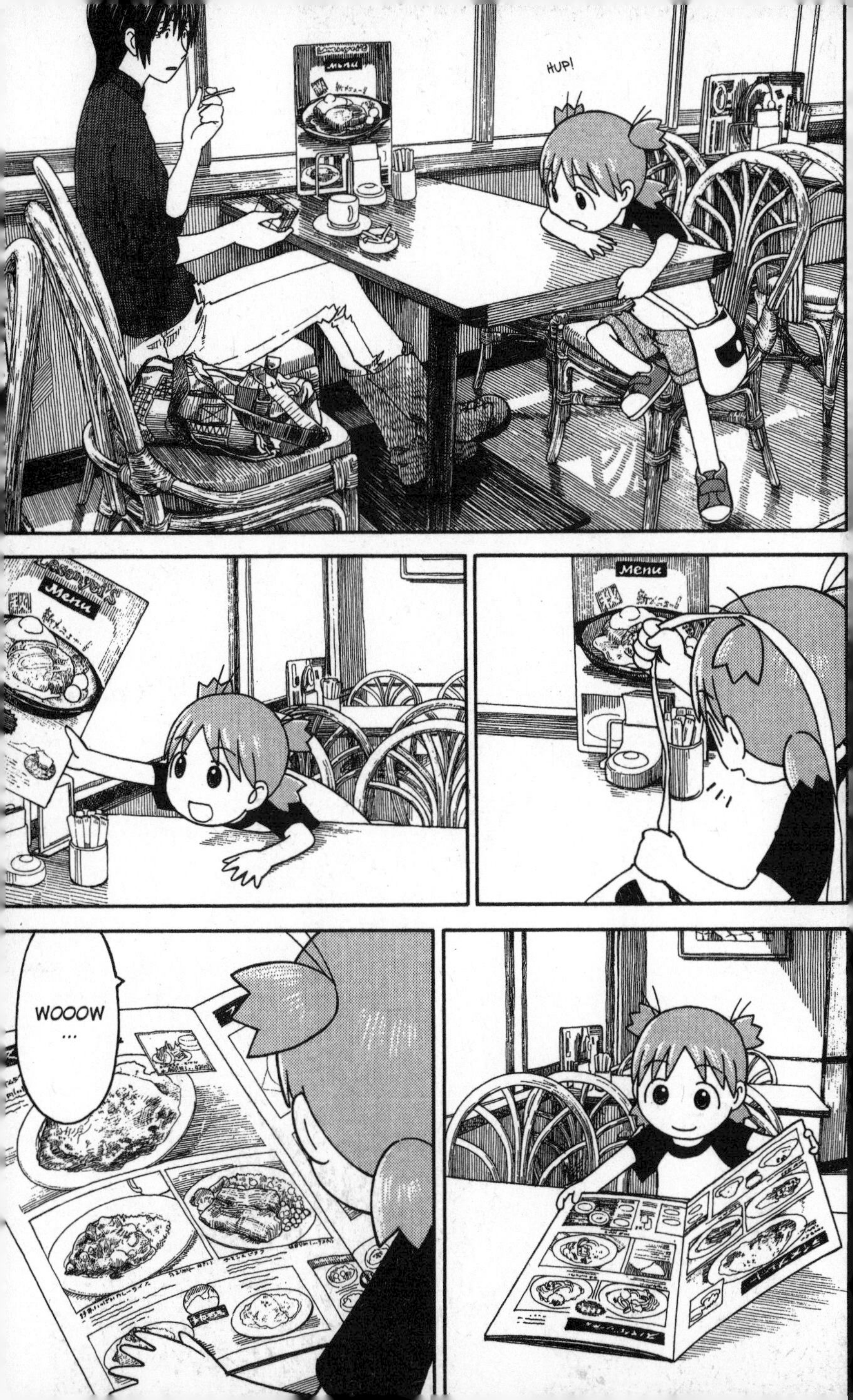
HUP!
WOOOW ...

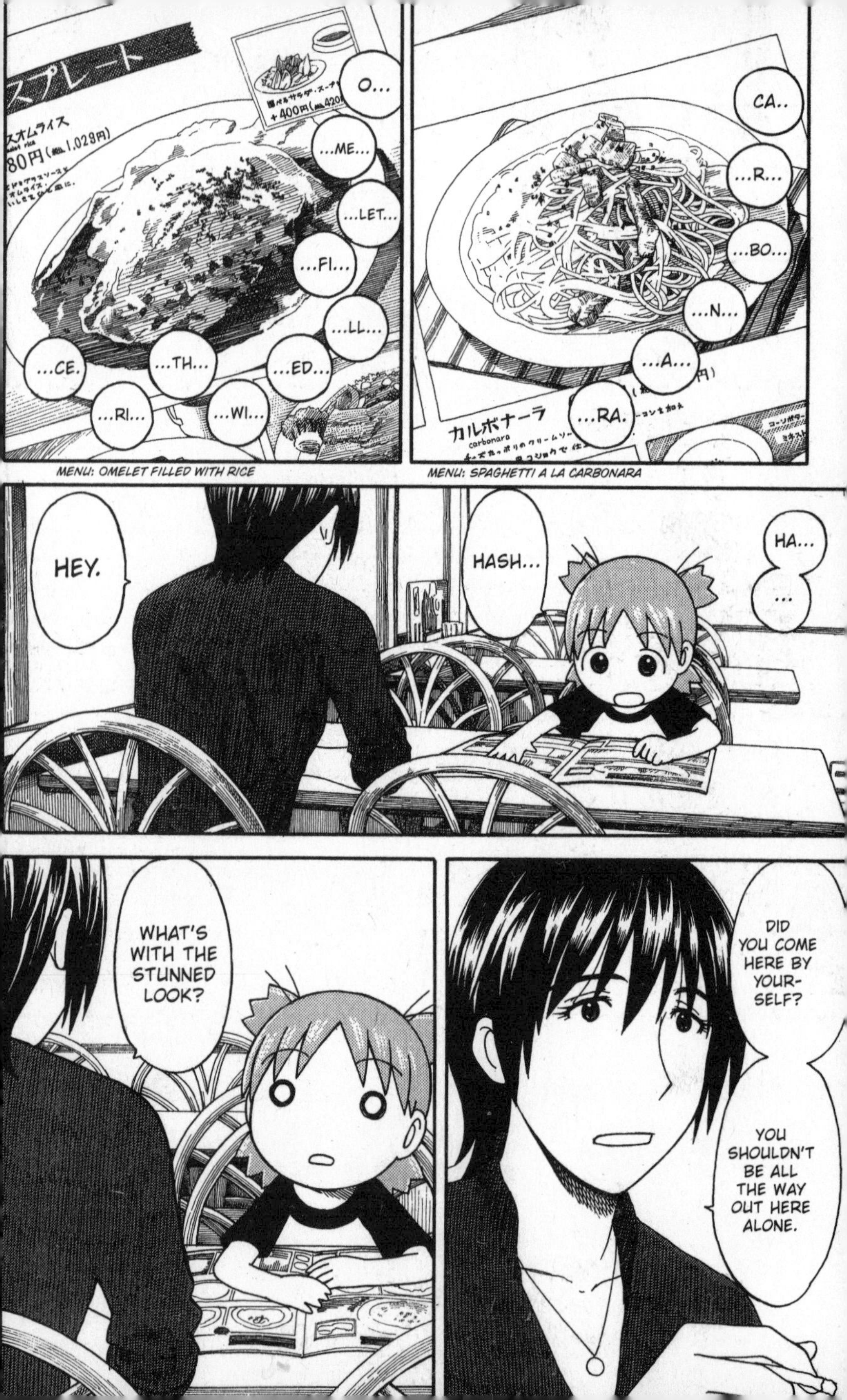

CA..
...R...
...BO...
...N...
...A...
...RA.
カルボナーラ
carbonara
MENU: SPAGHETTI A LA CARBONARA
O...
...ME...
...LET...
...FI...
...LL...
...ED...
...WI...
...TH...
...RI...
...CE.
MENU: OMELET FILLED WITH RICE
HA... ...
HASH...
HEY.
DID YOU COME HERE BY YOUR-SELF?
YOU SHOULDN'T BE ALL THE WAY OUT HERE ALONE.
WHAT'S WITH THE STUNNED LOOK?

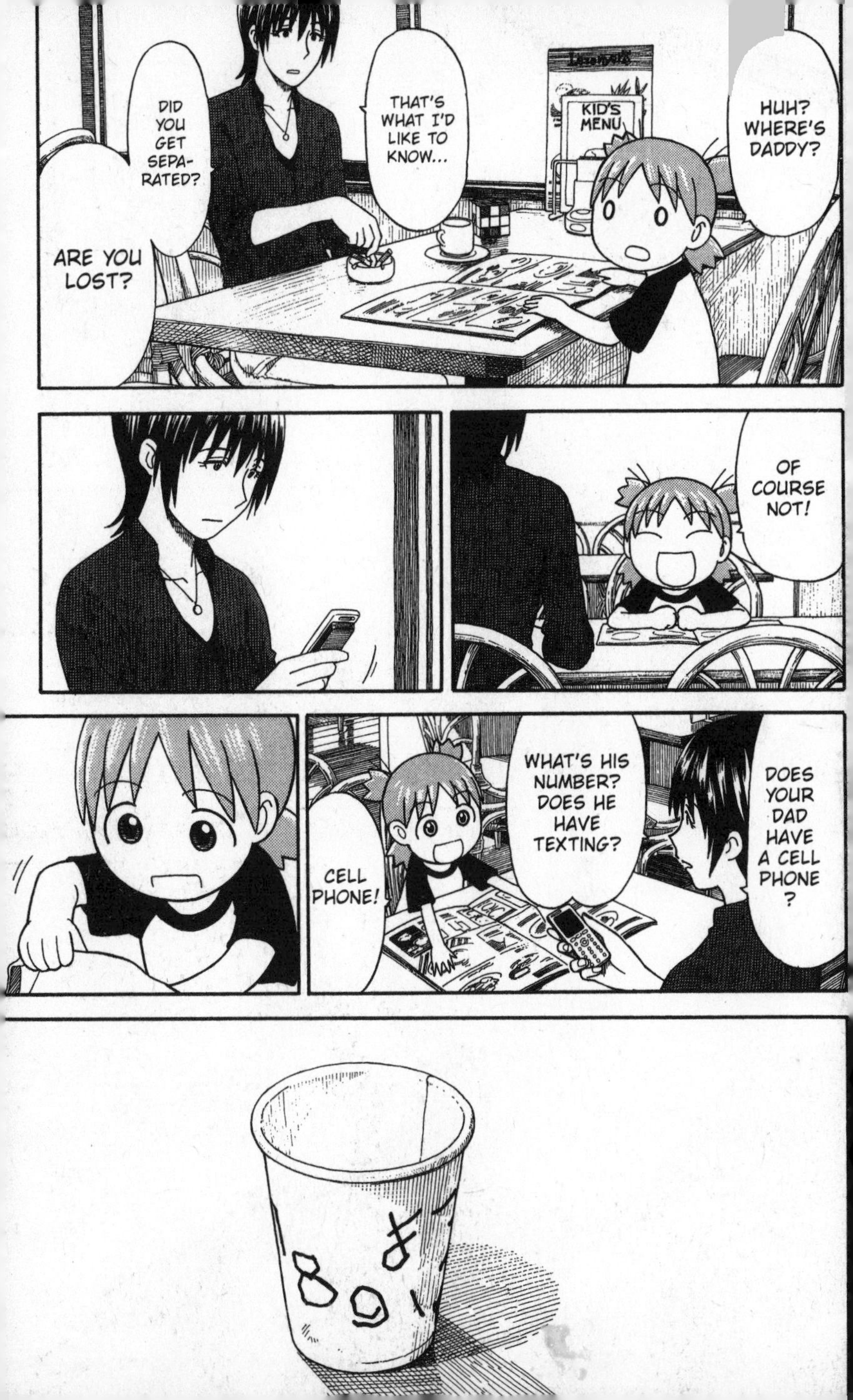
KID'S MENU
HUH? WHERE'S DADDY?
THAT'S WHAT I'D LIKE TO KNOW...
DID YOU GET SEPA-RATED?
ARE YOU LOST?
OF COURSE NOT!
DOES YOUR DAD HAVE A CELL PHONE?
WHAT'S HIS NUMBER? DOES HE HAVE TEXTING?
CELL PHONE!

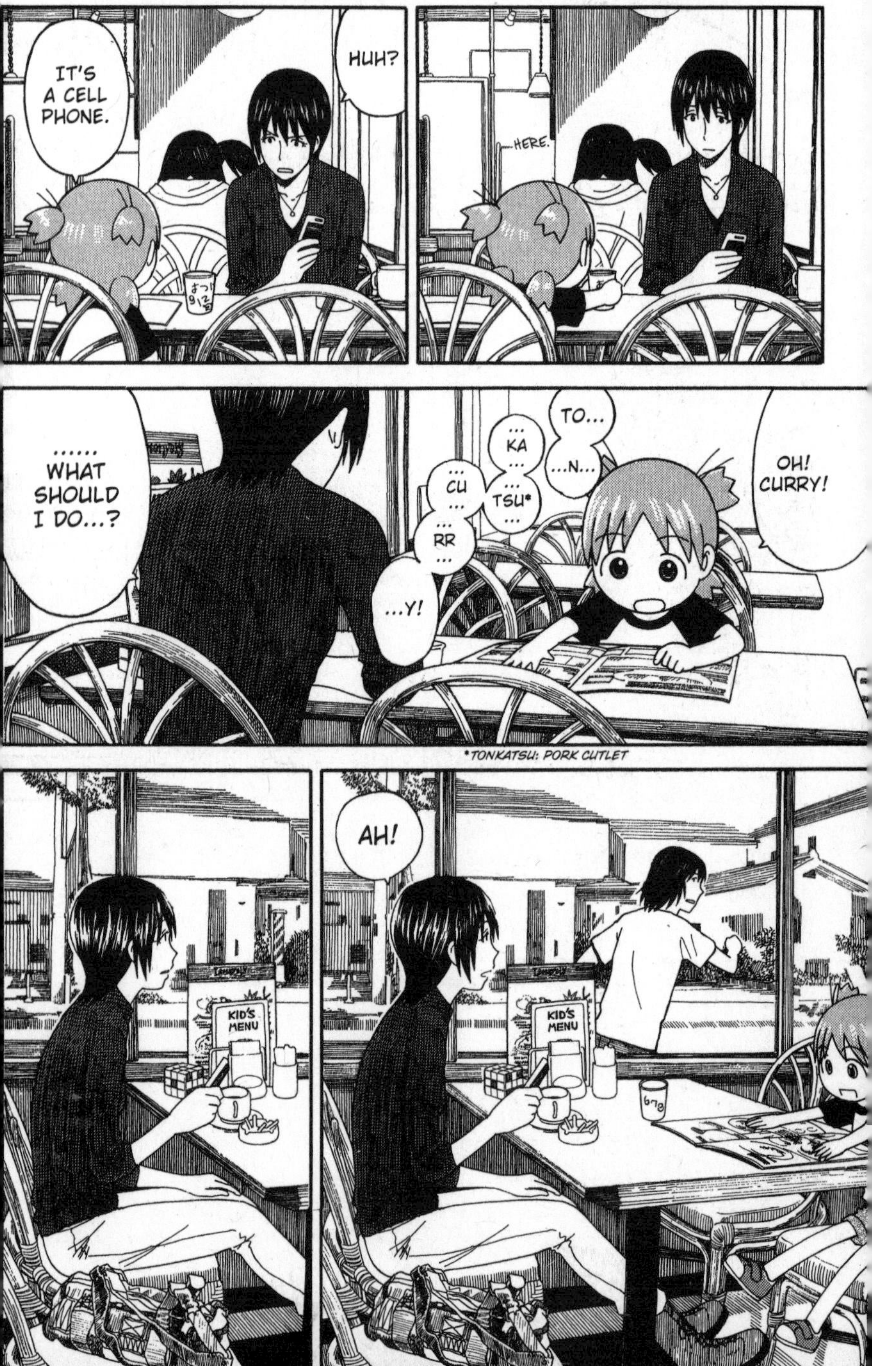
HERE.
HUH?
IT'S A CELL PHONE.
OH! CURRY!
TO...
...N...
...KA...
...TSU*...
...CU...
...RR...
...Y!
...... WHAT SHOULD I DO...?
*TONKATSU: PORK CUTLET
AH!
KID'S MENU
KID'S MENU

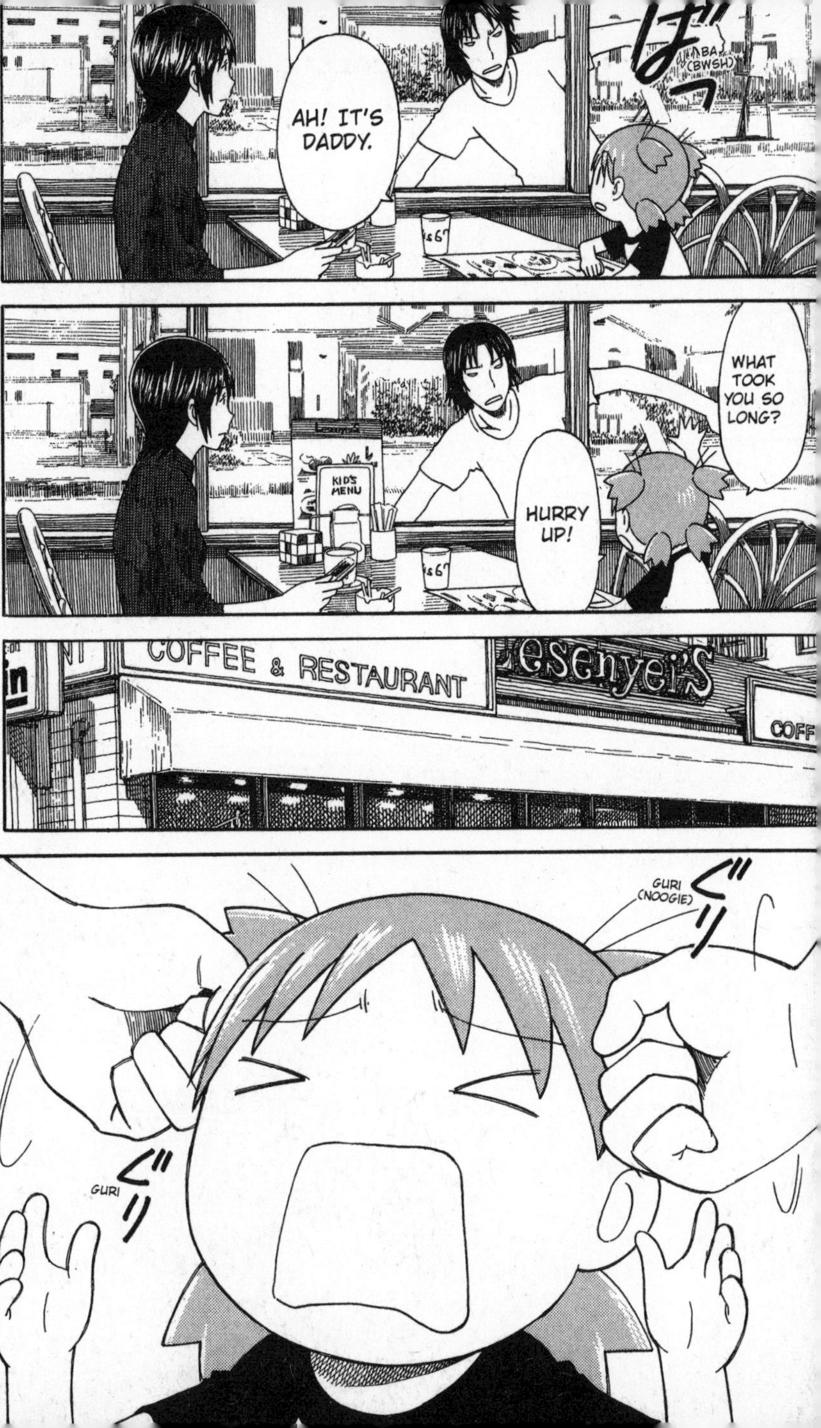
ばっ
BA (BWSH)
AH! IT'S DADDY.
WHAT TOOK YOU SO LONG?
HURRY UP!
COFFEE & RESTAURANT
esenyei's
COFF
ぐり
GURI (NOOGIE)
ぐり
GURI

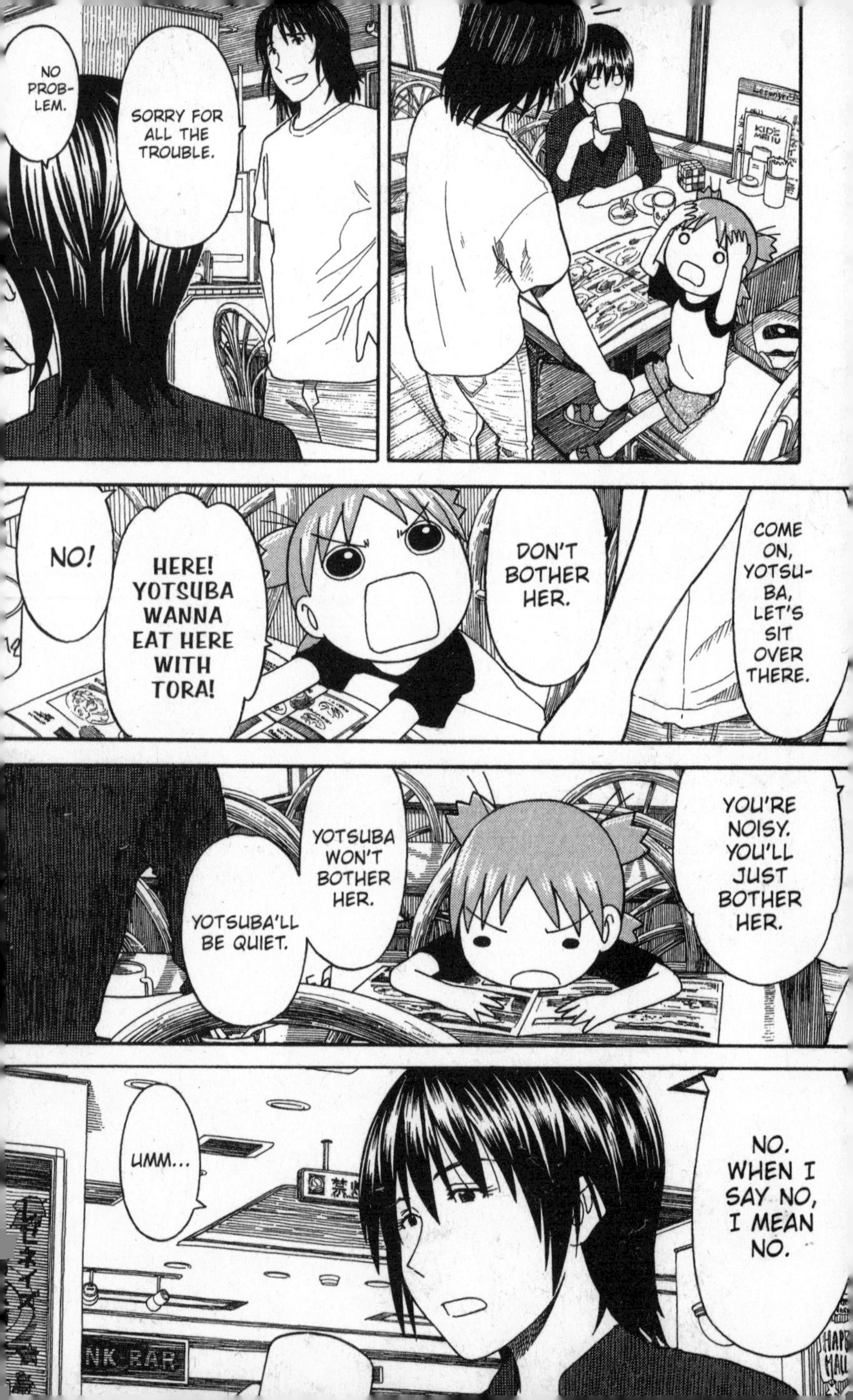
KIDS MENU
SORRY FOR ALL THE TROUBLE.
NO PROBLEM.
COME ON, YOTSUBA, LET'S SIT OVER THERE.
DON'T BOTHER HER.
HERE! YOTSUBA WANNA EAT HERE WITH TORA!
NO!
YOU'RE NOISY. YOU'LL JUST BOTHER HER.
YOTSUBA WON'T BOTHER HER.
YOTSUBA'LL BE QUIET.
NO. WHEN I SAY NO, I MEAN NO.
UMM...

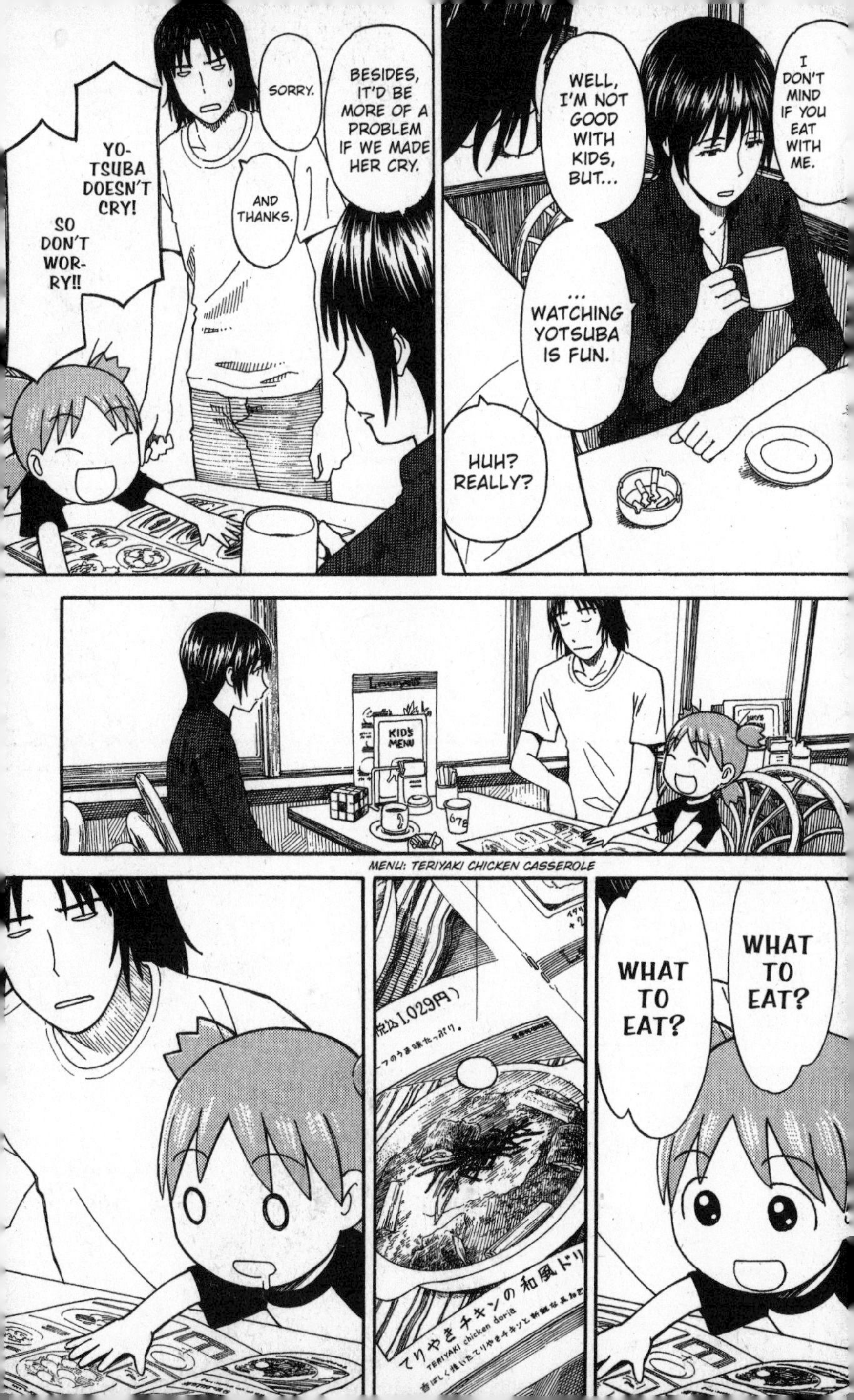
I DON'T MIND IF YOU EAT WITH ME.
WELL, I'M NOT GOOD WITH KIDS, BUT...
...WATCHING YOTSUBA IS FUN.
HUH? REALLY?
BESIDES, IT'D BE MORE OF A PROBLEM IF WE MADE HER CRY.
SORRY.
AND THANKS.
YOTSUBA DOESN'T CRY!
SO DON'T WORRY!!
KID'S MENU
MENU: TERIYAKI CHICKEN CASSEROLE
WHAT TO EAT?
WHAT TO EAT?
1,029円
TERIYAKI chicken doria

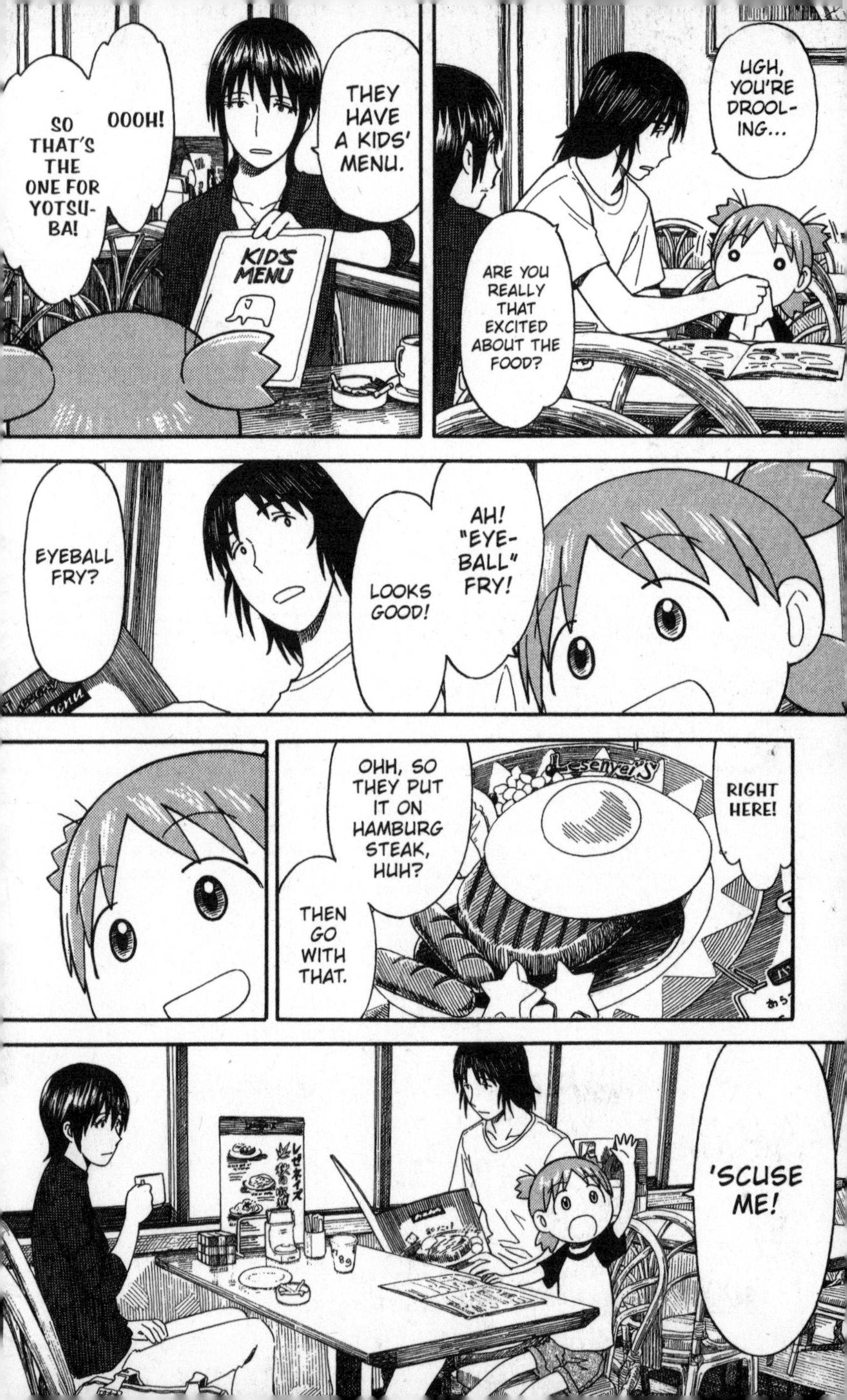
UGH, YOU'RE DROOLING...
ARE YOU REALLY THAT EXCITED ABOUT THE FOOD?
THEY HAVE A KIDS' MENU.
KID'S MENU
OOOH!
SO THAT'S THE ONE FOR YOTSUBA!
AH! "EYEBALL" FRY!
LOOKS GOOD!
EYEBALL FRY?
RIGHT HERE!
OHH, SO THEY PUT IT ON HAMBURG STEAK, HUH?
THEN GO WITH THAT.
'SCUSE ME!

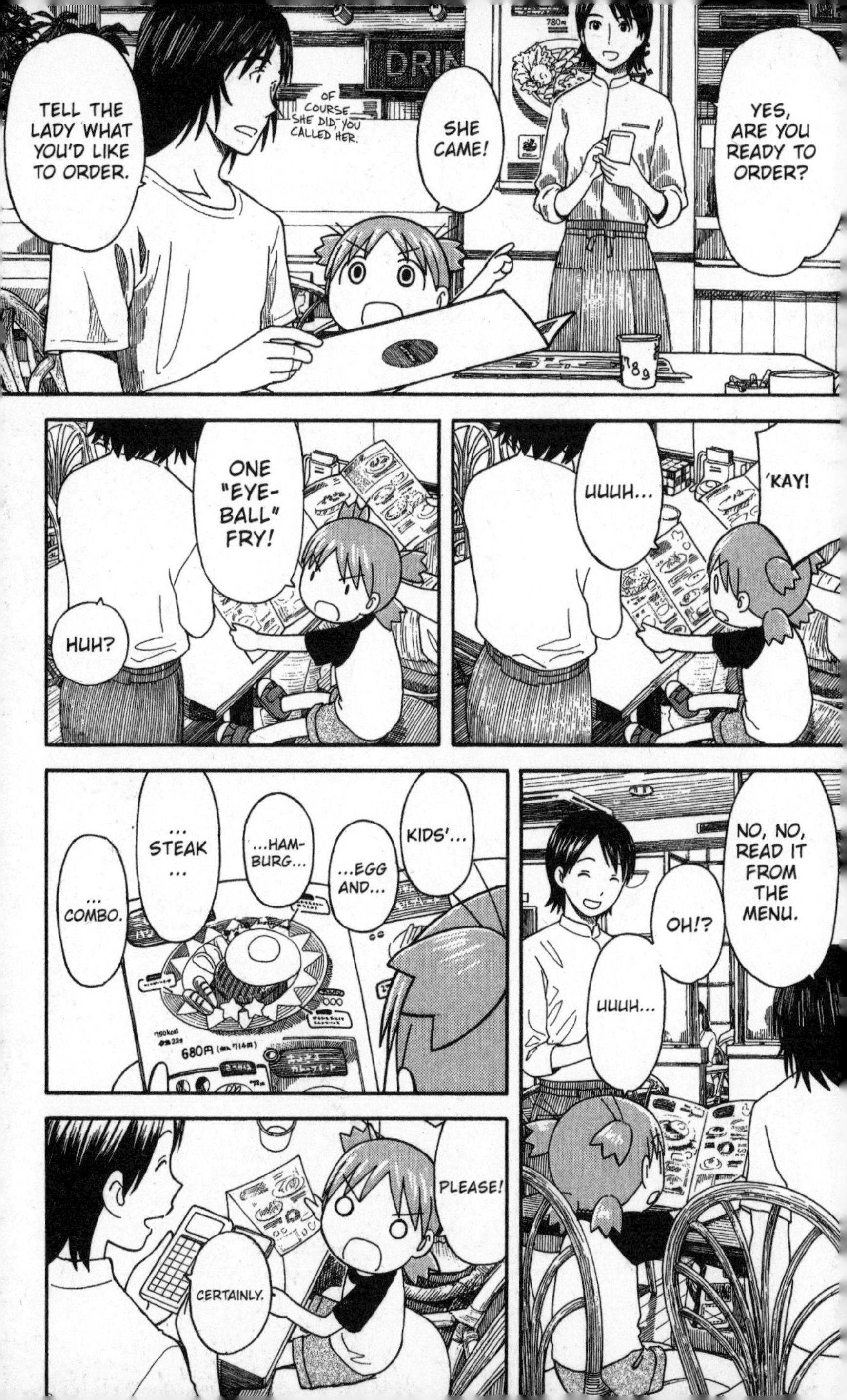
YES, ARE YOU READY TO ORDER?
SHE CAME!
OF COURSE SHE DID, YOU CALLED HER.
TELL THE LADY WHAT YOU'D LIKE TO ORDER.
'KAY!
UUUH...
ONE "EYE-BALL" FRY!
HUH?
NO, NO, READ IT FROM THE MENU.
OH!?
UUUH...
KIDS'...
...EGG AND...
...HAM-BURG...
... STEAK ...
... COMBO.
PLEASE!
CERTAINLY.

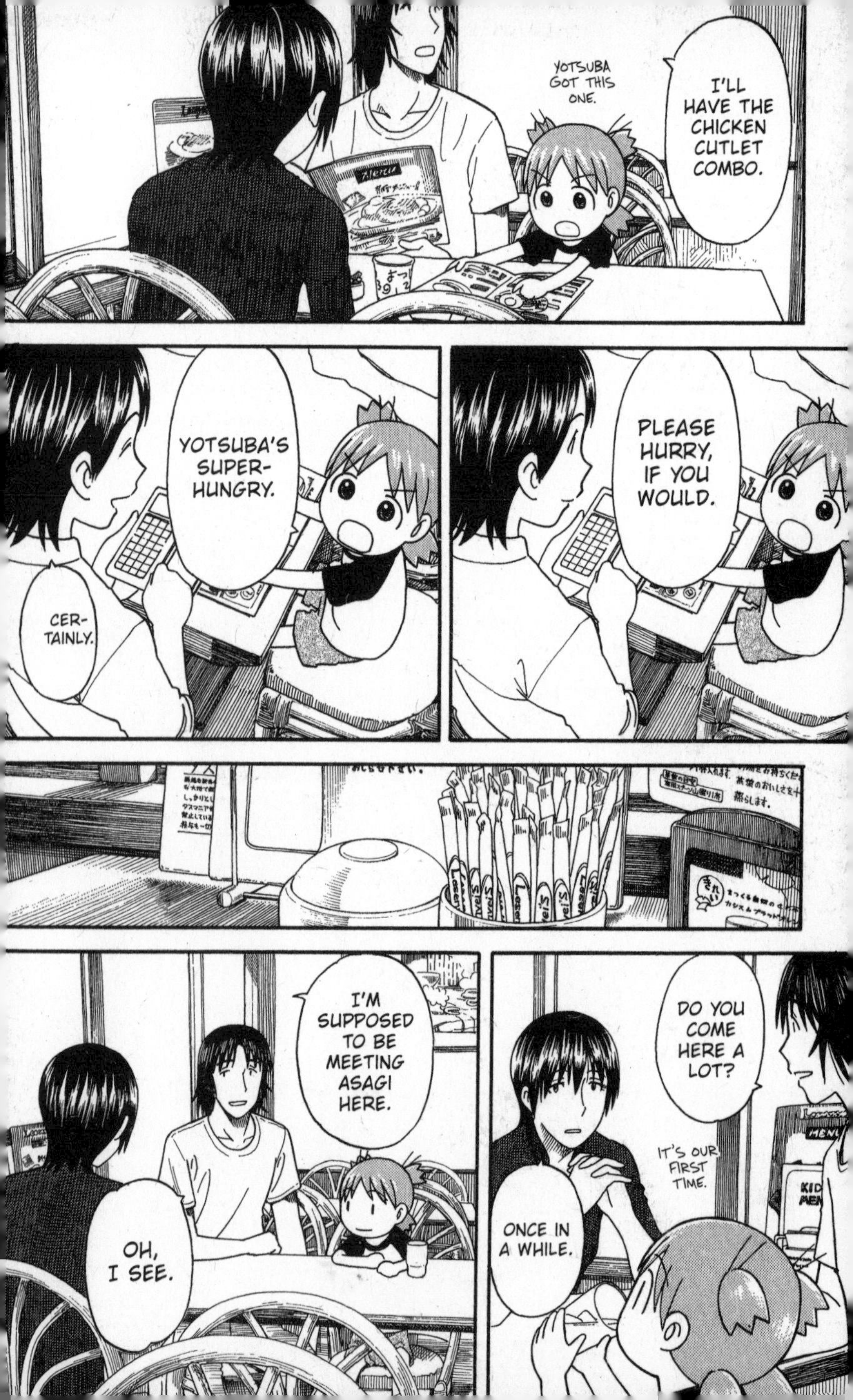
I'LL HAVE THE CHICKEN CUTLET COMBO.
YOTSUBA GOT THIS ONE.
PLEASE HURRY, IF YOU WOULD.
YOTSUBA'S SUPER-HUNGRY.
CER-TAINLY.
DO YOU COME HERE A LOT?
IT'S OUR FIRST TIME.
ONCE IN A WHILE.
I'M SUPPOSED TO BE MEETING ASAGI HERE.
OH, I SEE.

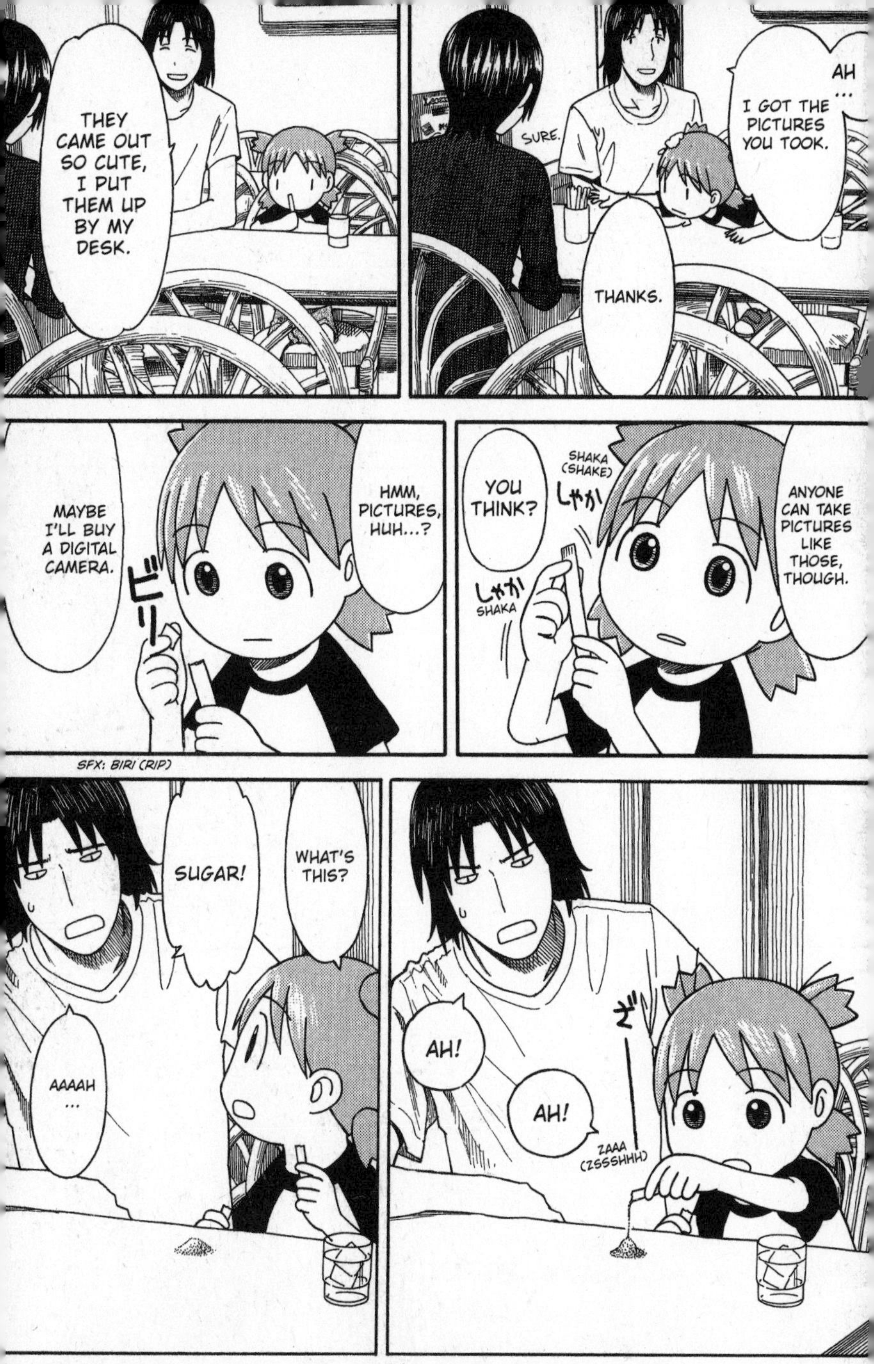
AH ... I GOT THE PICTURES YOU TOOK.
SURE.
THANKS.
THEY CAME OUT SO CUTE, I PUT THEM UP BY MY DESK.
ANYONE CAN TAKE PICTURES LIKE THOSE, THOUGH.
しゃか
SHAKA (SHAKE)
YOU THINK?
しゃか
SHAKA
HMM, PICTURES, HUH...?
ビリ
MAYBE I'LL BUY A DIGITAL CAMERA.
SFX: BIRI (RIP)
ざ
ZAAA (ZSSSHHH)
AH!
AH!
WHAT'S THIS?
SUGAR!
AAAAH ...

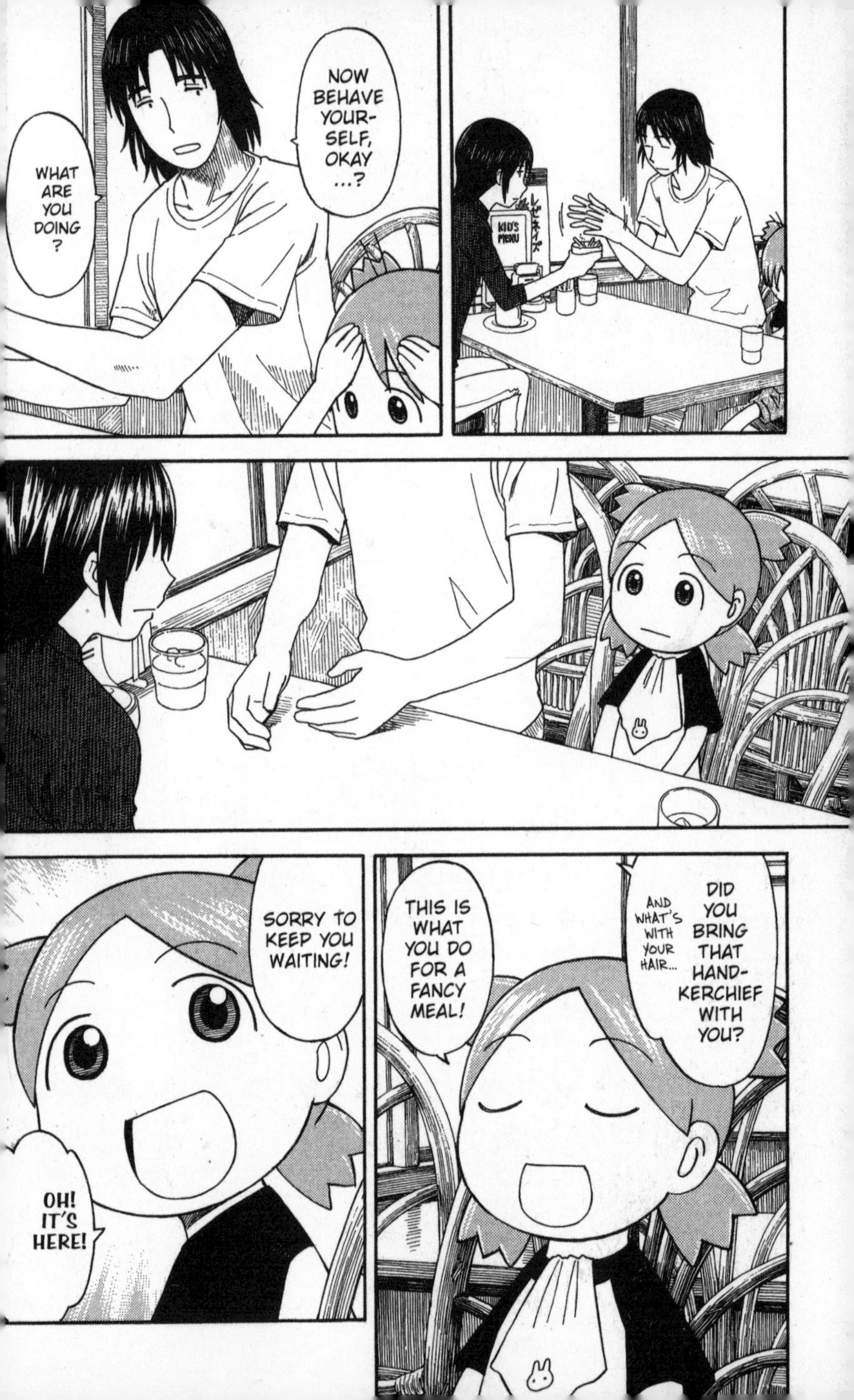
KID'S MENU
NOW BEHAVE YOUR-SELF, OKAY ...?
WHAT ARE YOU DOING?
DID YOU BRING THAT HAND-KERCHIEF WITH YOU?
AND WHAT'S WITH YOUR HAIR...
THIS IS WHAT YOU DO FOR A FANCY MEAL!
SORRY TO KEEP YOU WAITING!
OH! IT'S HERE!

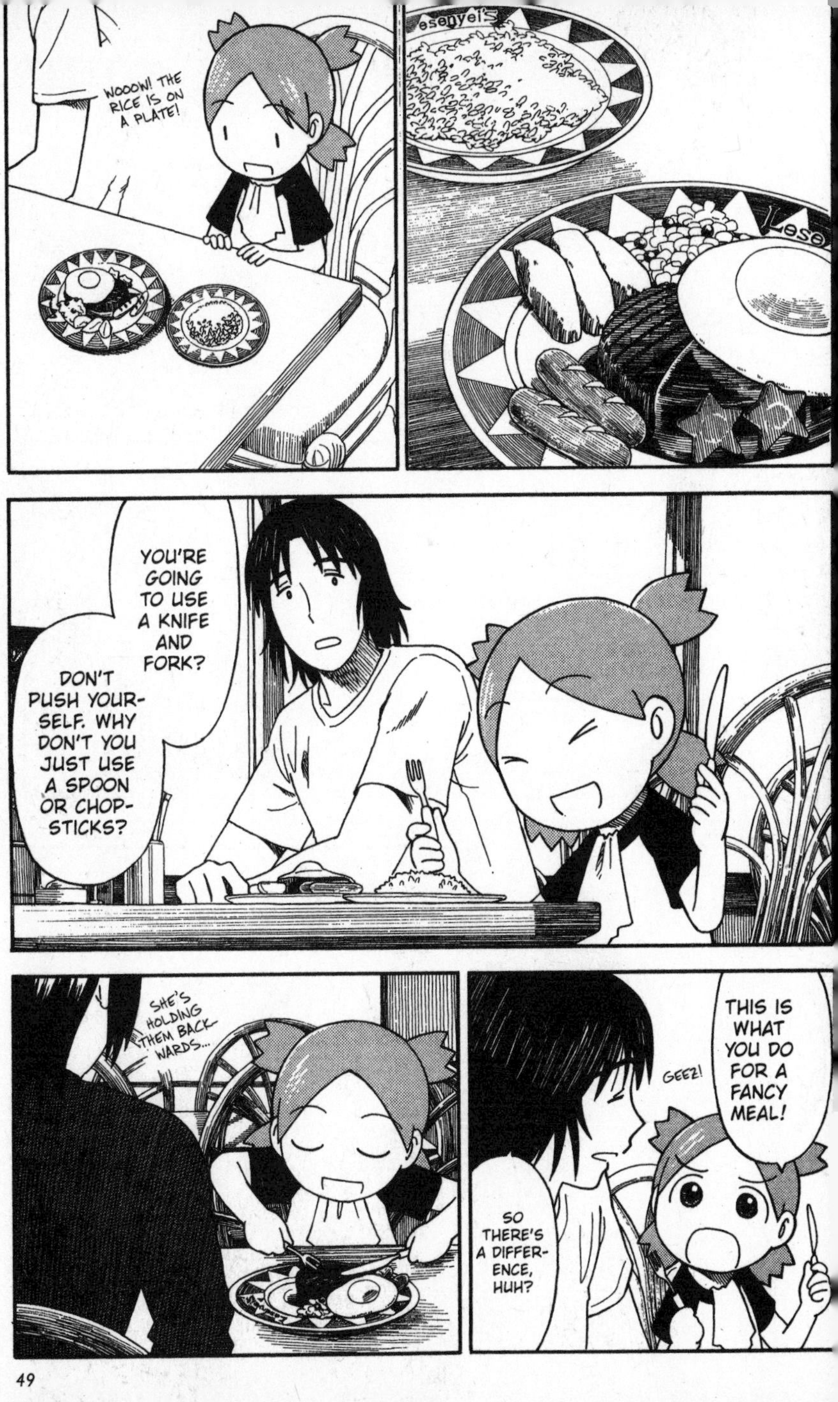
WOOOW! THE RICE IS ON A PLATE!
YOU'RE GOING TO USE A KNIFE AND FORK?
DON'T PUSH YOURSELF. WHY DON'T YOU JUST USE A SPOON OR CHOPSTICKS?
THIS IS WHAT YOU DO FOR A FANCY MEAL!
GEEZ!
SO THERE'S A DIFFERENCE, HUH?
SHE'S HOLDING THEM BACKWARDS...

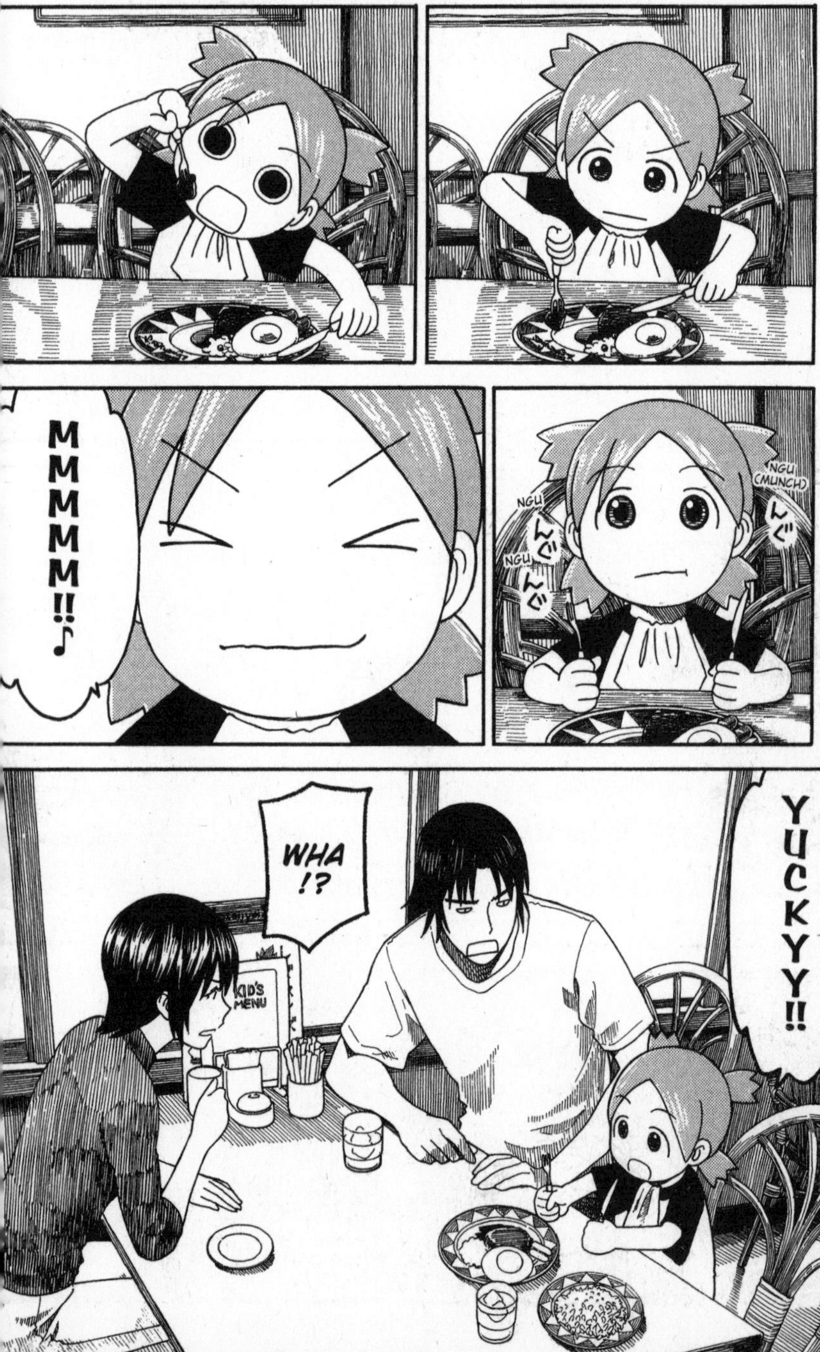
NGU (MUNCH)
んぐ
NGU
んぐ
NGU
んぐ
MMMMM!!♪
YUCKYY!!
WHA!?
KID'S MENU

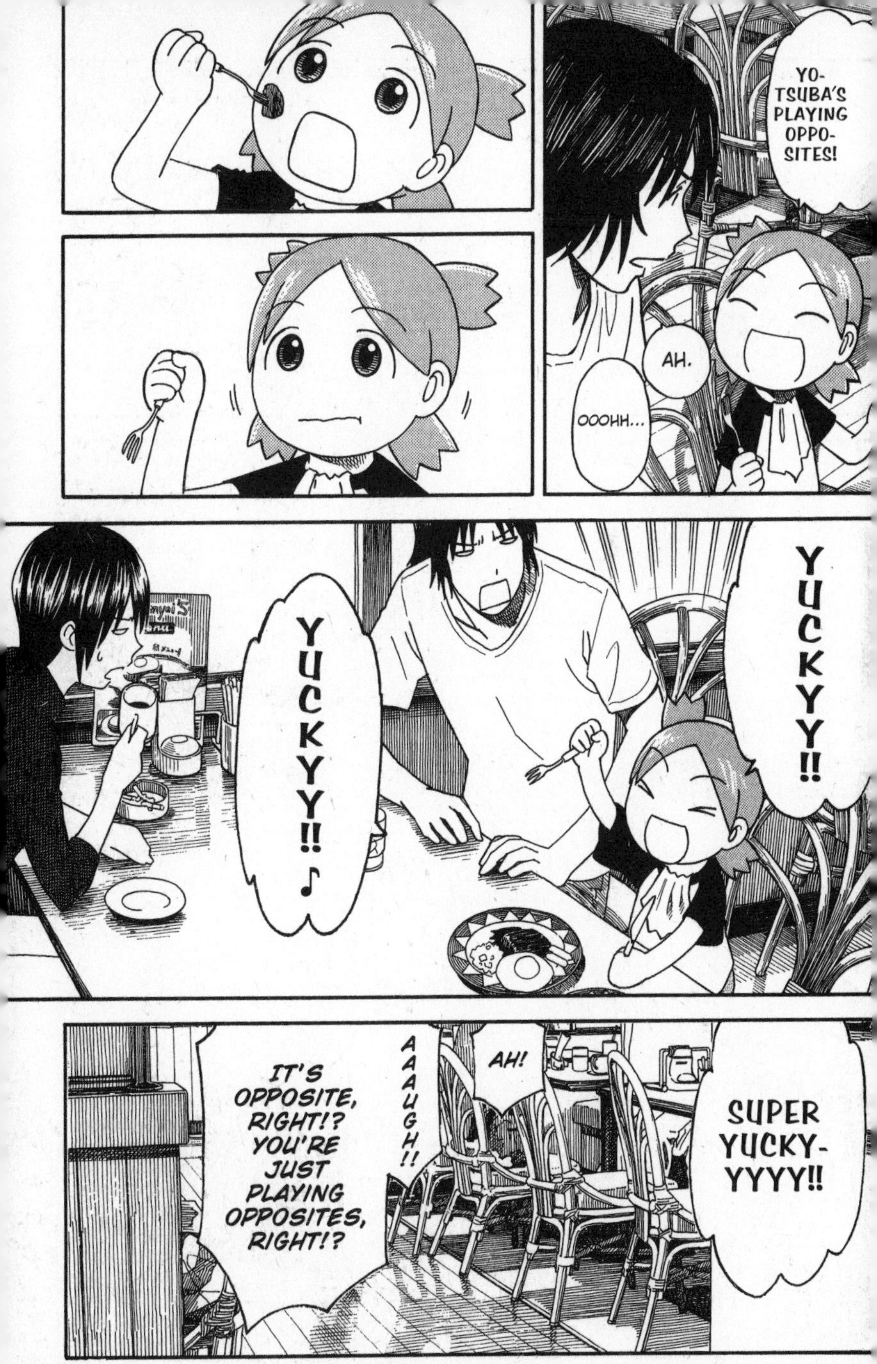
YO-TSUBA'S PLAYING OPPO-SITES!
AH.
OOOHH...
YUCKYY!!
YUCKYY!! ♪
SUPER YUCKY-YYYY!!
AH!
AAAAUGH!!
IT'S OPPOSITE, RIGHT!? YOU'RE JUST PLAYING OPPOSITES, RIGHT!?

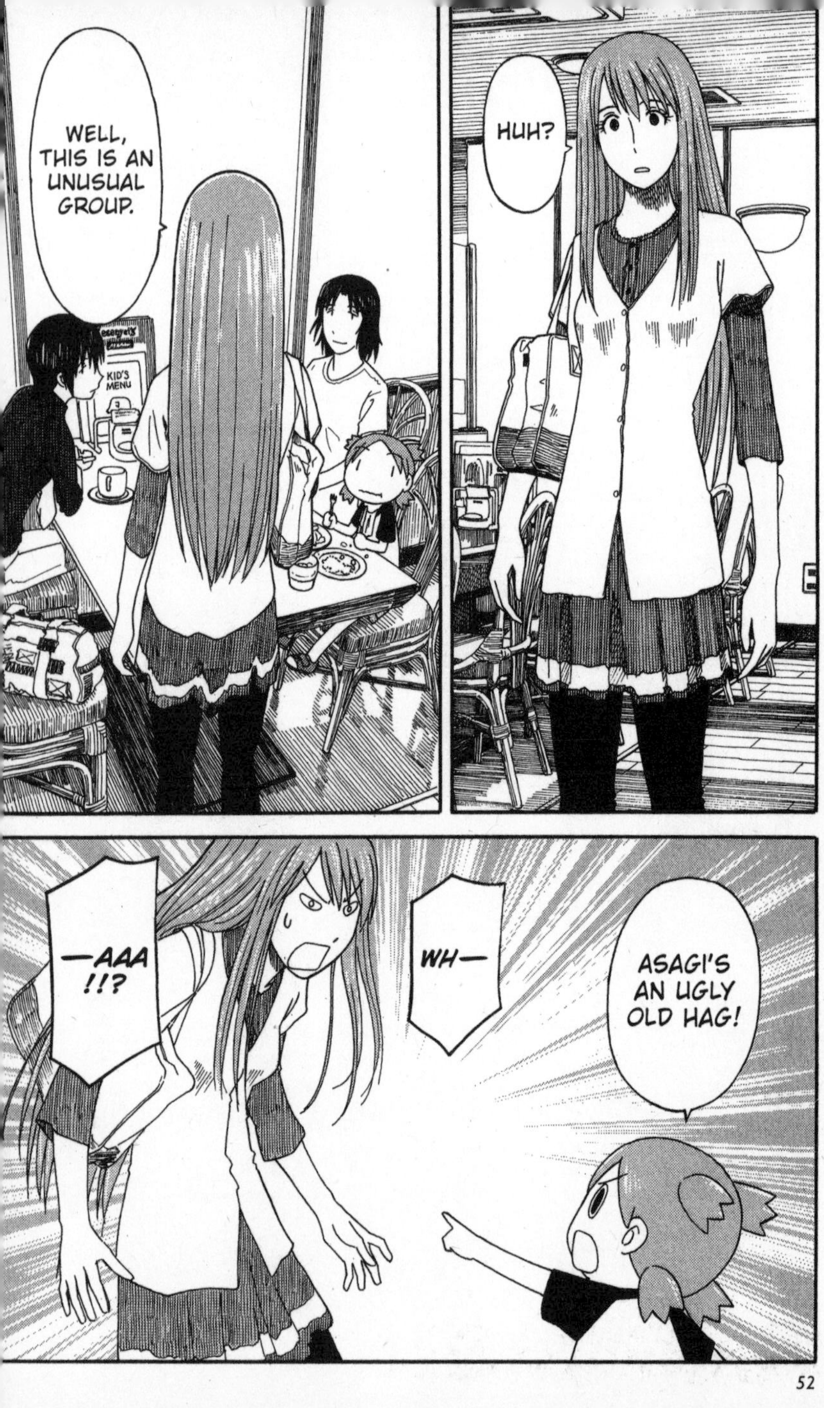
HUH?
WELL, THIS IS AN UNUSUAL GROUP.
KID'S MENU
ASAGI'S AN UGLY OLD HAG!
WH—
—AAA !!?

YOTSUBA&!

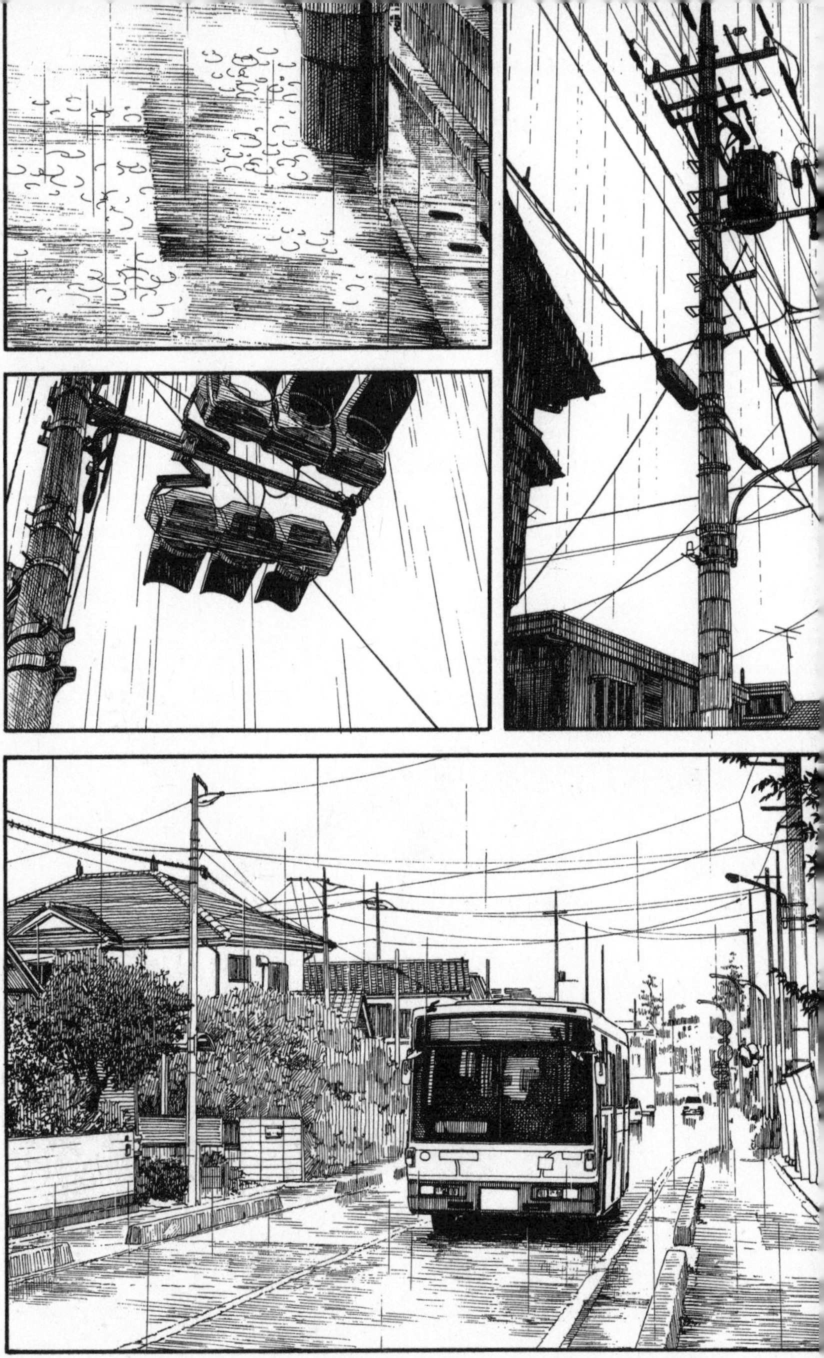

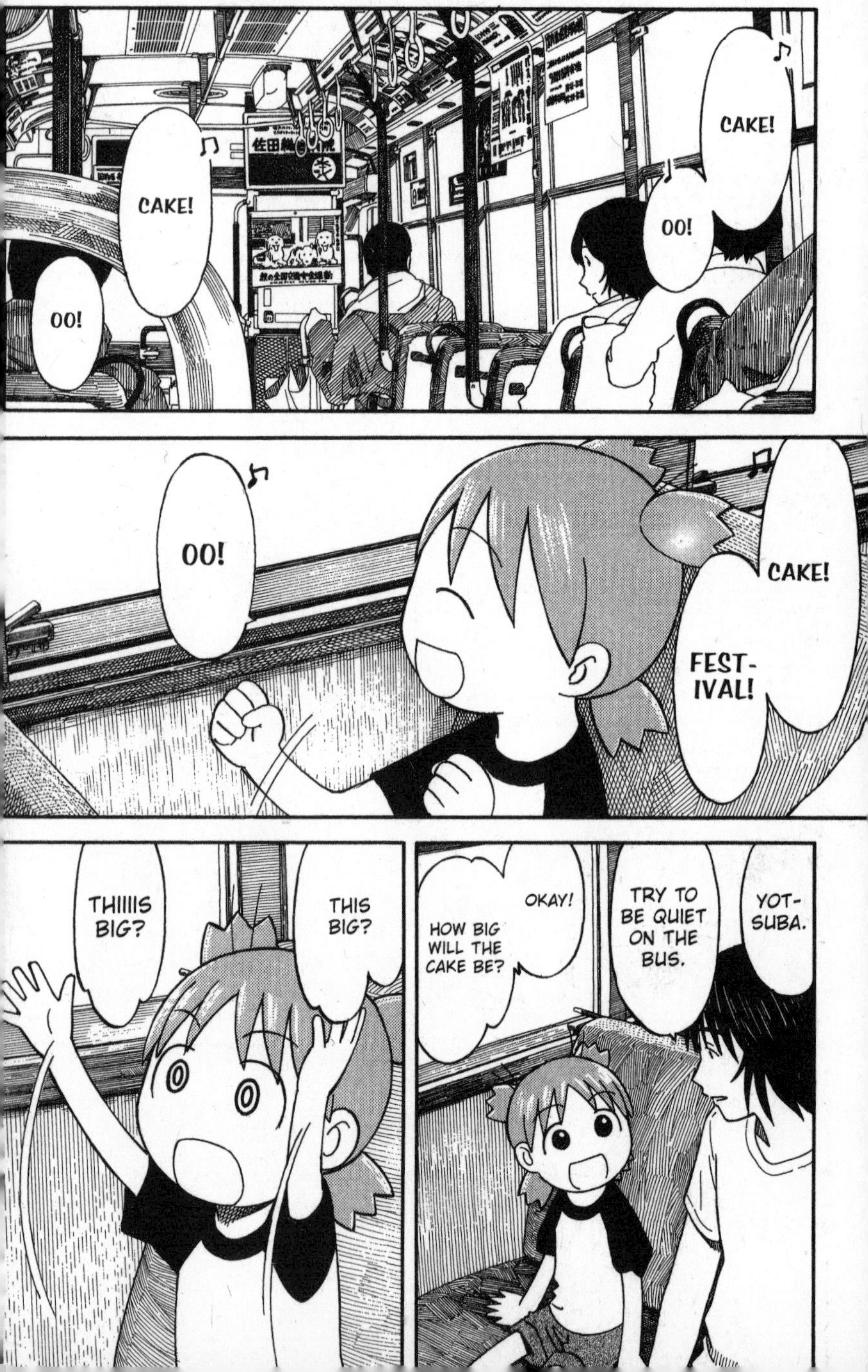
CAKE!
OO!
CAKE!
OO!
CAKE! FEST-IVAL!
OO!
YOT-SUBA.
TRY TO BE QUIET ON THE BUS.
OKAY! HOW BIG WILL THE CAKE BE?
THIS BIG?
THIIIIS BIG?

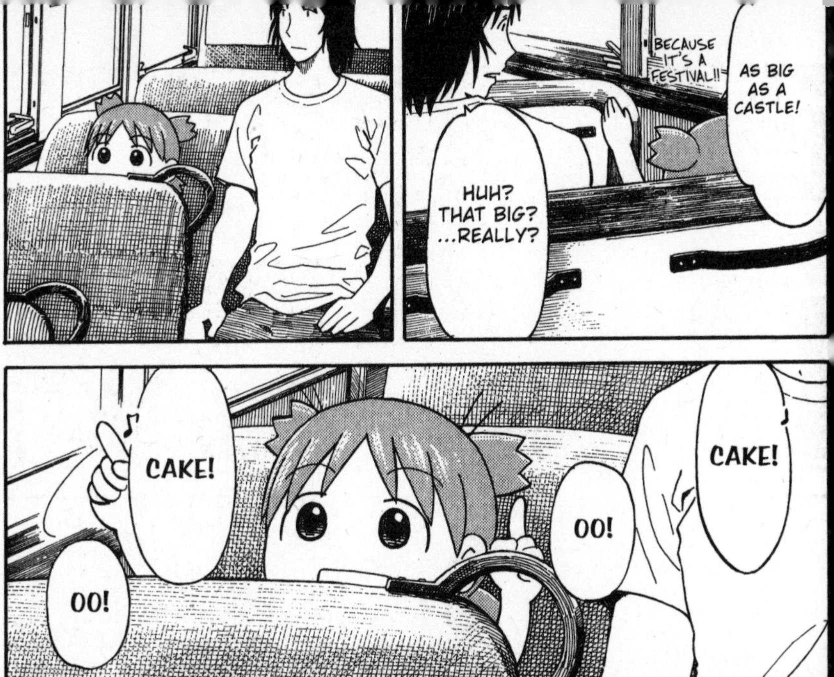
AS BIG AS A CASTLE!
BECAUSE IT'S A FESTIVAL!!
HUH? THAT BIG? ...REALLY?
CAKE!
OO!
CAKE!
OO!
CAKE!
FEST-IVAL!
OO! ♪
QUIETER, YOTSUBA.

SIGN: AJISAI WEST HIGH

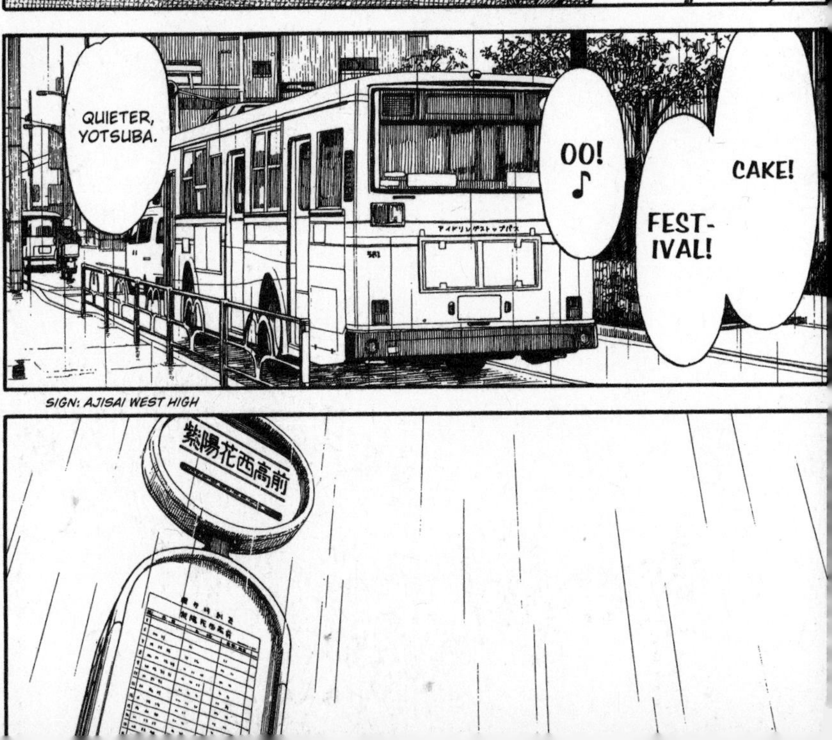
紫陽花西高前

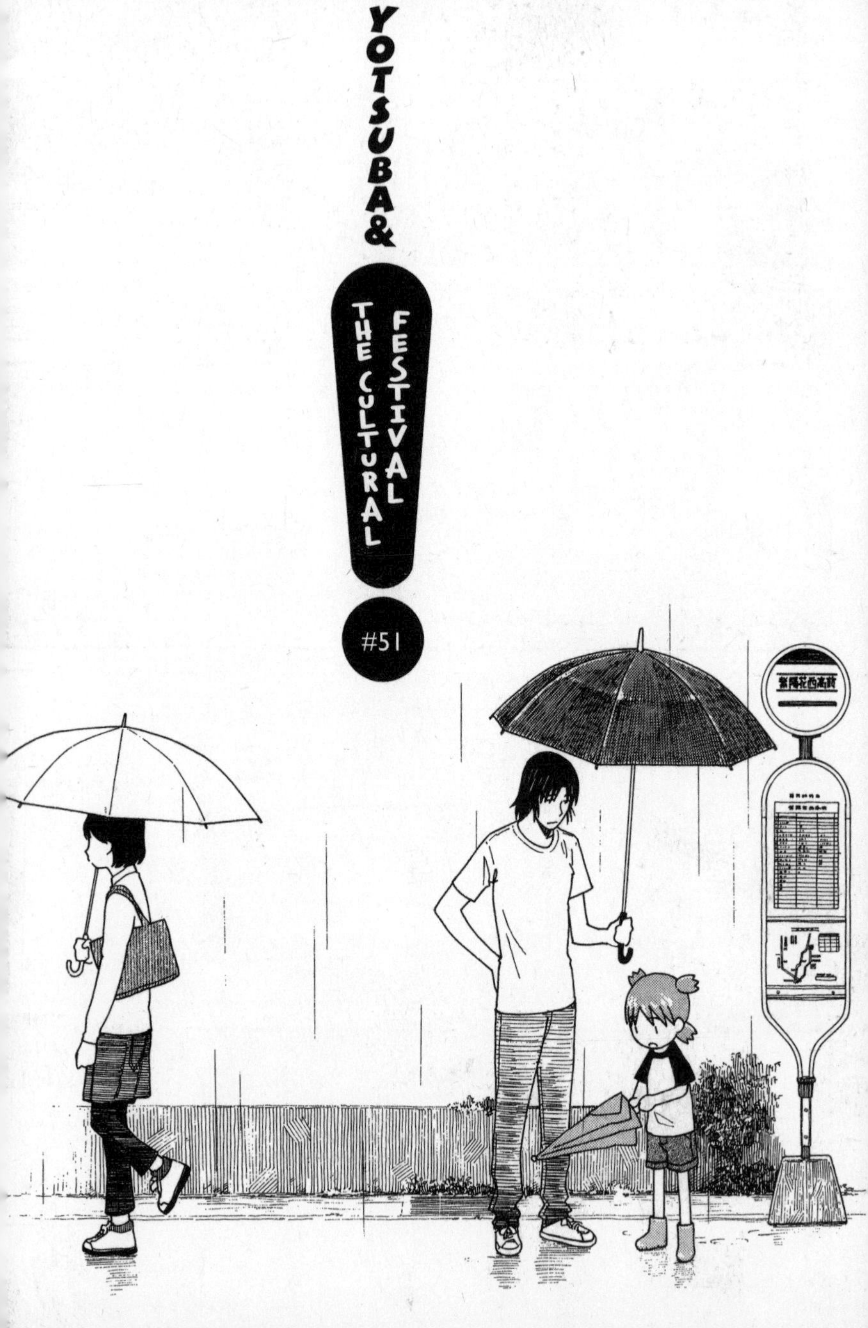
YOTSUBA&
THE CULTURAL FESTIVAL!
#51

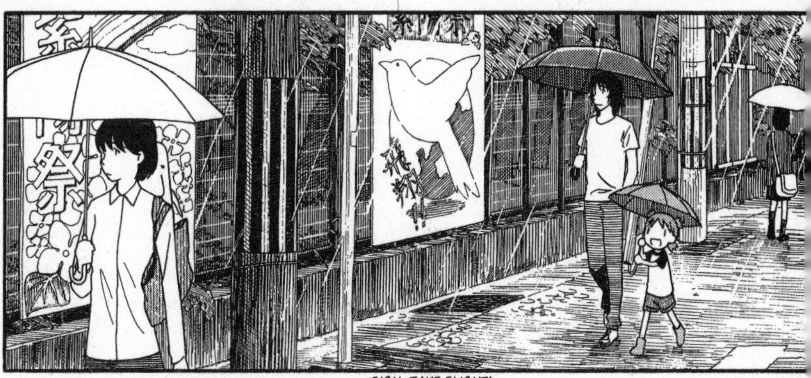

SIGN: TAKE FLIGHT!

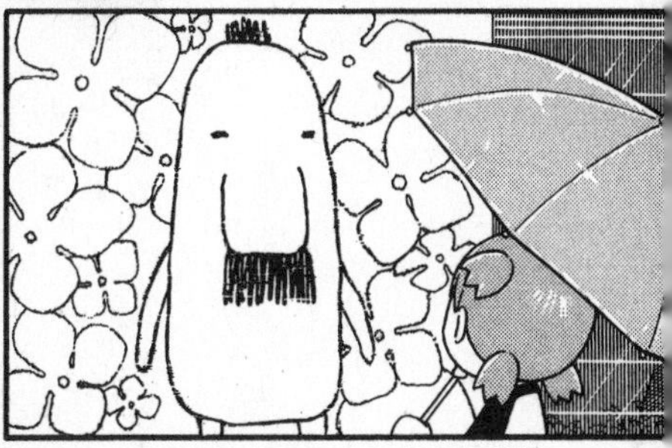

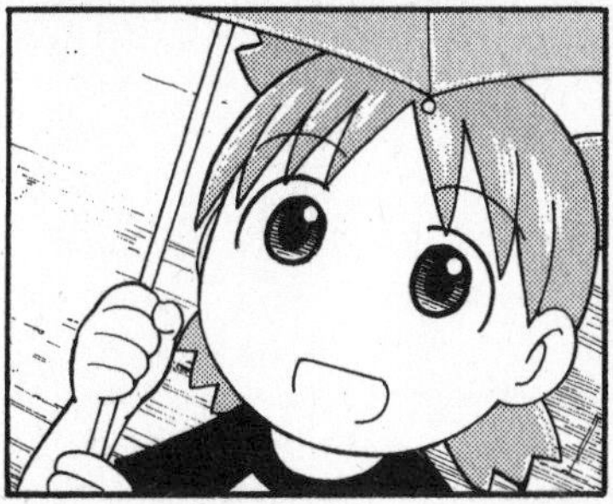

SIGN: 59TH AJISAI-LEBRATION

SIGNS: TREASURE HUNT, 1-4 / 1-6, HOTCAKES

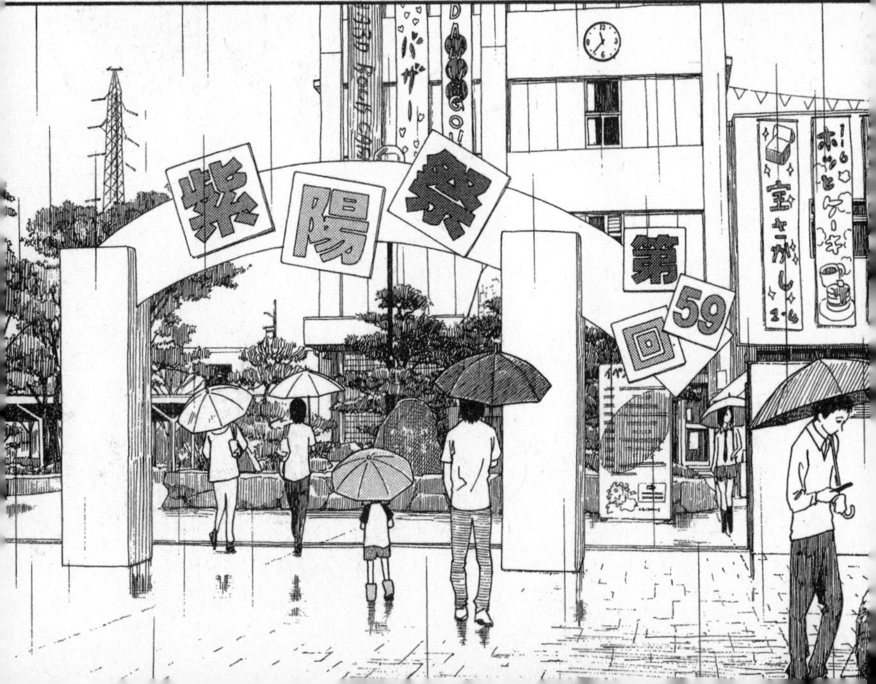
紫陽祭
第59回

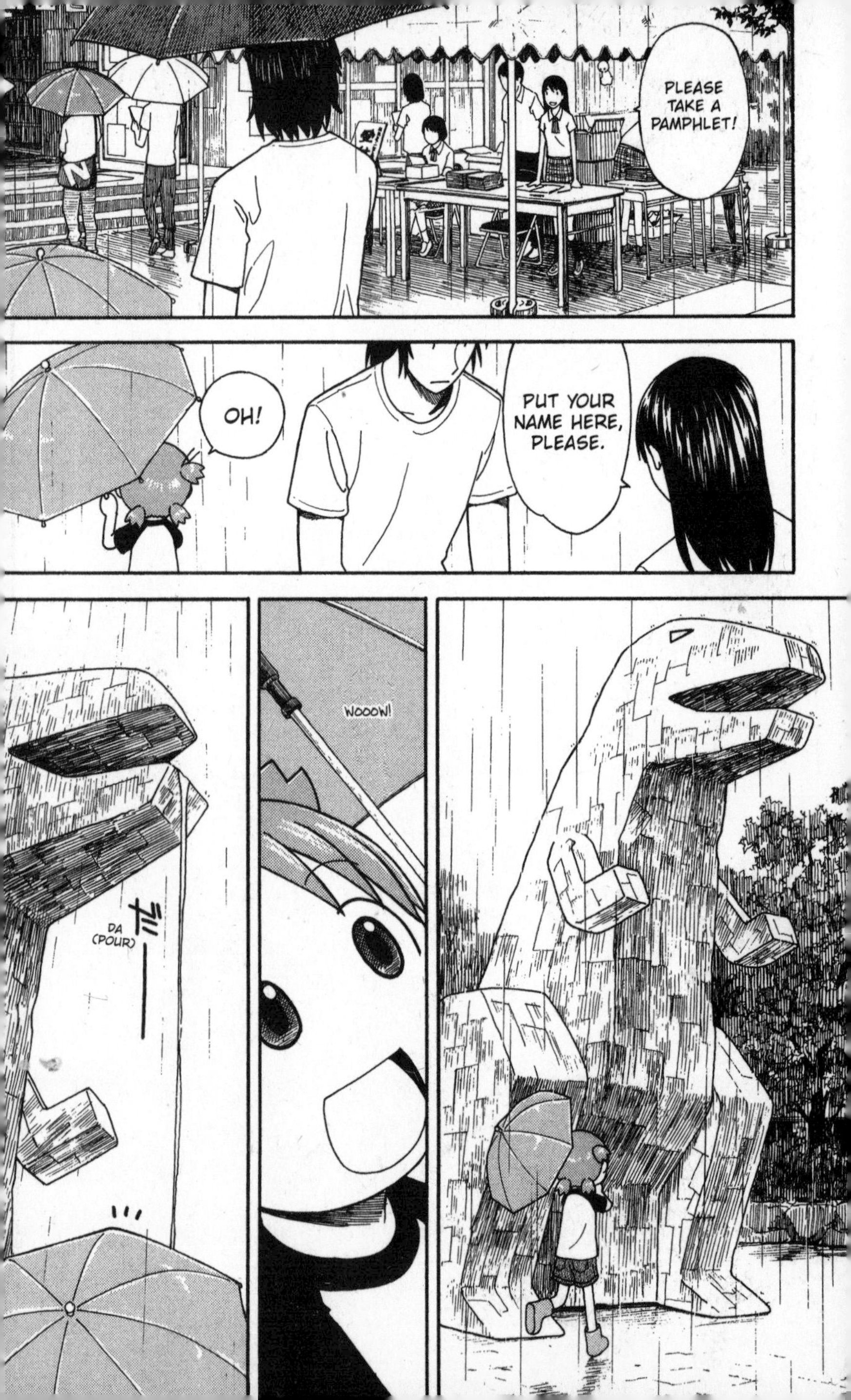
PLEASE TAKE A PAMPHLET!
PUT YOUR NAME HERE, PLEASE.
OH!
WOOOW!
DA (POUR)

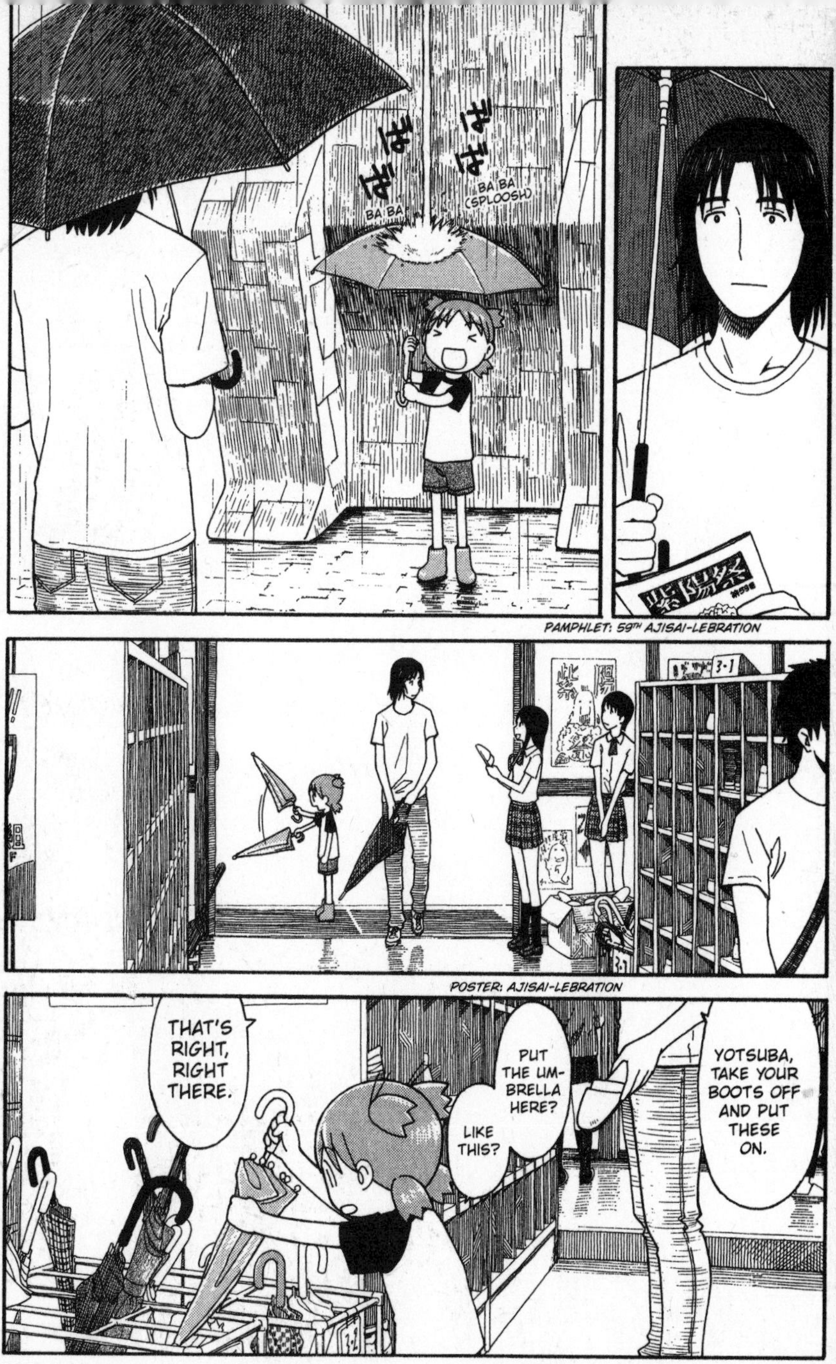
PAMPHLET: 59TH AJISAI-LEBRATION
BA BA (SPLOOSH)
BA BA
POSTER: AJISAI-LEBRATION
YOTSUBA, TAKE YOUR BOOTS OFF AND PUT THESE ON.
PUT THE UMBRELLA HERE?
LIKE THIS?
THAT'S RIGHT, RIGHT THERE.

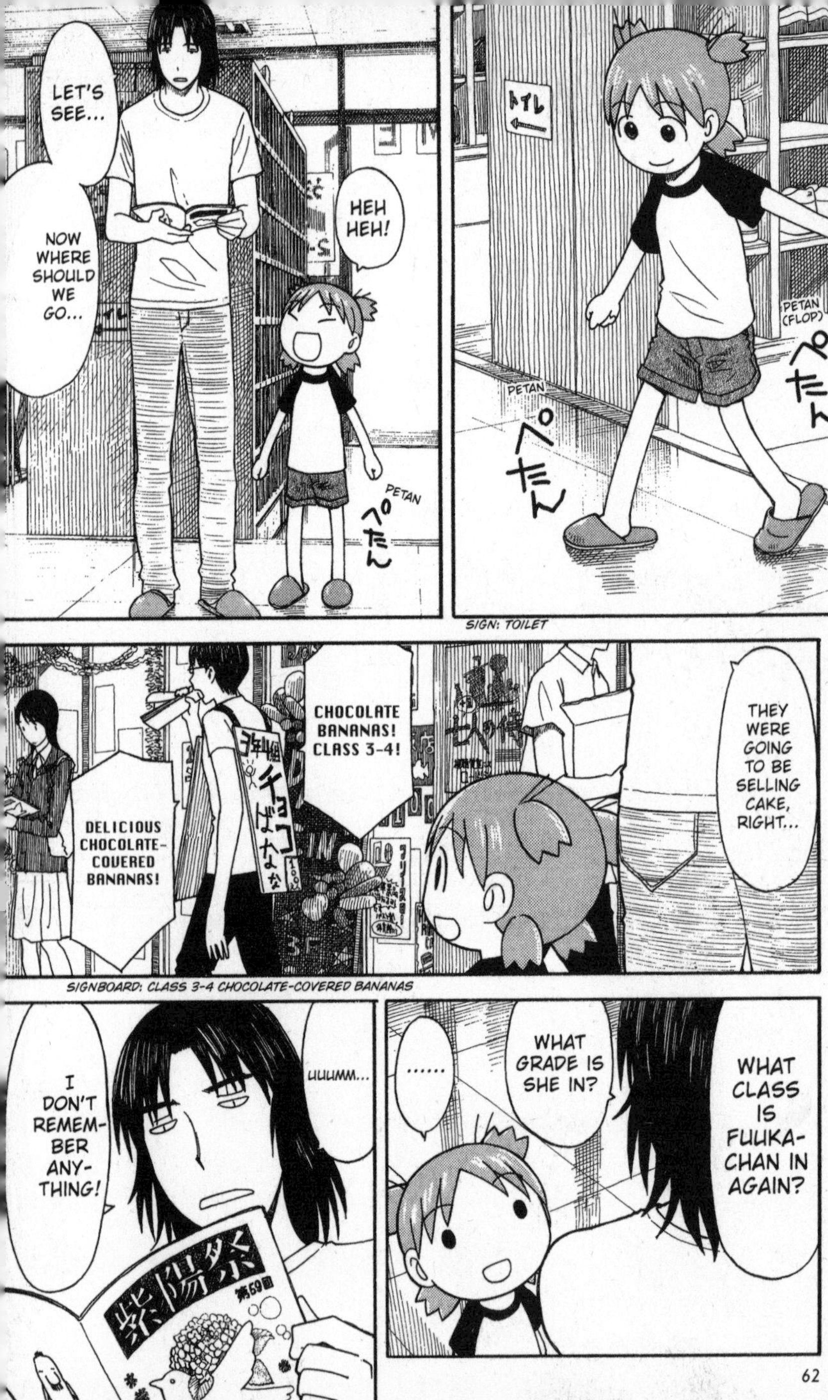
トイレ
PETAN (FLOP)
ぺたん
PETAN
ぺたん
LET'S SEE...
NOW WHERE SHOULD WE GO...
HEH HEH!
PETAN
ぺたん
SIGN: TOILET
THEY WERE GOING TO BE SELLING CAKE, RIGHT...
CHOCOLATE BANANAS! CLASS 3-4!
DELICIOUS CHOCOLATE-COVERED BANANAS!
3年4組
チョコばなな
SIGNBOARD: CLASS 3-4 CHOCOLATE-COVERED BANANAS
WHAT CLASS IS FUUKA-CHAN IN AGAIN?
WHAT GRADE IS SHE IN?
......
UUUMM...
I DON'T REMEMBER ANYTHING!
紫陽祭
第69回

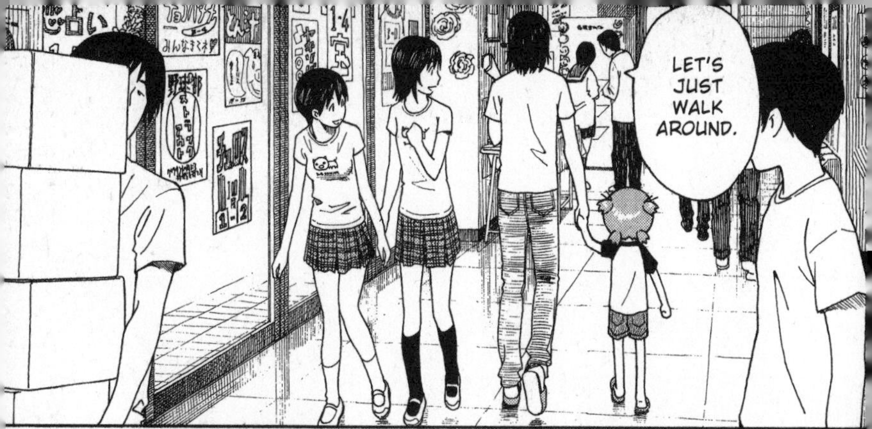
LET'S JUST WALK AROUND.
POSTERS: LOVE FORTUNE-TELLING, CHURROS, BASEBALL CLUB STRIKE OUT, CHOCOLATE-COVERED BANANAS, TONKATSU, 1-4 TREASURE

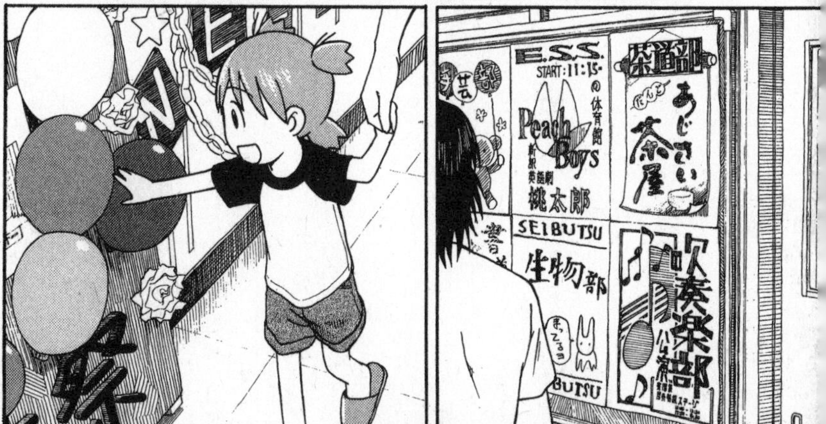
E.S.S.
START: 11:15~
Peach Boys
SEIBUTSU
BUTSU
POSTERS: CRAFT CLUB / E.S.S / NEW ENGLISH TRANSLATION, MOMOTARO (PEACH BOY LEGEND) / TEA CLUB / ANIMAL CLUB (I'M WAITING!) / WIND ENSEMBLE

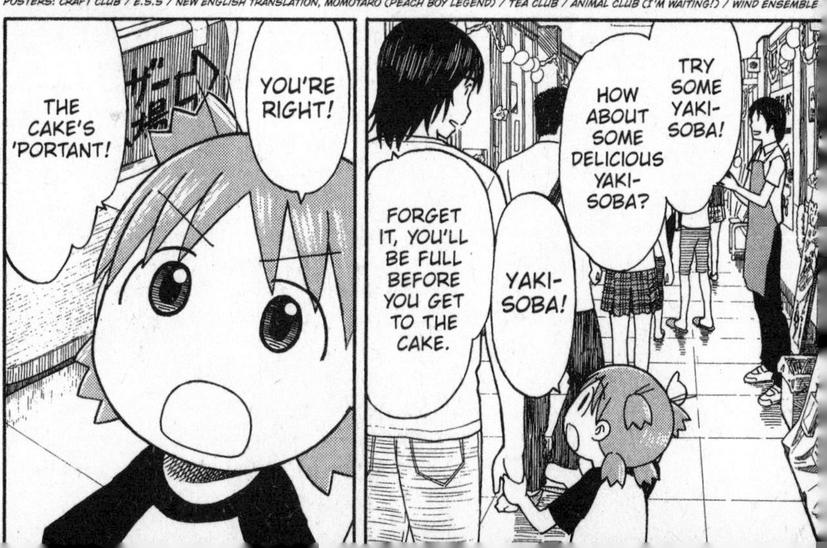
TRY SOME YAKI-SOBA!
HOW ABOUT SOME DELICIOUS YAKI-SOBA?
YAKI-SOBA!
FORGET IT, YOU'LL BE FULL BEFORE YOU GET TO THE CAKE.
YOU'RE RIGHT!
THE CAKE'S 'PORTANT!

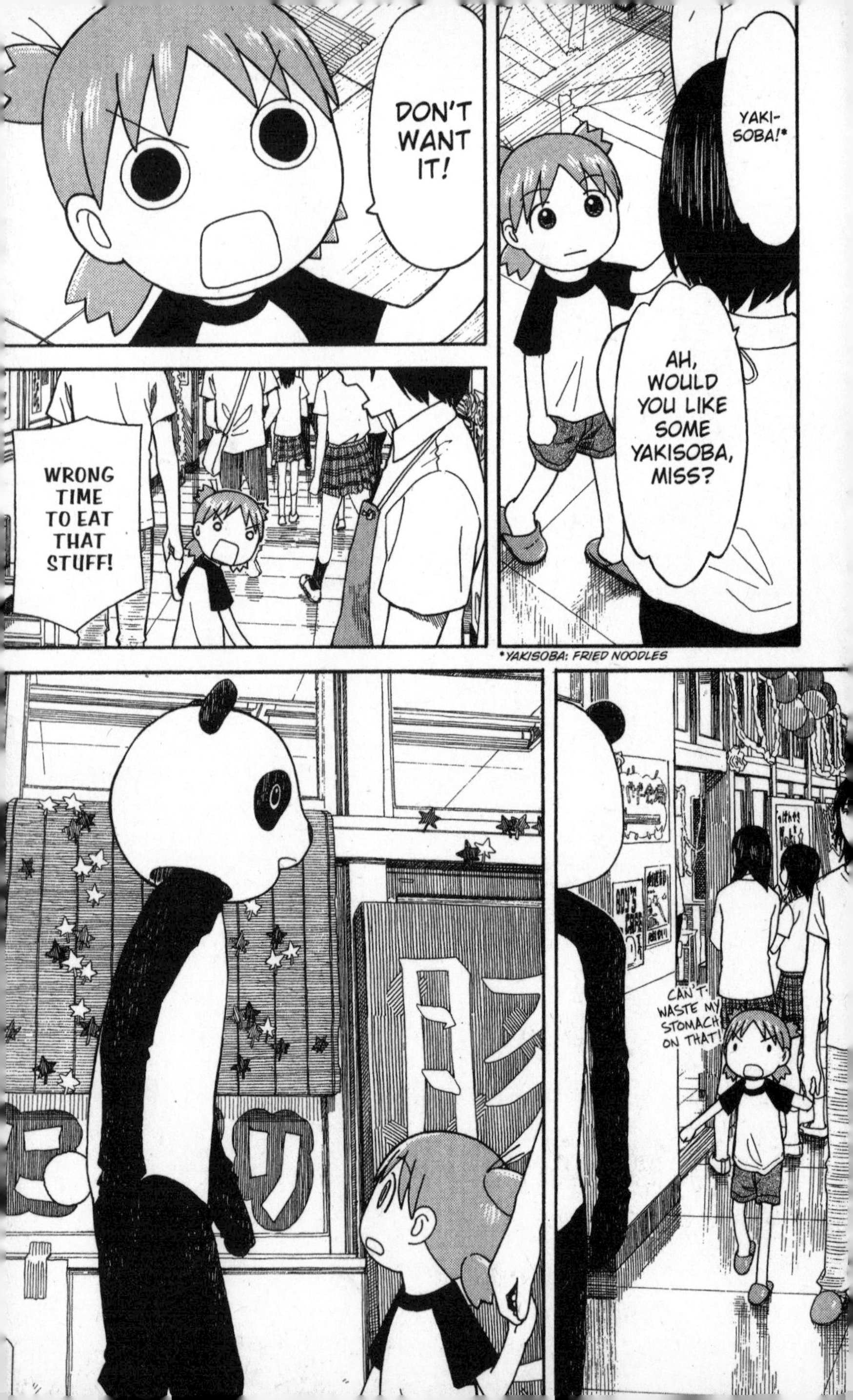
YAKI-SOBA!*
AH, WOULD YOU LIKE SOME YAKISOBA, MISS?
DON'T WANT IT!
WRONG TIME TO EAT THAT STUFF!
CAN'T WASTE MY STOMACH ON THAT!
*YAKISOBA: FRIED NOODLES

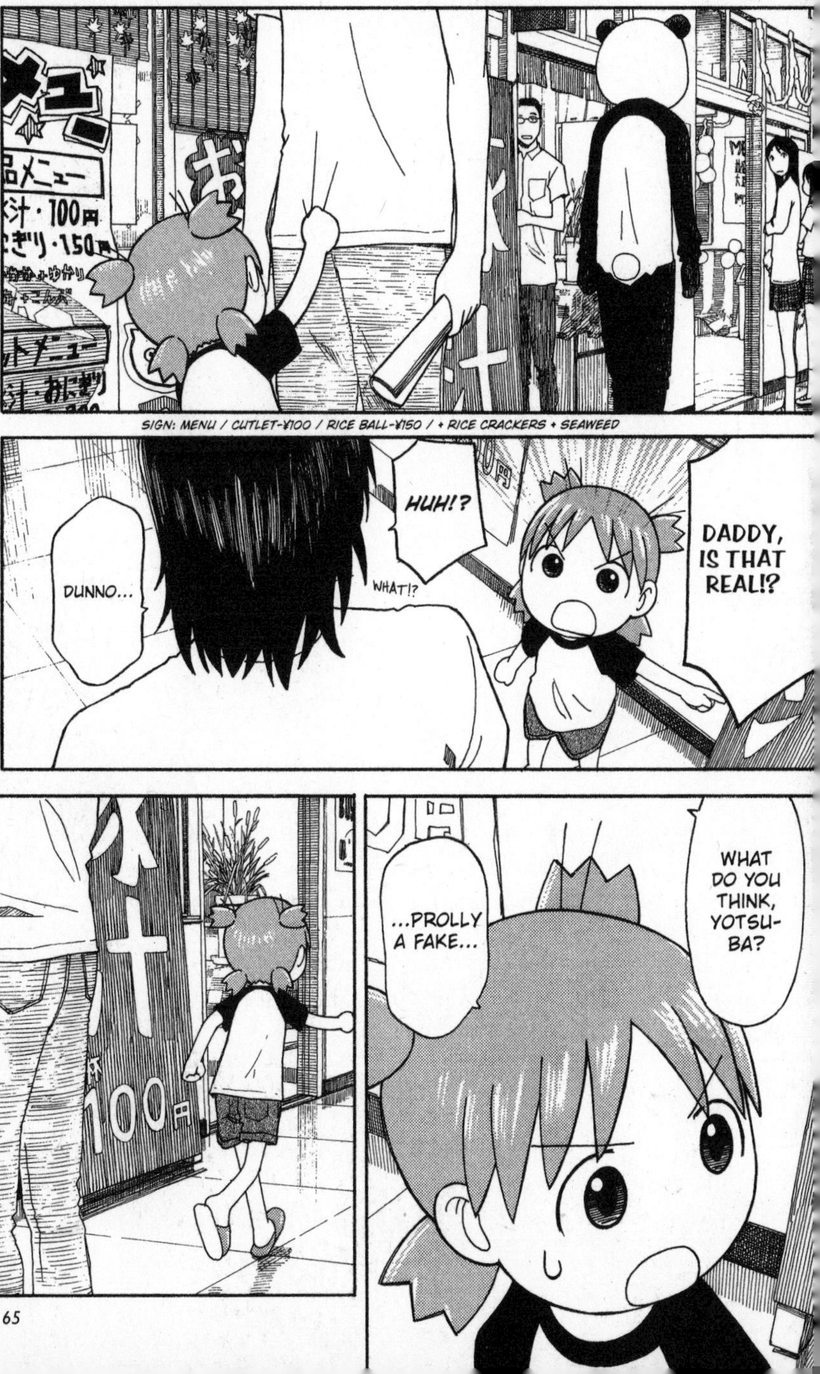
SIGN: MENU / CUTLET-¥100 / RICE BALL-¥150 / + RICE CRACKERS + SEAWEED
DADDY, IS THAT REAL!?
HUH!?
WHAT!?
DUNNO...
WHAT DO YOU THINK, YOTSUBA?
...PROLLY A FAKE...

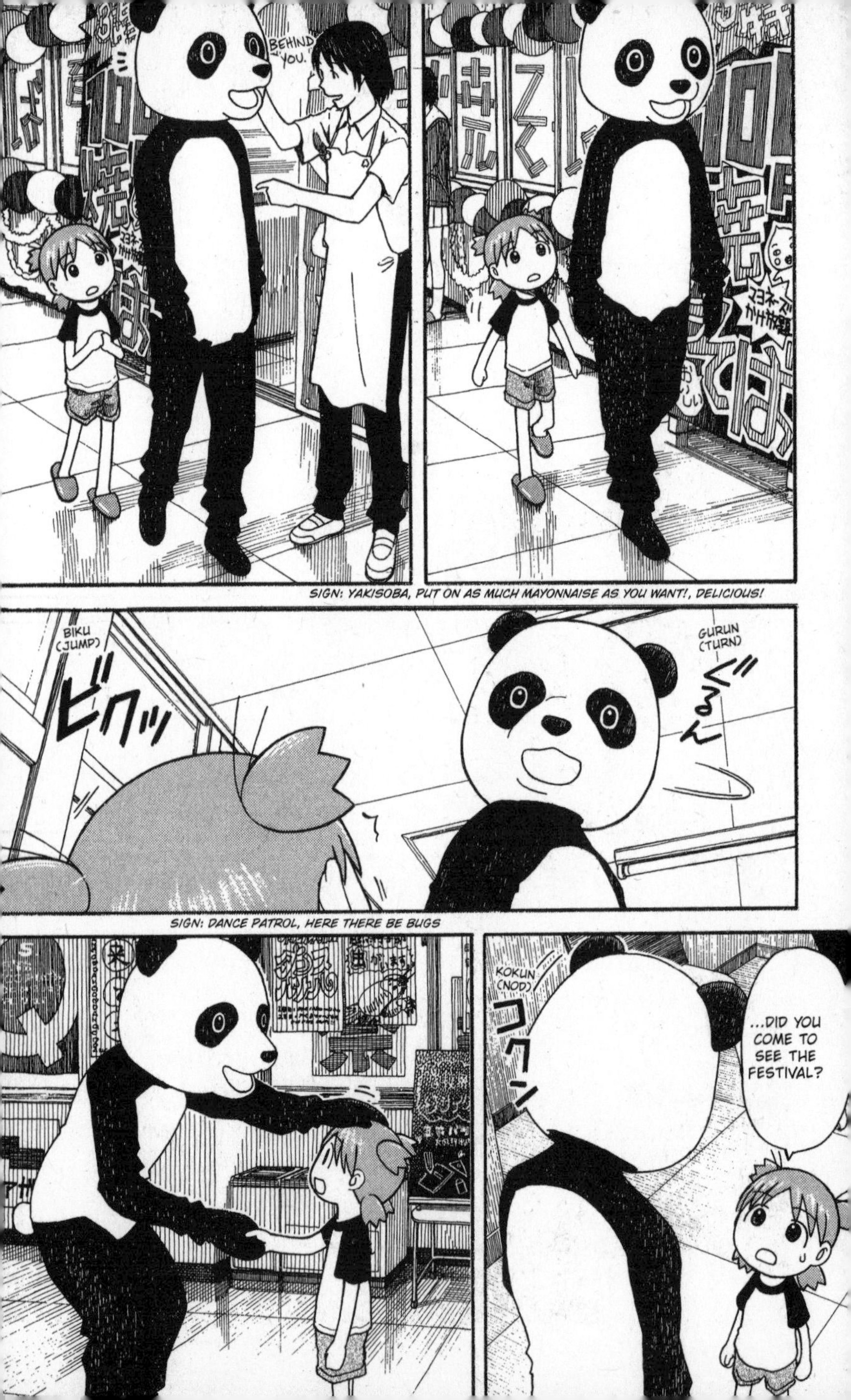

BEHIND YOU.
SIGN: YAKISOBA, PUT ON AS MUCH MAYONNAISE AS YOU WANT!, DELICIOUS!
GURUN (TURN)
BIKU (JUMP)
SIGN: DANCE PATROL, HERE THERE BE BUGS
...DID YOU COME TO SEE THE FESTIVAL?
KOKUN (NOD)

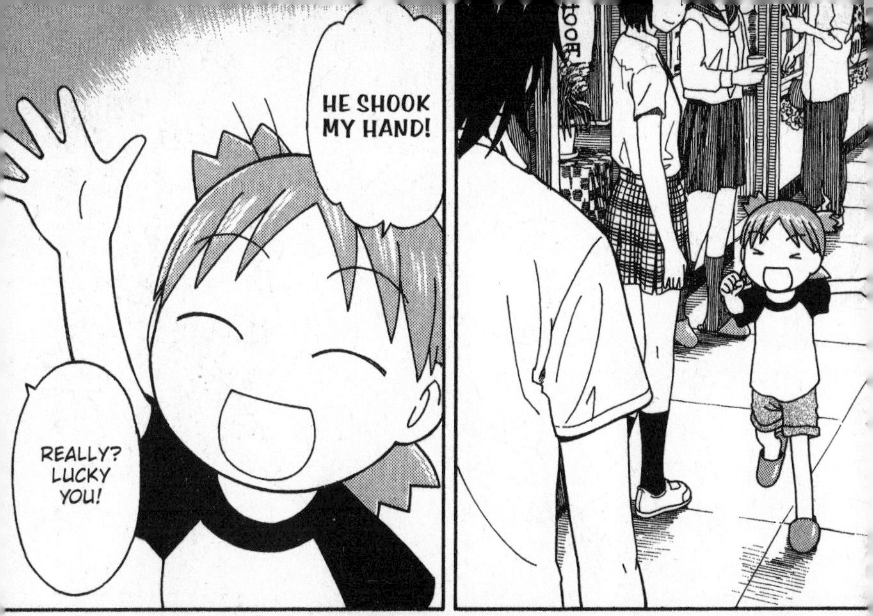
HE SHOOK MY HAND!
REALLY? LUCKY YOU!

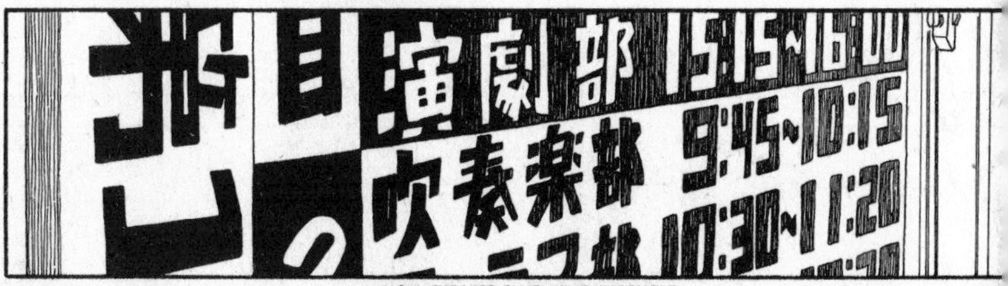
演劇部 15:15~16:00
吹奏楽部 9:45~10:15
10:30~11:20

SIGN: THEATER CLUB, WIND ENSEMBLE

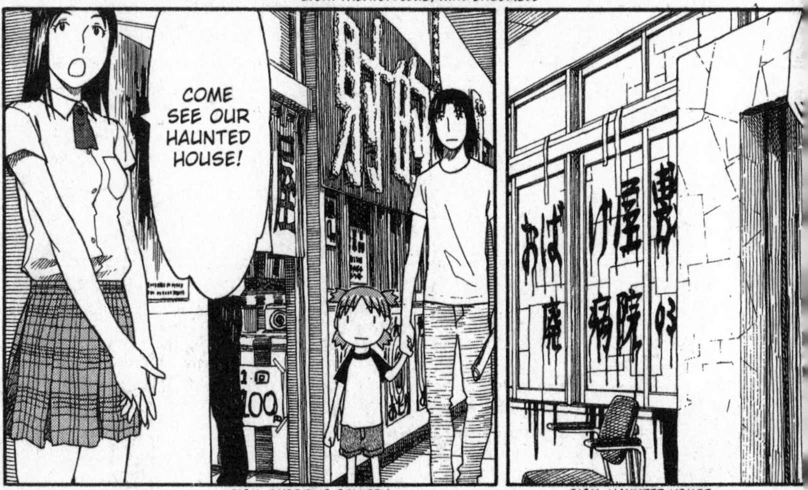
おばけ屋敷
廃病院03
射的
1回 100円
COME SEE OUR HAUNTED HOUSE!

SIGN: SHOOTING GALLERY

SIGN: HAUNTED HOUSE, DESERTED HOSPITAL 03

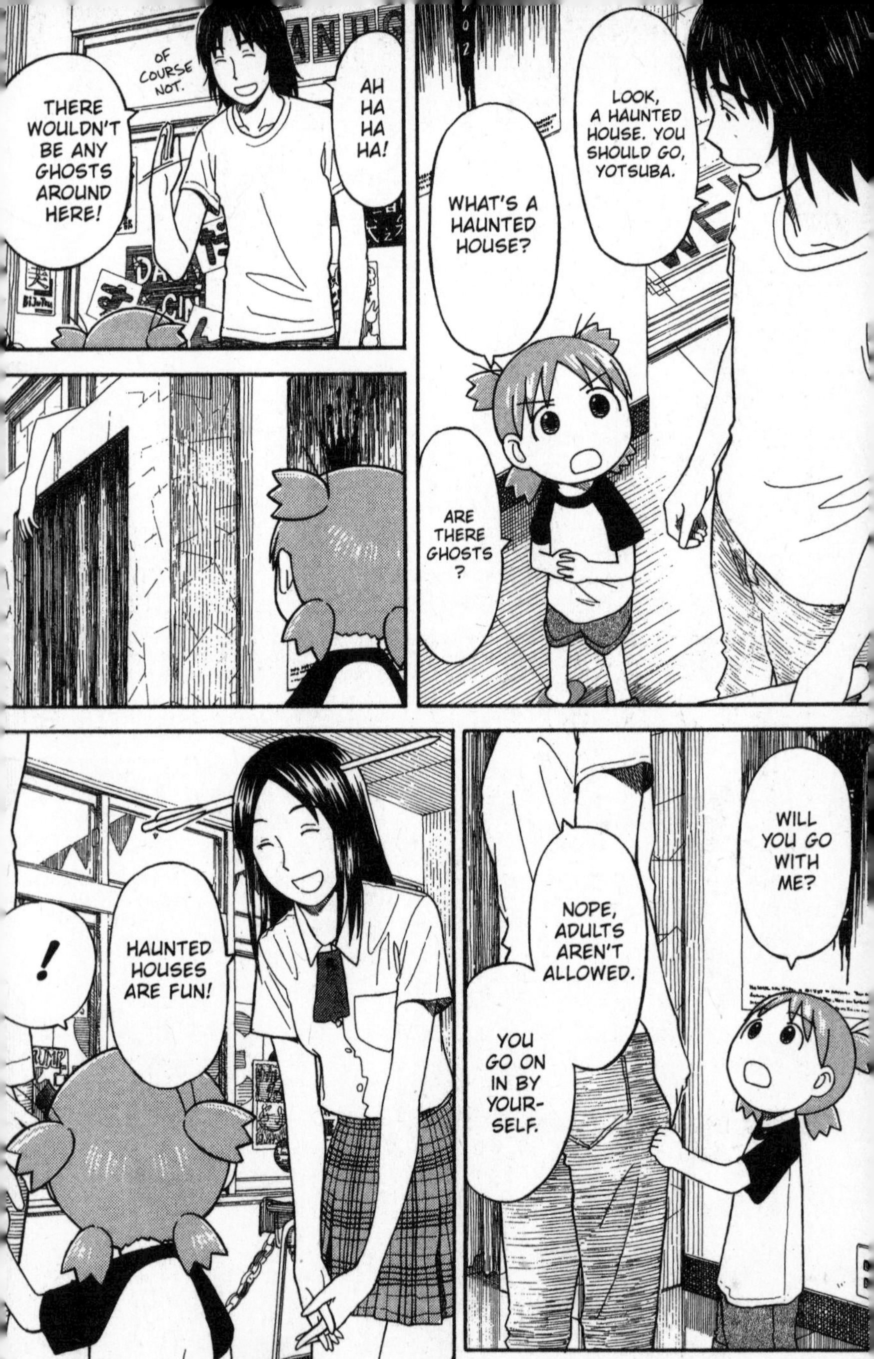
LOOK, A HAUNTED HOUSE. YOU SHOULD GO, YOTSUBA.
WHAT'S A HAUNTED HOUSE?
ARE THERE GHOSTS?
AH HA HA HA!
OF COURSE NOT.
THERE WOULDN'T BE ANY GHOSTS AROUND HERE!
WILL YOU GO WITH ME?
NOPE, ADULTS AREN'T ALLOWED.
YOU GO ON IN BY YOUR-SELF.
HAUNTED HOUSES ARE FUN!
!

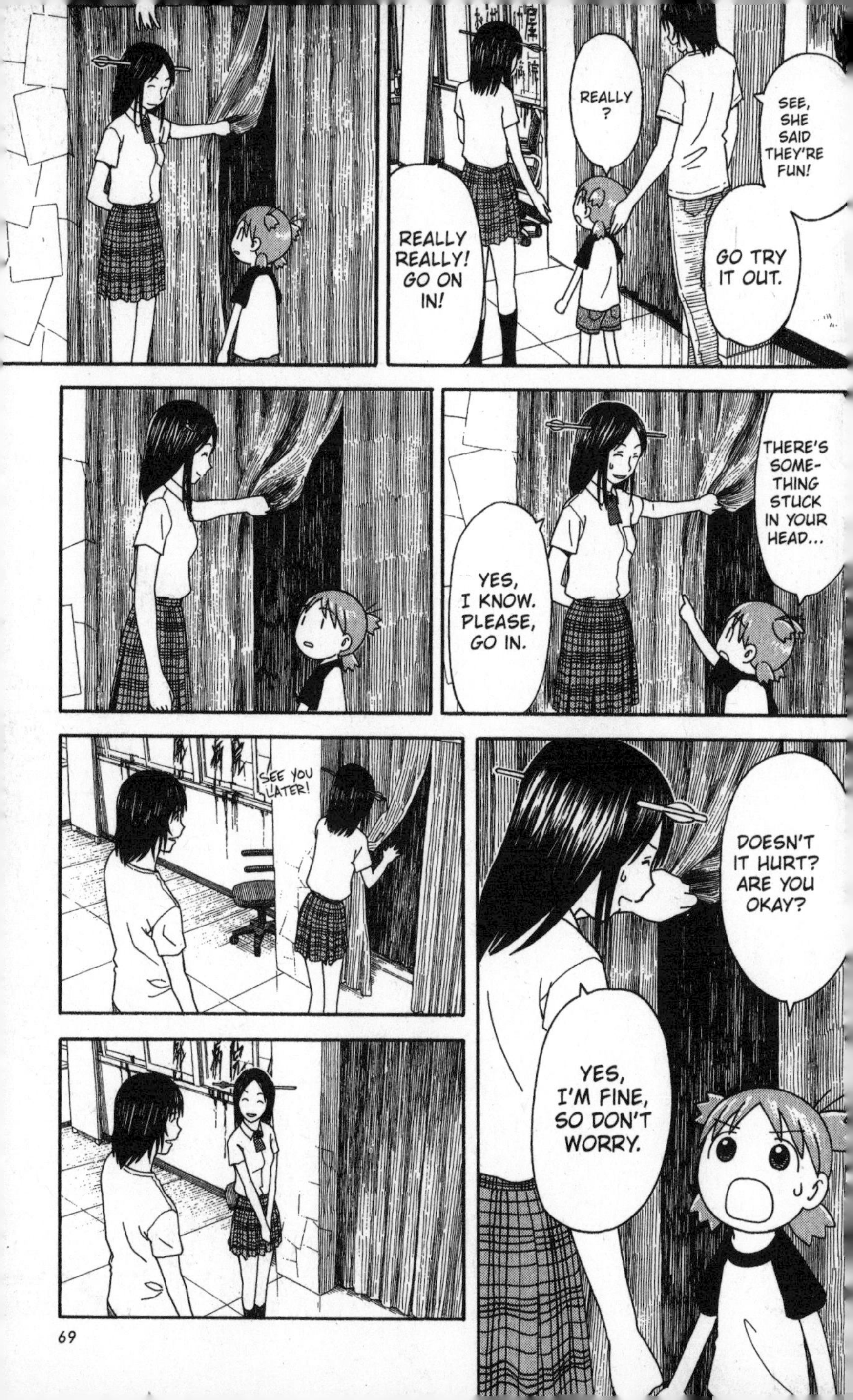
SEE, SHE SAID THEY'RE FUN!
REALLY ?
GO TRY IT OUT.
REALLY REALLY! GO ON IN!
THERE'S SOME-THING STUCK IN YOUR HEAD...
YES, I KNOW. PLEASE, GO IN.
DOESN'T IT HURT? ARE YOU OKAY?
YES, I'M FINE, SO DON'T WORRY.
SEE YOU LATER!

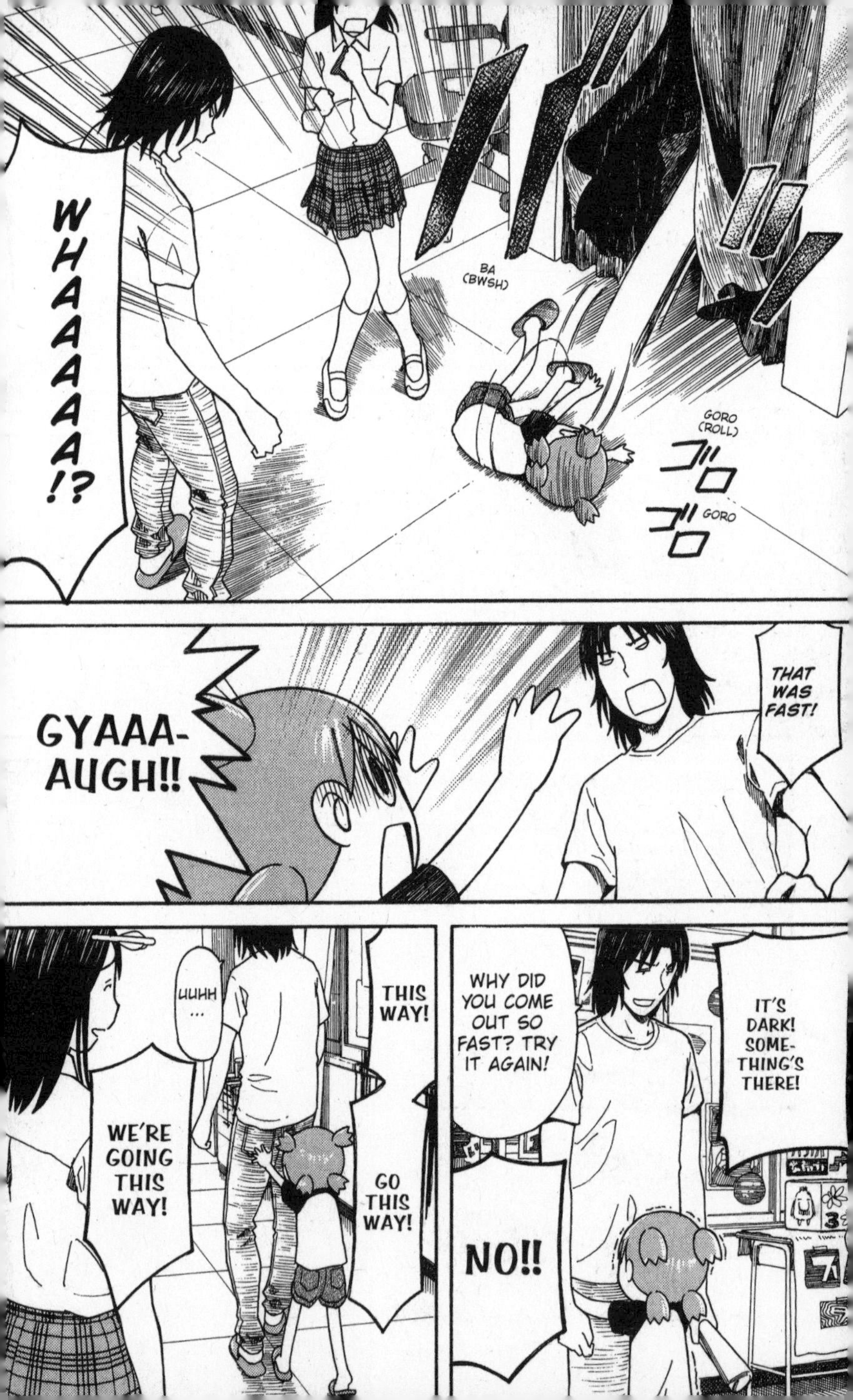
BA (BWSH)
GORO (ROLL)
ゴロ
GORO
ゴロ
WHAAAAAAA!?
THAT WAS FAST!
GYAAA-AUGH!!
IT'S DARK! SOME-THING'S THERE!
WHY DID YOU COME OUT SO FAST? TRY IT AGAIN!
NO!!
THIS WAY!
GO THIS WAY!
UUHH ...
WE'RE GOING THIS WAY!

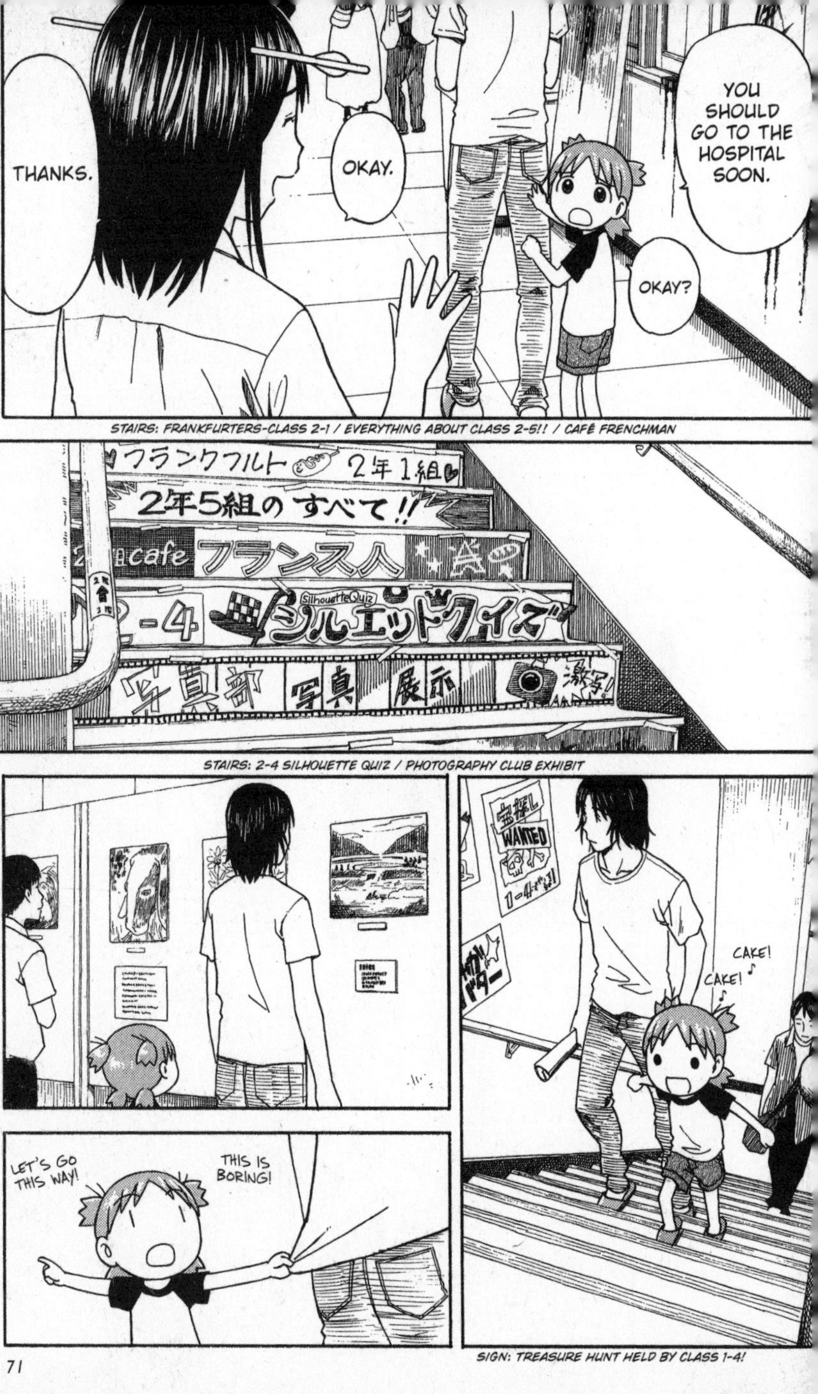
YOU SHOULD GO TO THE HOSPITAL SOON.
OKAY?
OKAY.
THANKS.
フランクフルト 2年1組
2年5組のすべて!!
cafe フランス人
SilhouetteQuiz
2-4 シルエットクイズ
写真部 写真 展示 激写!
宝探し
WANTED
CAKE!
CAKE!
THIS IS BORING!
LET'S GO THIS WAY!
STAIRS: FRANKFURTERS-CLASS 2-1 / EVERYTHING ABOUT CLASS 2-5!! / CAFÉ FRENCHMAN

STAIRS: 2-4 SILHOUETTE QUIZ / PHOTOGRAPHY CLUB EXHIBIT

SIGN: TREASURE HUNT HELD BY CLASS 1-4!

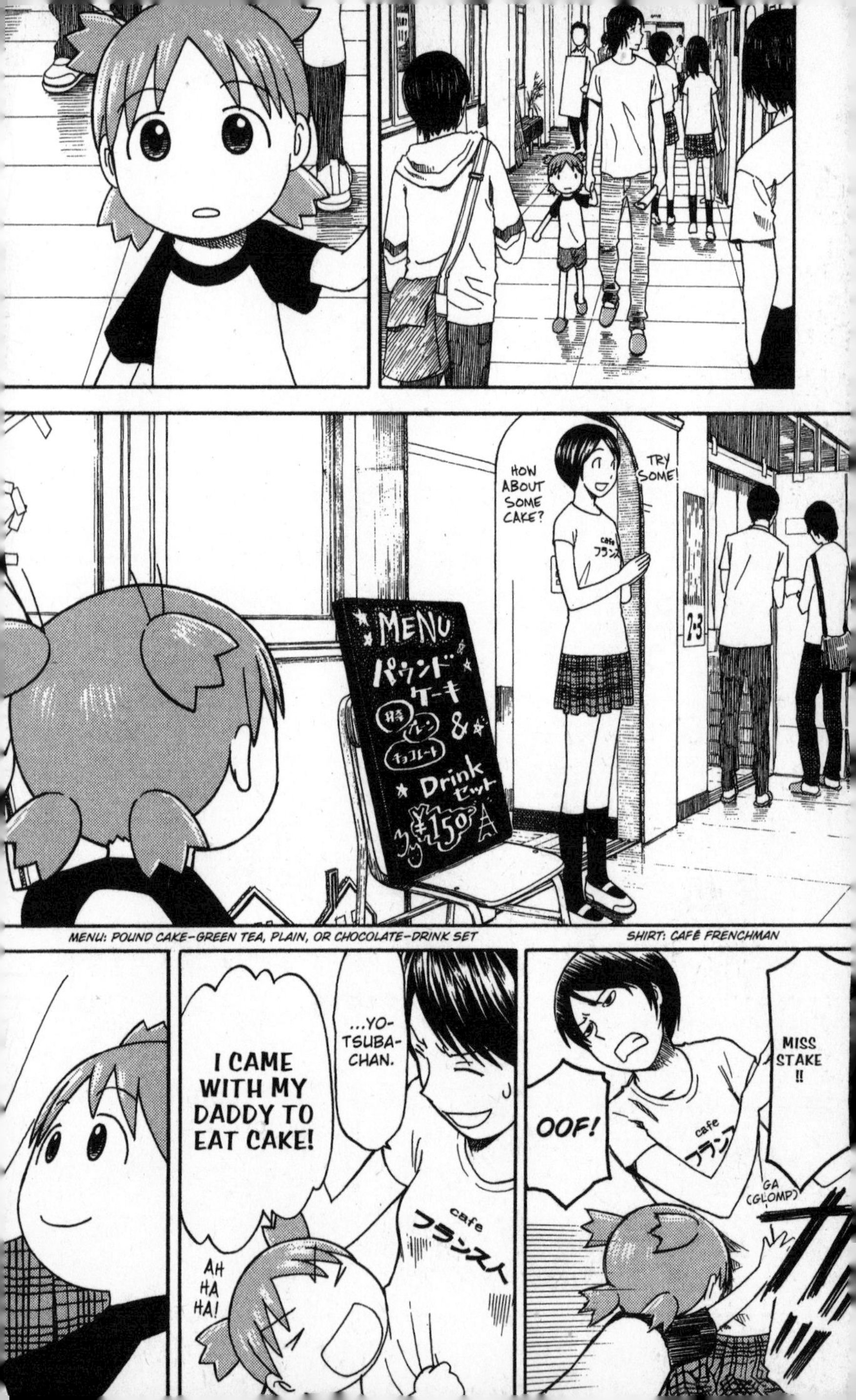
TRY SOME!
HOW ABOUT SOME CAKE?
MENU
パウンドケーキ
プレーン
チョコレート
&
Drink セット
¥150
cafe フランス人
MENU: POUND CAKE-GREEN TEA, PLAIN, OR CHOCOLATE-DRINK SET
SHIRT: CAFÉ FRENCHMAN
MISS STAKE !!
OOF!
GA (GLOMP)
cafe フランス
...YO-TSUBA-CHAN.
I CAME WITH MY DADDY TO EAT CAKE!
cafe フランス人
AH HA HA!

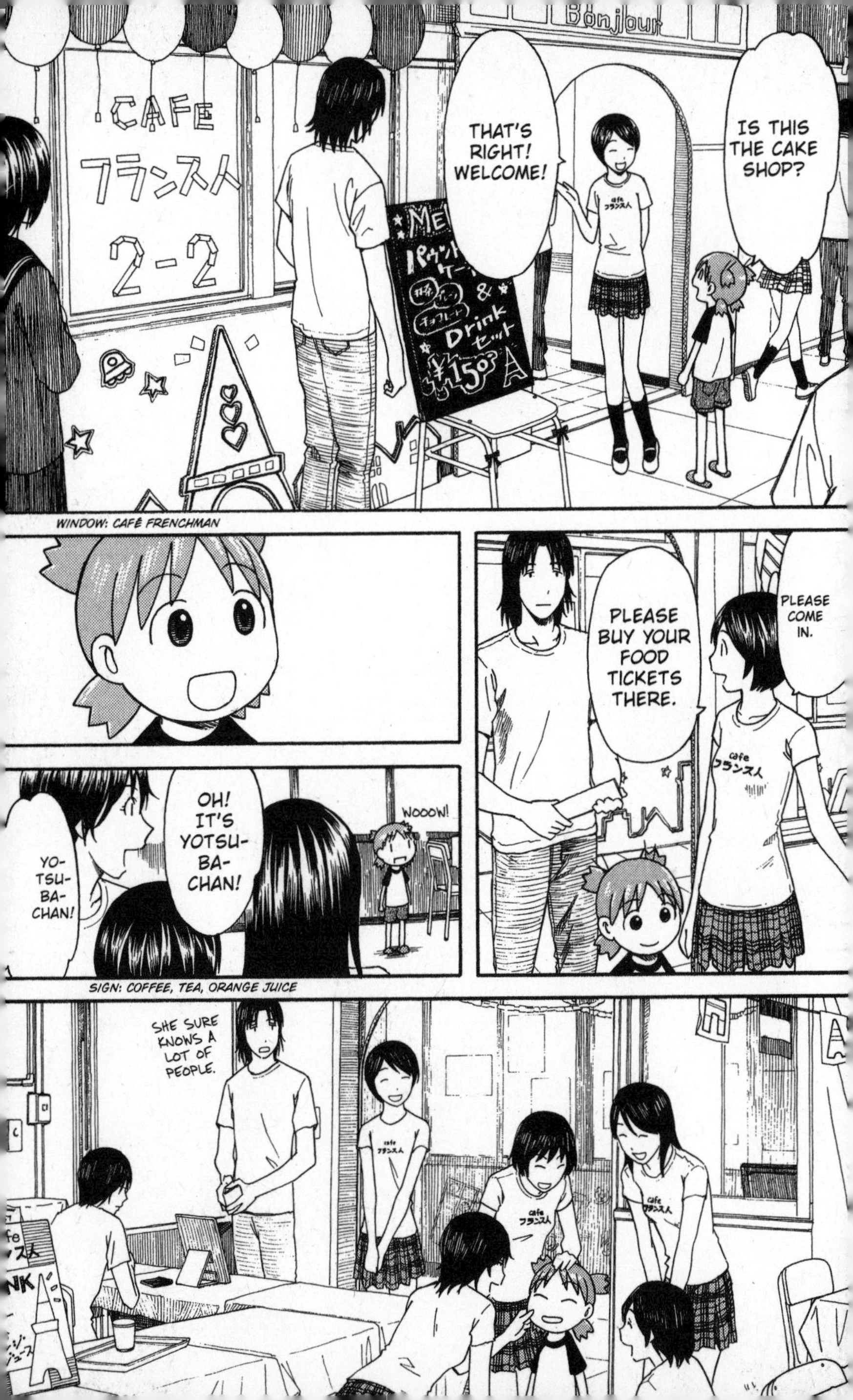
Bonjour
CAFE
フランス人
2-2
Drink
¥150
IS THIS THE CAKE SHOP?
THAT'S RIGHT! WELCOME!
WINDOW: CAFÉ FRENCHMAN
PLEASE COME IN.
PLEASE BUY YOUR FOOD TICKETS THERE.
WOOOW!
OH! IT'S YOTSU-BA-CHAN!
YO-TSU-BA-CHAN!
SIGN: COFFEE, TEA, ORANGE JUICE
SHE SURE KNOWS A LOT OF PEOPLE.

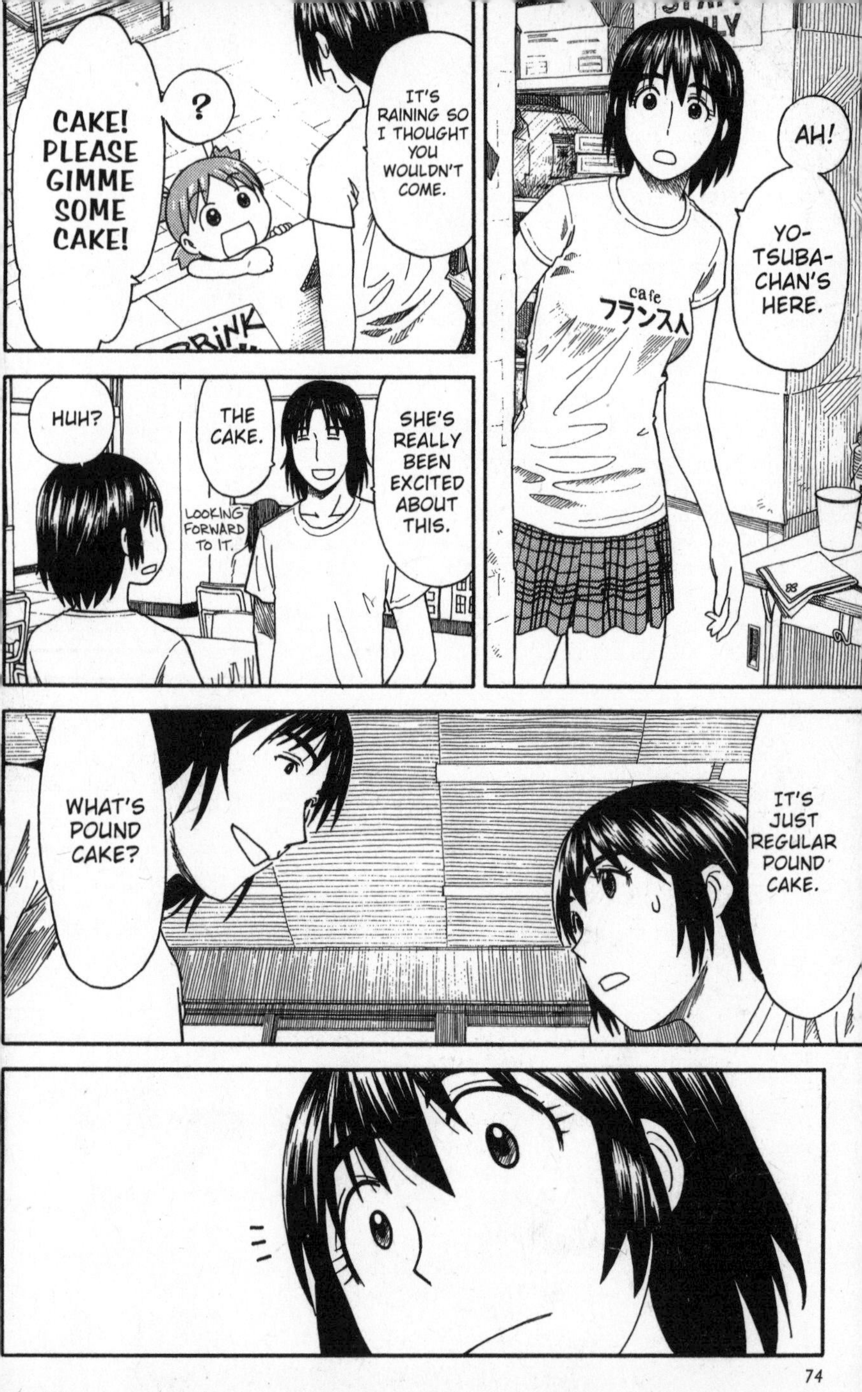
AH!
YO-TSUBA-CHAN'S HERE.
cafe フランス人
IT'S RAINING SO I THOUGHT YOU WOULDN'T COME.
?
CAKE! PLEASE GIMME SOME CAKE!
SHE'S REALLY BEEN EXCITED ABOUT THIS.
LOOKING FORWARD TO IT.
THE CAKE.
HUH?
IT'S JUST REGULAR POUND CAKE.
WHAT'S POUND CAKE?

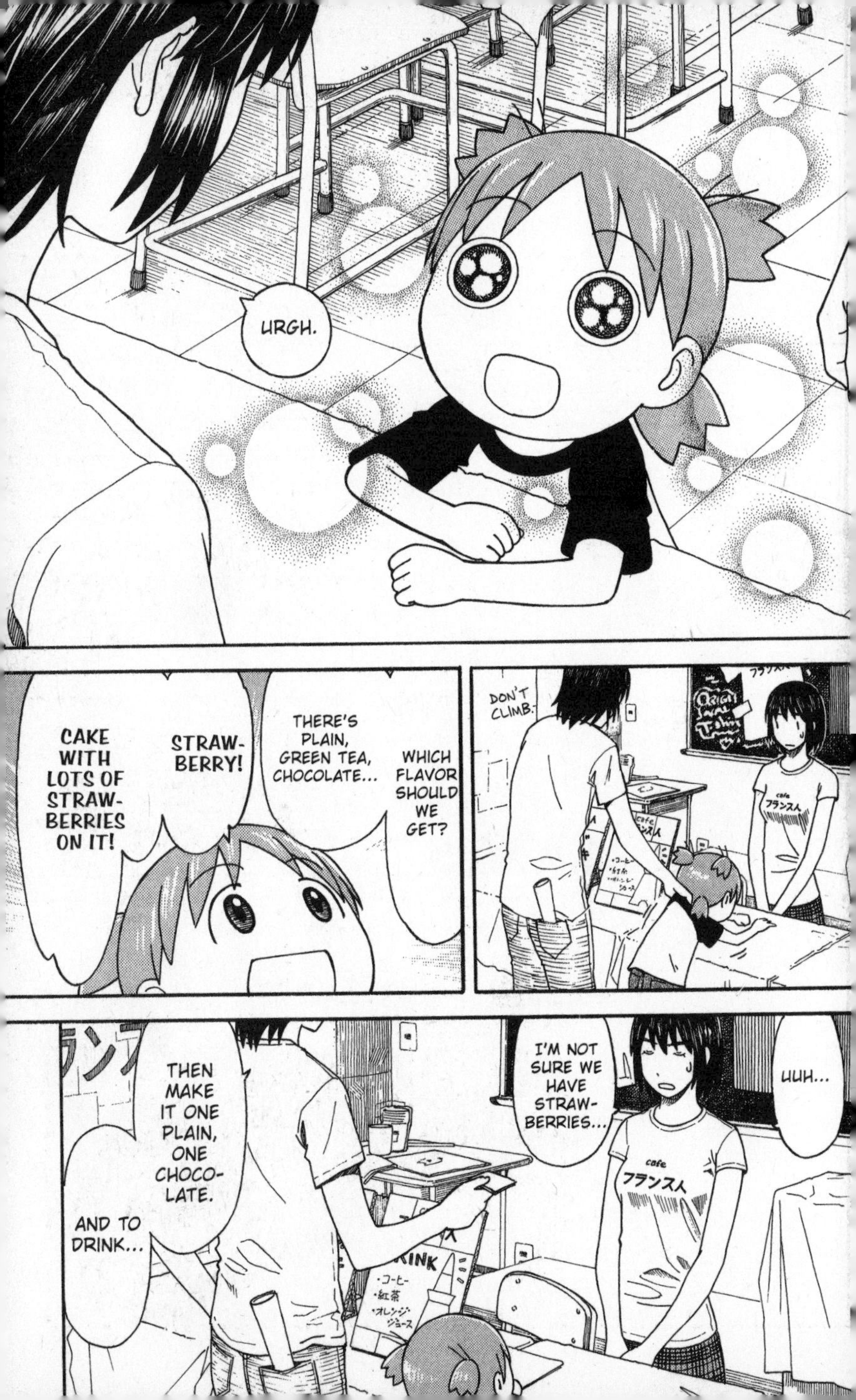
URGH.
DON'T CLIMB.
cafe フランス人
WHICH FLAVOR SHOULD WE GET?
THERE'S PLAIN, GREEN TEA, CHOCOLATE...
STRAW-BERRY!
CAKE WITH LOTS OF STRAW-BERRIES ON IT!
UUH...
I'M NOT SURE WE HAVE STRAW-BERRIES...
cafe フランス人
THEN MAKE IT ONE PLAIN, ONE CHOCO-LATE.
AND TO DRINK...
・コーヒー
・紅茶
・オレンジジュース

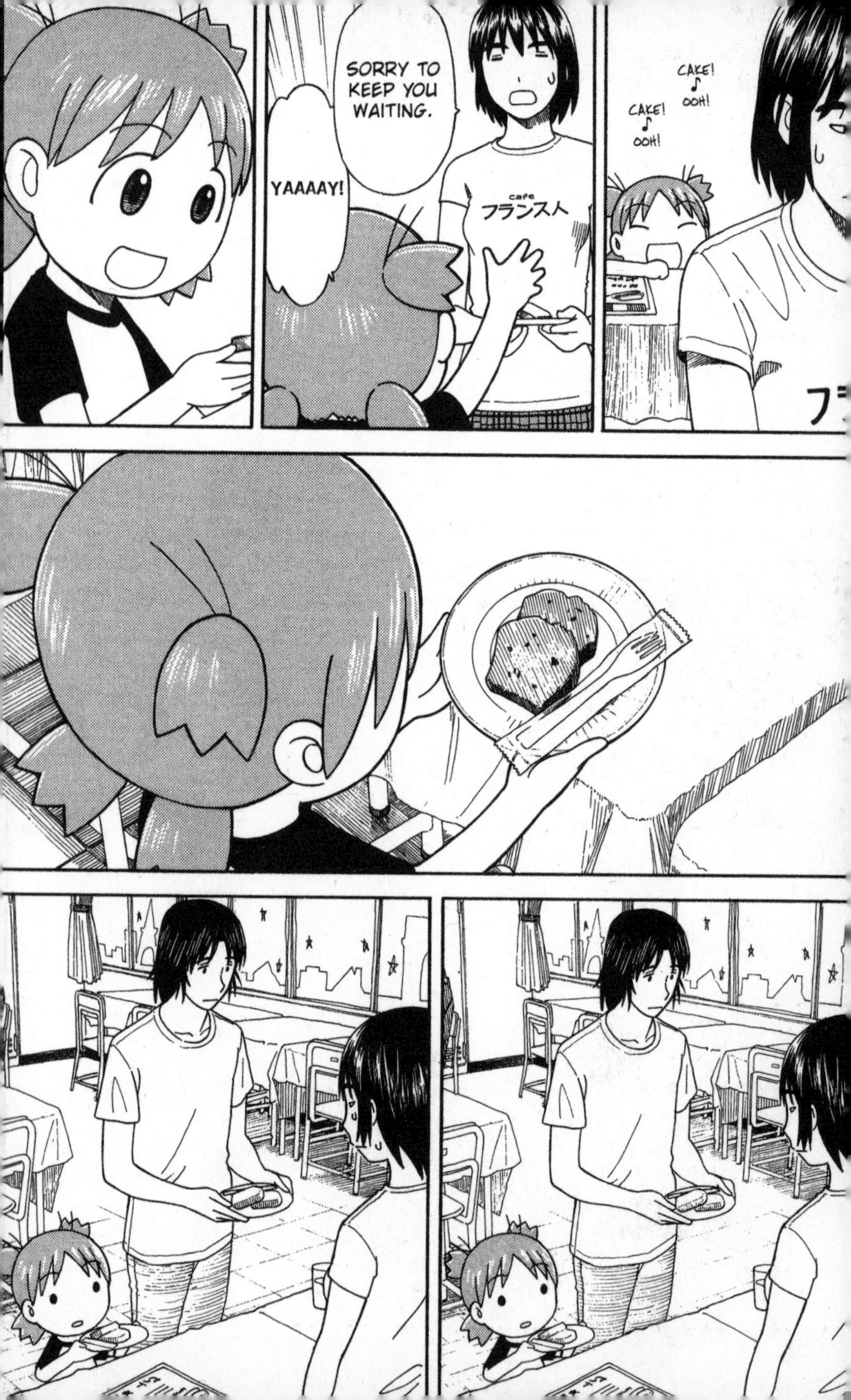

CAKE! ♪ OOH!
CAKE! ♪ OOH!
SORRY TO KEEP YOU WAITING.
cafe フランス人
YAAAAY!

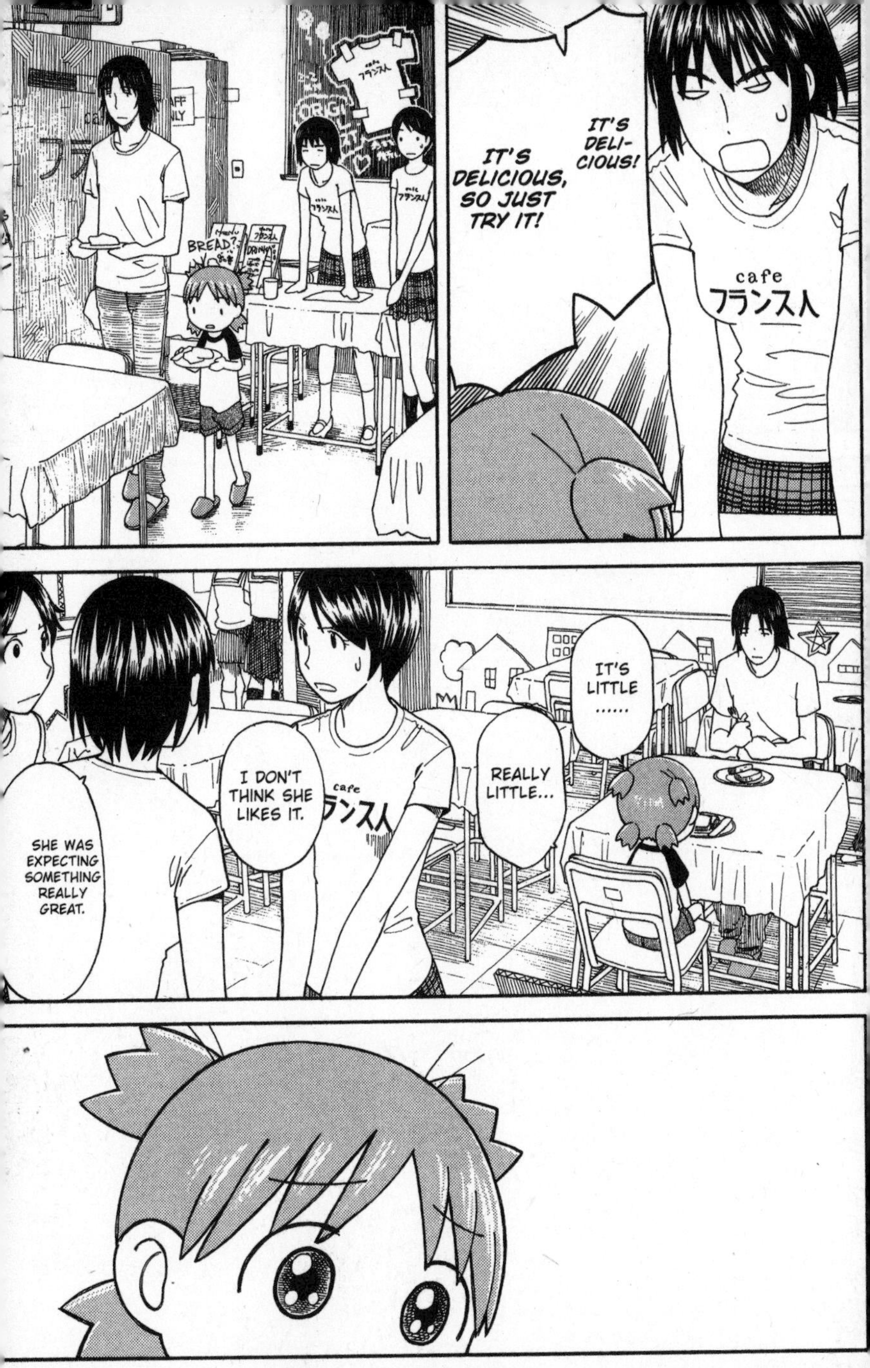

IT'S DELI- CIOUS!
IT'S DELICIOUS, SO JUST TRY IT!
cafe フランス人
BREAD?
IT'S LITTLE ......
REALLY LITTLE...
I DON'T THINK SHE LIKES IT.
SHE WAS EXPECTING SOMETHING REALLY GREAT.

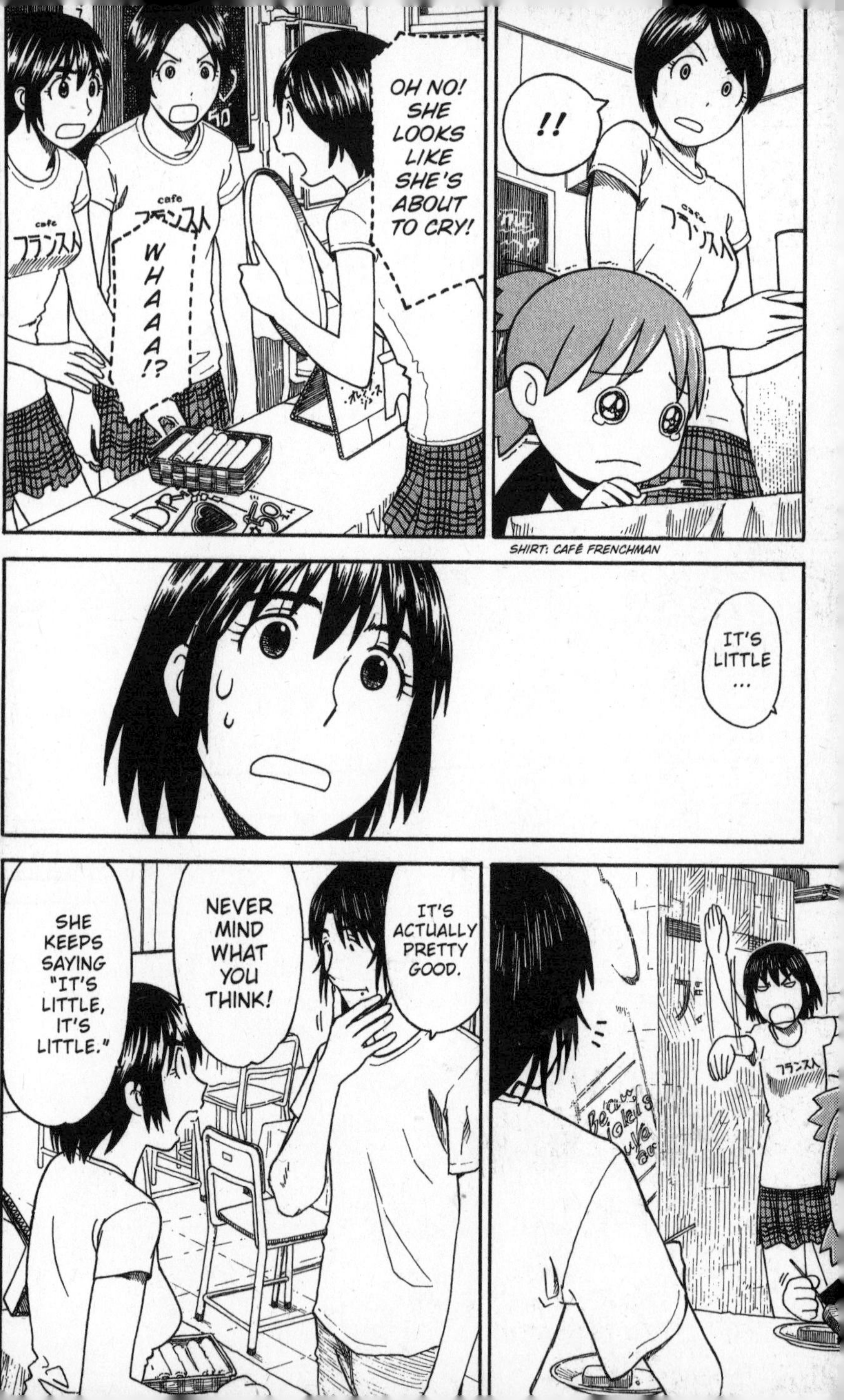
!!
OH NO! SHE LOOKS LIKE SHE'S ABOUT TO CRY!
WHAAAA!?
SHIRT: CAFÉ FRENCHMAN
IT'S LITTLE ...
IT'S ACTUALLY PRETTY GOOD.
NEVER MIND WHAT YOU THINK!
SHE KEEPS SAYING "IT'S LITTLE, IT'S LITTLE."

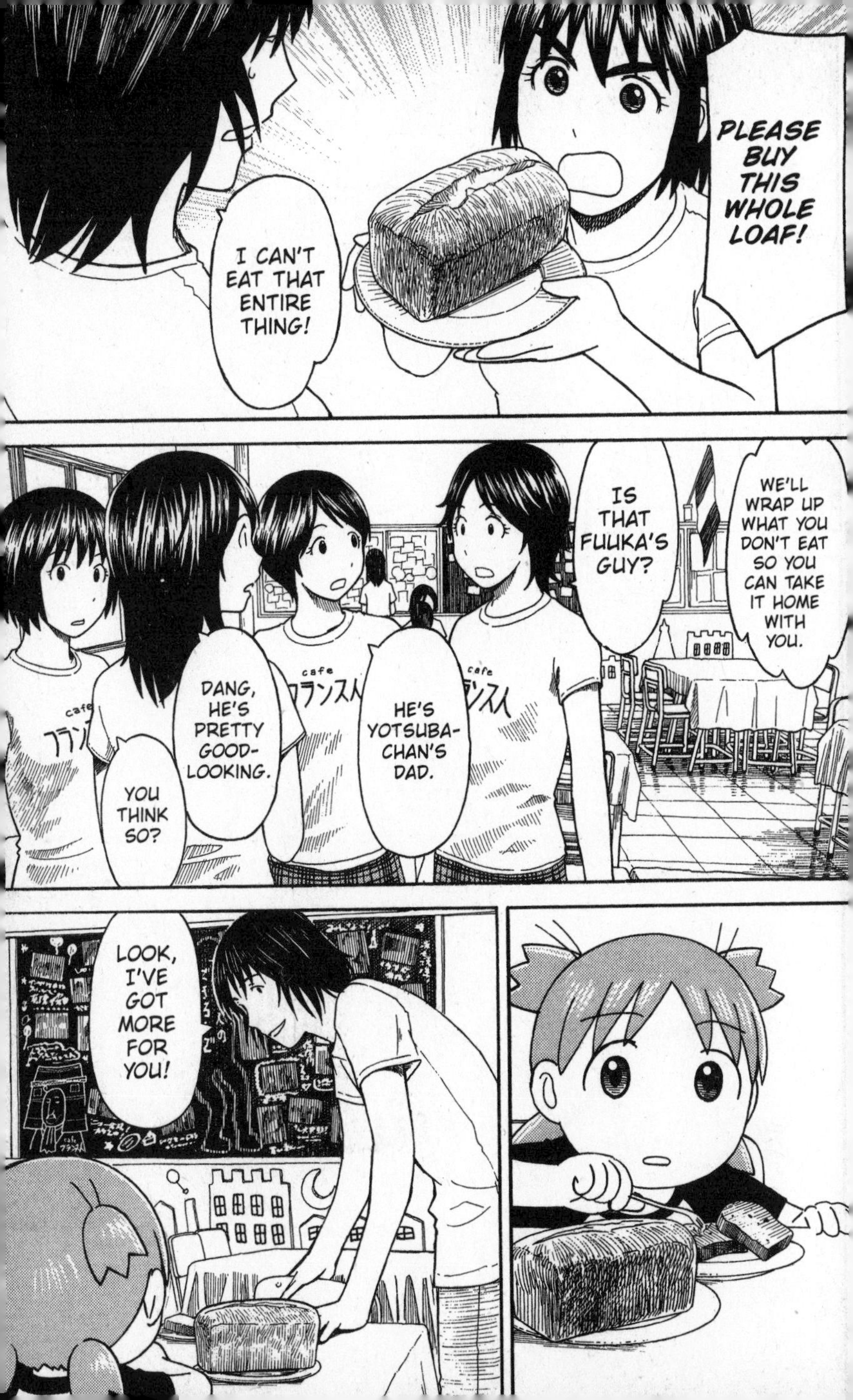
PLEASE BUY THIS WHOLE LOAF!
I CAN'T EAT THAT ENTIRE THING!
WE'LL WRAP UP WHAT YOU DON'T EAT SO YOU CAN TAKE IT HOME WITH YOU.
IS THAT FUUKA'S GUY?
HE'S YOTSUBA-CHAN'S DAD.
DANG, HE'S PRETTY GOOD-LOOKING.
YOU THINK SO?
LOOK, I'VE GOT MORE FOR YOU!

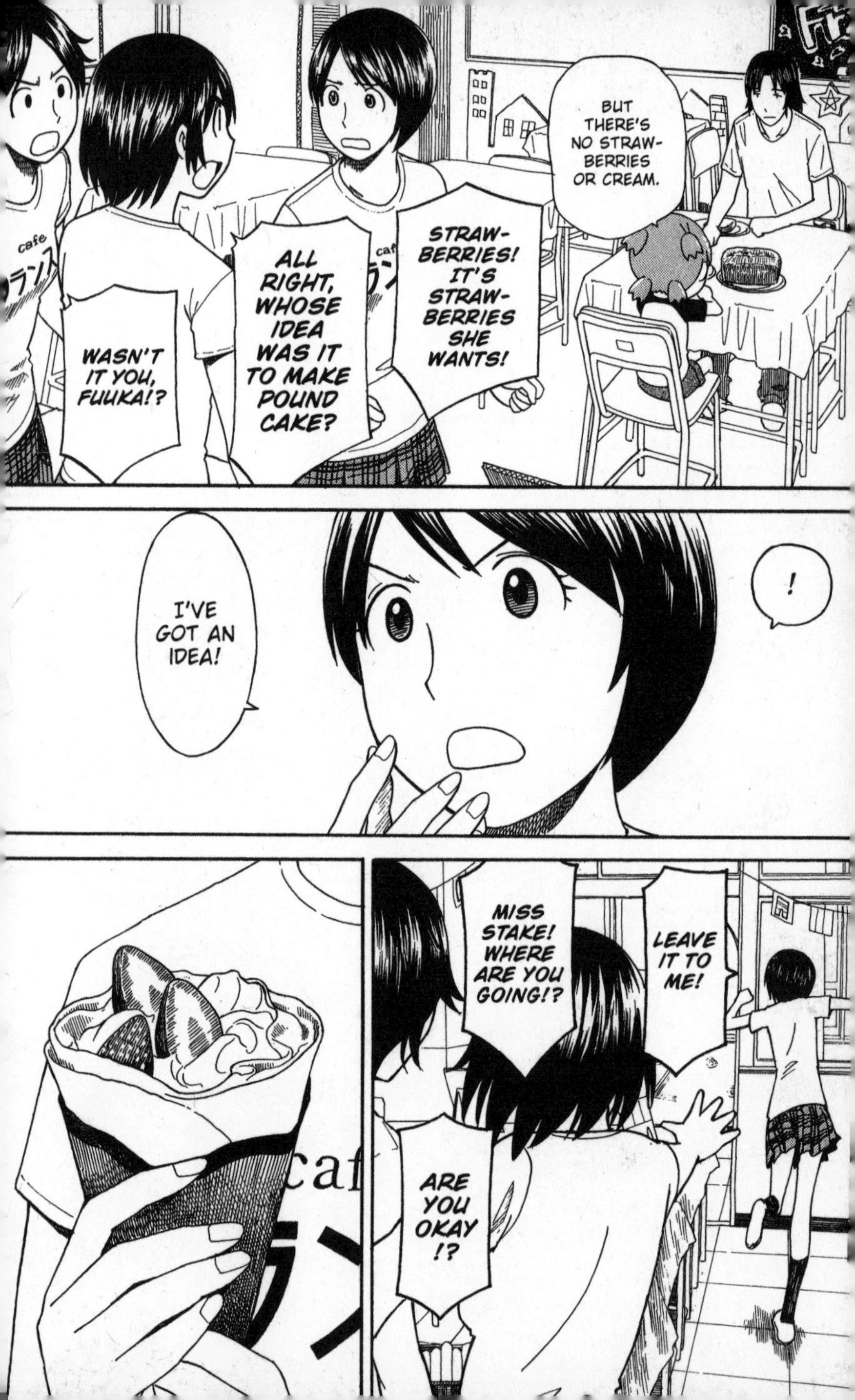
BUT THERE'S NO STRAWBERRIES OR CREAM.
STRAWBERRIES! IT'S STRAWBERRIES SHE WANTS!
ALL RIGHT, WHOSE IDEA WAS IT TO MAKE POUND CAKE?
WASN'T IT YOU, FUUKA!?
!
I'VE GOT AN IDEA!
LEAVE IT TO ME!
MISS STAKE! WHERE ARE YOU GOING!?
ARE YOU OKAY !?

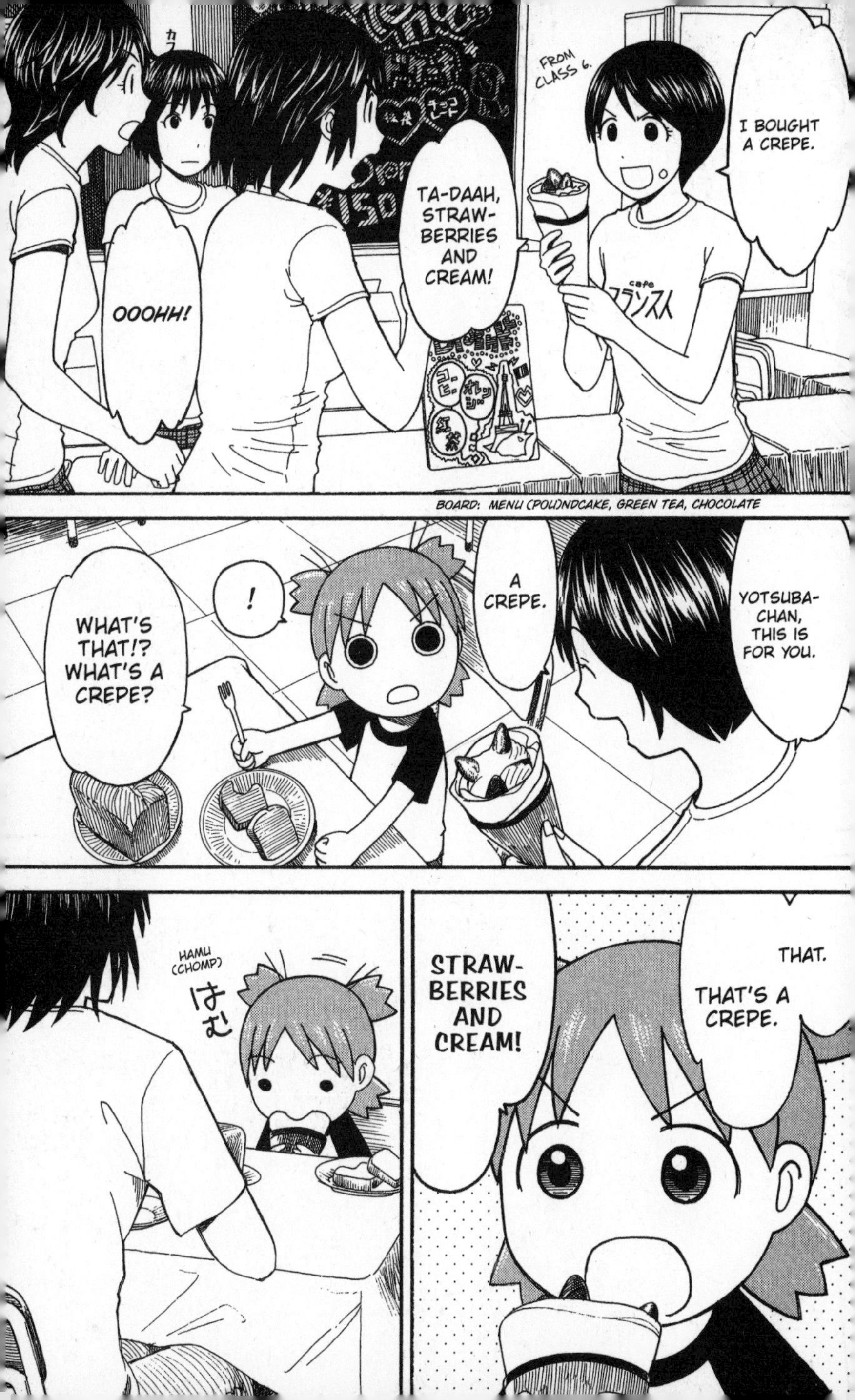
FROM CLASS 6.
I BOUGHT A CREPE.
TA-DAAH, STRAWBERRIES AND CREAM!
OOOHH!
BOARD: MENU (POU)NDCAKE, GREEN TEA, CHOCOLATE
YOTSUBA-CHAN, THIS IS FOR YOU.
A CREPE.
!
WHAT'S THAT!? WHAT'S A CREPE?
THAT.
THAT'S A CREPE.
STRAWBERRIES AND CREAM!
HAMU (CHOMP)
はむ

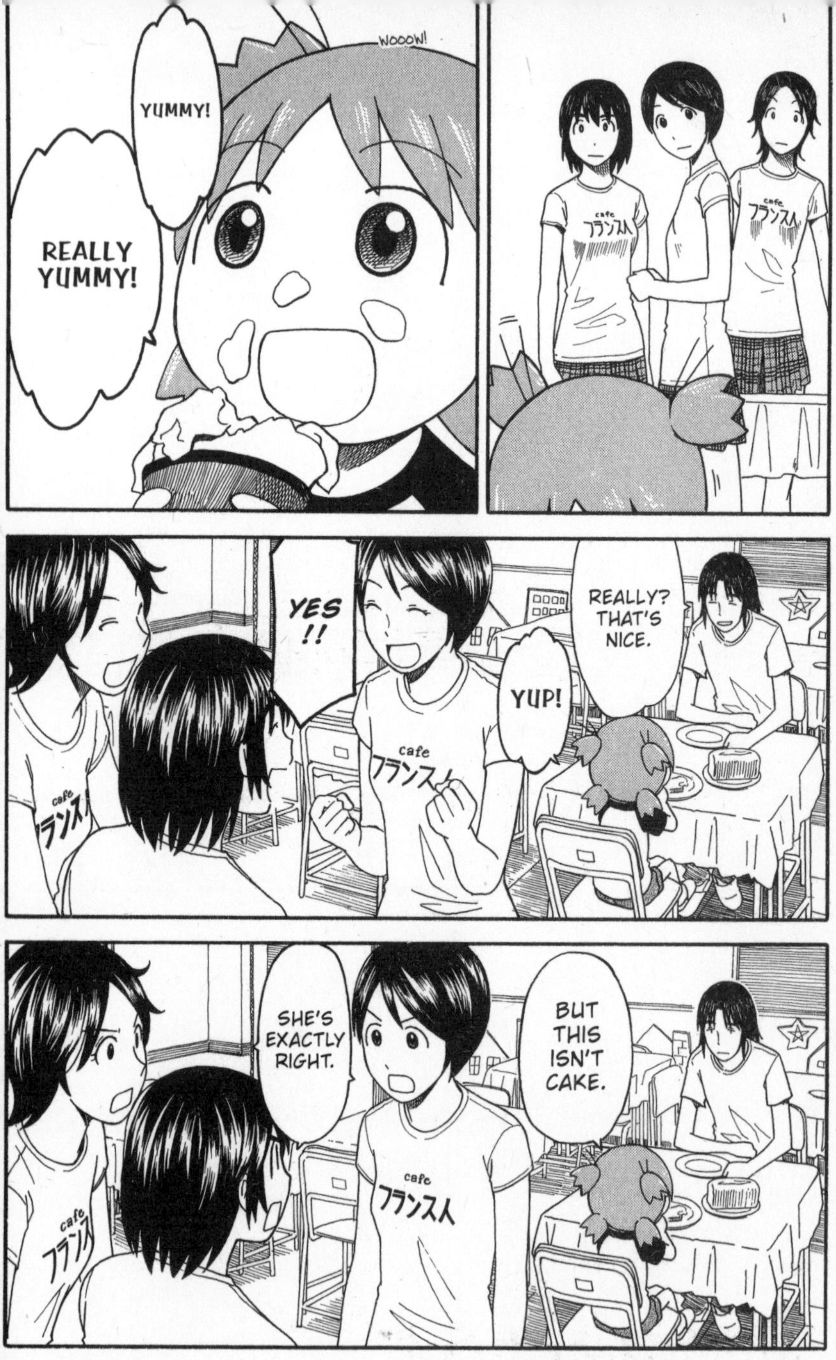
cafe フランス人
WOOOW!
YUMMY!
REALLY YUMMY!
REALLY? THAT'S NICE.
YUP!
YES !!
BUT THIS ISN'T CAKE.
SHE'S EXACTLY RIGHT.

YOTSUBA&!

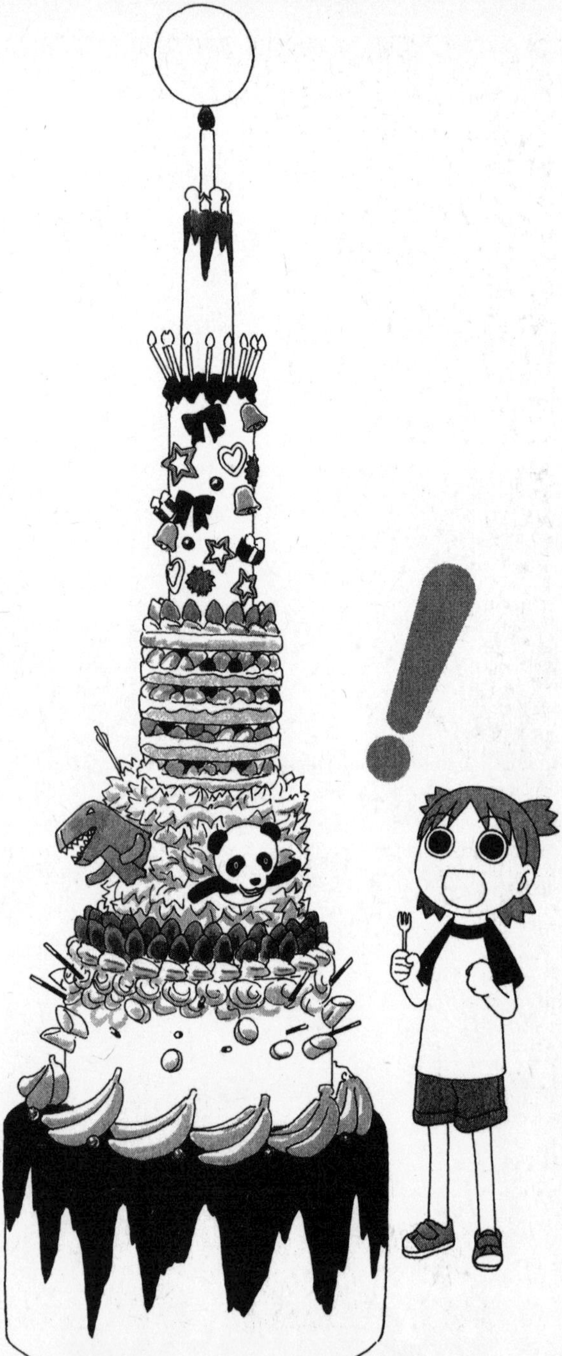

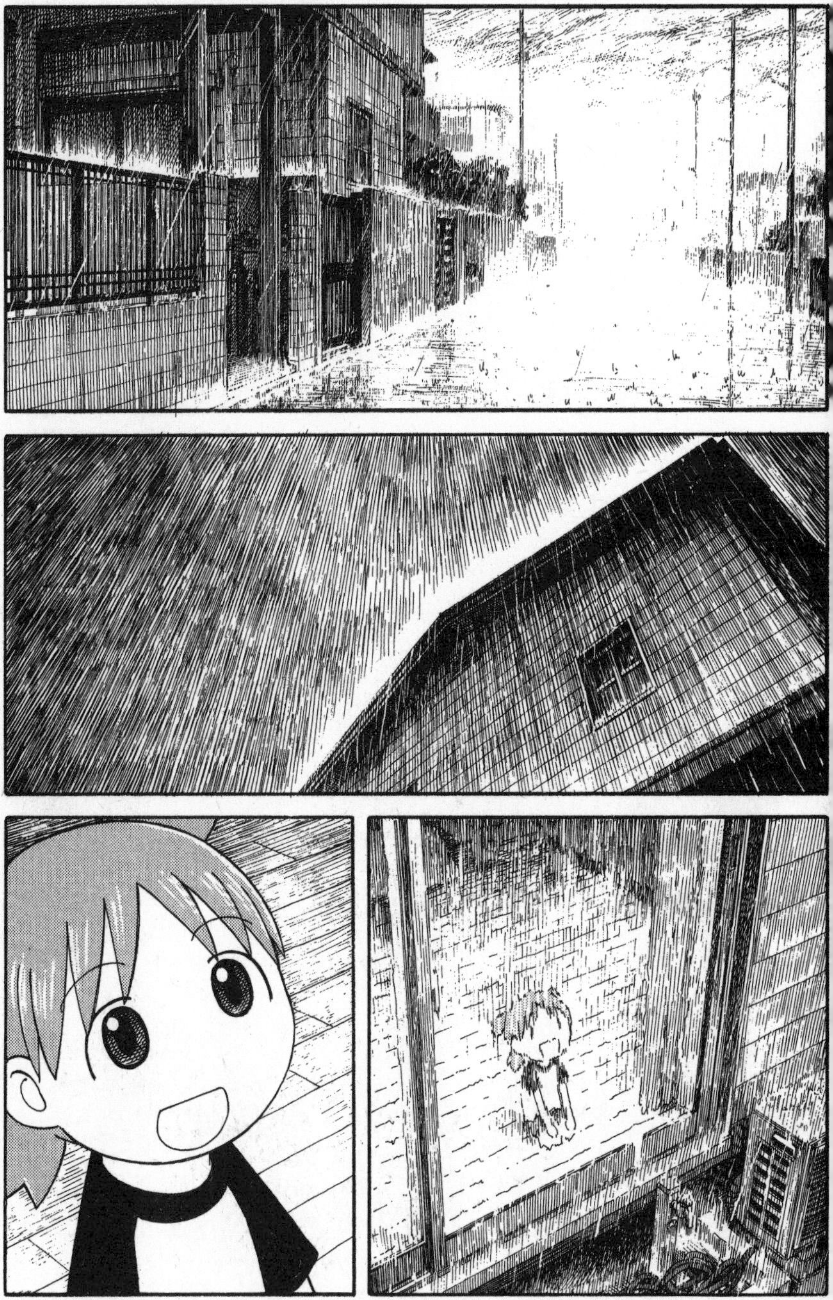

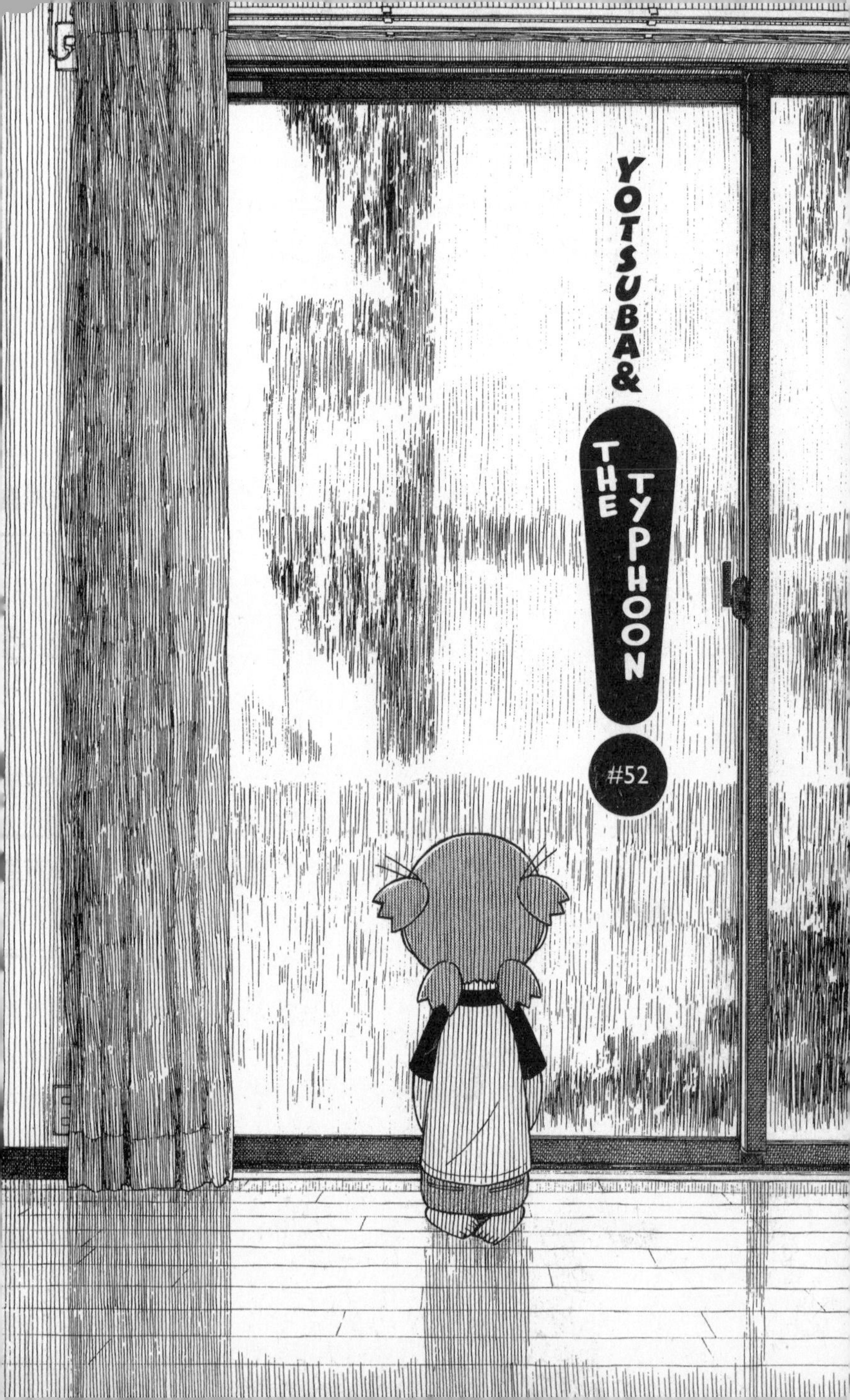
YOTSUBA&
THE TYPHOON
#52

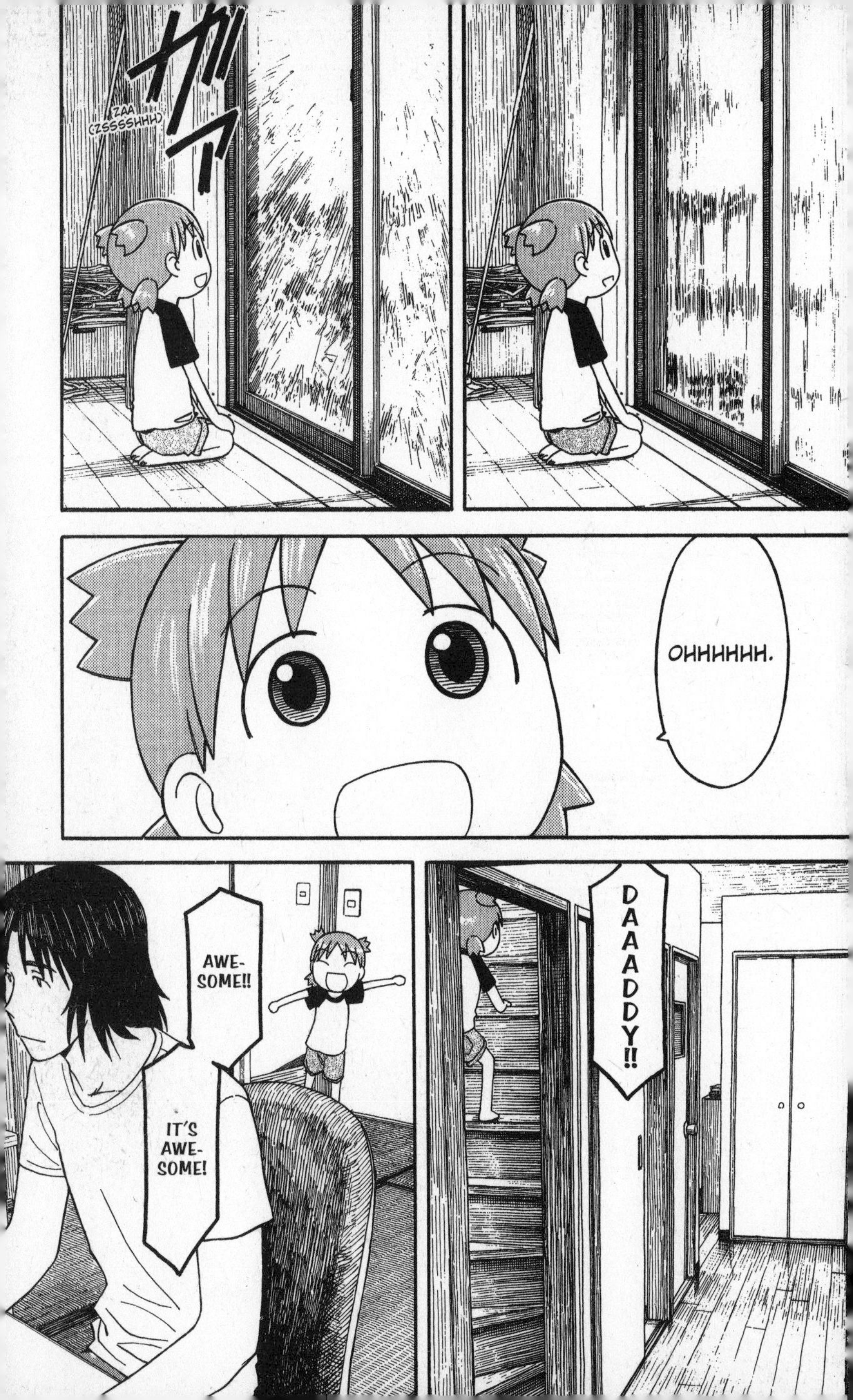
ZAA (ZSSSSHHH)
OHHHHHH.
DAAAADDY!!
AWE-SOME!!
IT'S AWE-SOME!

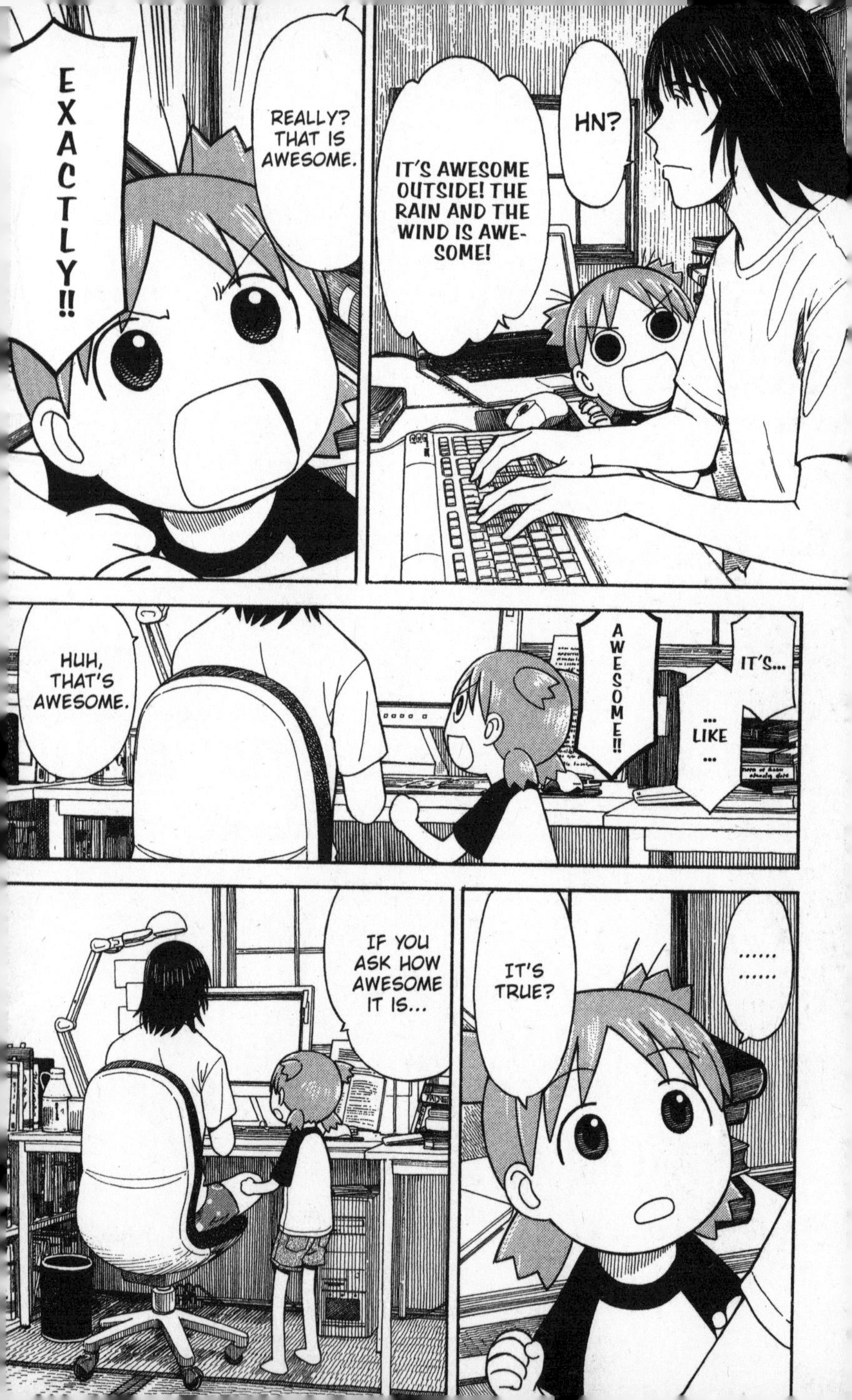
HN?
IT'S AWESOME OUTSIDE! THE RAIN AND THE WIND IS AWE-SOME!
REALLY? THAT IS AWESOME.
EXACTLY!!
IT'S...
...LIKE...
AWESOME!!
HUH, THAT'S AWESOME.
......
......
IT'S TRUE?
IF YOU ASK HOW AWESOME IT IS...

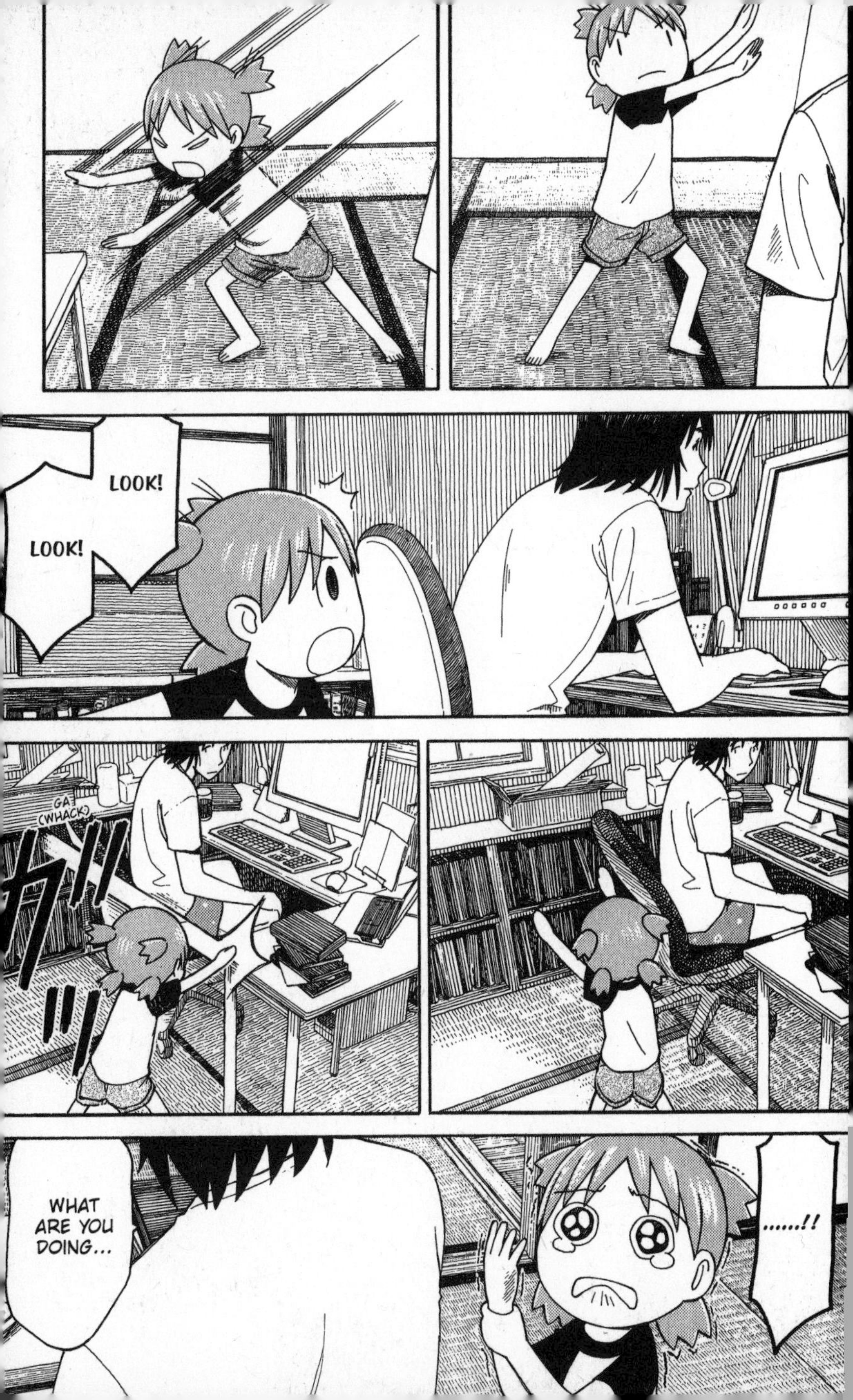
LOOK!
LOOK!
GA (WHACK)
......!!
WHAT ARE YOU DOING...

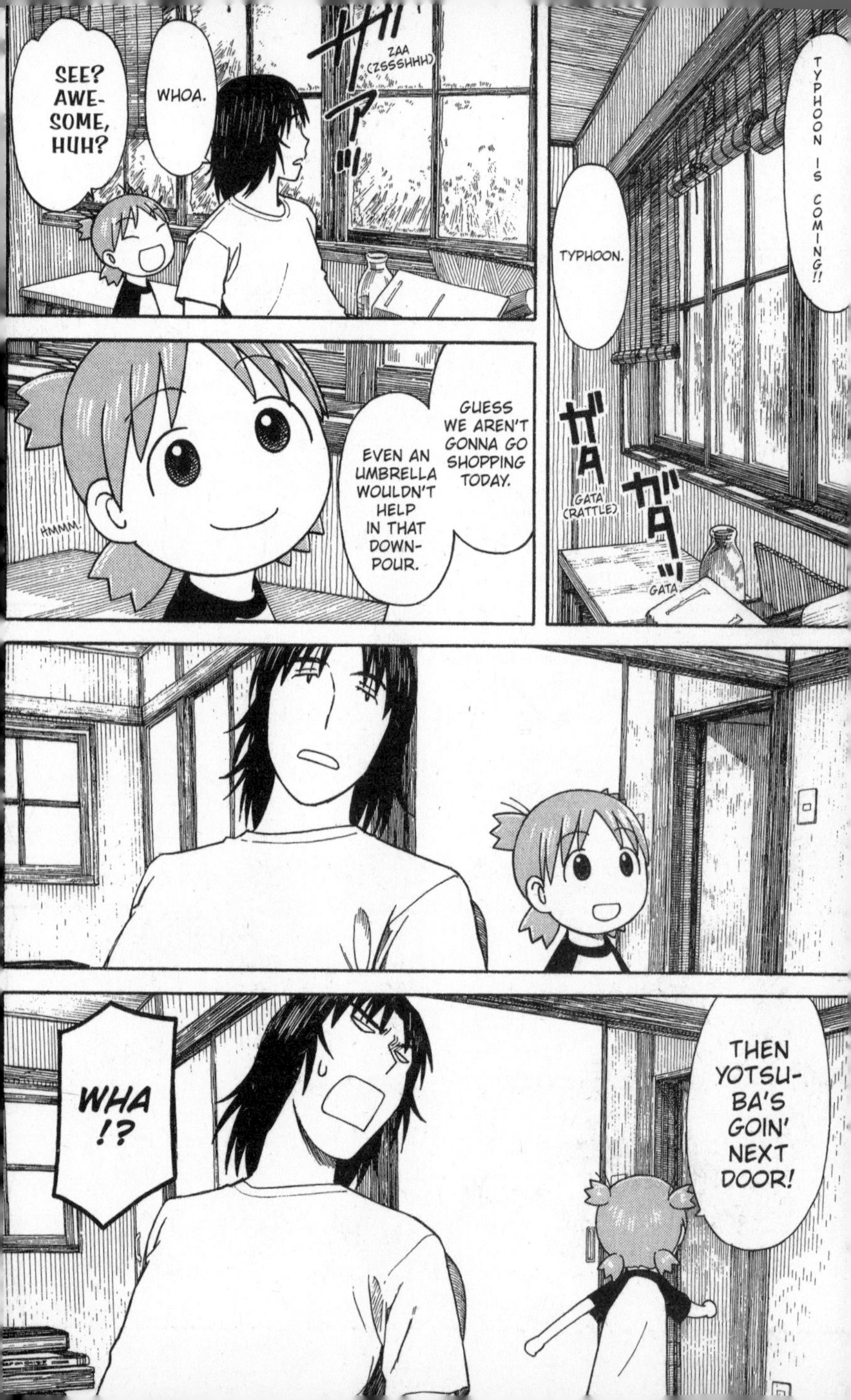
TYPHOON IS COMING!!
TYPHOON.
GATA (RATTLE)
GATA
ZAA (ZSSSHHH)
WHOA.
SEE? AWE-SOME, HUH?
GUESS WE AREN'T GONNA GO SHOPPING TODAY.
EVEN AN UMBRELLA WOULDN'T HELP IN THAT DOWN-POUR.
HMMM.
THEN YOTSU-BA'S GOIN' NEXT DOOR!
WHA!?

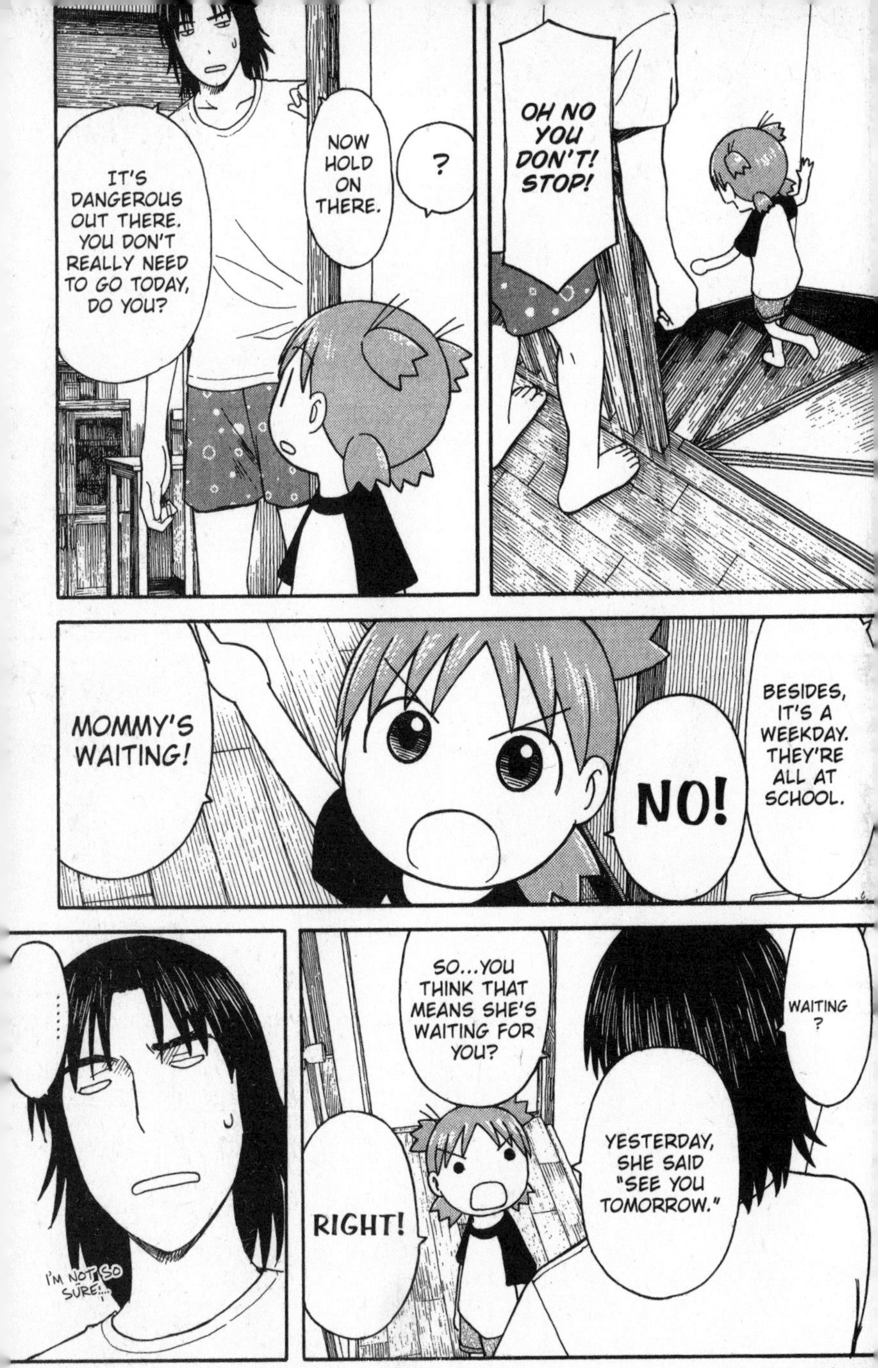
OH NO YOU DON'T! STOP!
?
NOW HOLD ON THERE.
IT'S DANGEROUS OUT THERE. YOU DON'T REALLY NEED TO GO TODAY, DO YOU?
BESIDES, IT'S A WEEKDAY. THEY'RE ALL AT SCHOOL.
NO!
MOMMY'S WAITING!
WAITING?
YESTERDAY, SHE SAID "SEE YOU TOMORROW."
SO...YOU THINK THAT MEANS SHE'S WAITING FOR YOU?
RIGHT!
......
I'M NOT SO SURE!...

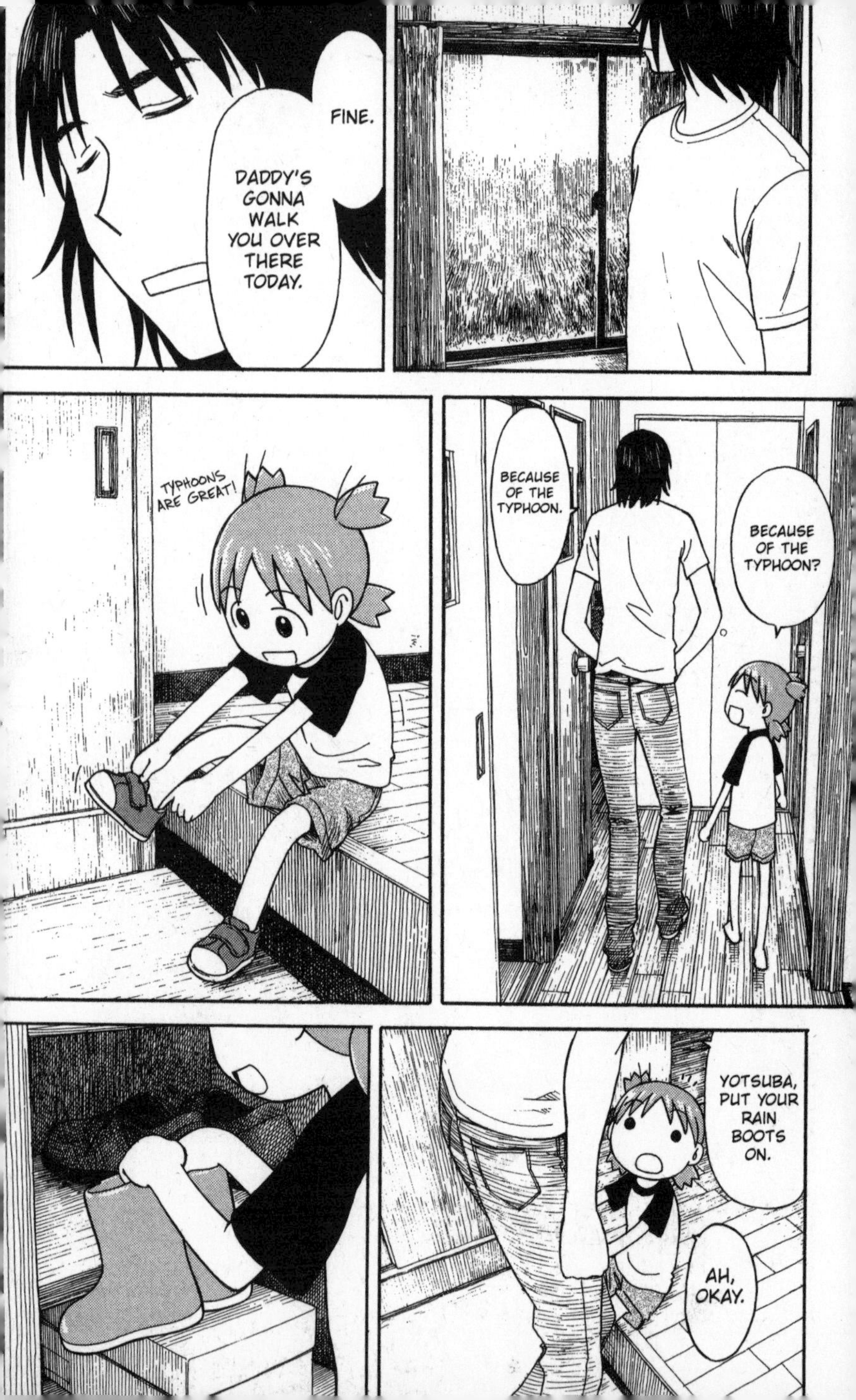
FINE.
DADDY'S GONNA WALK YOU OVER THERE TODAY.
BECAUSE OF THE TYPHOON?
BECAUSE OF THE TYPHOON.
TYPHOONS ARE GREAT!
YOTSUBA, PUT YOUR RAIN BOOTS ON.
AH, OKAY.

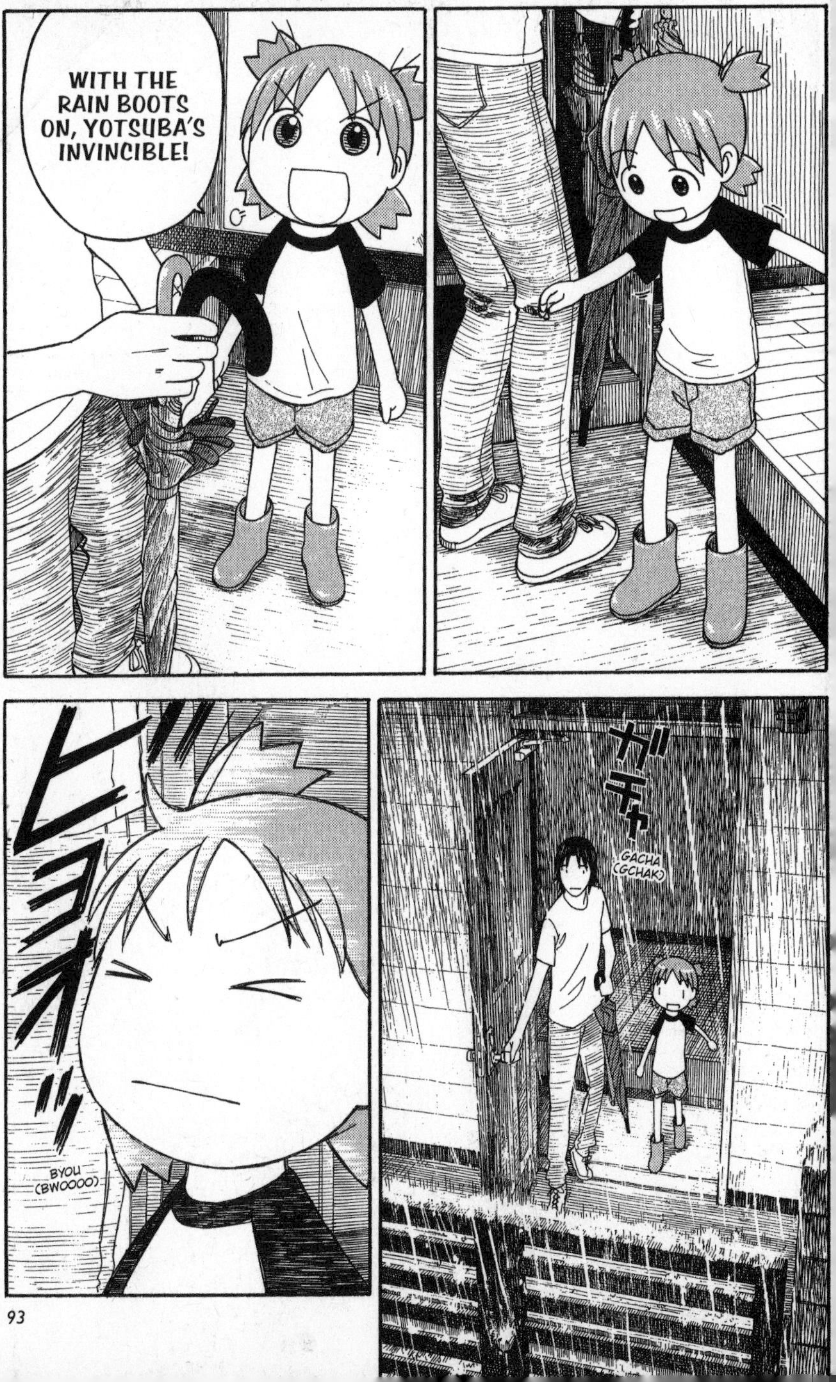
WITH THE RAIN BOOTS ON, YOTSUBA'S INVINCIBLE!
ガチャ
GACHA (GCHAK)
BYOU (BWOOOO)

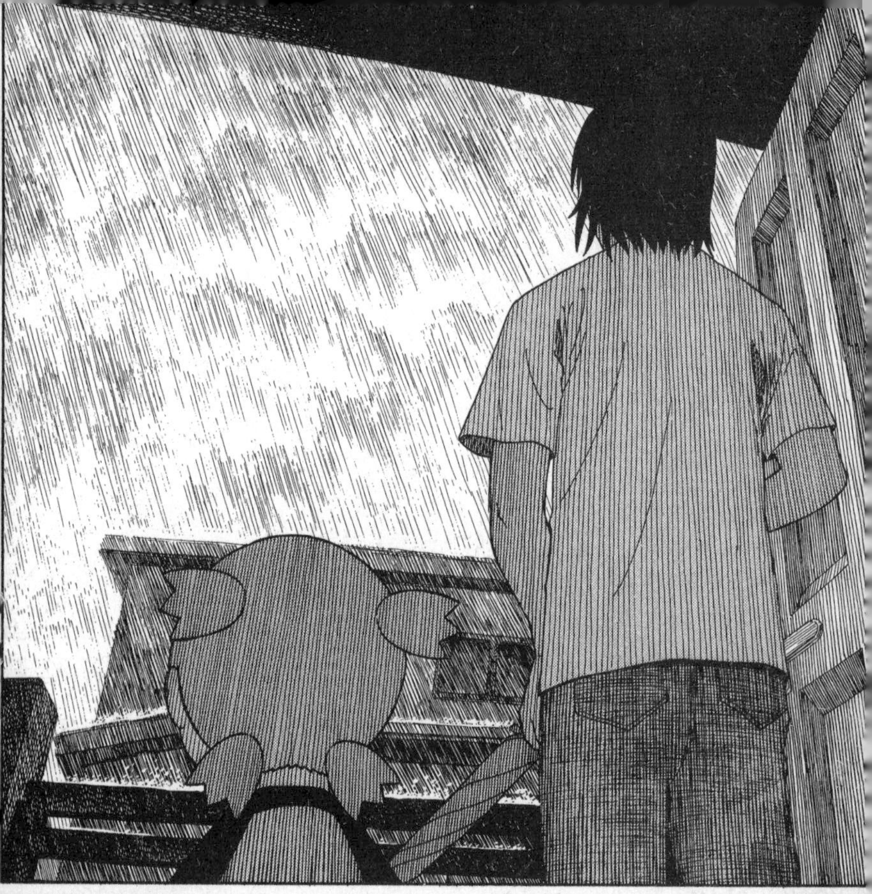
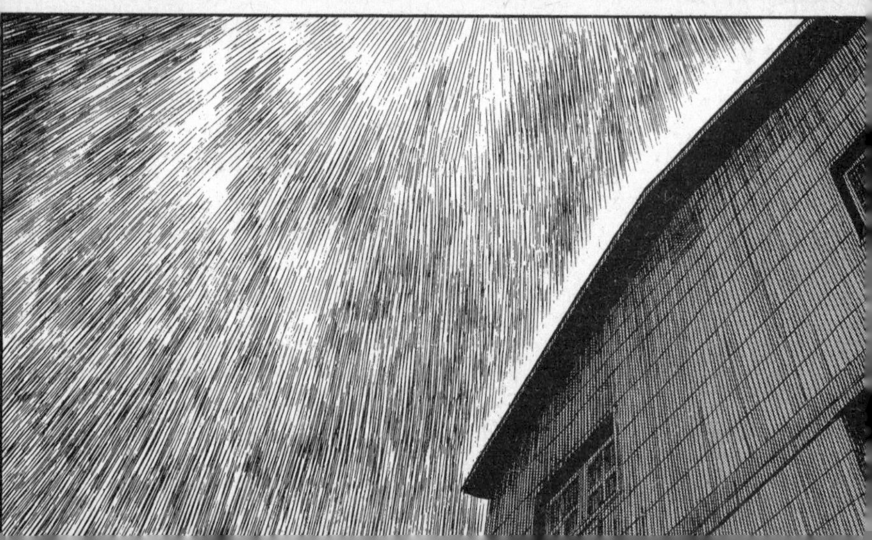

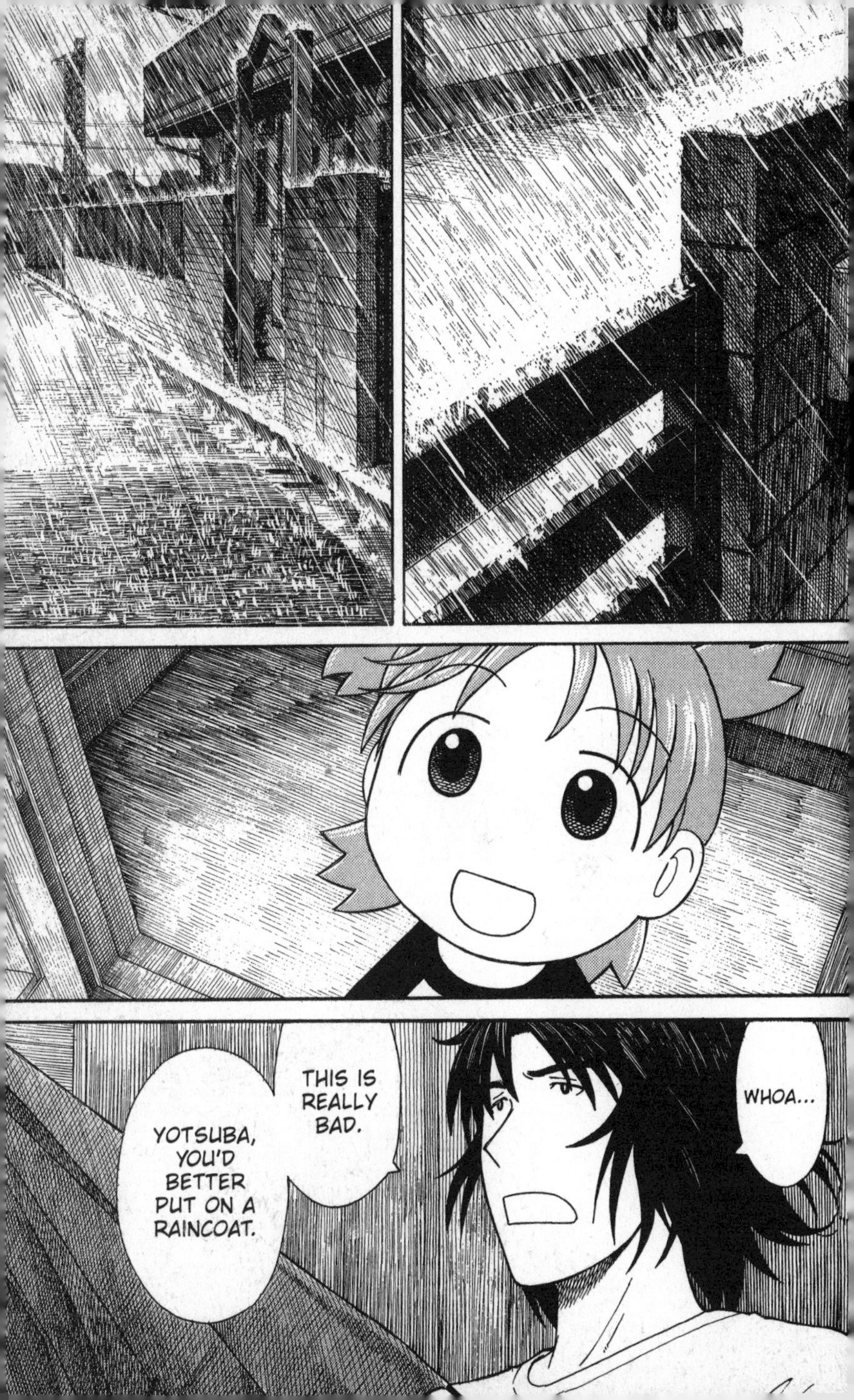
WHOA...
THIS IS REALLY BAD.
YOTSUBA, YOU'D BETTER PUT ON A RAINCOAT.

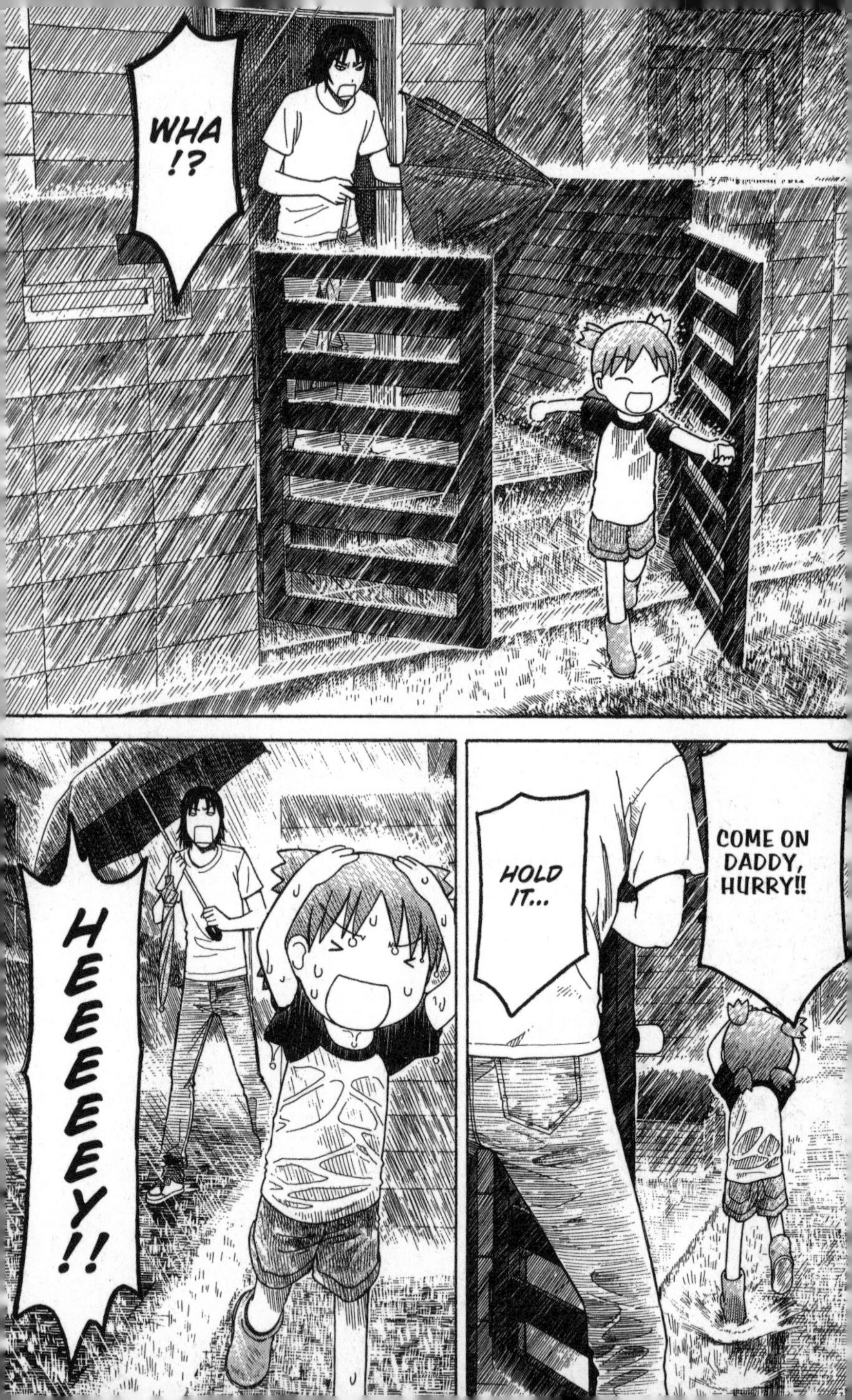
WHA!?
COME ON DADDY, HURRY!!
HOLD IT...
HEEEEEY!!

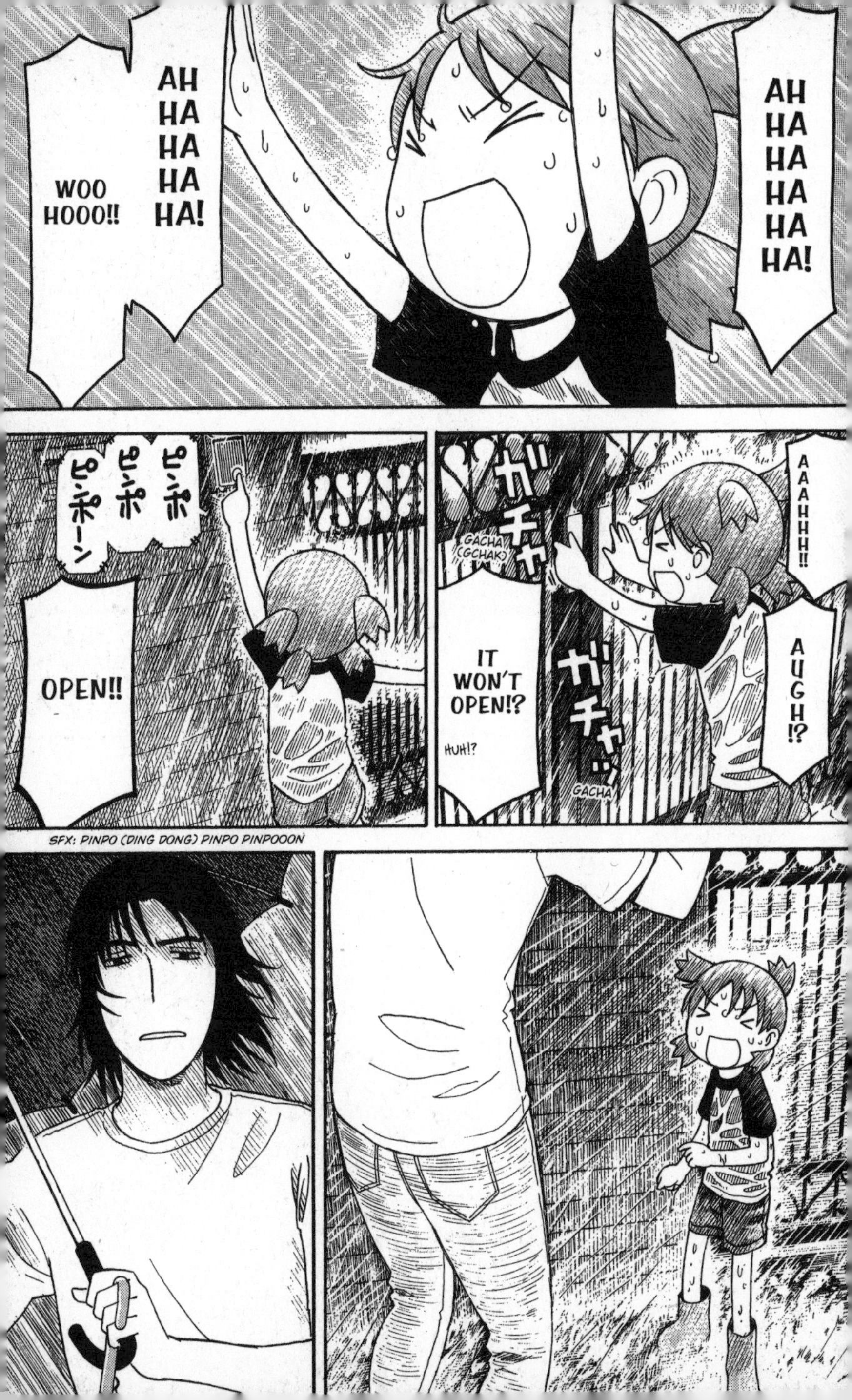
AH HA HA HA HA HA HA!
AH HA HA HA HA!
WOO HOOO!!
AAAAHHH!!
AUGH!?
ガチャ
GACHA (GCHAK)
ガチャッ
GACHA
IT WON'T OPEN!?
HUH!?
ピンポ ピンポ ピンポーン
OPEN!!
SFX: PINPO (DING DONG) PINPO PINPOOON

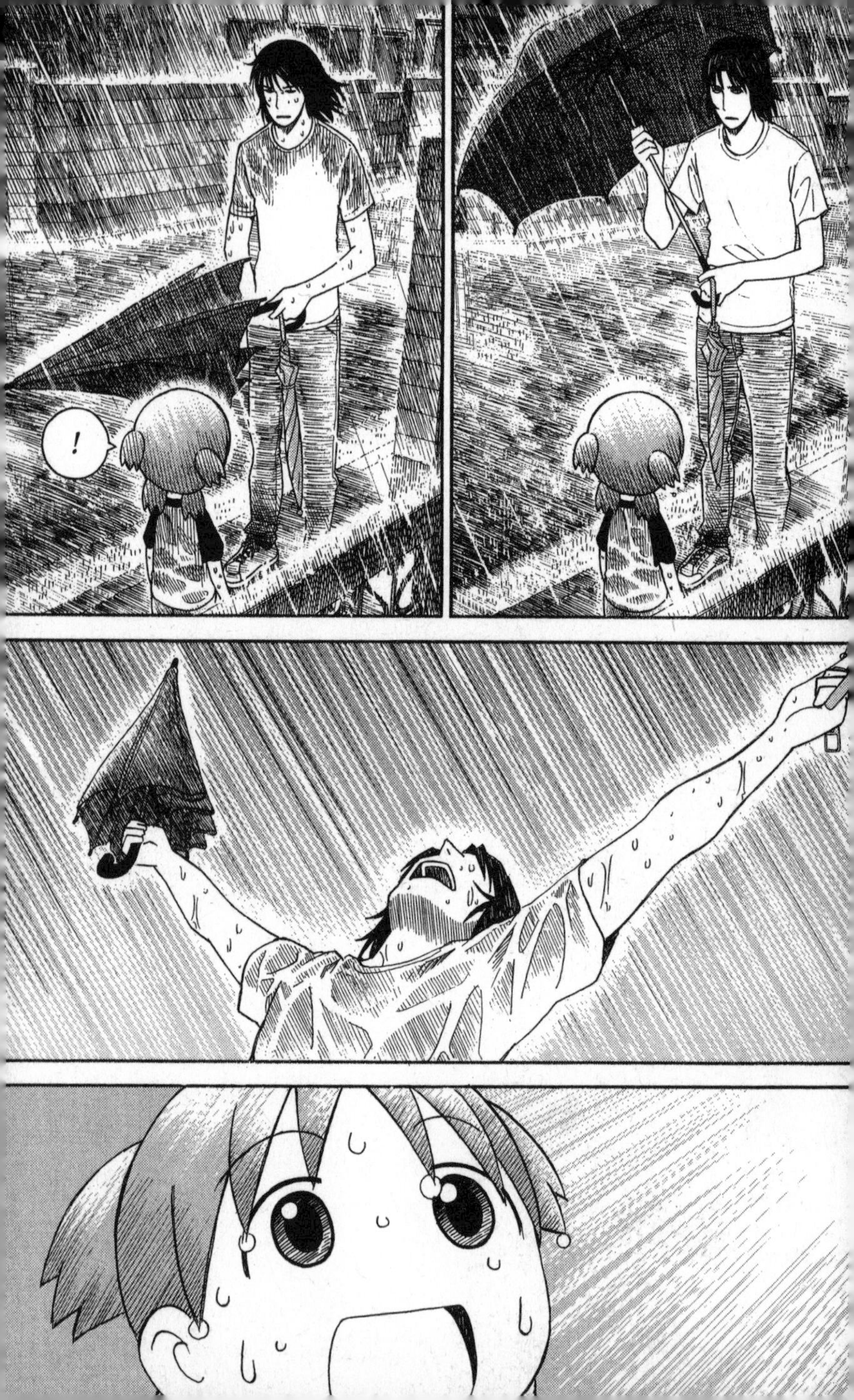
!

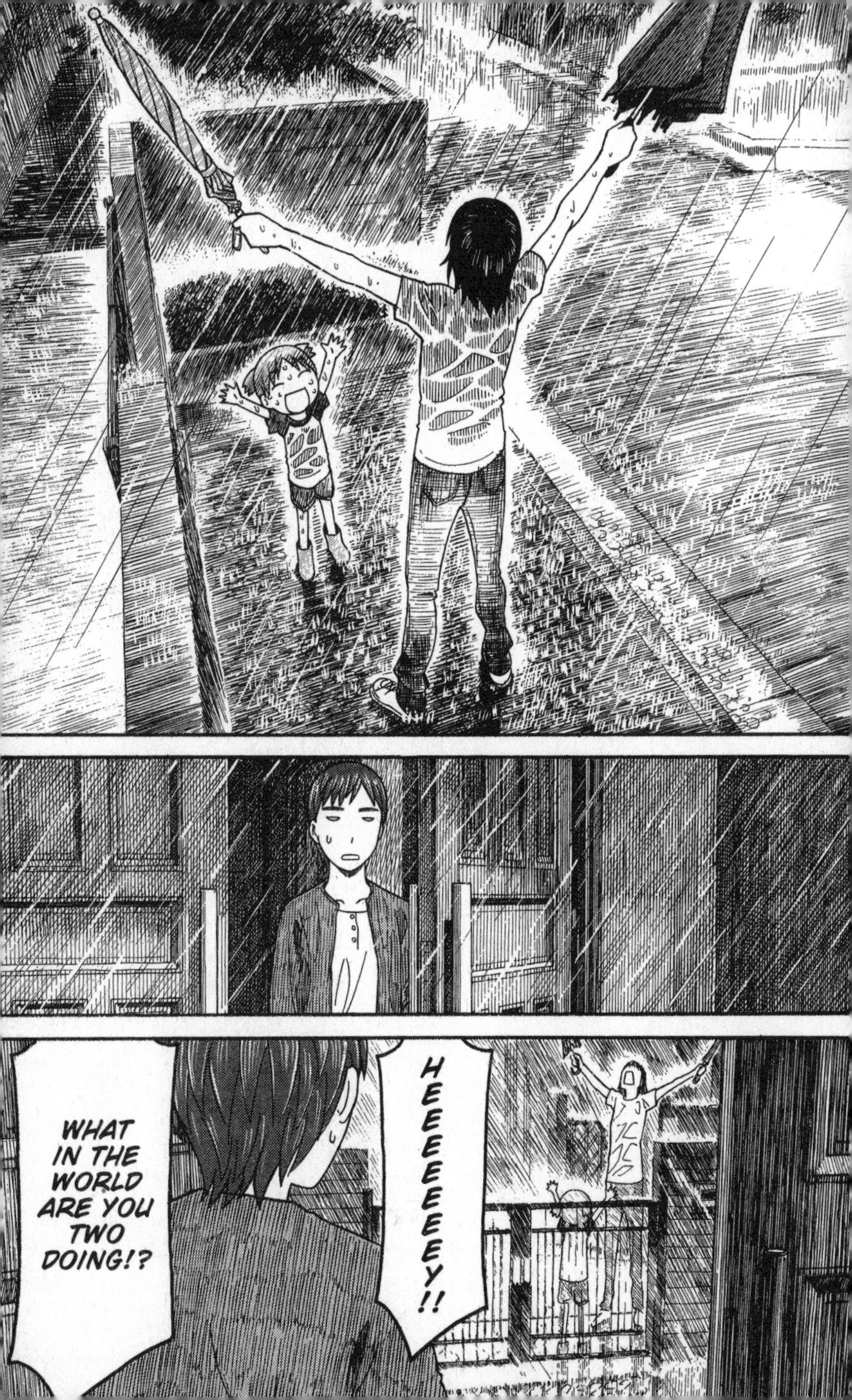
HEEEEEEEY!!
WHAT IN THE WORLD ARE YOU TWO DOING!?

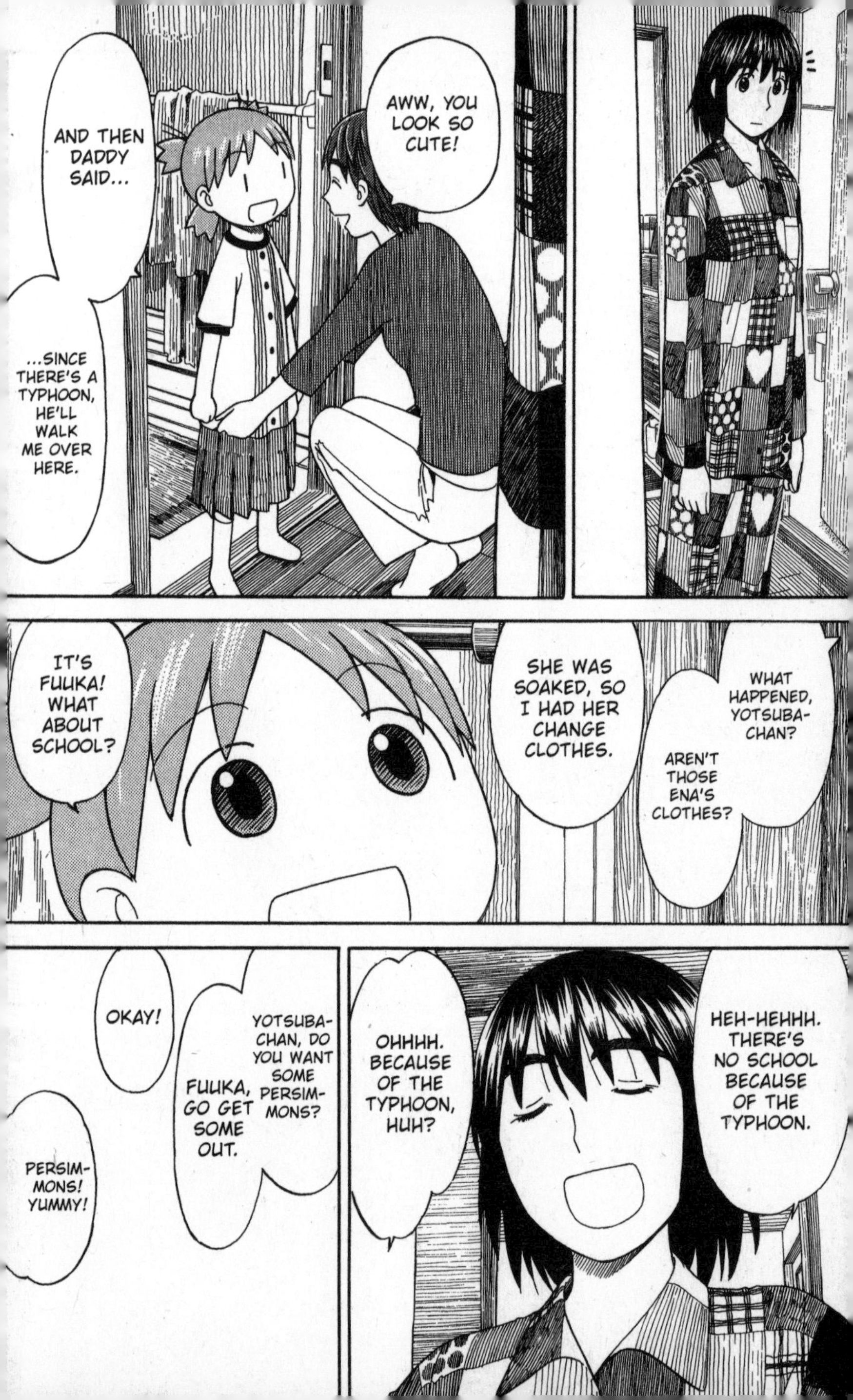
AWW, YOU LOOK SO CUTE!
AND THEN DADDY SAID...
...SINCE THERE'S A TYPHOON, HE'LL WALK ME OVER HERE.
WHAT HAPPENED, YOTSUBA-CHAN?
AREN'T THOSE ENA'S CLOTHES?
SHE WAS SOAKED, SO I HAD HER CHANGE CLOTHES.
IT'S FUUKA! WHAT ABOUT SCHOOL?
HEH-HEHHH. THERE'S NO SCHOOL BECAUSE OF THE TYPHOON.
OHHHH. BECAUSE OF THE TYPHOON, HUH?
YOTSUBA-CHAN, DO YOU WANT SOME PERSIM-MONS?
FUUKA, GO GET SOME OUT.
OKAY!
PERSIM-MONS! YUMMY!

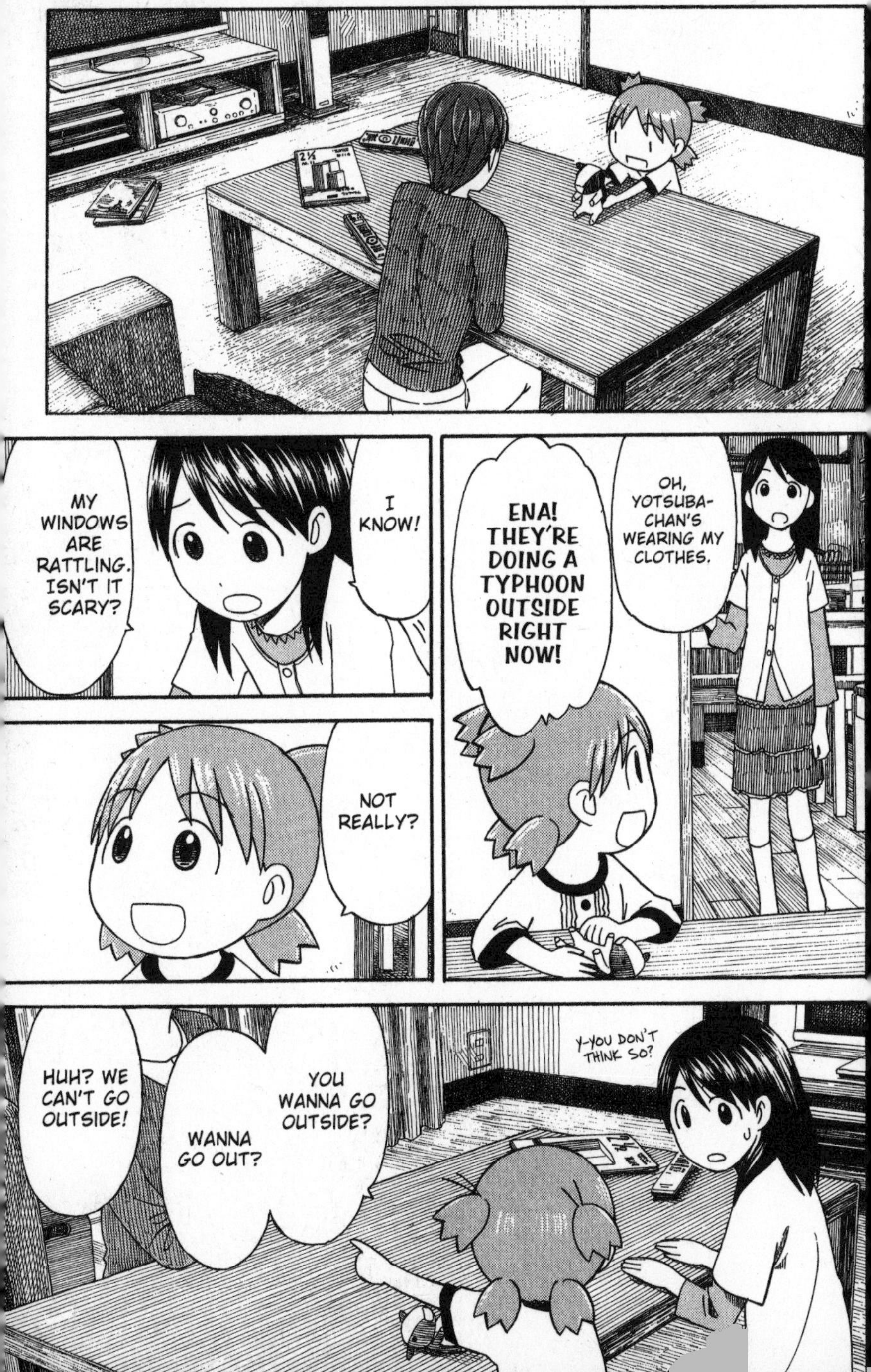
OH, YOTSUBA-CHAN'S WEARING MY CLOTHES.
ENA! THEY'RE DOING A TYPHOON OUTSIDE RIGHT NOW!
I KNOW!
MY WINDOWS ARE RATTLING. ISN'T IT SCARY?
NOT REALLY?
Y-YOU DON'T THINK SO?
YOU WANNA GO OUTSIDE?
WANNA GO OUT?
HUH? WE CAN'T GO OUTSIDE!

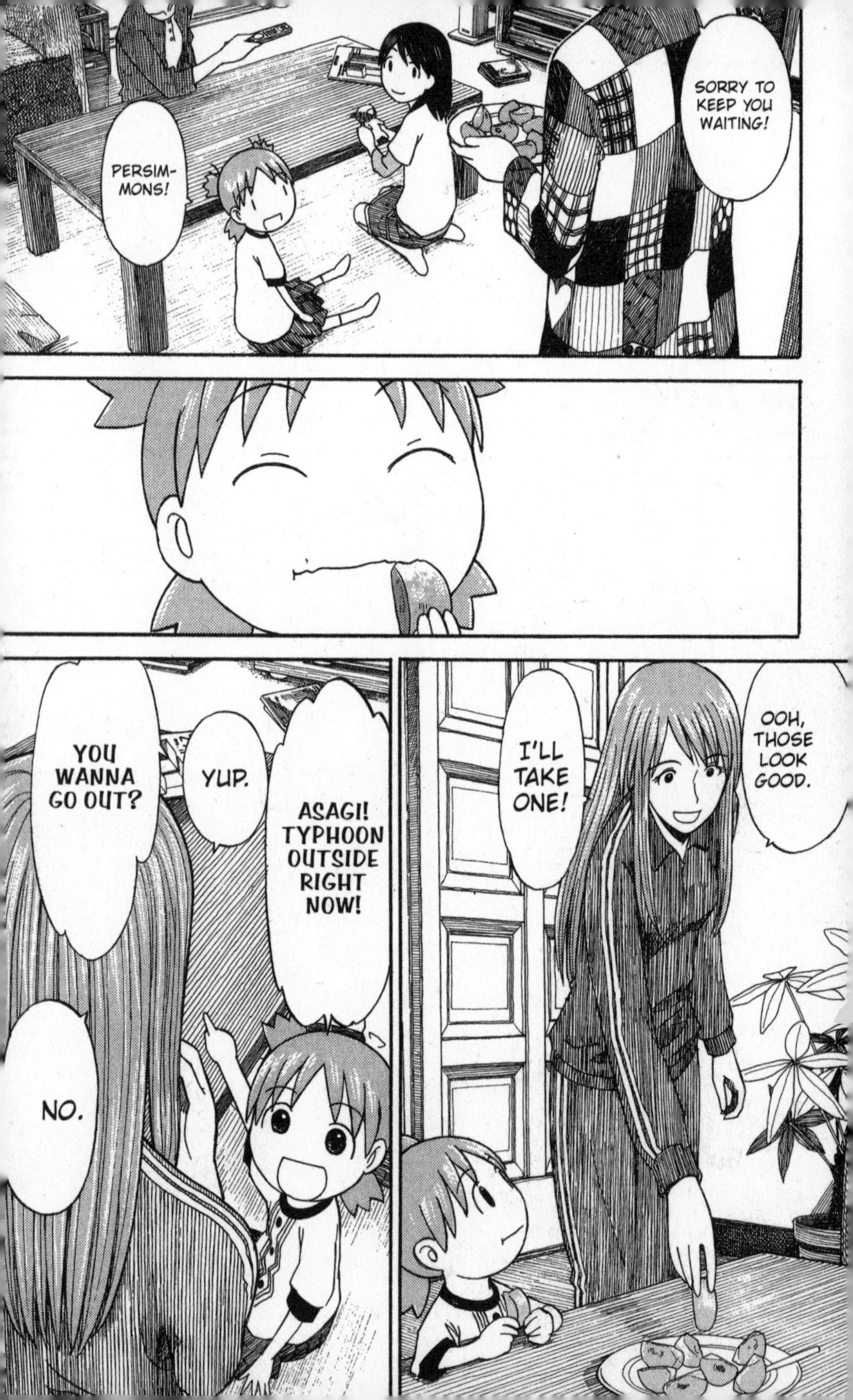
SORRY TO KEEP YOU WAITING!
PERSIM-MONS!
OOH, THOSE LOOK GOOD.
I'LL TAKE ONE!
ASAGI! TYPHOON OUTSIDE RIGHT NOW!
YUP.
YOU WANNA GO OUT?
NO.

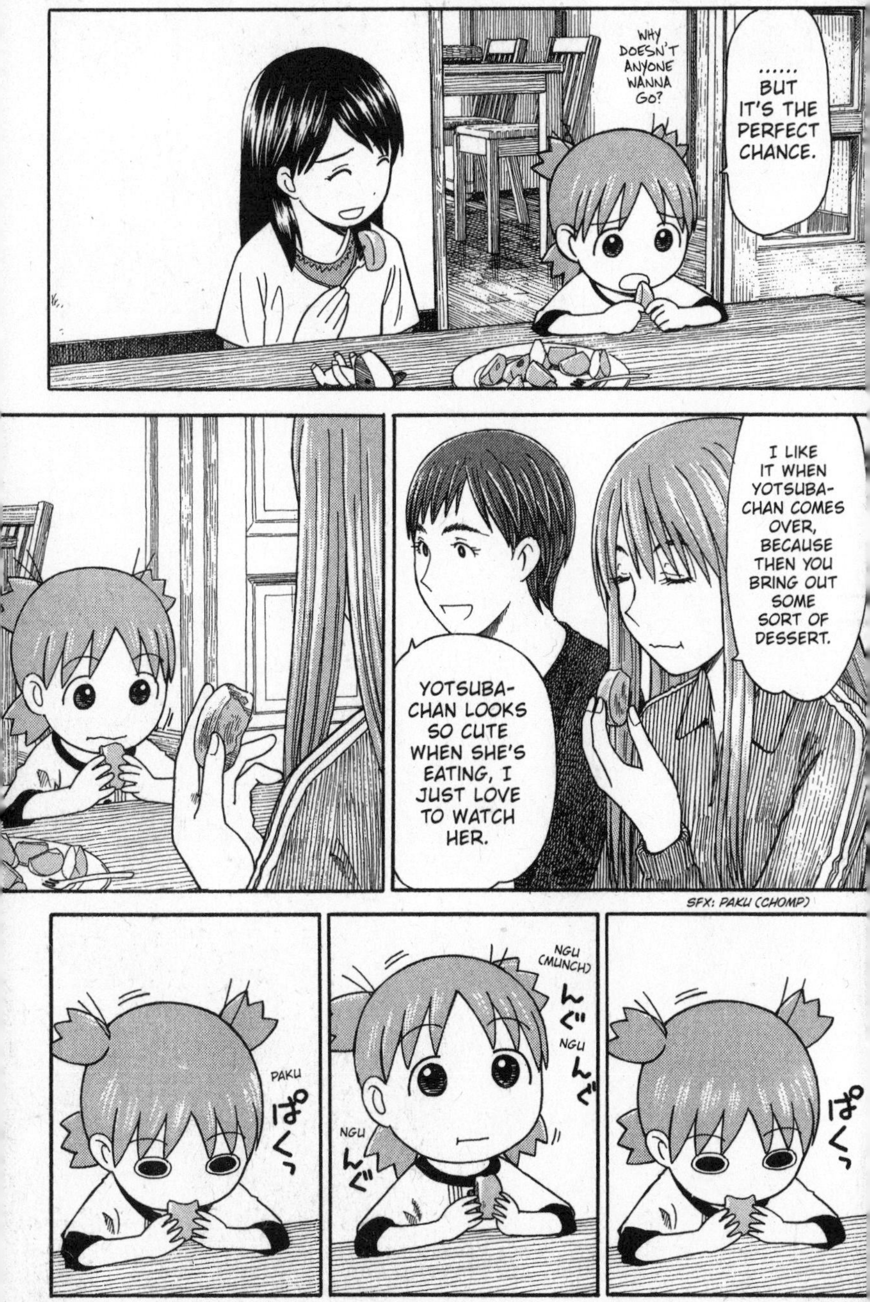

......
BUT IT'S THE PERFECT CHANCE.
WHY DOESN'T ANYONE WANNA GO?
I LIKE IT WHEN YOTSUBA-CHAN COMES OVER, BECAUSE THEN YOU BRING OUT SOME SORT OF DESSERT.
YOTSUBA-CHAN LOOKS SO CUTE WHEN SHE'S EATING, I JUST LOVE TO WATCH HER.
SFX: PAKU (CHOMP)
ぱくっ
NGU (MUNCH)
んぐ
NGU
んぐ
NGU
んぐ
PAKU
ぱくっ

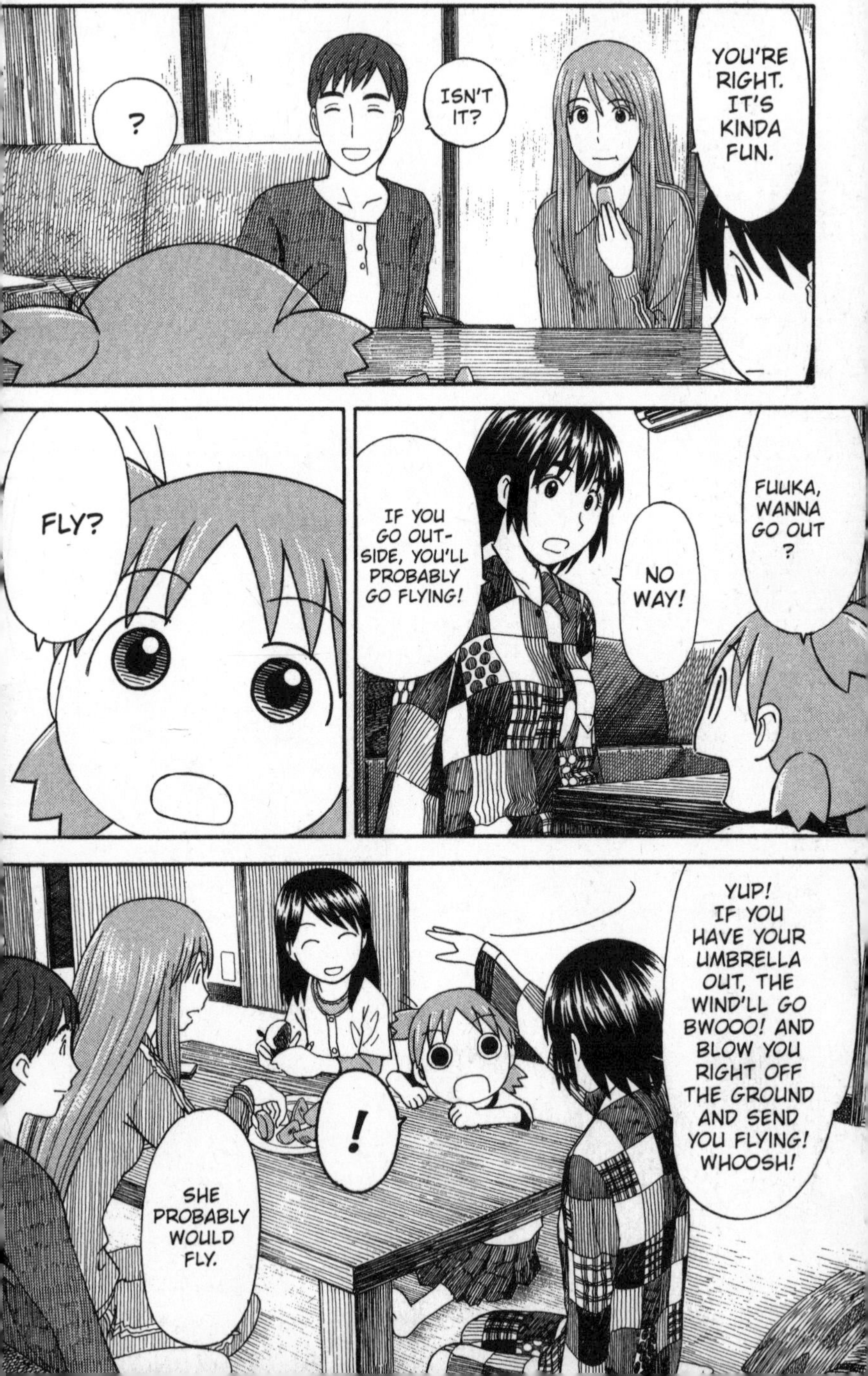
YOU'RE RIGHT. IT'S KINDA FUN.
ISN'T IT?
?
FUUKA, WANNA GO OUT?
NO WAY!
IF YOU GO OUT-SIDE, YOU'LL PROBABLY GO FLYING!
FLY?
YUP! IF YOU HAVE YOUR UMBRELLA OUT, THE WIND'LL GO BWOOO! AND BLOW YOU RIGHT OFF THE GROUND AND SEND YOU FLYING! WHOOSH!
!
SHE PROBABLY WOULD FLY.

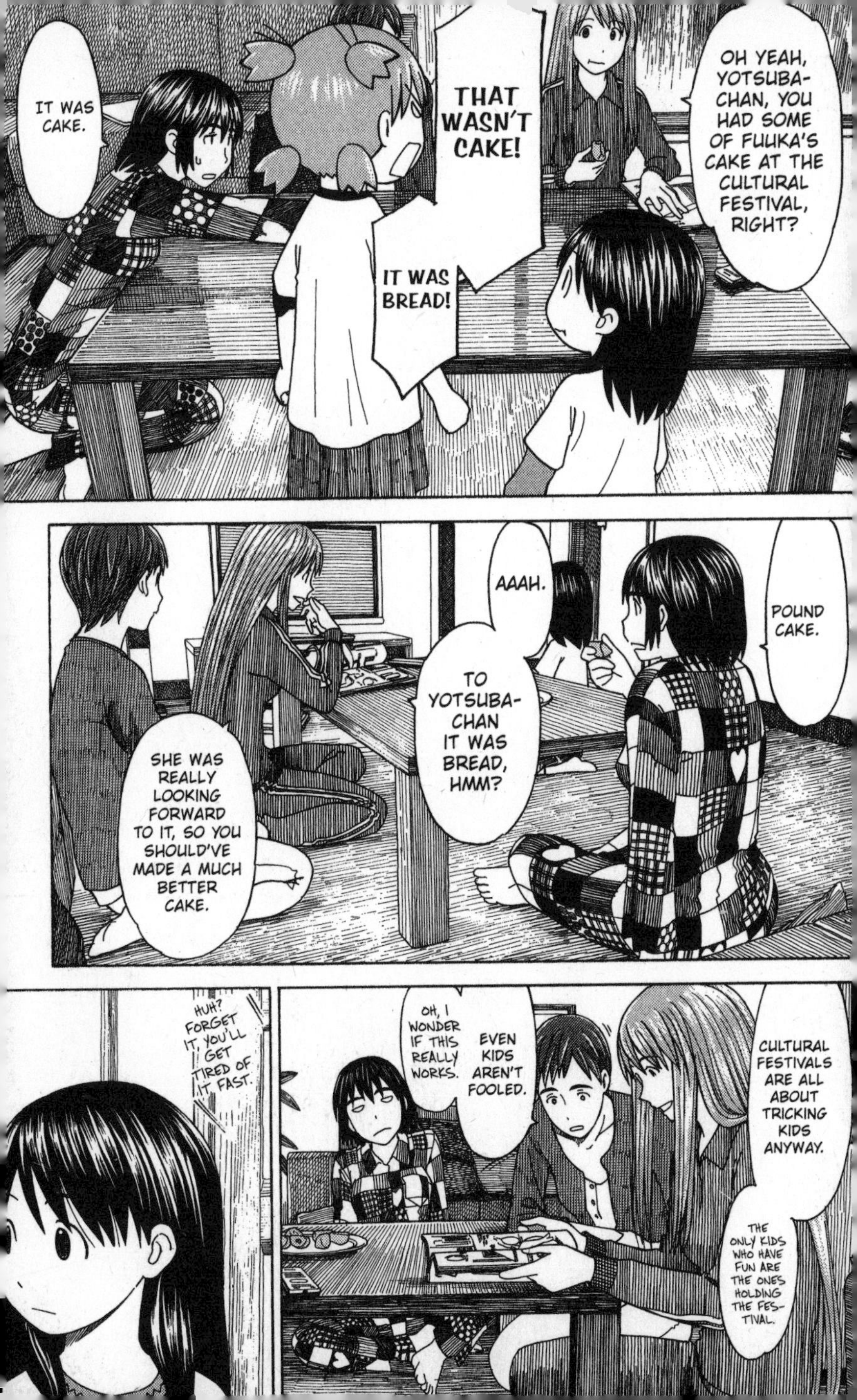
OH YEAH, YOTSUBA-CHAN, YOU HAD SOME OF FUUKA'S CAKE AT THE CULTURAL FESTIVAL, RIGHT?
THAT WASN'T CAKE!
IT WAS BREAD!
IT WAS CAKE.
POUND CAKE.
AAAH.
TO YOTSUBA-CHAN IT WAS BREAD, HMM?
SHE WAS REALLY LOOKING FORWARD TO IT, SO YOU SHOULD'VE MADE A MUCH BETTER CAKE.
CULTURAL FESTIVALS ARE ALL ABOUT TRICKING KIDS ANYWAY.
THE ONLY KIDS WHO HAVE FUN ARE THE ONES HOLDING THE FES-TIVAL.
EVEN KIDS AREN'T FOOLED.
OH, I WONDER IF THIS REALLY WORKS.
HUH? FORGET IT, YOU'LL GET TIRED OF IT FAST.

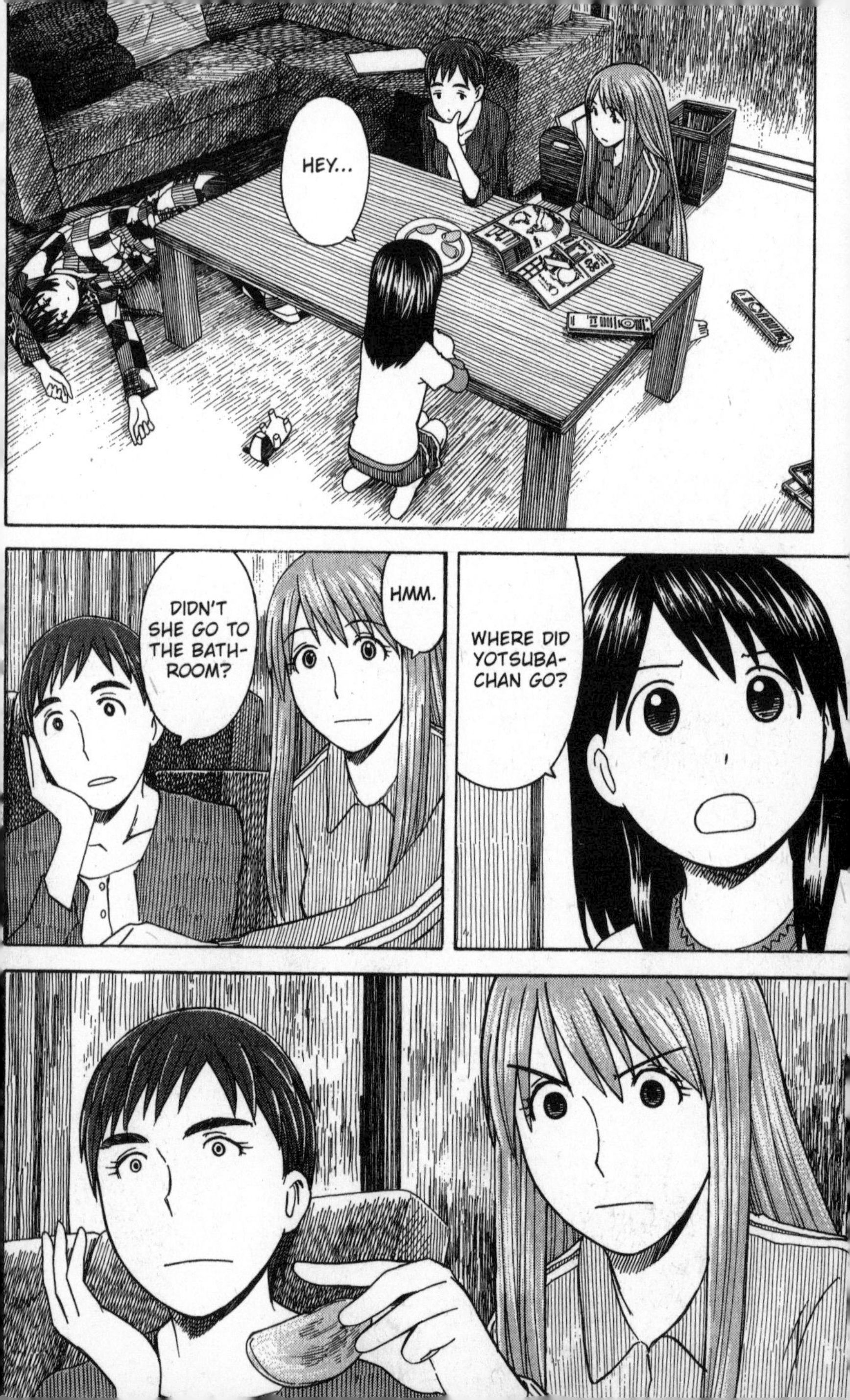
HEY...
WHERE DID YOTSUBA-CHAN GO?
HMM.
DIDN'T SHE GO TO THE BATH-ROOM?

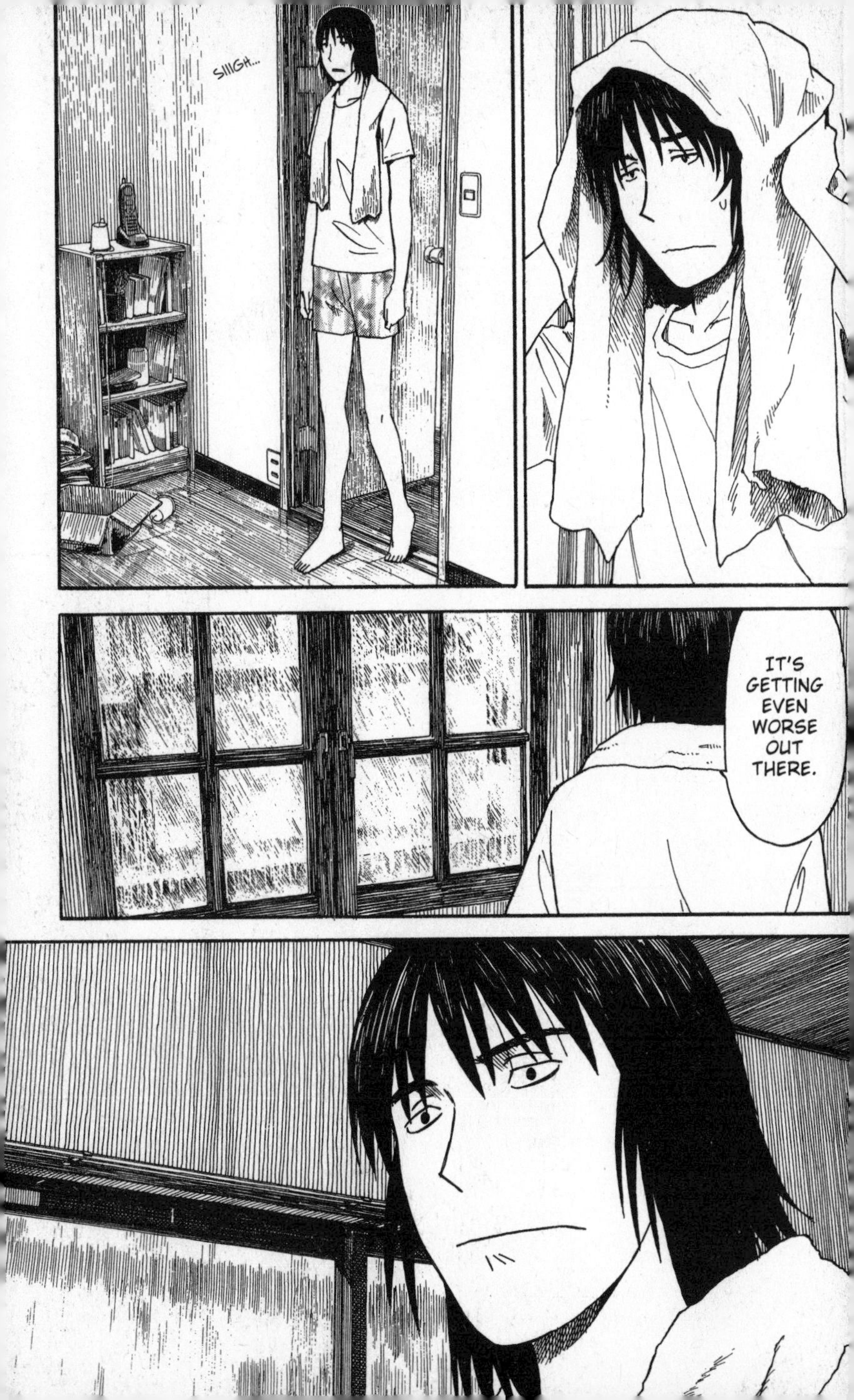
SIIIGH...
IT'S GETTING EVEN WORSE OUT THERE.

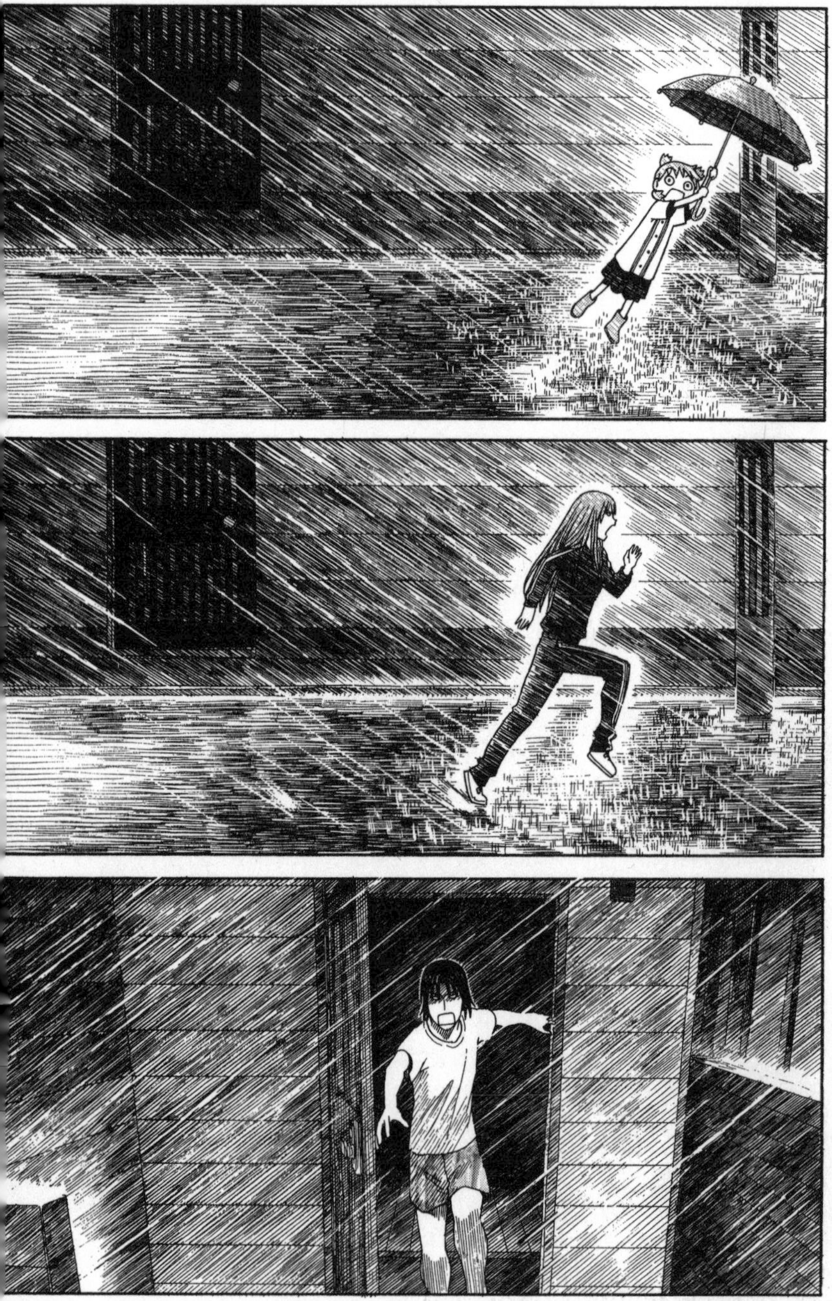

YOTSUBA&!

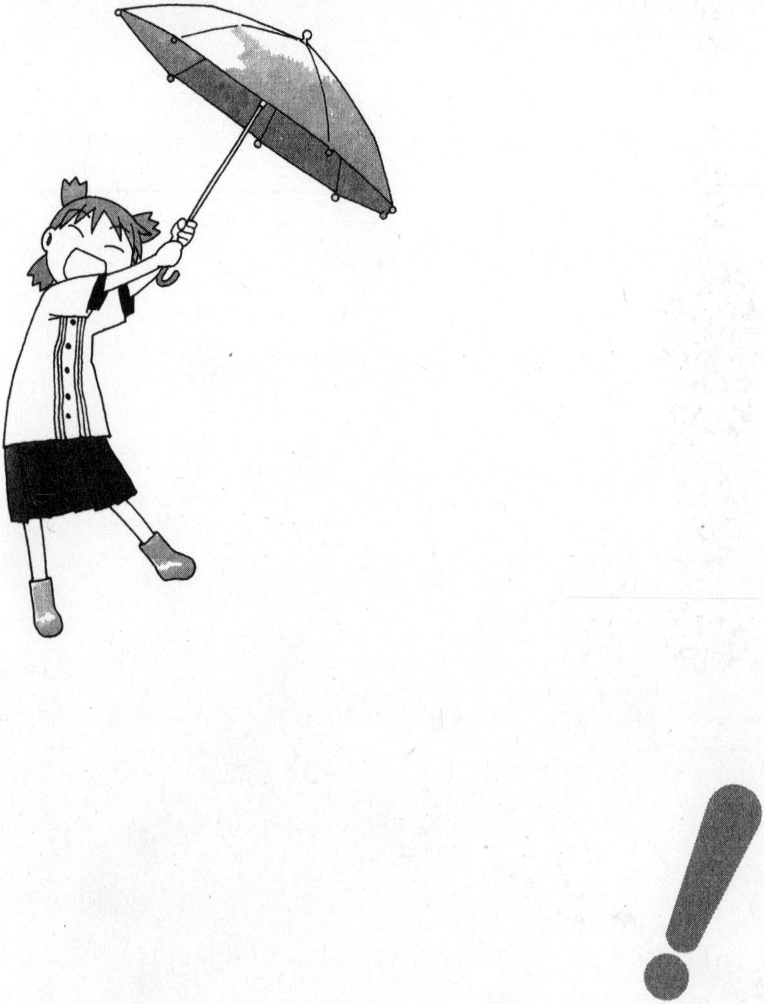
!

YOTSUBA& WATCHING THE HOUSE

#53

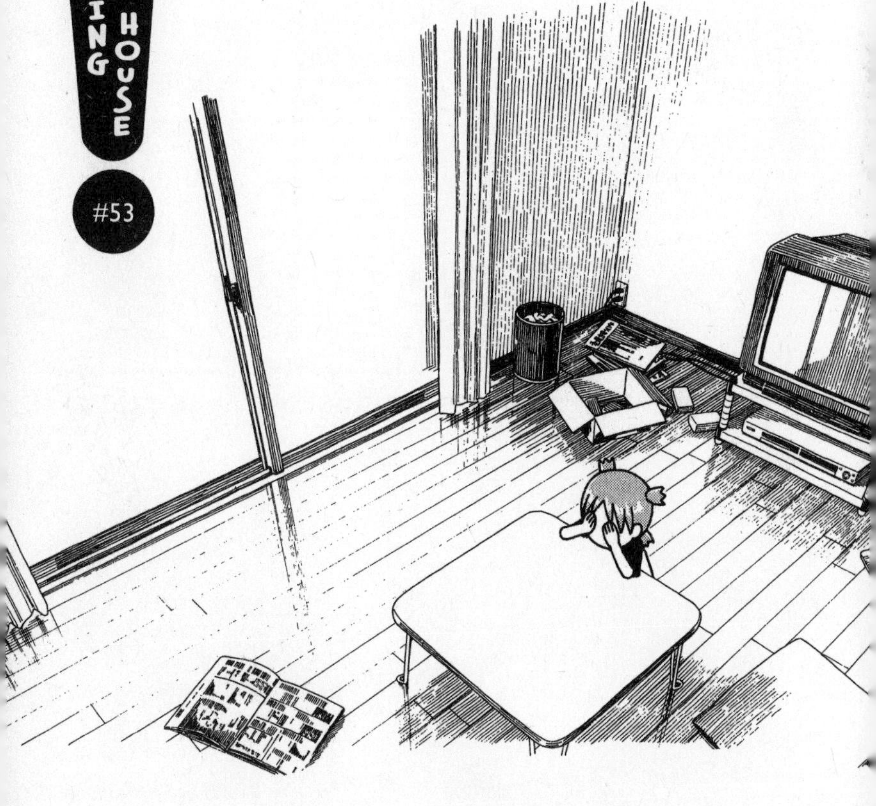

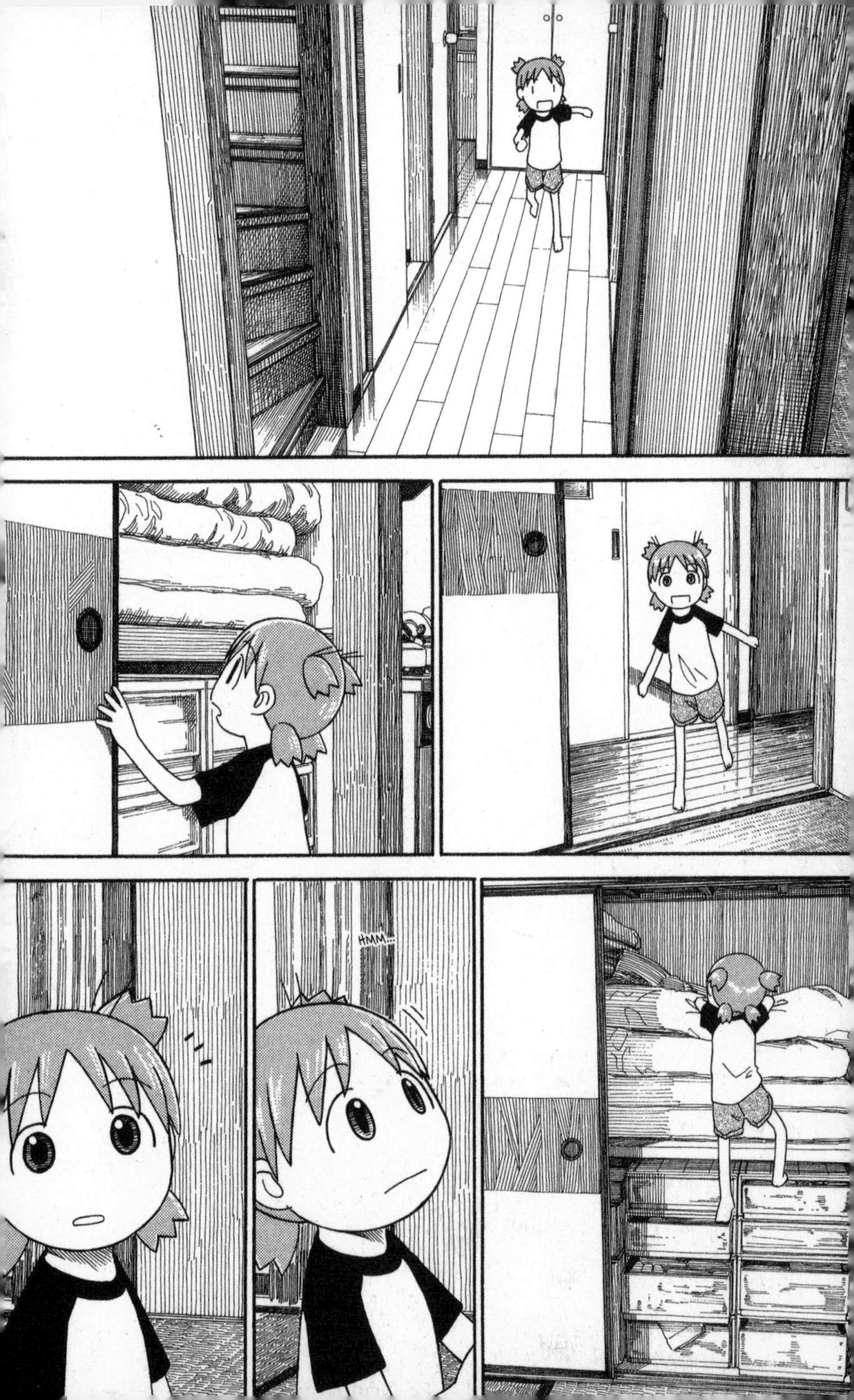
HMM...

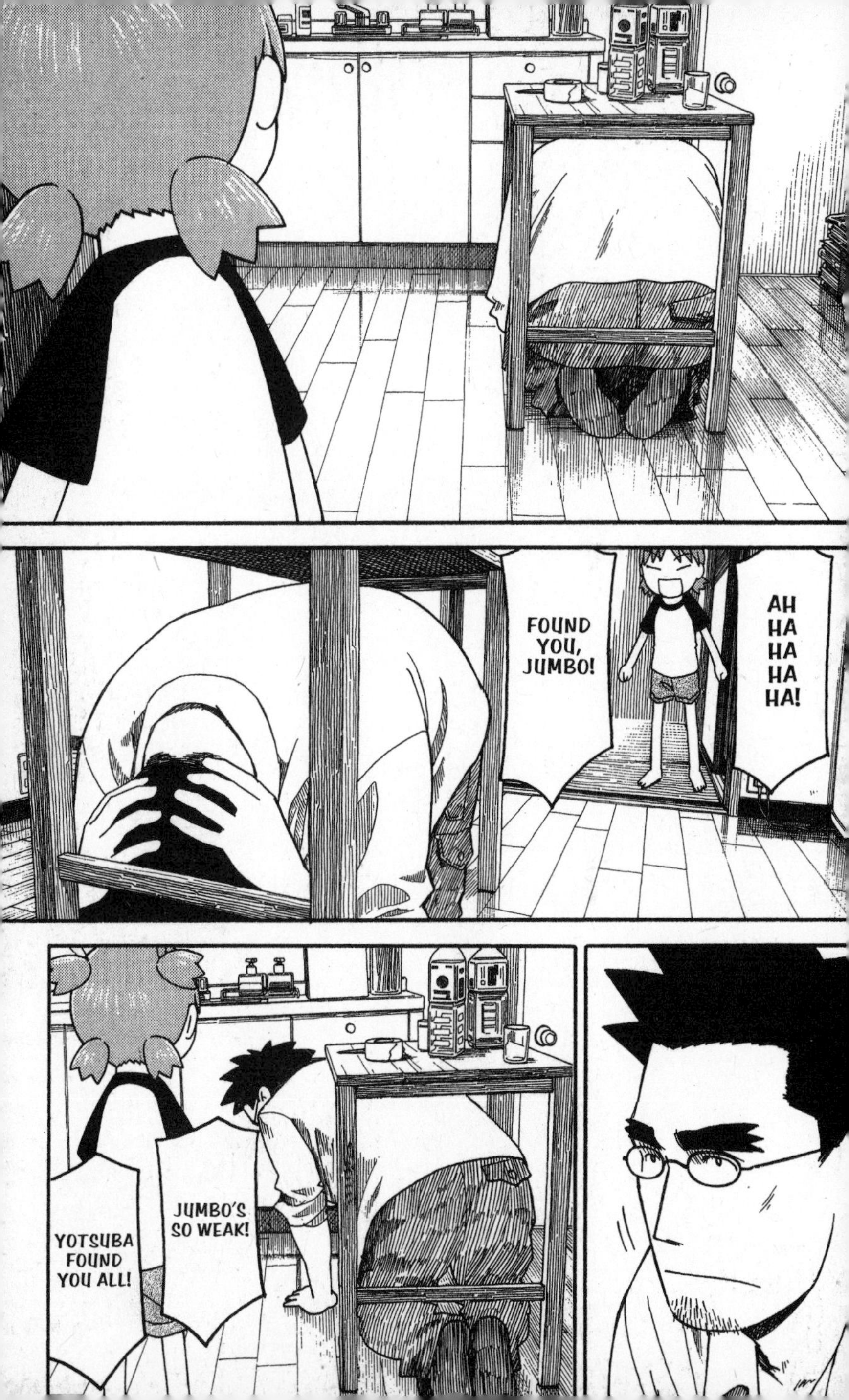
AH HA HA HA HA!
FOUND YOU, JUMBO!
JUMBO'S SO WEAK!
YOTSUBA FOUND YOU ALL!

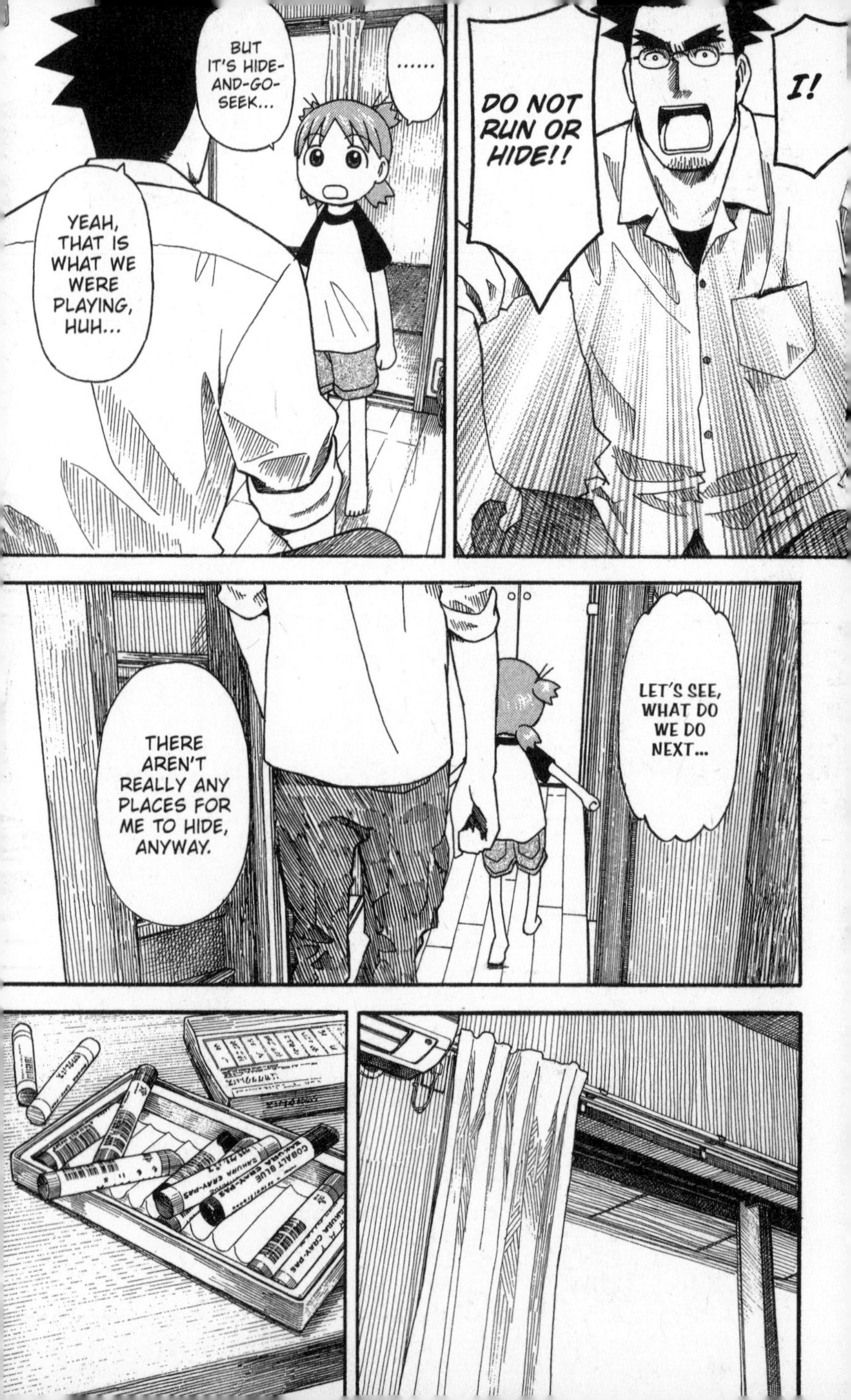
I!
DO NOT RUN OR HIDE!!
......
BUT IT'S HIDE-AND-GO-SEEK...
YEAH, THAT IS WHAT WE WERE PLAYING, HUH...
LET'S SEE, WHAT DO WE DO NEXT...
THERE AREN'T REALLY ANY PLACES FOR ME TO HIDE, ANYWAY.

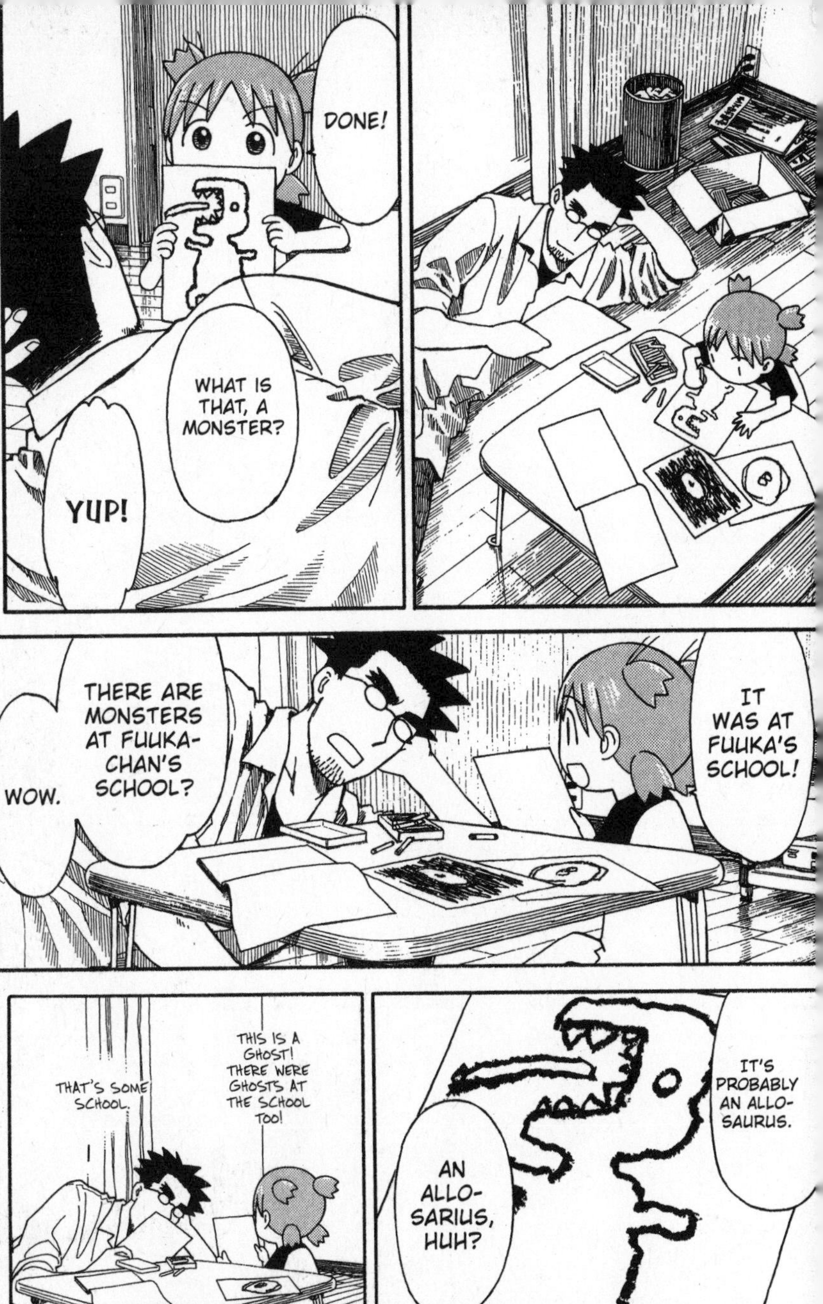
DONE!
WHAT IS THAT, A MONSTER?
YUP!
IT WAS AT FUUKA'S SCHOOL!
THERE ARE MONSTERS AT FUUKA-CHAN'S SCHOOL?
WOW.
IT'S PROBABLY AN ALLO-SAURUS.
AN ALLO-SARIUS, HUH?
THIS IS A GHOST! THERE WERE GHOSTS AT THE SCHOOL TOO!
THAT'S SOME SCHOOL.

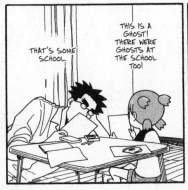

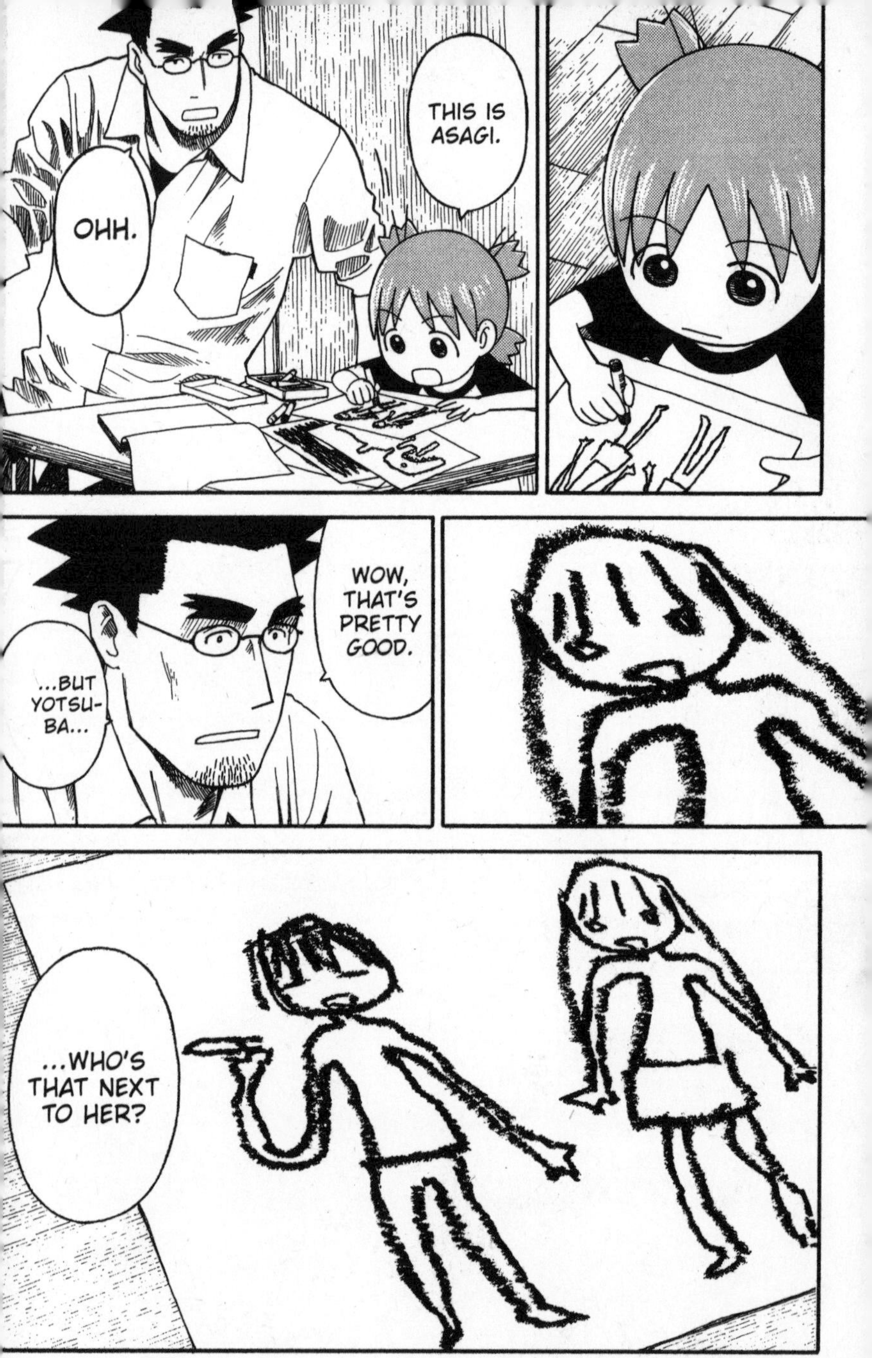
THIS IS ASAGI.
OHH.
WOW, THAT'S PRETTY GOOD.
...BUT YOTSUBA...
...WHO'S THAT NEXT TO HER?

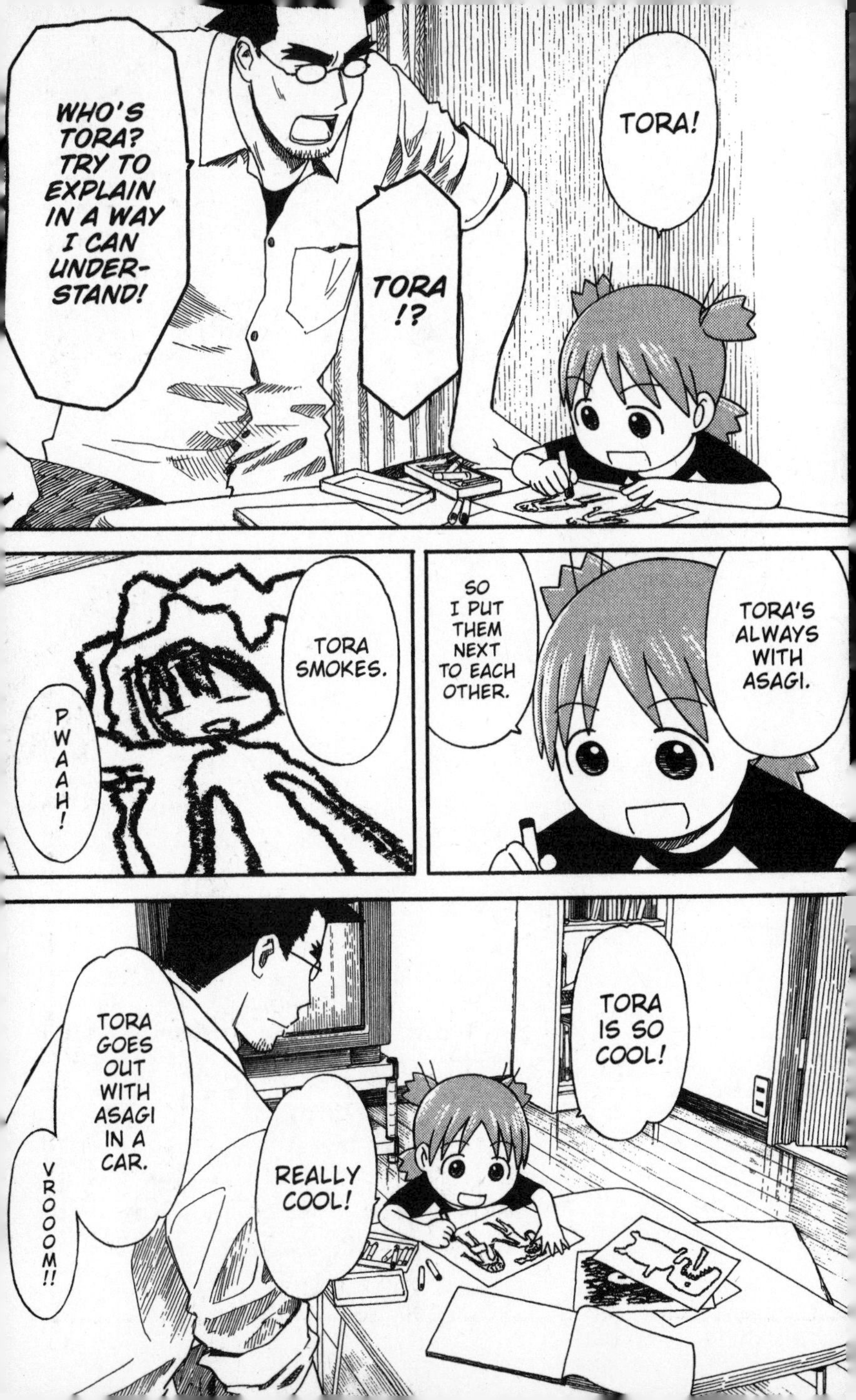
TORA!
TORA!?
WHO'S TORA? TRY TO EXPLAIN IN A WAY I CAN UNDER-STAND!
TORA'S ALWAYS WITH ASAGI.
SO I PUT THEM NEXT TO EACH OTHER.
TORA SMOKES.
PWAAH!
TORA IS SO COOL!
REALLY COOL!
TORA GOES OUT WITH ASAGI IN A CAR.
VROOOOM!!

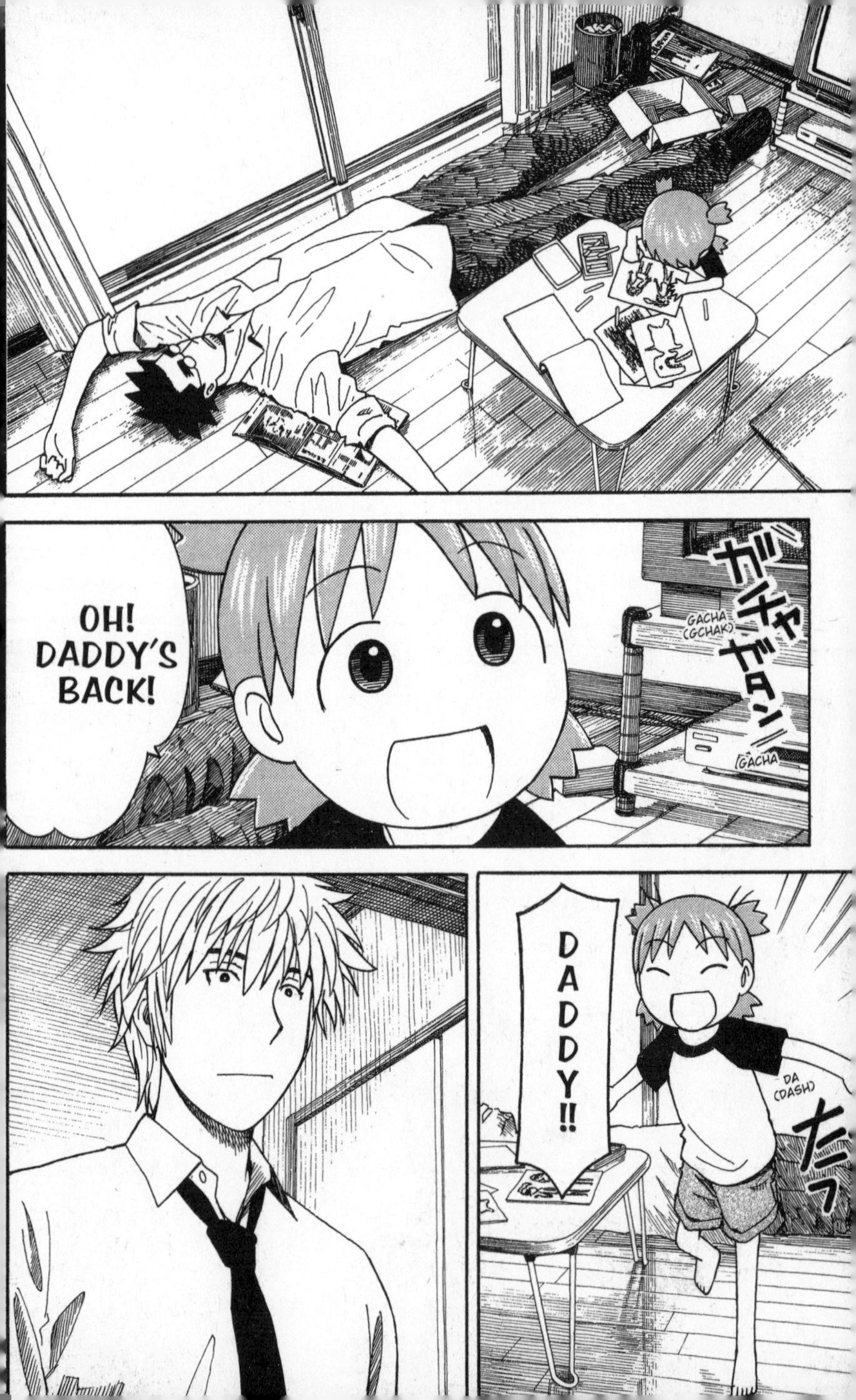
ガチャ
GACHA (GCHAK)
ガタン
GACHA
OH! DADDY'S BACK!
DADDY!!
たっ
DA (DASH)

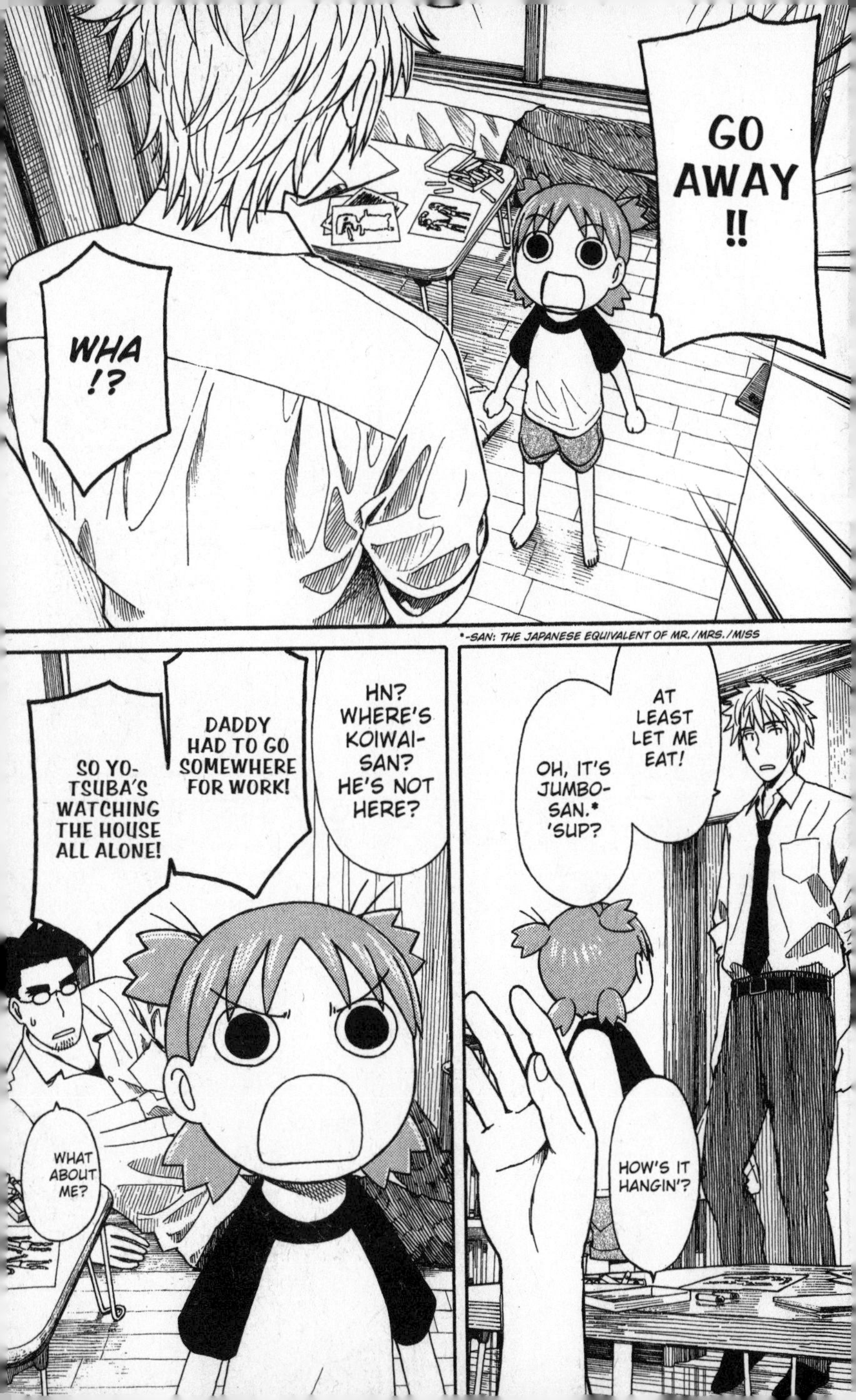
GO AWAY !!
WHA !?
AT LEAST LET ME EAT!
OH, IT'S JUMBO-SAN.* 'SUP?
HOW'S IT HANGIN'?
HN? WHERE'S KOIWAI-SAN? HE'S NOT HERE?
DADDY HAD TO GO SOMEWHERE FOR WORK!
SO YO-TSUBA'S WATCHING THE HOUSE ALL ALONE!
WHAT ABOUT ME?

*-SAN: THE JAPANESE EQUIVALENT OF MR./MRS./MISS

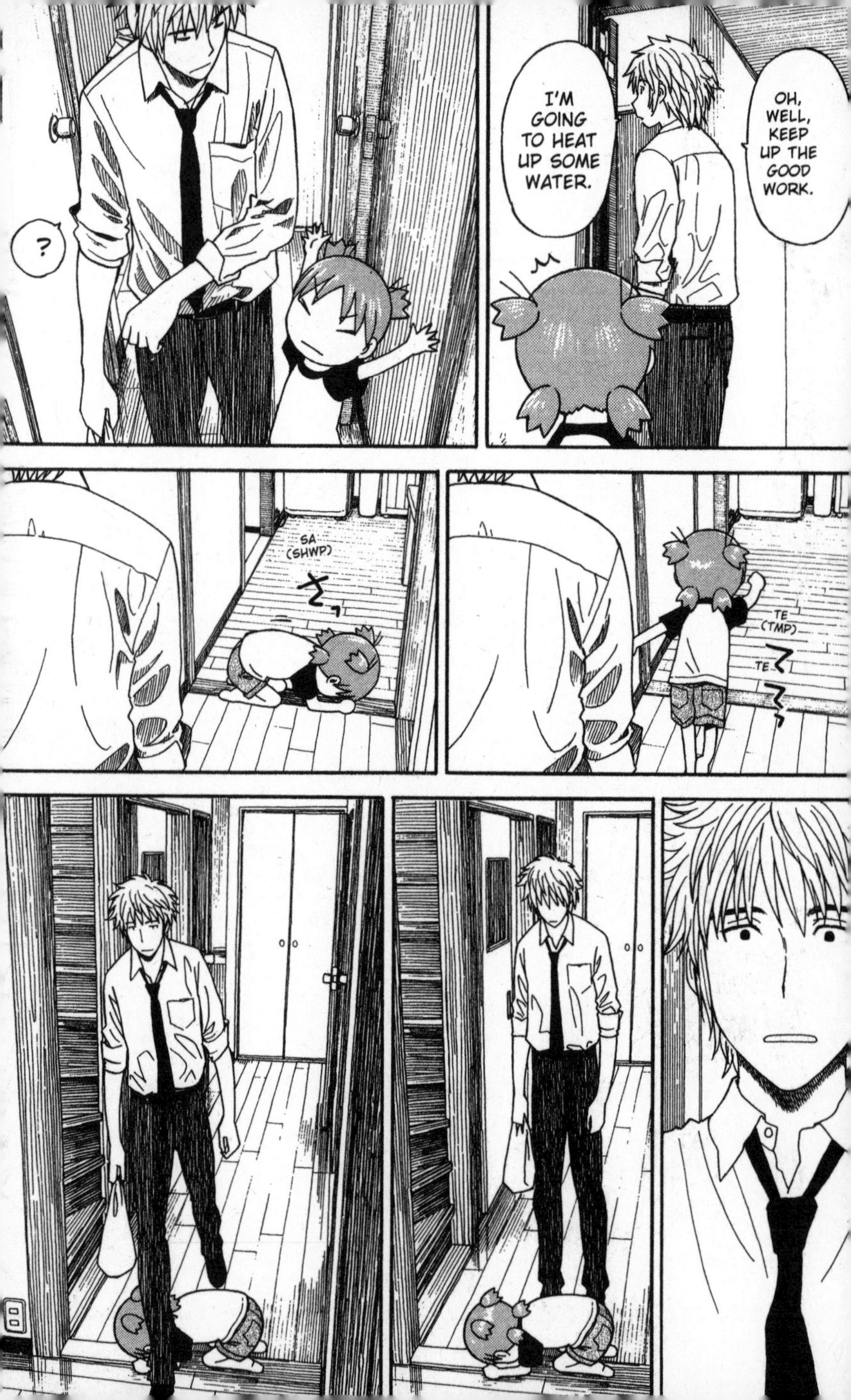
OH, WELL, KEEP UP THE GOOD WORK.
I'M GOING TO HEAT UP SOME WATER.
?
TE (TMP)
TE
SA (SHWP)

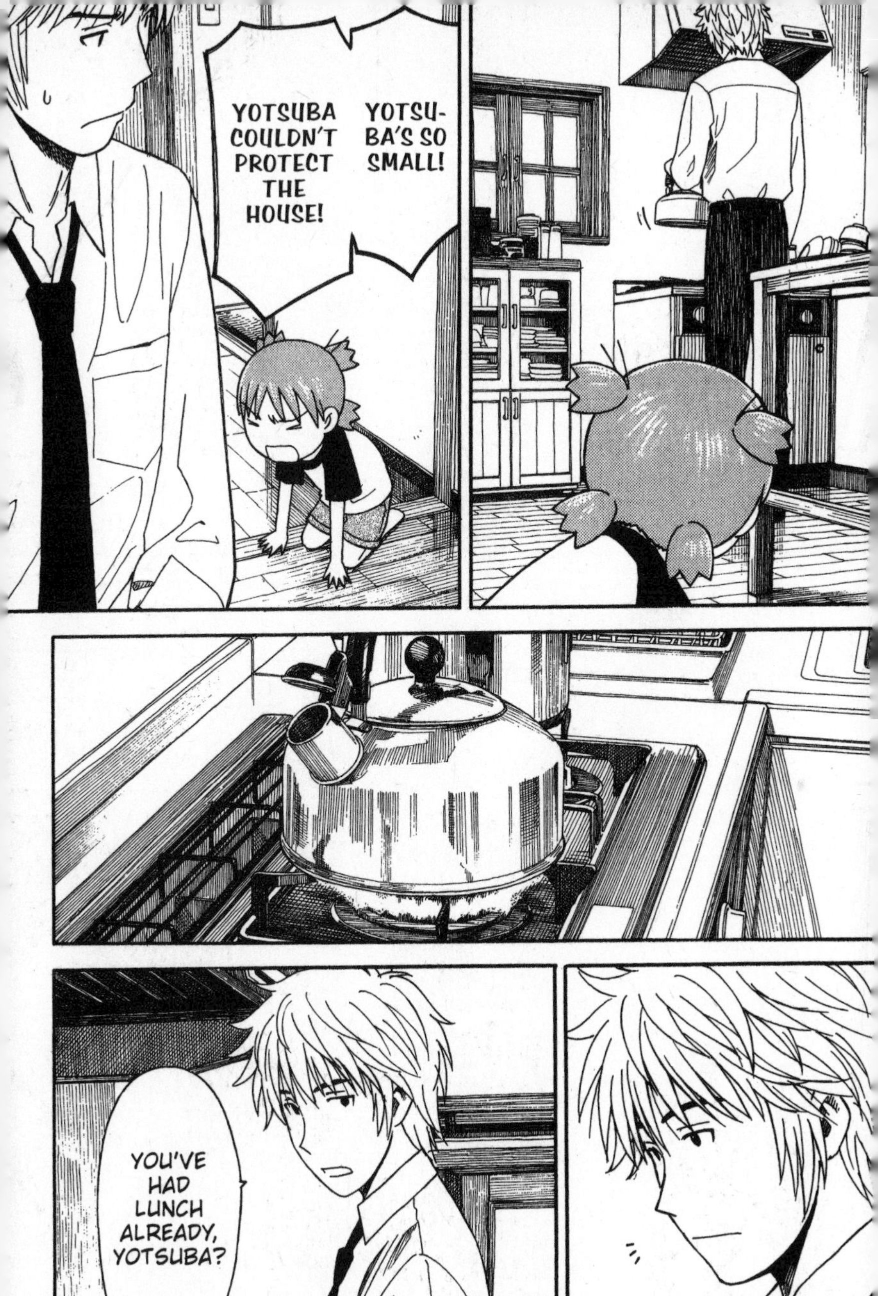
YOTSU-BA'S SO SMALL!
YOTSUBA COULDN'T PROTECT THE HOUSE!
YOU'VE HAD LUNCH ALREADY, YOTSUBA?

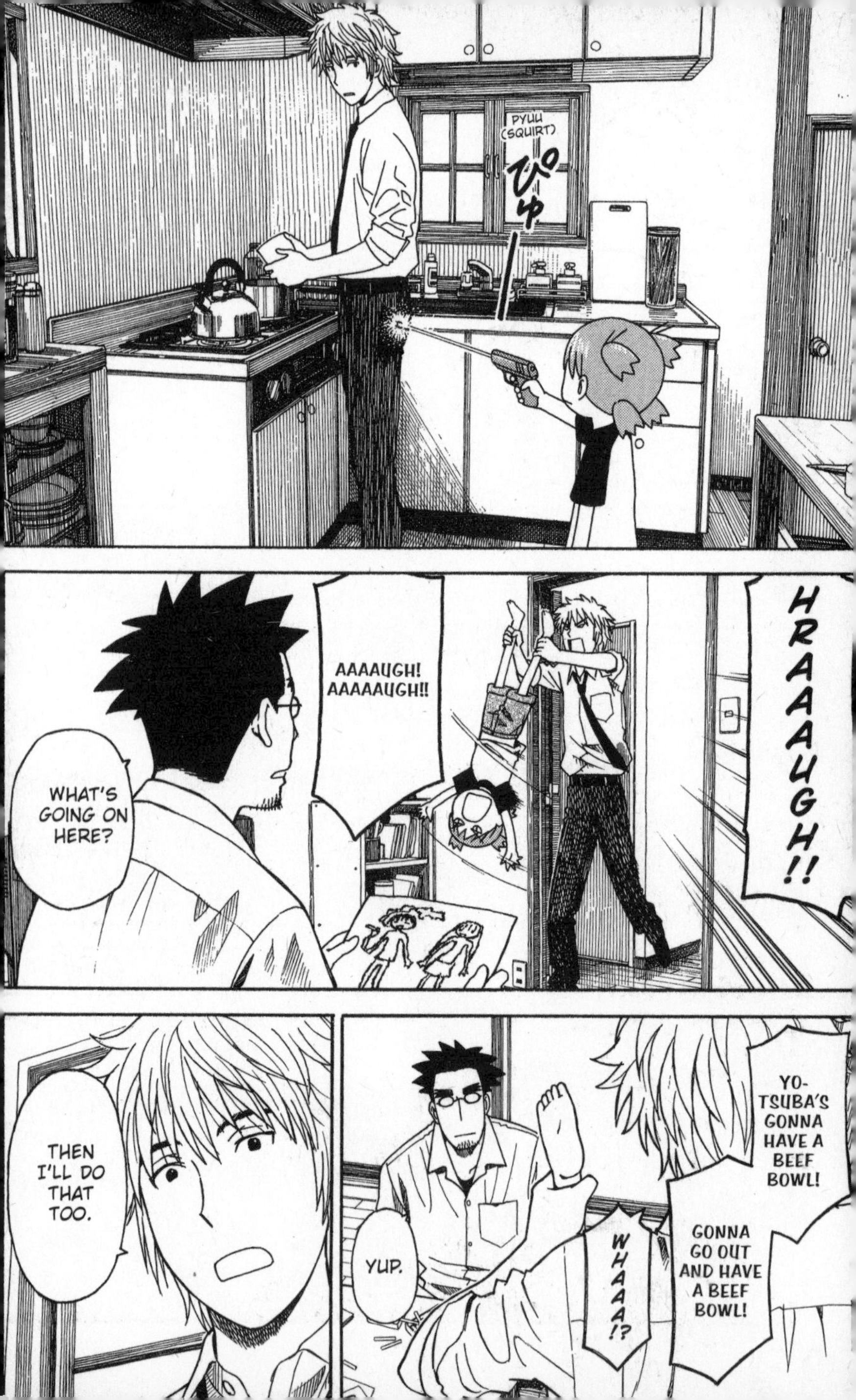
PYUU (SQUIRT)
ぴゅ
HRAAAAUGH!!
AAAAUGH! AAAAAUGH!!
WHAT'S GOING ON HERE?
YO-TSUBA'S GONNA HAVE A BEEF BOWL!
GONNA GO OUT AND HAVE A BEEF BOWL!
WHAAAA!?
YUP.
THEN I'LL DO THAT TOO.

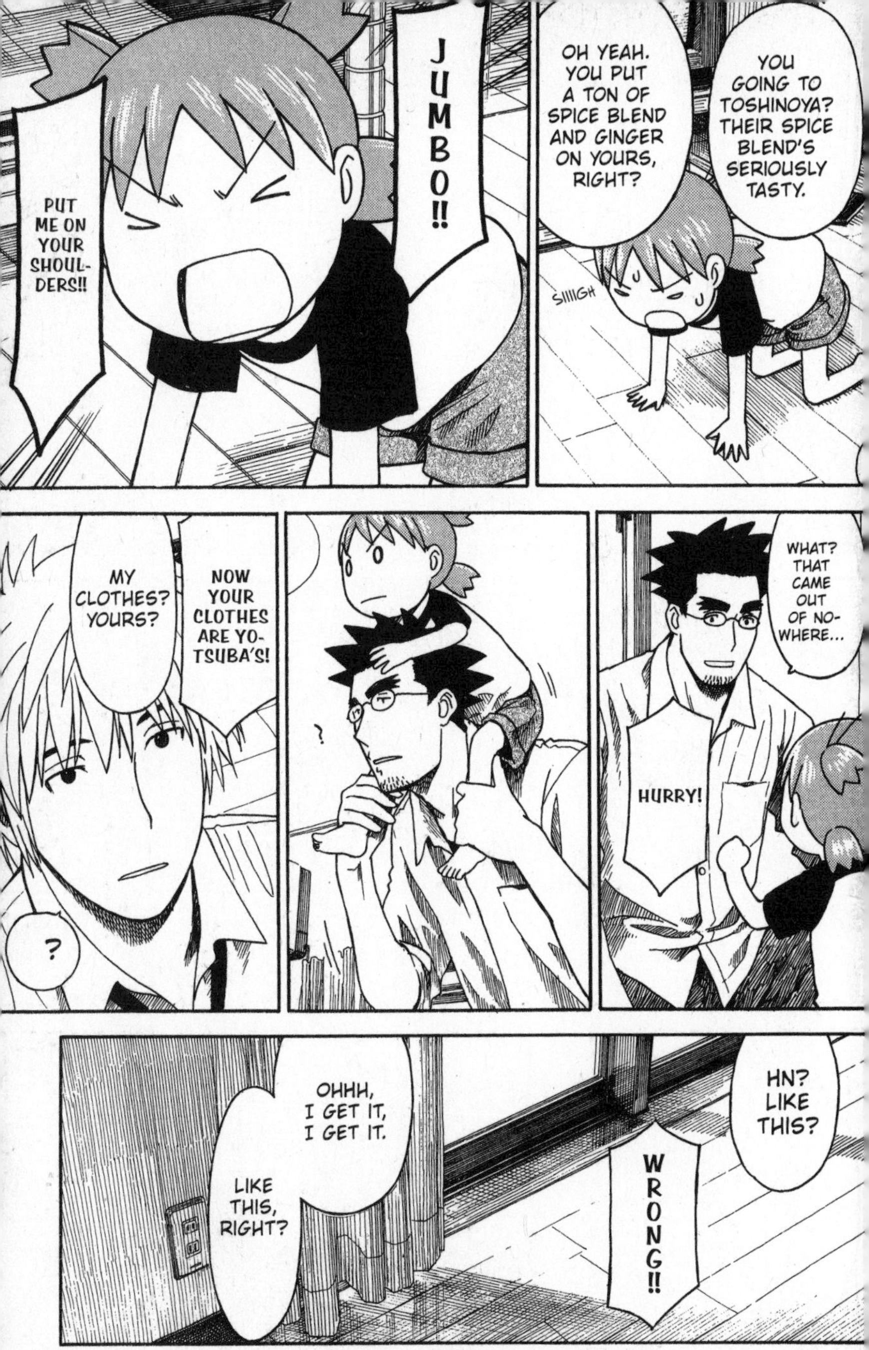
YOU GOING TO TOSHINOYA? THEIR SPICE BLEND'S SERIOUSLY TASTY.
OH YEAH. YOU PUT A TON OF SPICE BLEND AND GINGER ON YOURS, RIGHT?
SIIIGH
JUMBO!!
PUT ME ON YOUR SHOUL-DERS!!
WHAT? THAT CAME OUT OF NO-WHERE...
HURRY!
?
NOW YOUR CLOTHES ARE YO-TSUBA'S!
MY CLOTHES? YOURS?
?
HN? LIKE THIS?
WRONG!!
OHHH, I GET IT, I GET IT.
LIKE THIS, RIGHT?

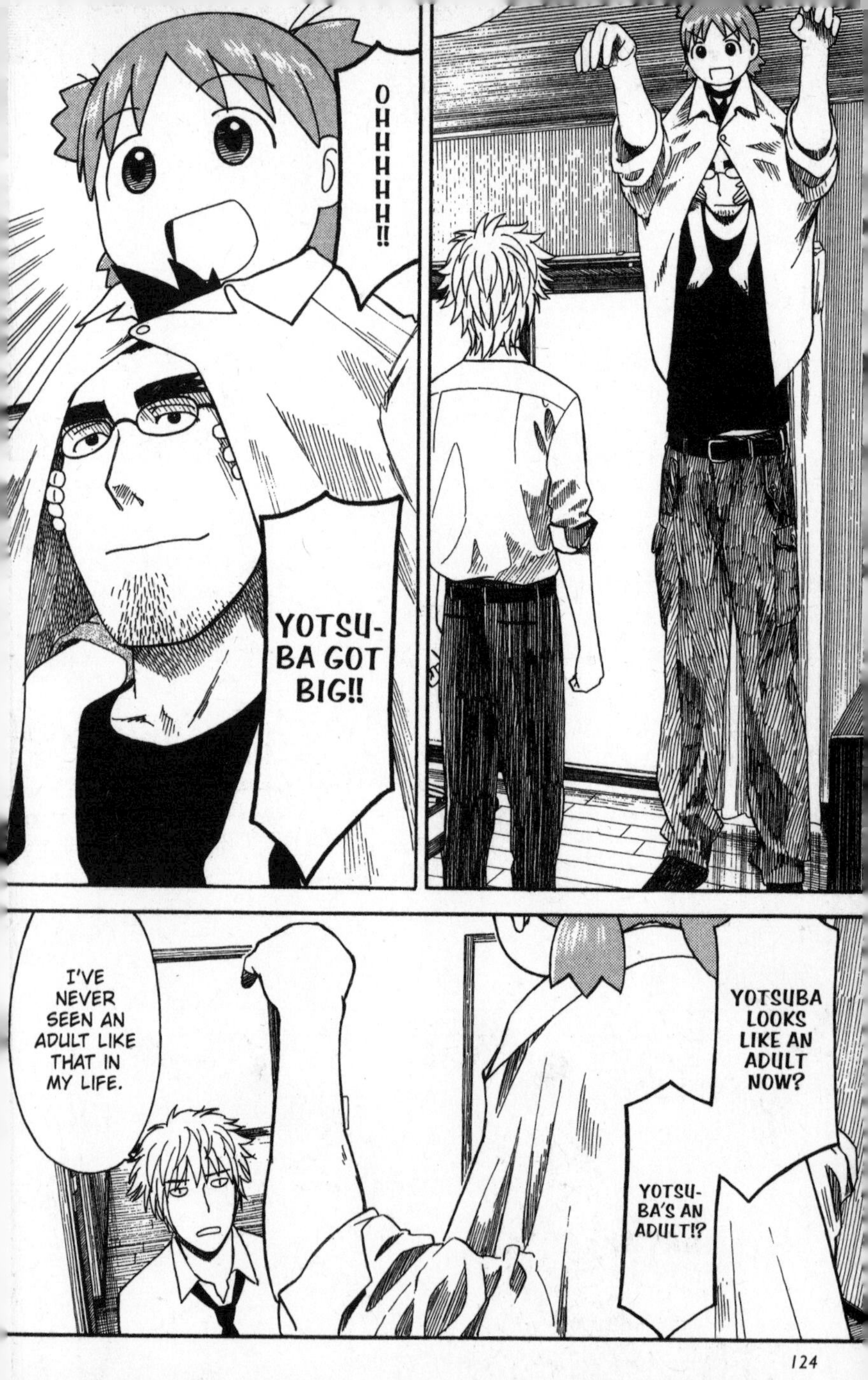
OHHHHHH!!
YOTSU-BA GOT BIG!!
YOTSUBA LOOKS LIKE AN ADULT NOW?
YOTSU-BA'S AN ADULT!?
I'VE NEVER SEEN AN ADULT LIKE THAT IN MY LIFE.

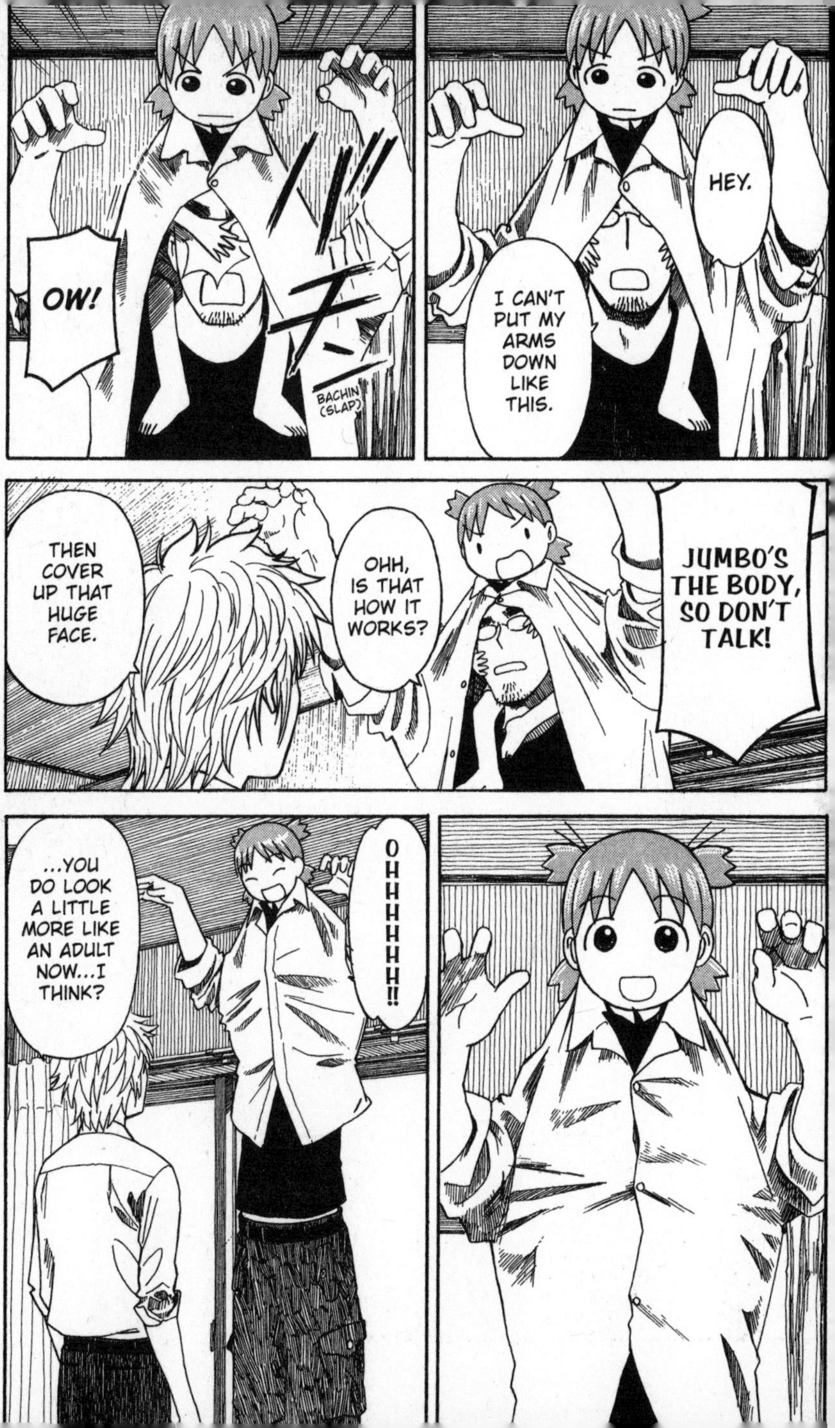
HEY.
I CAN'T PUT MY ARMS DOWN LIKE THIS.
BACHIN (SLAP)
OW!
JUMBO'S THE BODY, SO DON'T TALK!
OHH, IS THAT HOW IT WORKS?
THEN COVER UP THAT HUGE FACE.
OHHHHHHH!!
...YOU DO LOOK A LITTLE MORE LIKE AN ADULT NOW...I THINK?

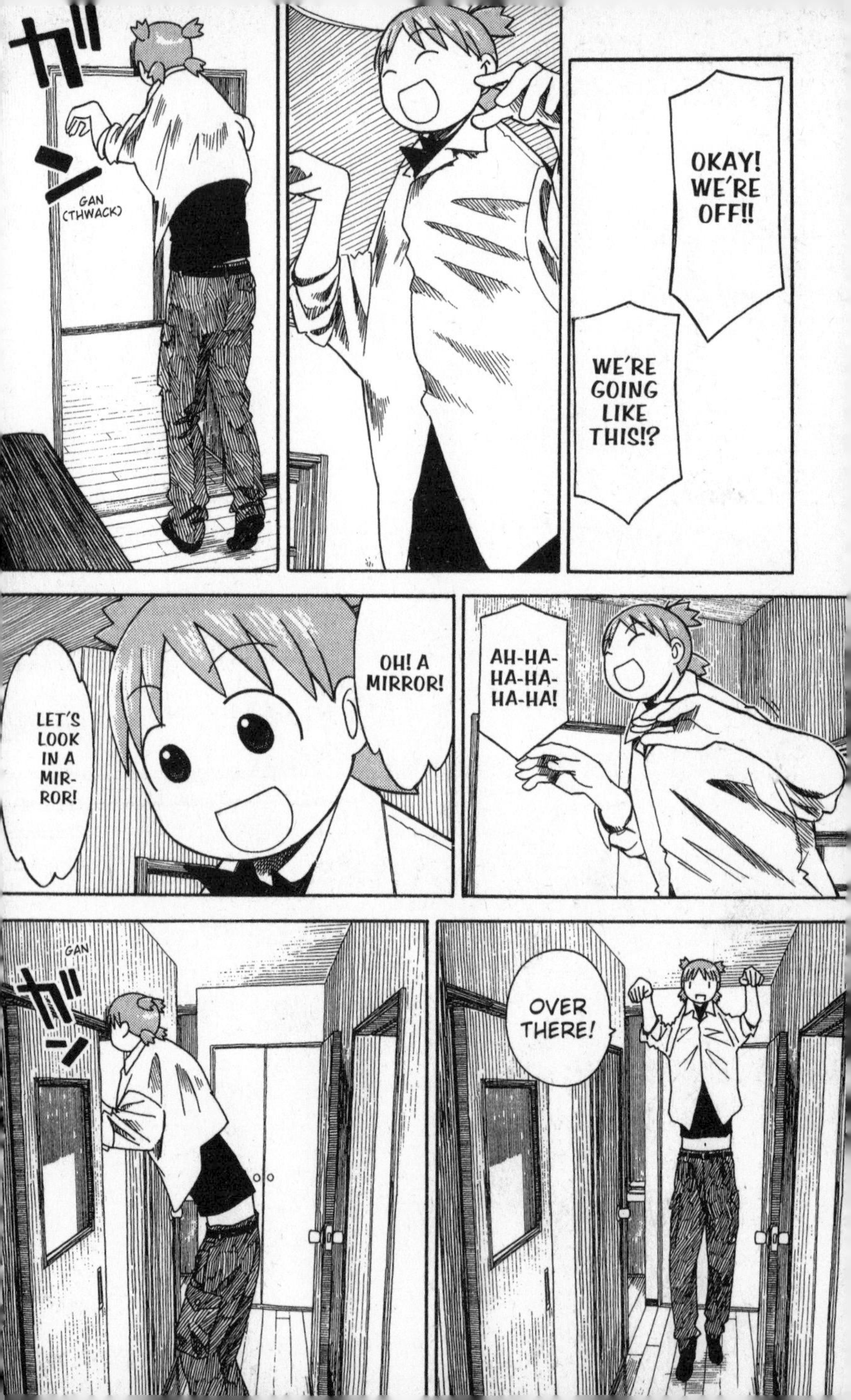
OKAY! WE'RE OFF!!
WE'RE GOING LIKE THIS!?
ガン
GAN (THWACK)
AH-HA-HA-HA-HA-HA!
OH! A MIRROR!
LET'S LOOK IN A MIR-ROR!
OVER THERE!
ガン
GAN

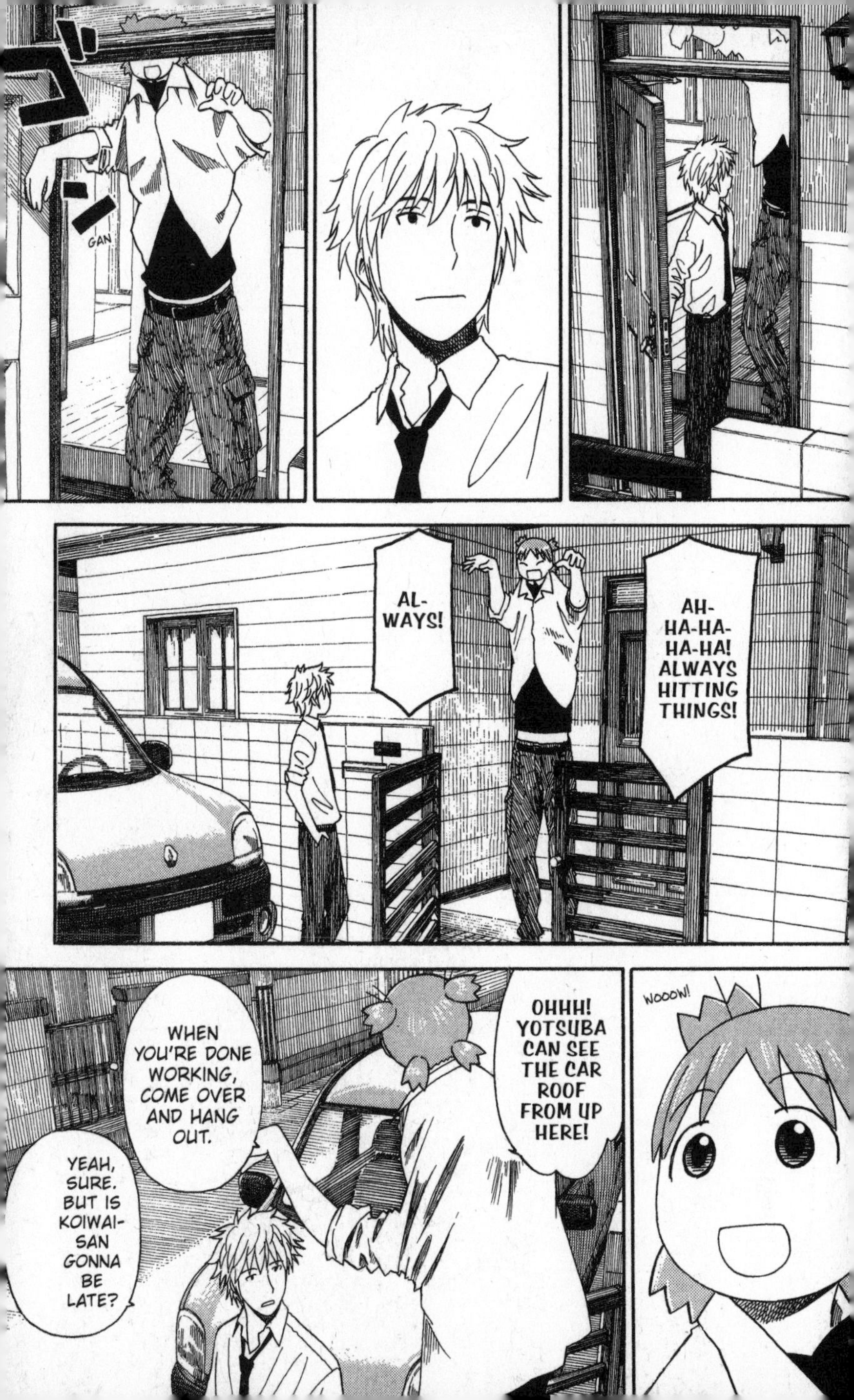
GAN
AH-HA-HA-HA-HA! ALWAYS HITTING THINGS!
AL-WAYS!
WOOOW!
OHHH! YOTSUBA CAN SEE THE CAR ROOF FROM UP HERE!
WHEN YOU'RE DONE WORKING, COME OVER AND HANG OUT.
YEAH, SURE. BUT IS KOIWAI-SAN GONNA BE LATE?

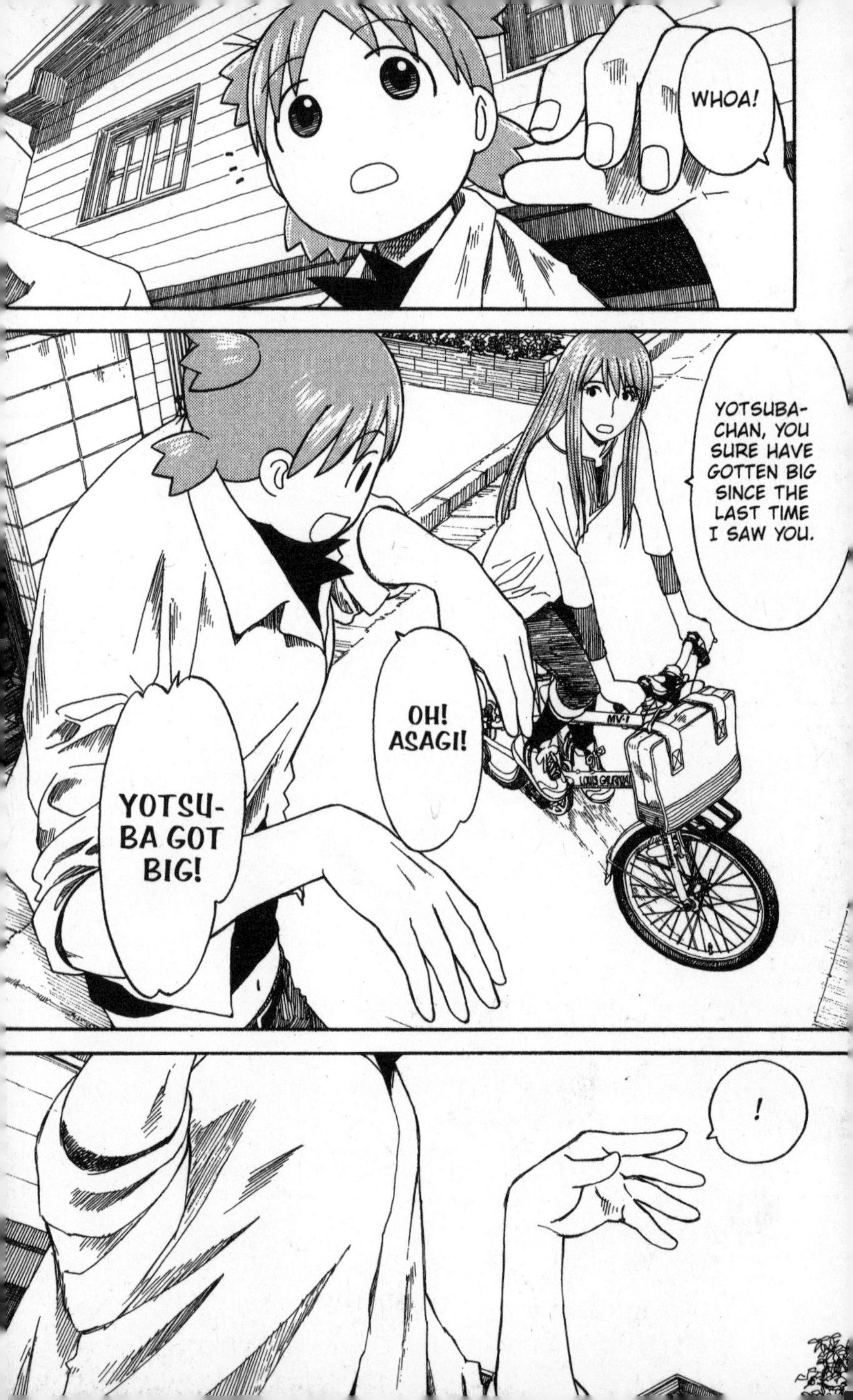
WHOA!
YOTSUBA-CHAN, YOU SURE HAVE GOTTEN BIG SINCE THE LAST TIME I SAW YOU.
OH! ASAGI!
YOTSU-BA GOT BIG!
!

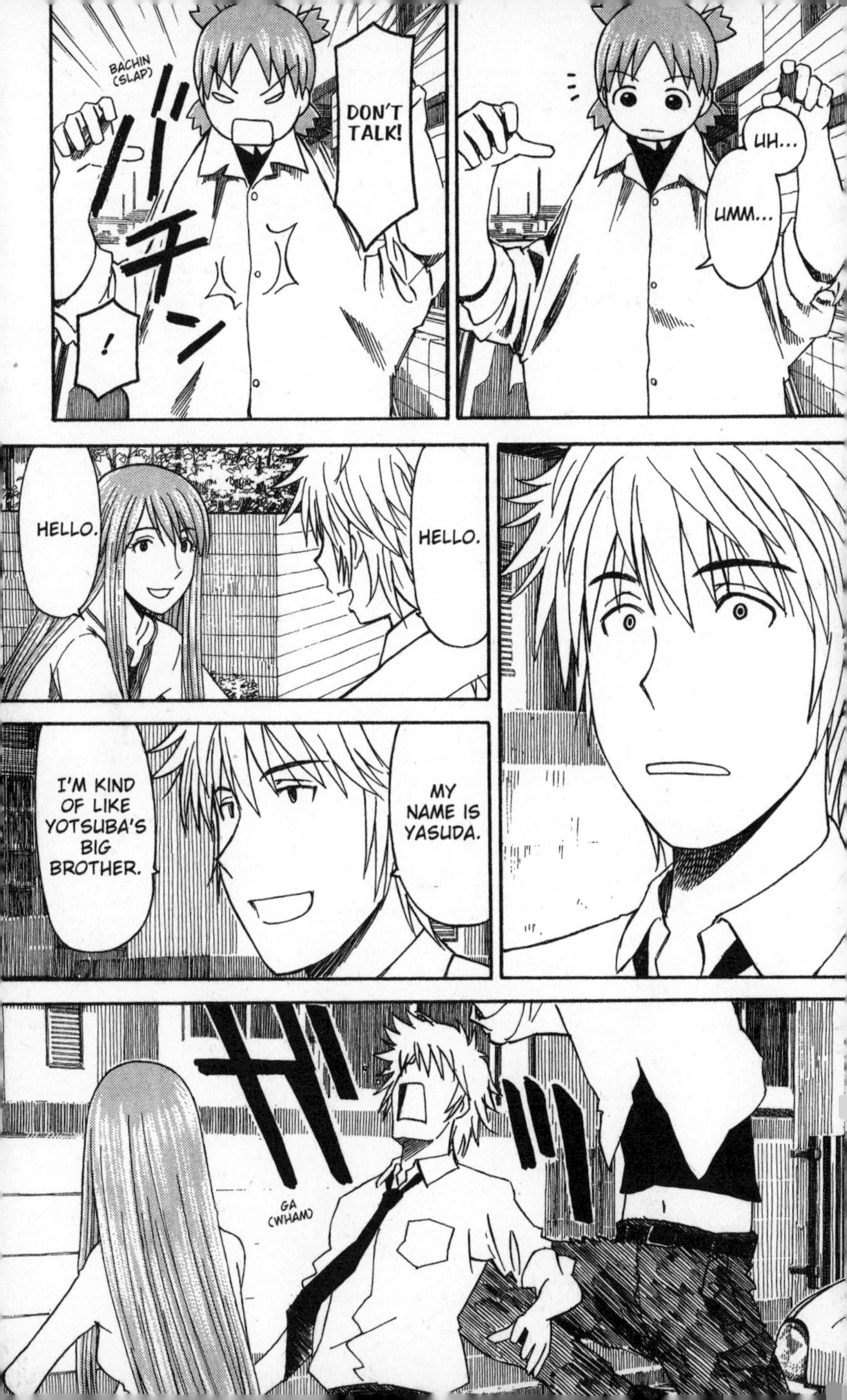
UH...
UMM...
DON'T TALK!
BACHIN (SLAP)
!
HELLO.
HELLO.
MY NAME IS YASUDA.
I'M KIND OF LIKE YOTSUBA'S BIG BROTHER.
GA (WHAM)

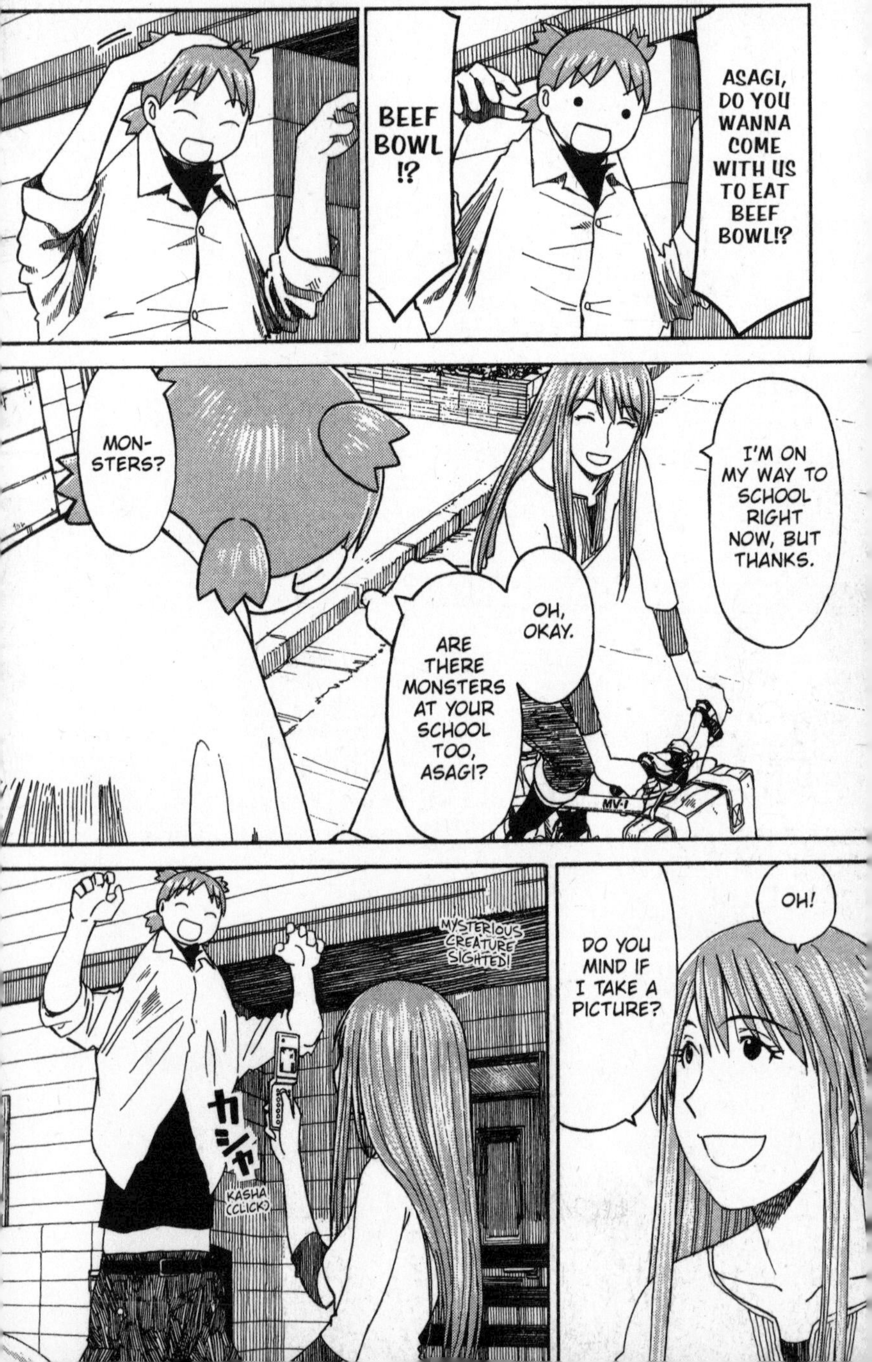
ASAGI, DO YOU WANNA COME WITH US TO EAT BEEF BOWL!?
BEEF BOWL !?
I'M ON MY WAY TO SCHOOL RIGHT NOW, BUT THANKS.
OH, OKAY.
ARE THERE MONSTERS AT YOUR SCHOOL TOO, ASAGI?
MON-STERS?
OH!
DO YOU MIND IF I TAKE A PICTURE?
MYSTERIOUS CREATURE SIGHTED!
カシャ
KASHA (CLICK)

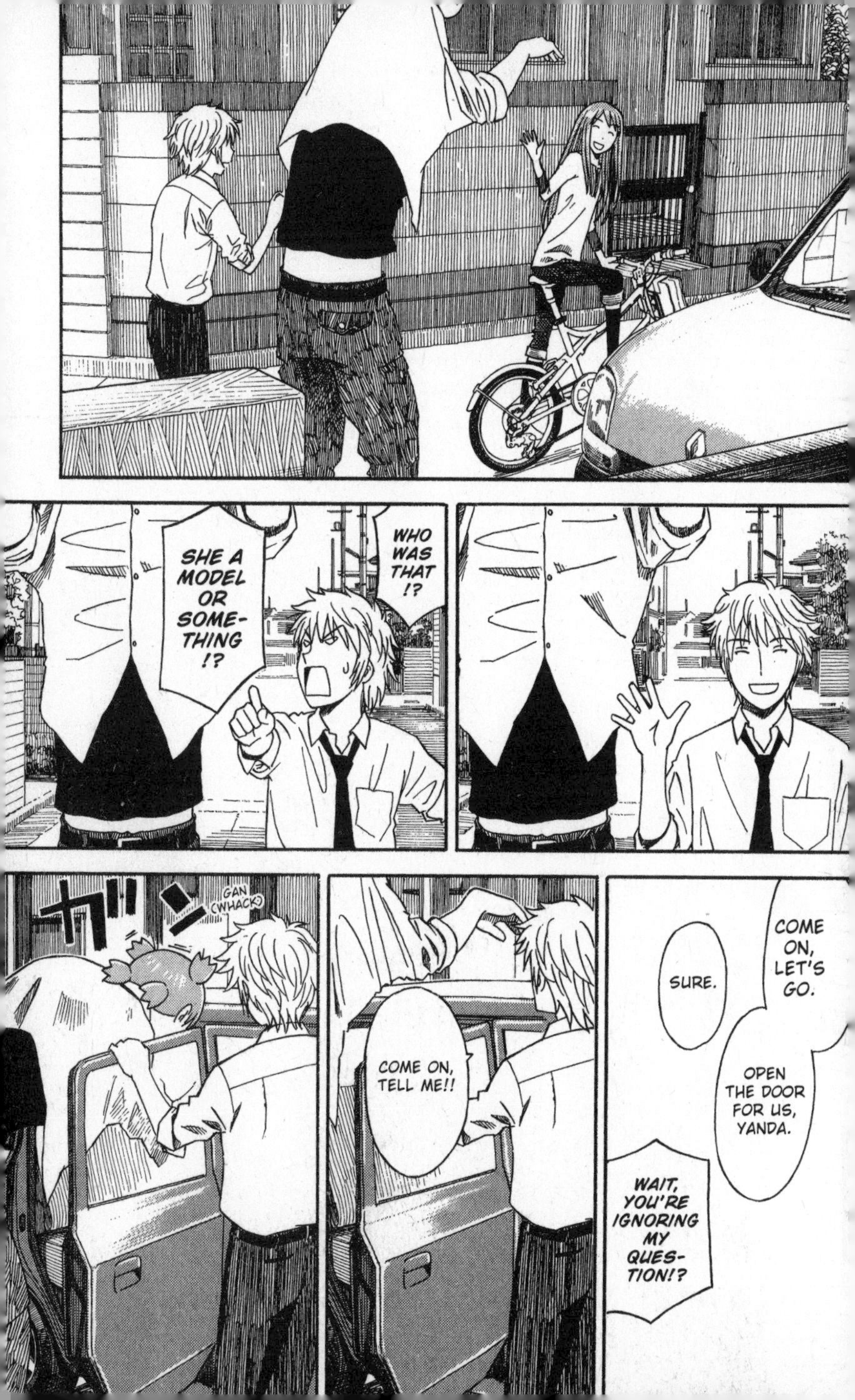
WHO WAS THAT!?
SHE A MODEL OR SOMETHING!?
COME ON, LET'S GO.
SURE.
OPEN THE DOOR FOR US, YANDA.
WAIT, YOU'RE IGNORING MY QUESTION!?
COME ON, TELL ME!!
GAN (WHACK)

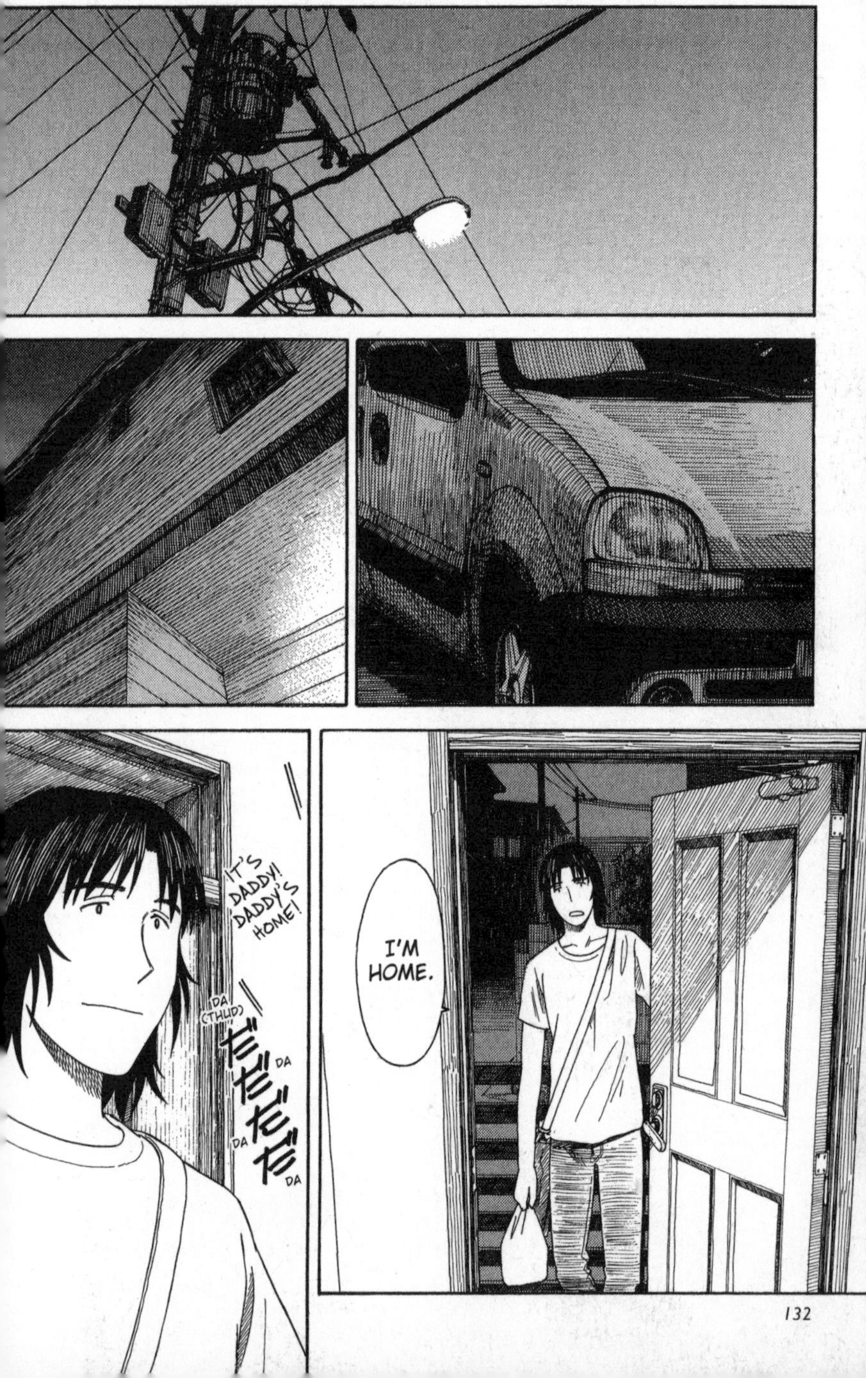
I'M HOME.
IT'S DADDY! DADDY'S HOME!
DA (THUD) だだだだ DA DA DA DA

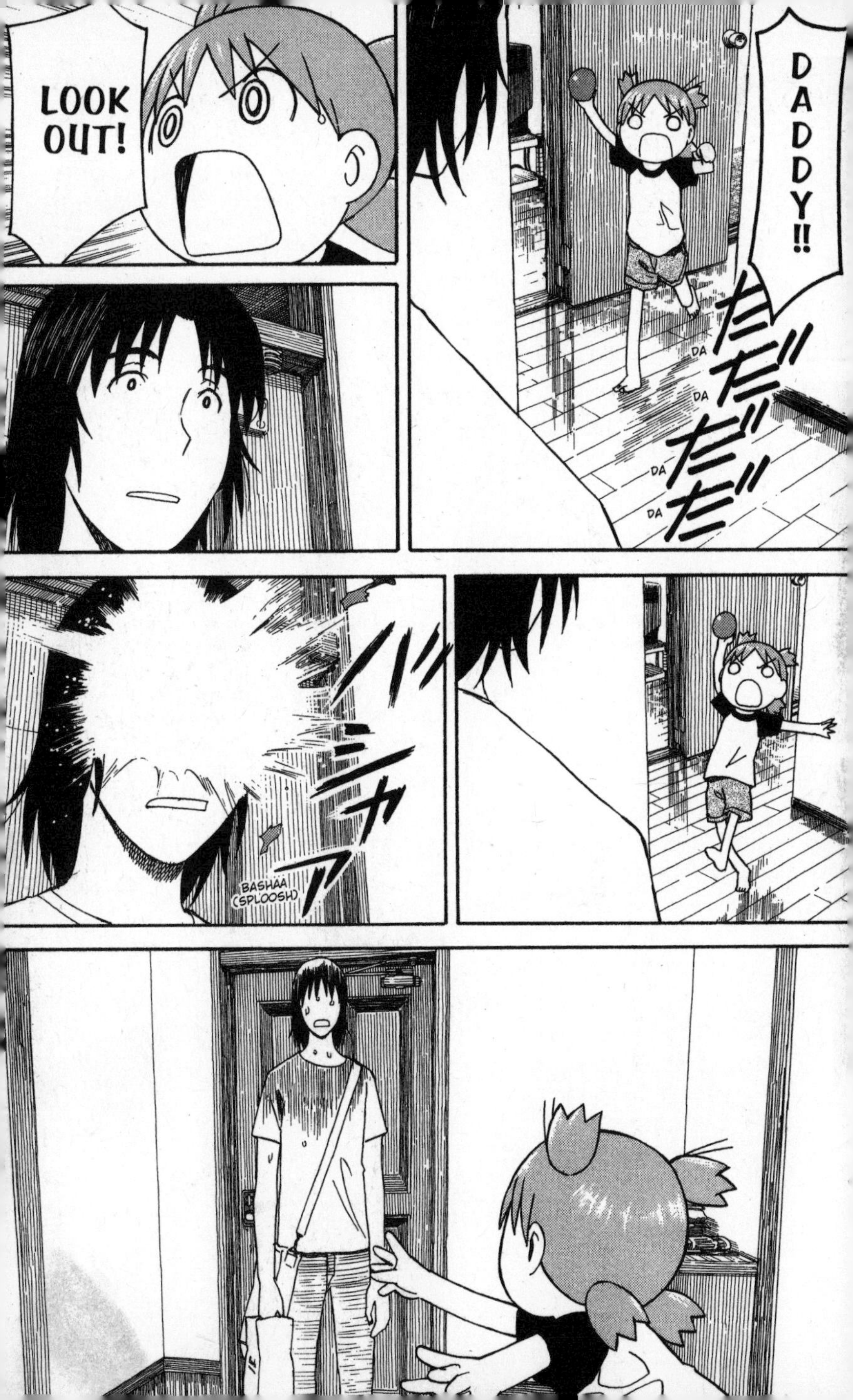
DADDY!!
だだだだ
DA DA DA DA
LOOK OUT!
バシャア
BASHAA (SPLOOSH)

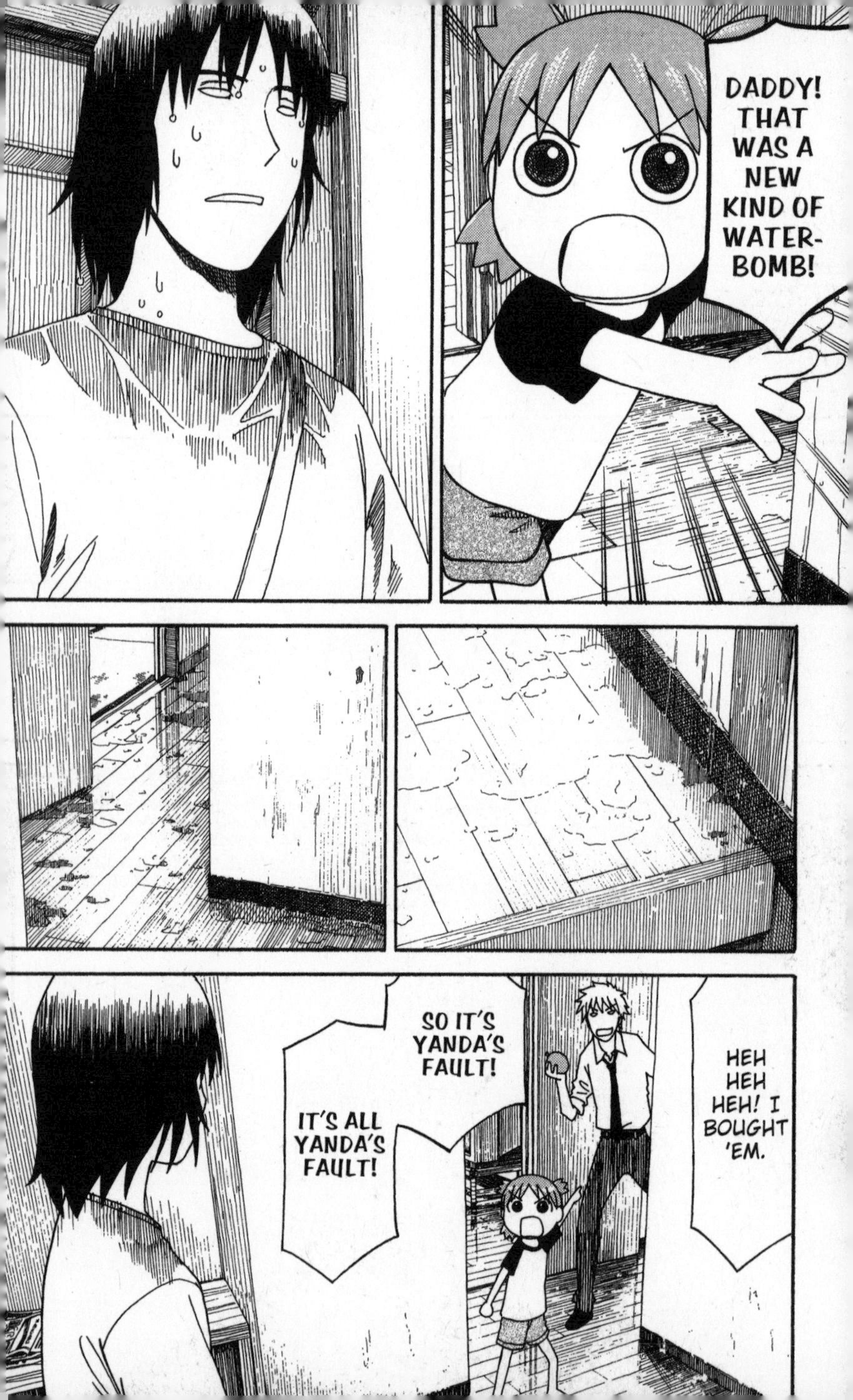
DADDY! THAT WAS A NEW KIND OF WATER-BOMB!
HEH HEH HEH! I BOUGHT 'EM.
SO IT'S YANDA'S FAULT!
IT'S ALL YANDA'S FAULT!

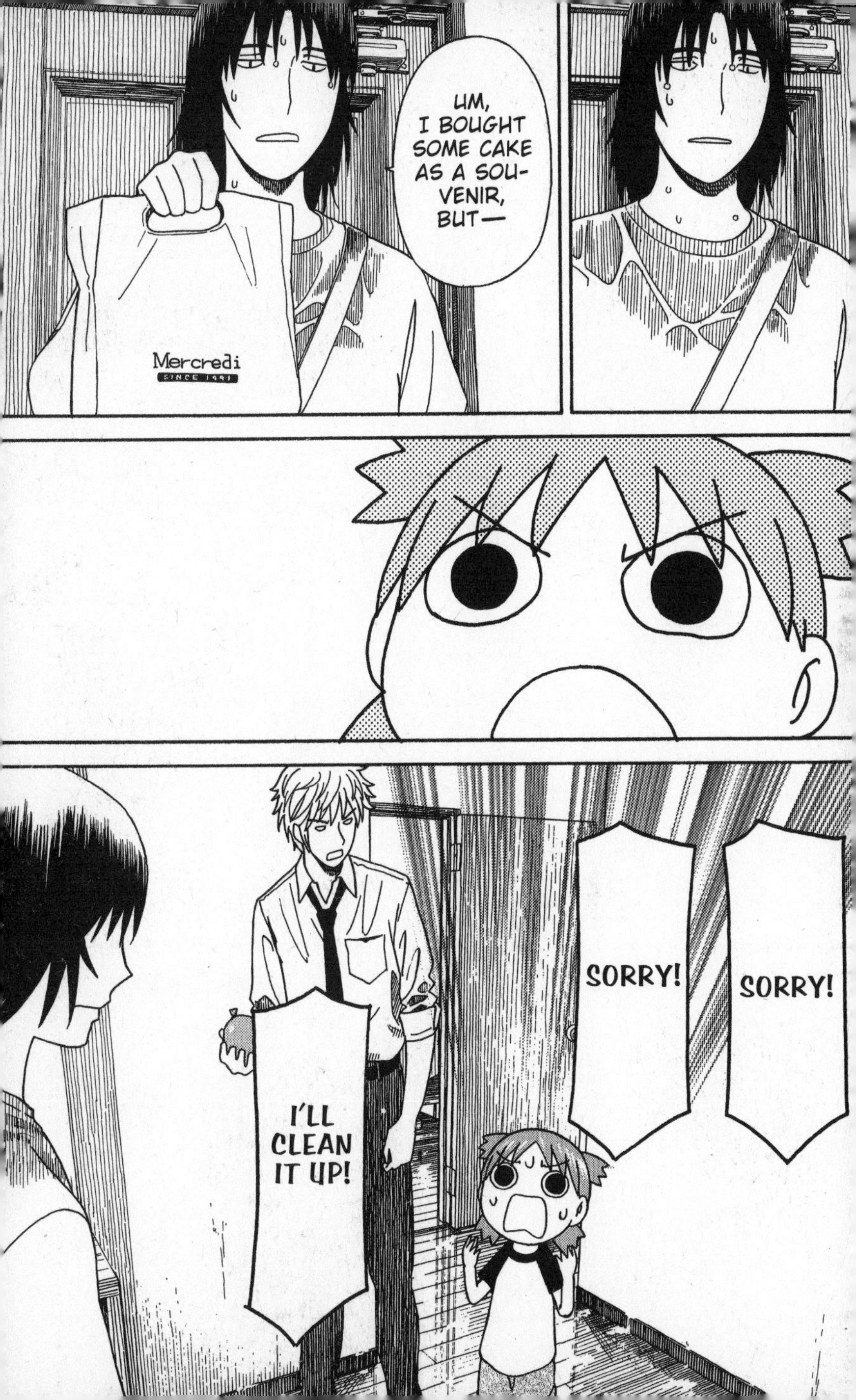
UM, I BOUGHT SOME CAKE AS A SOU-VENIR, BUT—
Mercredi
SINCE 1991
SORRY!
SORRY!
I'LL CLEAN IT UP!

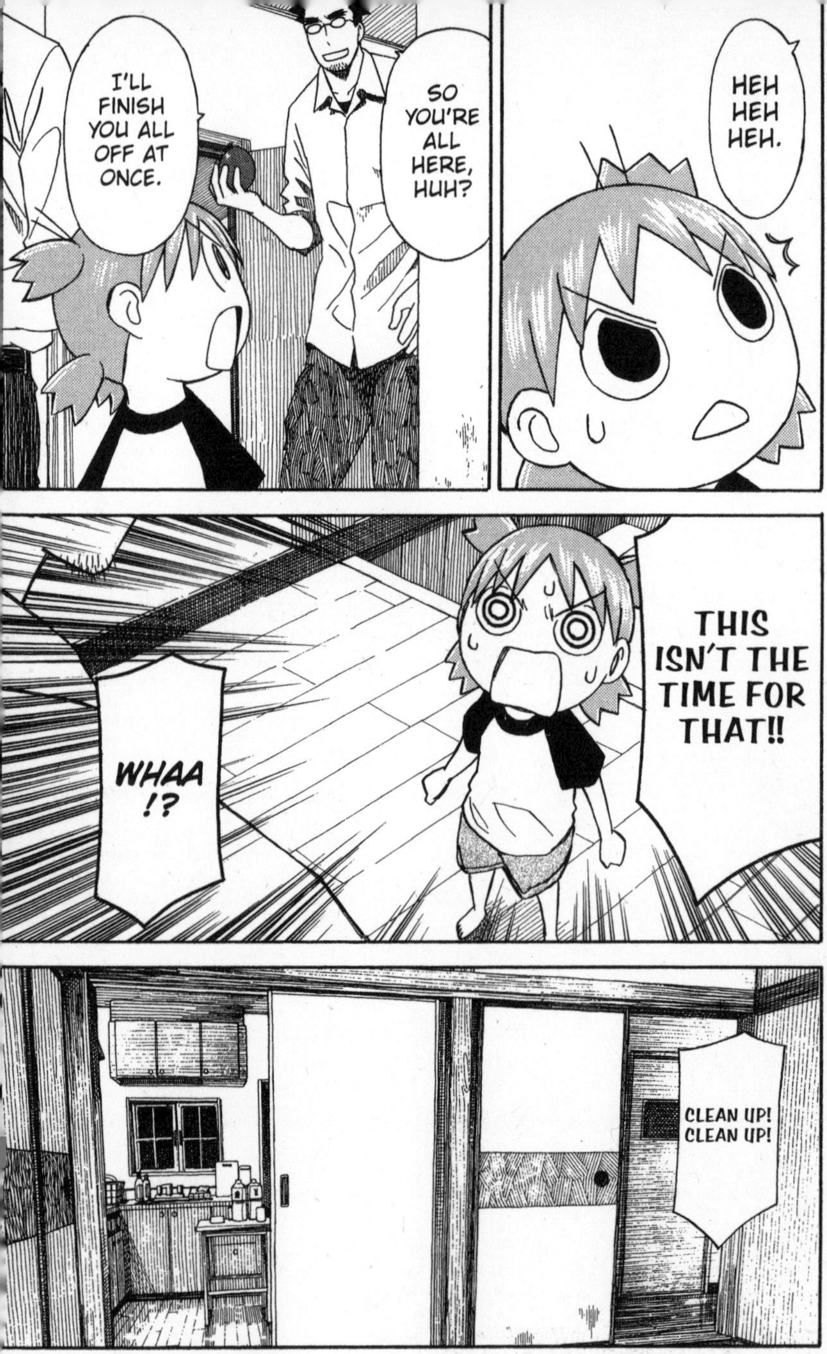
HEH HEH HEH.
SO YOU'RE ALL HERE, HUH?
I'LL FINISH YOU ALL OFF AT ONCE.
THIS ISN'T THE TIME FOR THAT!!
WHAA !?
CLEAN UP! CLEAN UP!

YOTSUBA&!

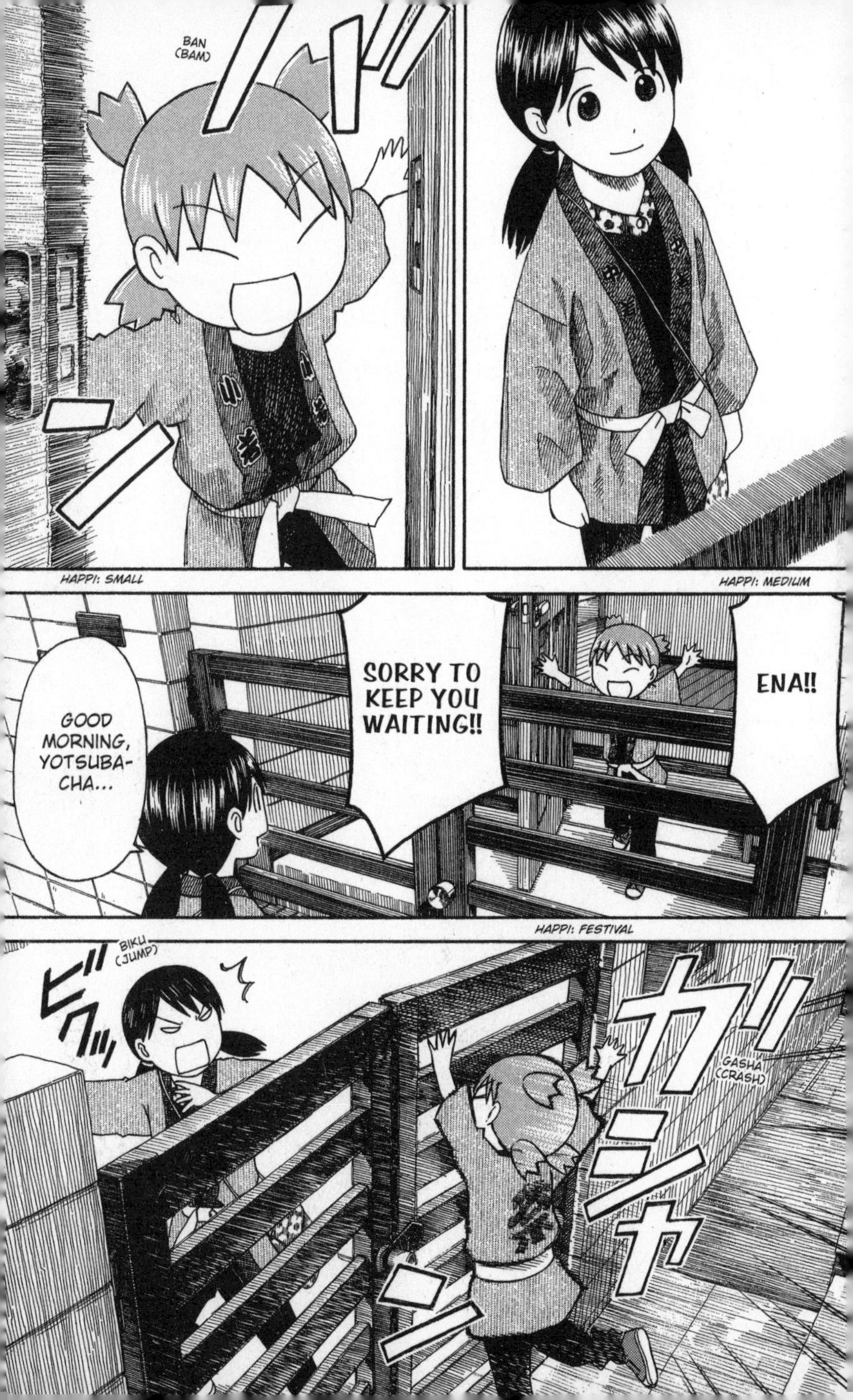
HAPPI: MEDIUM
BAN (BAM)
HAPPI: SMALL
ENA!!
SORRY TO KEEP YOU WAITING!!
GOOD MORNING, YOTSUBA-CHA...
HAPPI: FESTIVAL
GASHA (CRASH)
BIKU (JUMP)

*NOTICE THAT ALL OF THE HAPPI HAVE A KANJI CHARACTER ON THE BACK. IN SOME CASES, IT IS THE CHARACTER FOR "FESTIVAL." IN OTHER CASES, IT IS THE FIRST CHARACTER IN THE NAME OF THE PERSON'S TOWN. THE TOWN WHERE YOTSUBA AND THE GANG LIVE IS EMAIMACHI, AND THE FIRST CHARACTER, WHICH YOU SEE ON THE HAPPI, MEANS "BLOOM" AND/OR "SMILE."

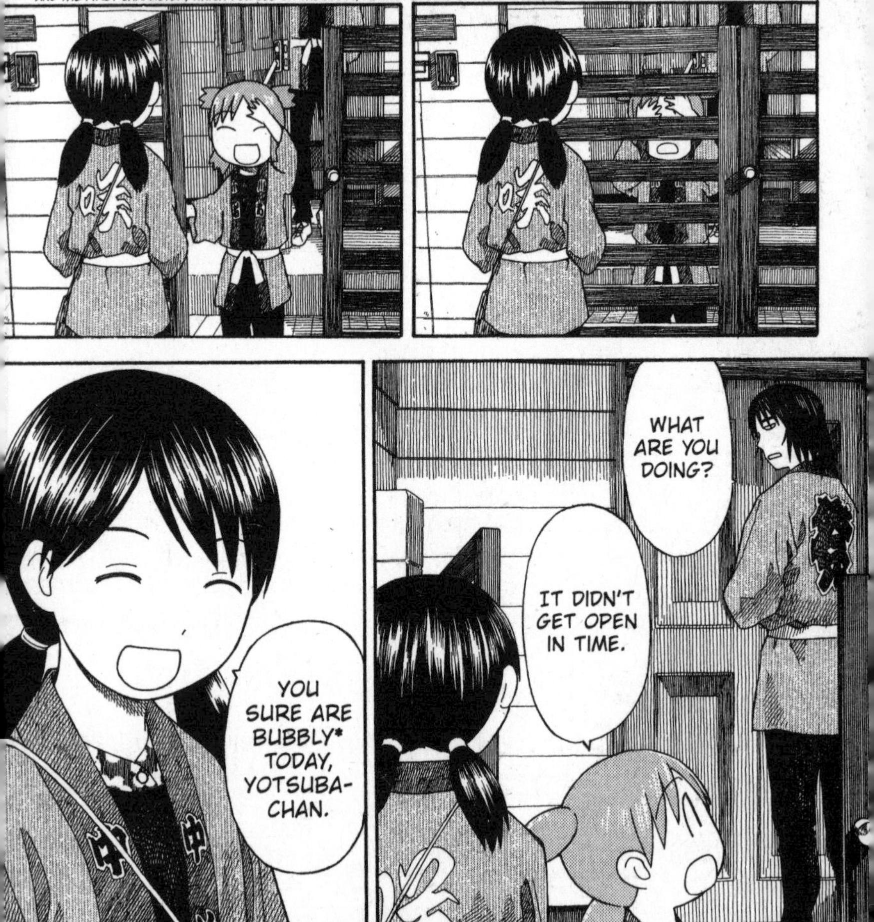
WHAT ARE YOU DOING?
IT DIDN'T GET OPEN IN TIME.
YOU SURE ARE BUBBLY* TODAY, YOTSUBA-CHAN.

*ENA SAYS THAT YOTSUBA IS "NORI-NORI" WHICH MEANS "ENERGETIC" AND "SPIRITED." YOTSUBA CONFUSES THIS WITH THE WORD "NORI," WHICH IS A TYPE OF SEAWEED USED IN JAPANESE COOKING. ONE DISH THAT IT IS USED IN IS TSUKUDANI, WHICH IS LITTLE BITS OF MEAT, SEAFOOD, OR SEAWEED SIMMERED IN SOY SAUCE AND MIRIN.

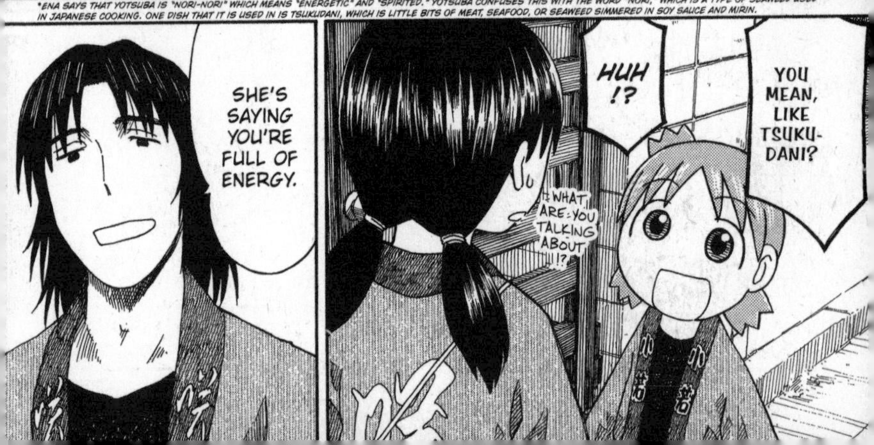
YOU MEAN, LIKE TSUKUDANI?
HUH!?
WHAT ARE YOU TALKING ABOUT!!!?
SHE'S SAYING YOU'RE FULL OF ENERGY.

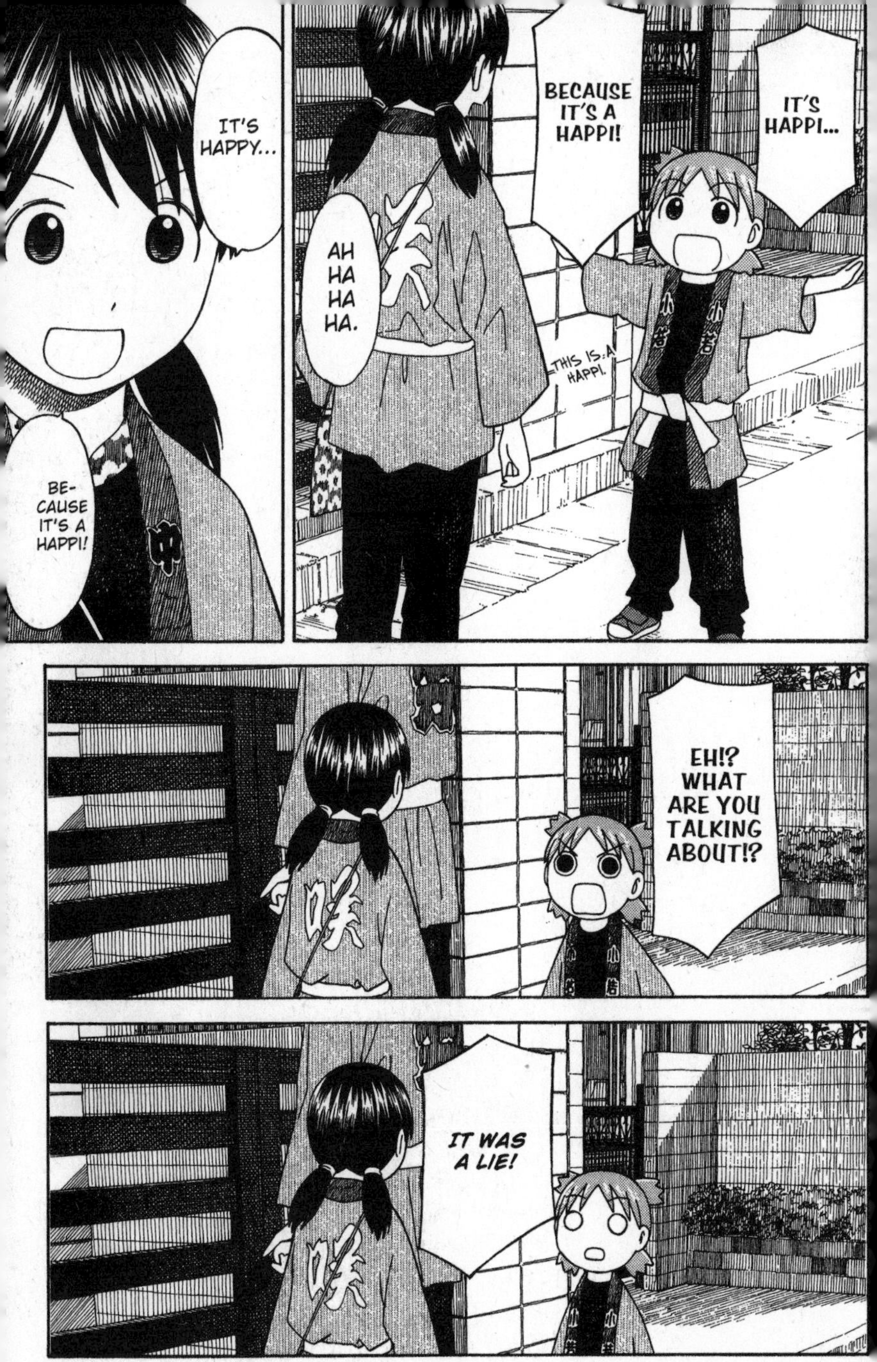
IT'S HAPPI...
BECAUSE IT'S A HAPPI!
AH HA HA HA.
THIS IS A HAPPI.
IT'S HAPPY...
BE-CAUSE IT'S A HAPPI!
EH!? WHAT ARE YOU TALKING ABOUT!?
IT WAS A LIE!

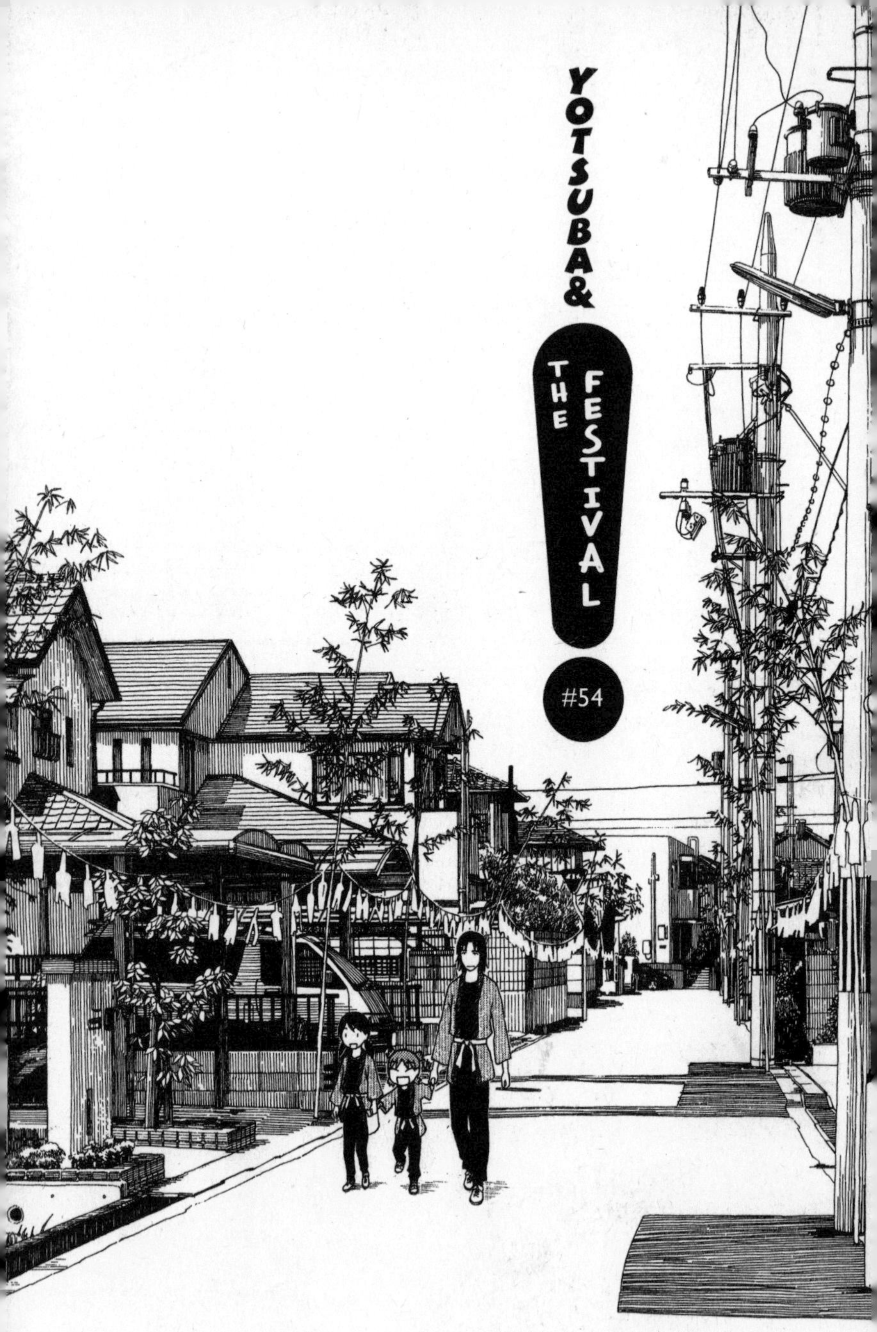
YOTSUBA&
THE FESTIVAL
#54

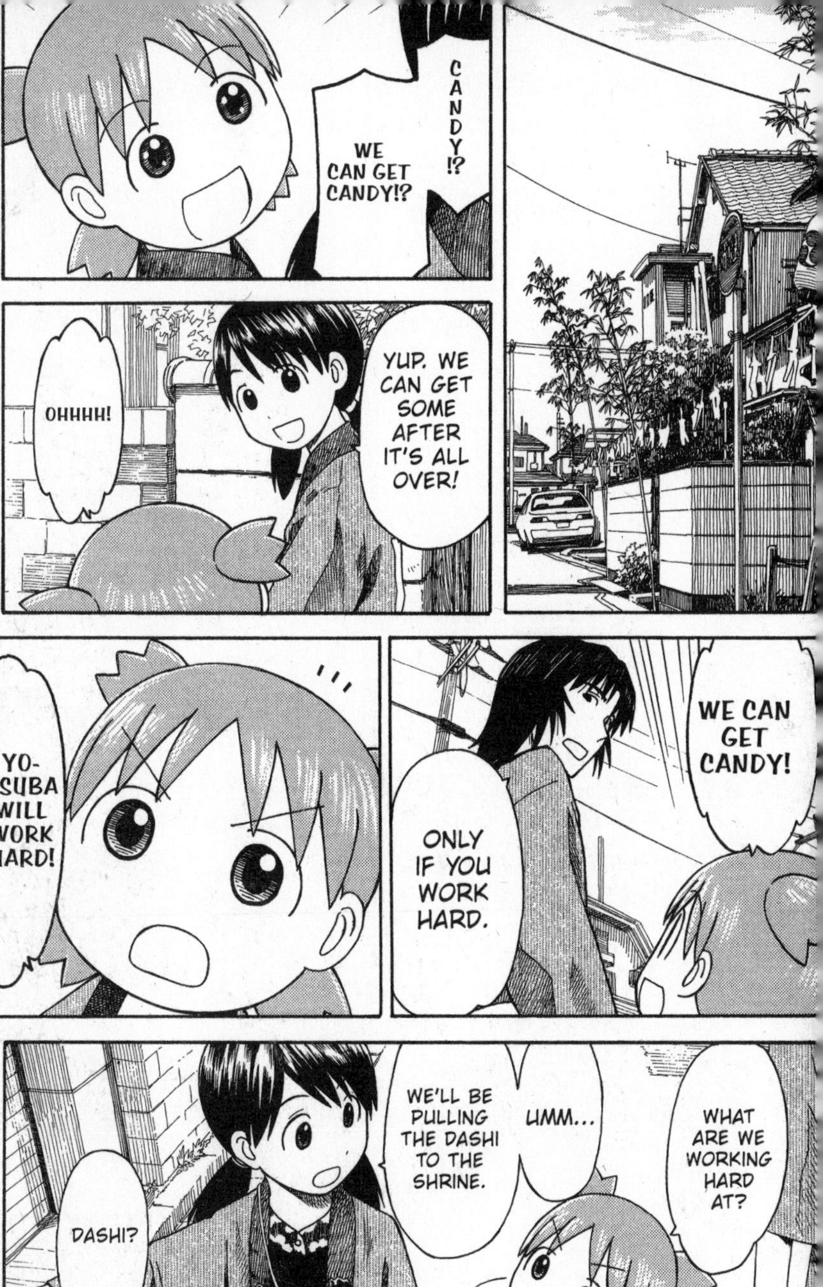
CANDY!?
WE CAN GET CANDY!?
YUP. WE CAN GET SOME AFTER IT'S ALL OVER!
OHHHH!
WE CAN GET CANDY!
ONLY IF YOU WORK HARD.
YO-TSUBA WILL WORK HARD!
WHAT ARE WE WORKING HARD AT?
UMM...
WE'LL BE PULLING THE DASHI TO THE SHRINE.
DASHI?

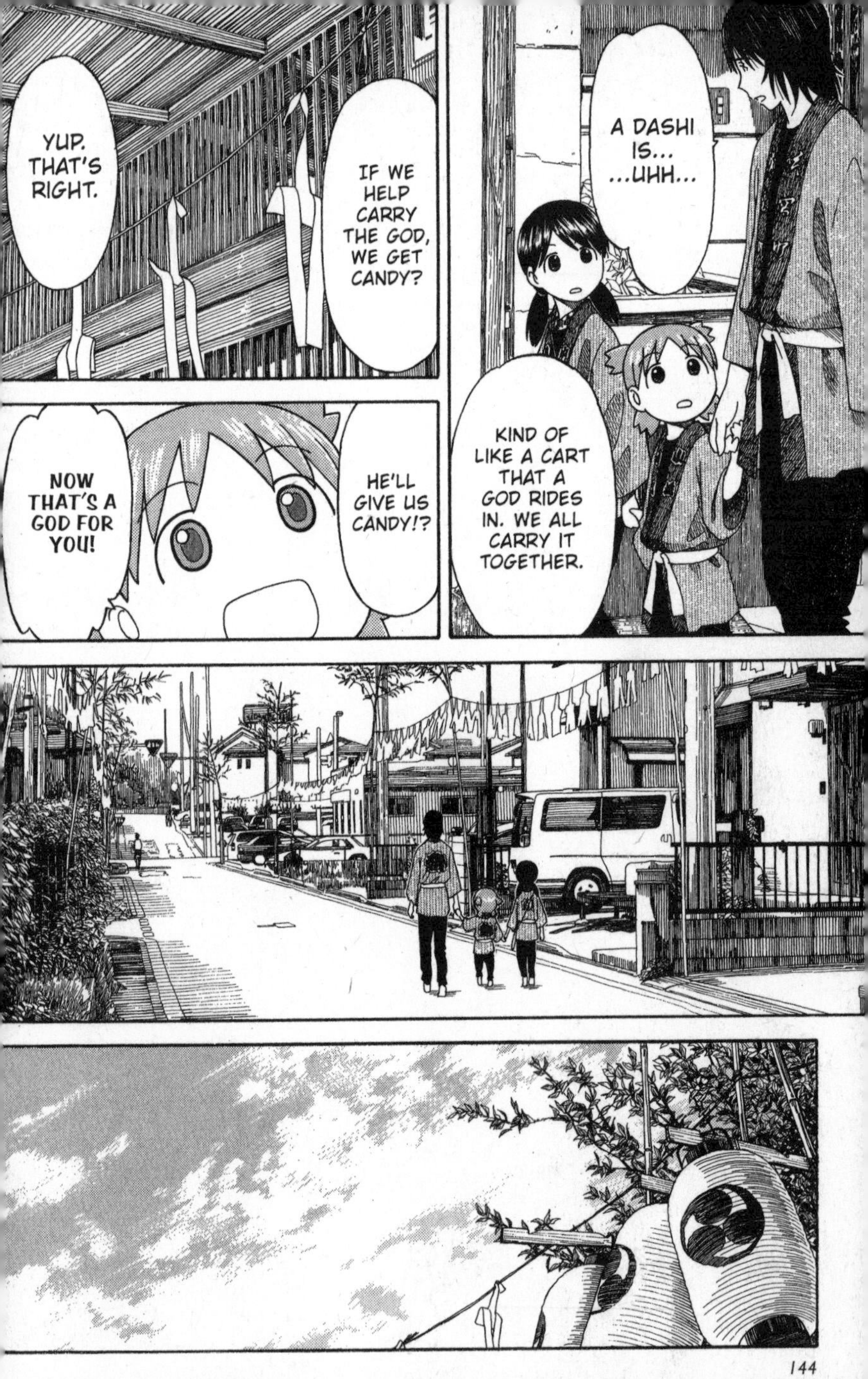
A DASHI IS... ...UHH...
KIND OF LIKE A CART THAT A GOD RIDES IN. WE ALL CARRY IT TOGETHER.
IF WE HELP CARRY THE GOD, WE GET CANDY?
YUP. THAT'S RIGHT.
HE'LL GIVE US CANDY!?
NOW THAT'S A GOD FOR YOU!

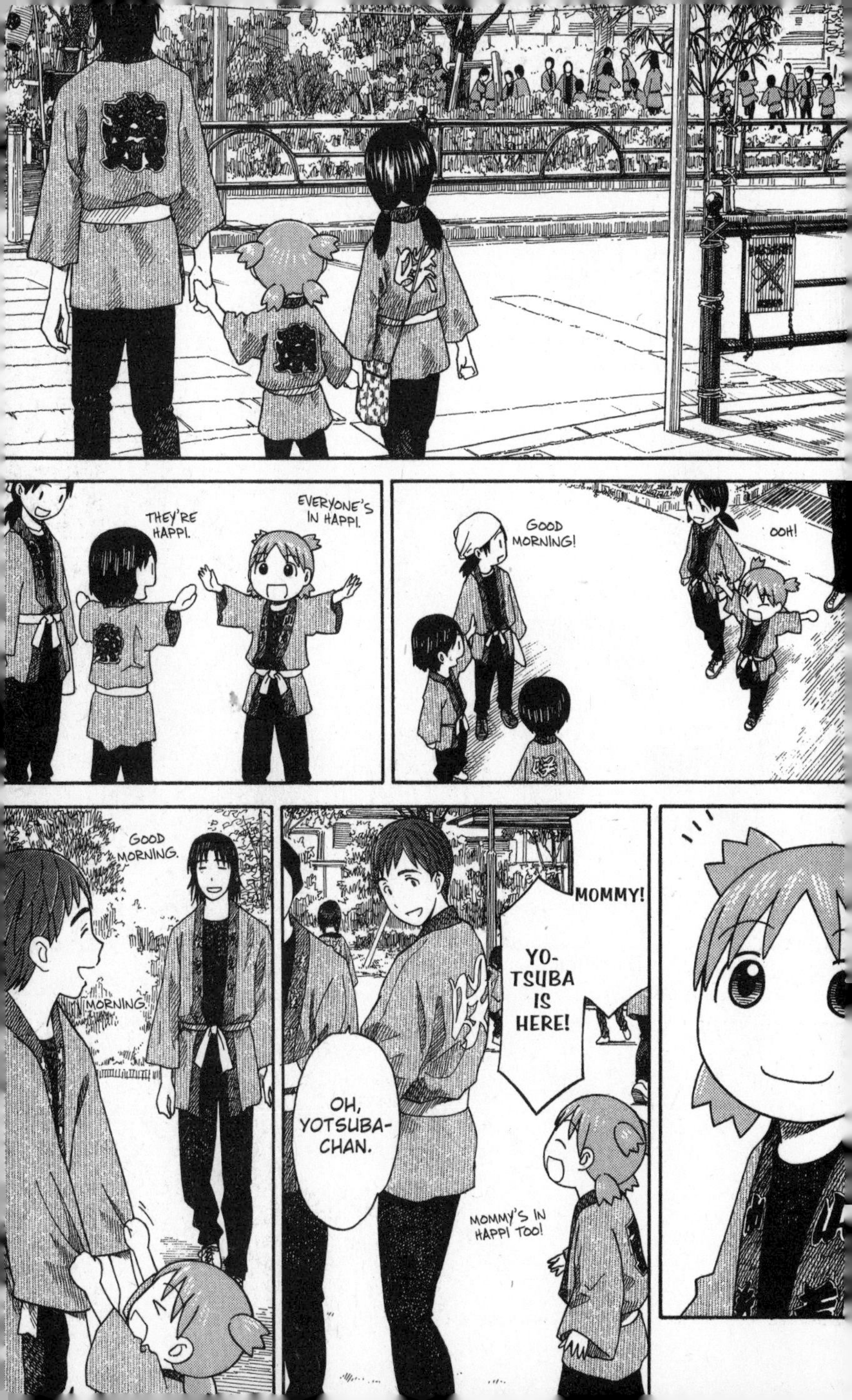
OOH!
GOOD MORNING!
EVERYONE'S IN HAPPI.
THEY'RE HAPPI.
MOMMY!
YO-TSUBA IS HERE!
OH, YOTSUBA-CHAN.
MOMMY'S IN HAPPI TOO!
GOOD MORNING.
MORNING.

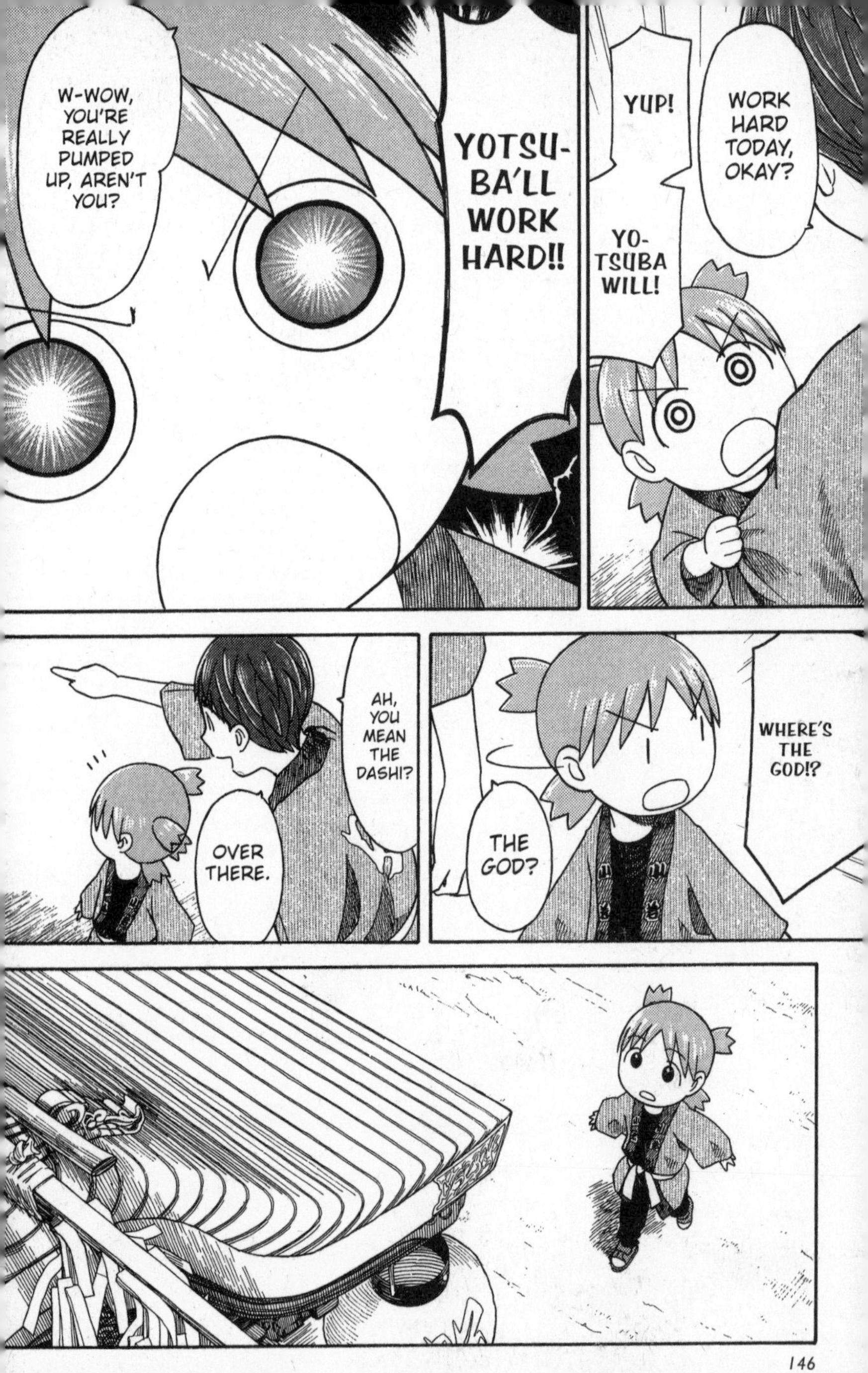
WORK HARD TODAY, OKAY?
YUP!
YO-TSUBA WILL!
YOTSU-BA'LL WORK HARD!!
W-WOW, YOU'RE REALLY PUMPED UP, AREN'T YOU?
WHERE'S THE GOD!?
THE GOD?
AH, YOU MEAN THE DASHI?
OVER THERE.

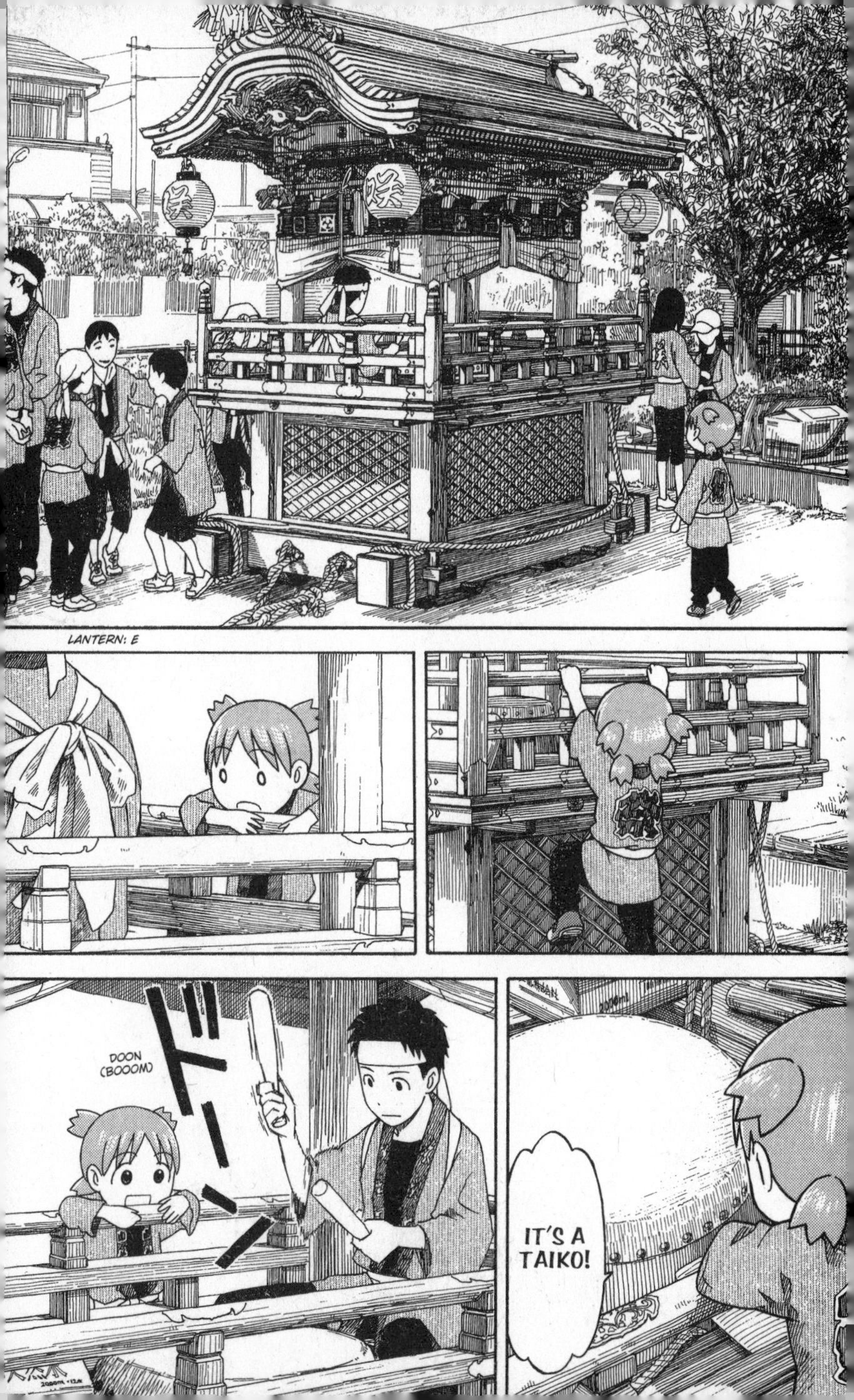
LANTERN: E
IT'S A TAIKO!
DOON (BOOOM)

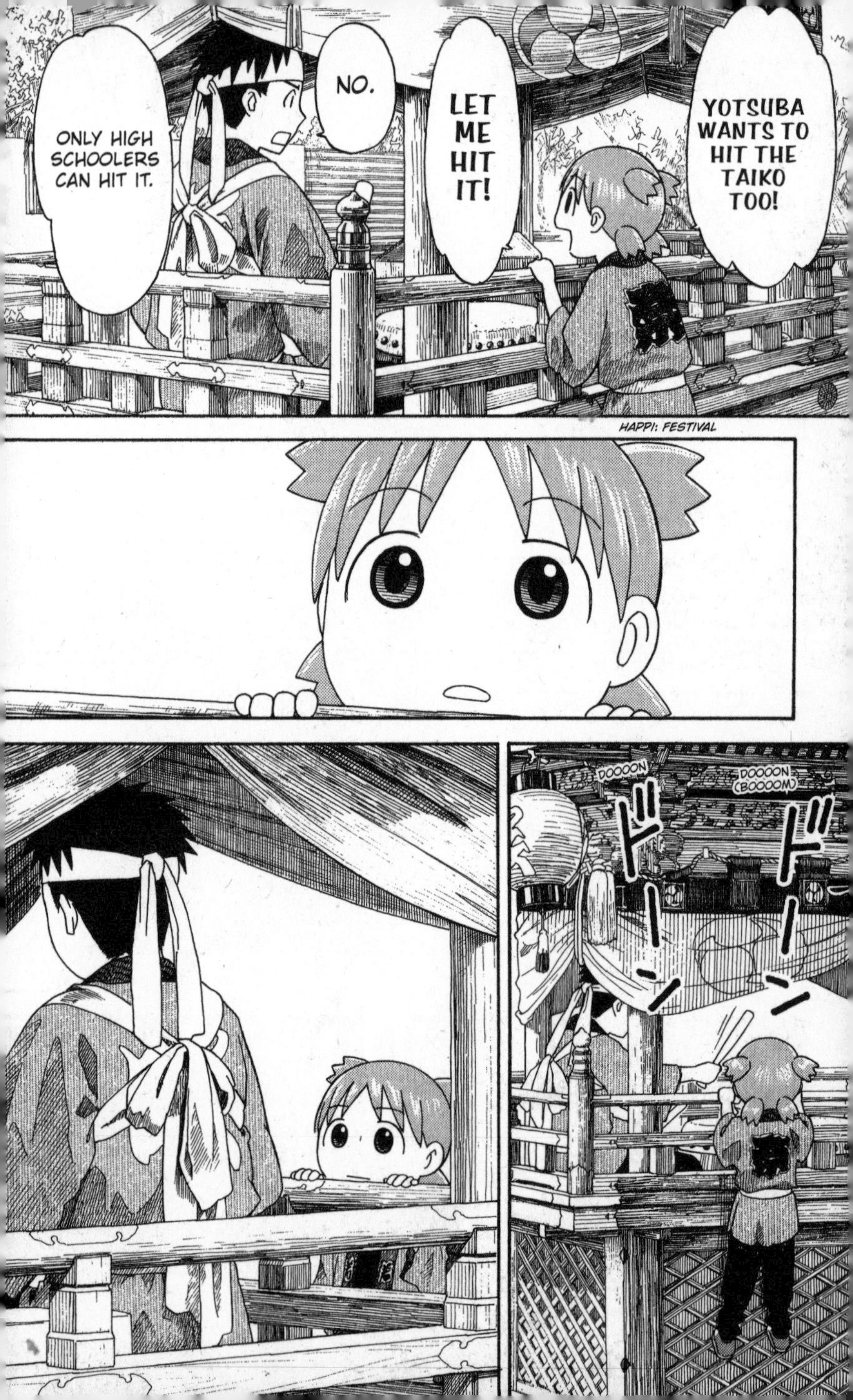
YOTSUBA WANTS TO HIT THE TAIKO TOO!
LET ME HIT IT!
NO.
ONLY HIGH SCHOOLERS CAN HIT IT.
HAPPI: FESTIVAL
DOOOON (BOOOOM)
DOOOON

FUUKA.

HIRO-KUN...

WHY DON'T YOU LET HER HIT IT, JUST A LITTLE BIT?

JUST THIS ONCE.

HE SAID YOU CAN!

THANK YOU!!

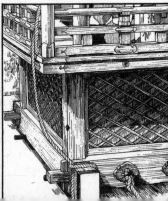

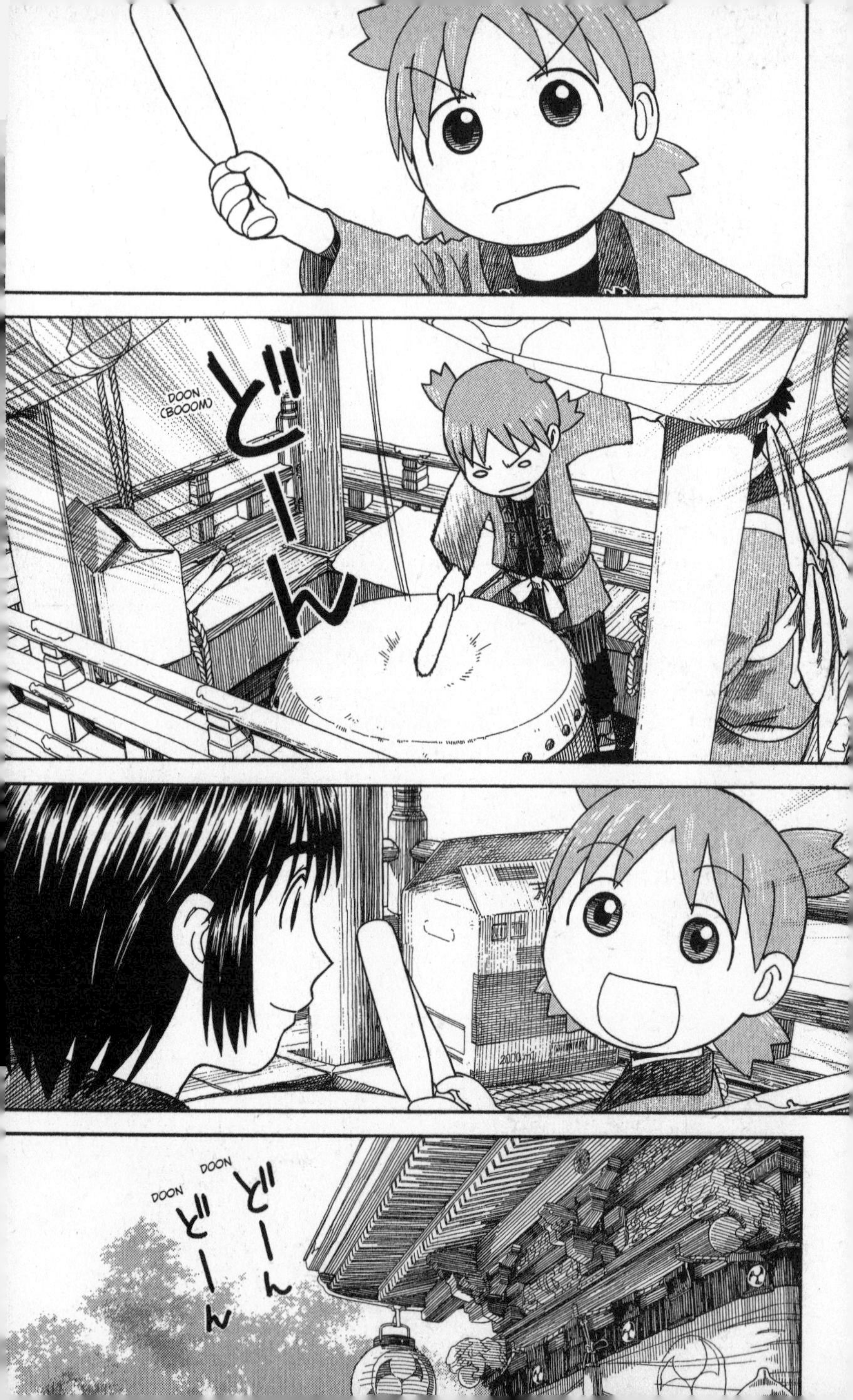

どーん
DOON (BOOOM)
どーん
DOON
どーん
DOON

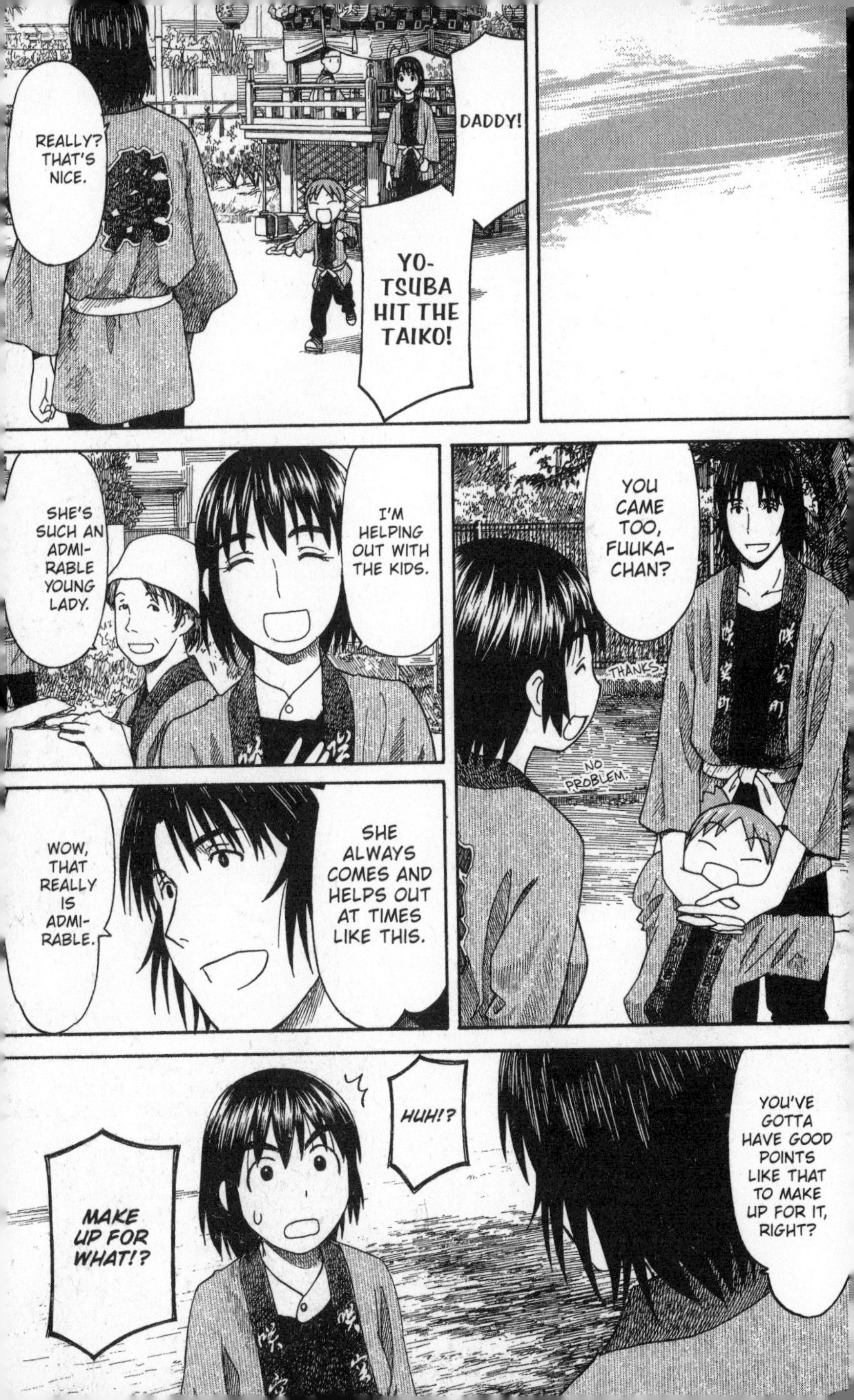
DADDY!
YO-TSUBA HIT THE TAIKO!
REALLY? THAT'S NICE.
YOU CAME TOO, FUUKA-CHAN?
THANKS.
NO PROBLEM.
I'M HELPING OUT WITH THE KIDS.
SHE'S SUCH AN ADMIRABLE YOUNG LADY.
SHE ALWAYS COMES AND HELPS OUT AT TIMES LIKE THIS.
WOW, THAT REALLY IS ADMIRABLE.
YOU'VE GOTTA HAVE GOOD POINTS LIKE THAT TO MAKE UP FOR IT, RIGHT?
HUH!?
MAKE UP FOR WHAT!?

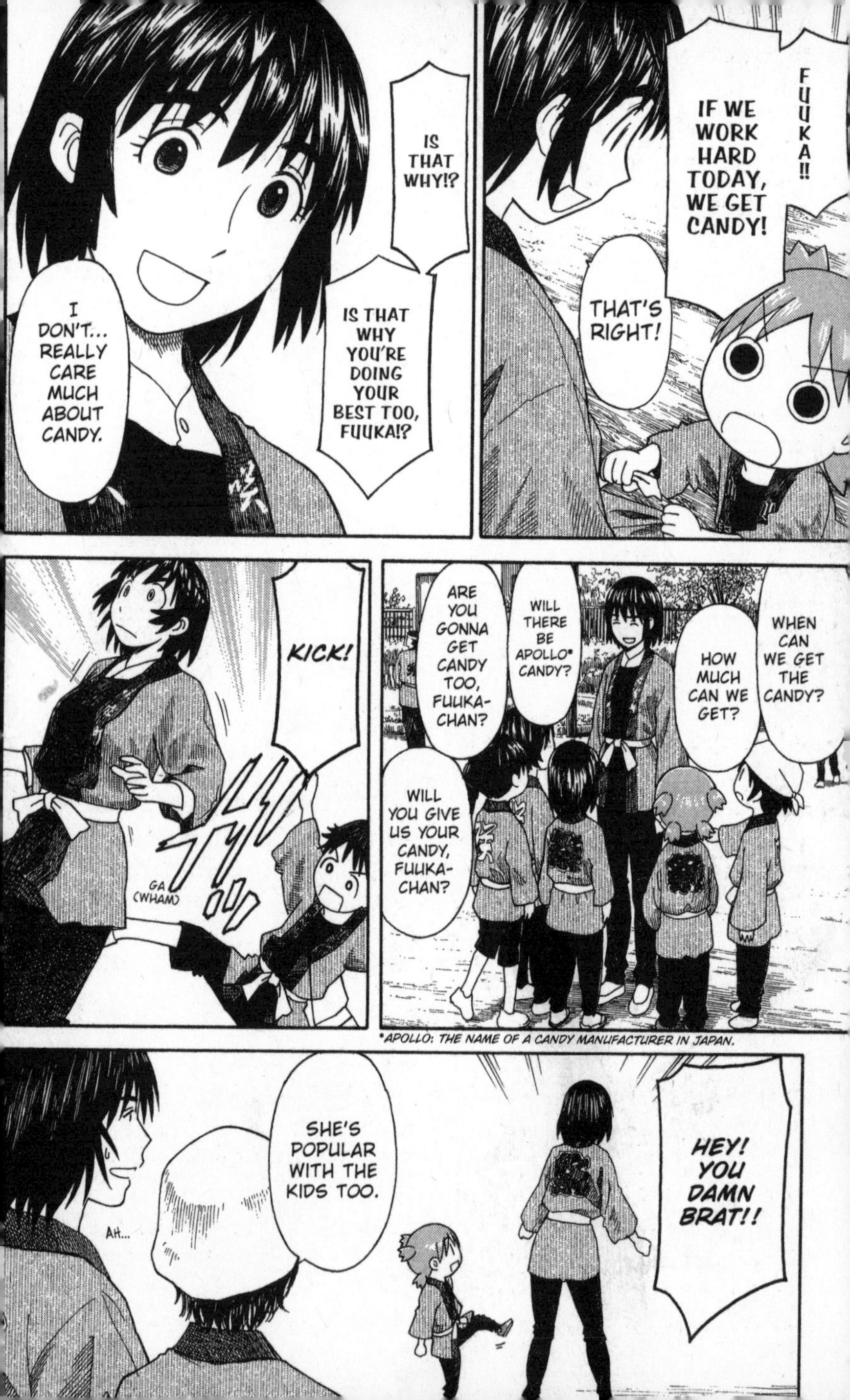
FUUKA!!
IF WE WORK HARD TODAY, WE GET CANDY!
THAT'S RIGHT!
IS THAT WHY!?
IS THAT WHY YOU'RE DOING YOUR BEST TOO, FUUKA!?
I DON'T... REALLY CARE MUCH ABOUT CANDY.
WHEN CAN WE GET THE CANDY?
HOW MUCH CAN WE GET?
WILL THERE BE APOLLO* CANDY?
ARE YOU GONNA GET CANDY TOO, FUUKA-CHAN?
WILL YOU GIVE US YOUR CANDY, FUUKA-CHAN?
KICK!
GA (WHAM)
HEY! YOU DAMN BRAT!!
SHE'S POPULAR WITH THE KIDS TOO.
AH...
*APOLLO: THE NAME OF A CANDY MANUFACTURER IN JAPAN.

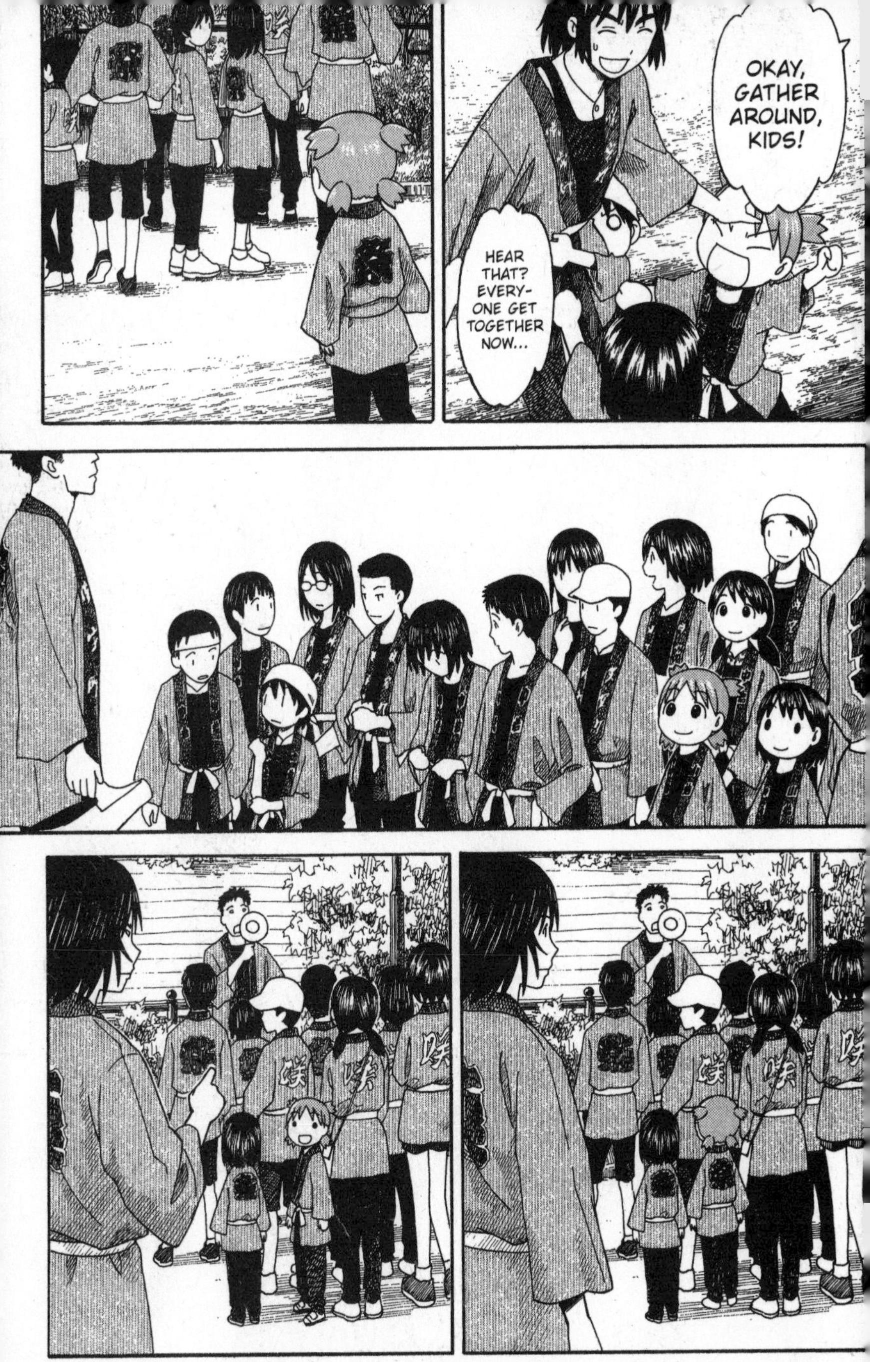
OKAY, GATHER AROUND, KIDS!
HEAR THAT? EVERY-ONE GET TOGETHER NOW...

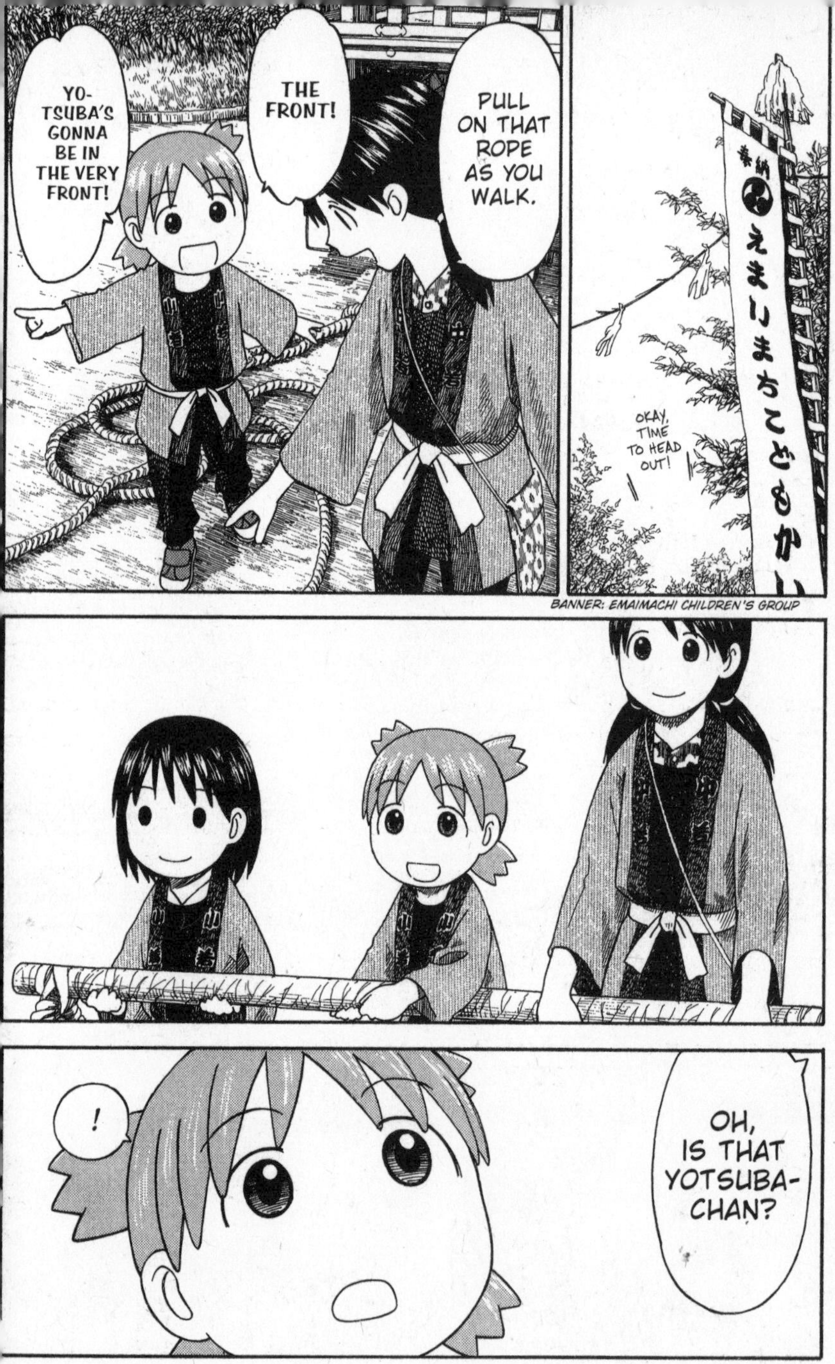

奉納
えまいまちこどもか
OKAY, TIME TO HEAD OUT!
PULL ON THAT ROPE AS YOU WALK.
THE FRONT!
YO-TSUBA'S GONNA BE IN THE VERY FRONT!
BANNER: EMAIMACHI CHILDREN'S GROUP
OH, IS THAT YOTSUBA-CHAN?
!

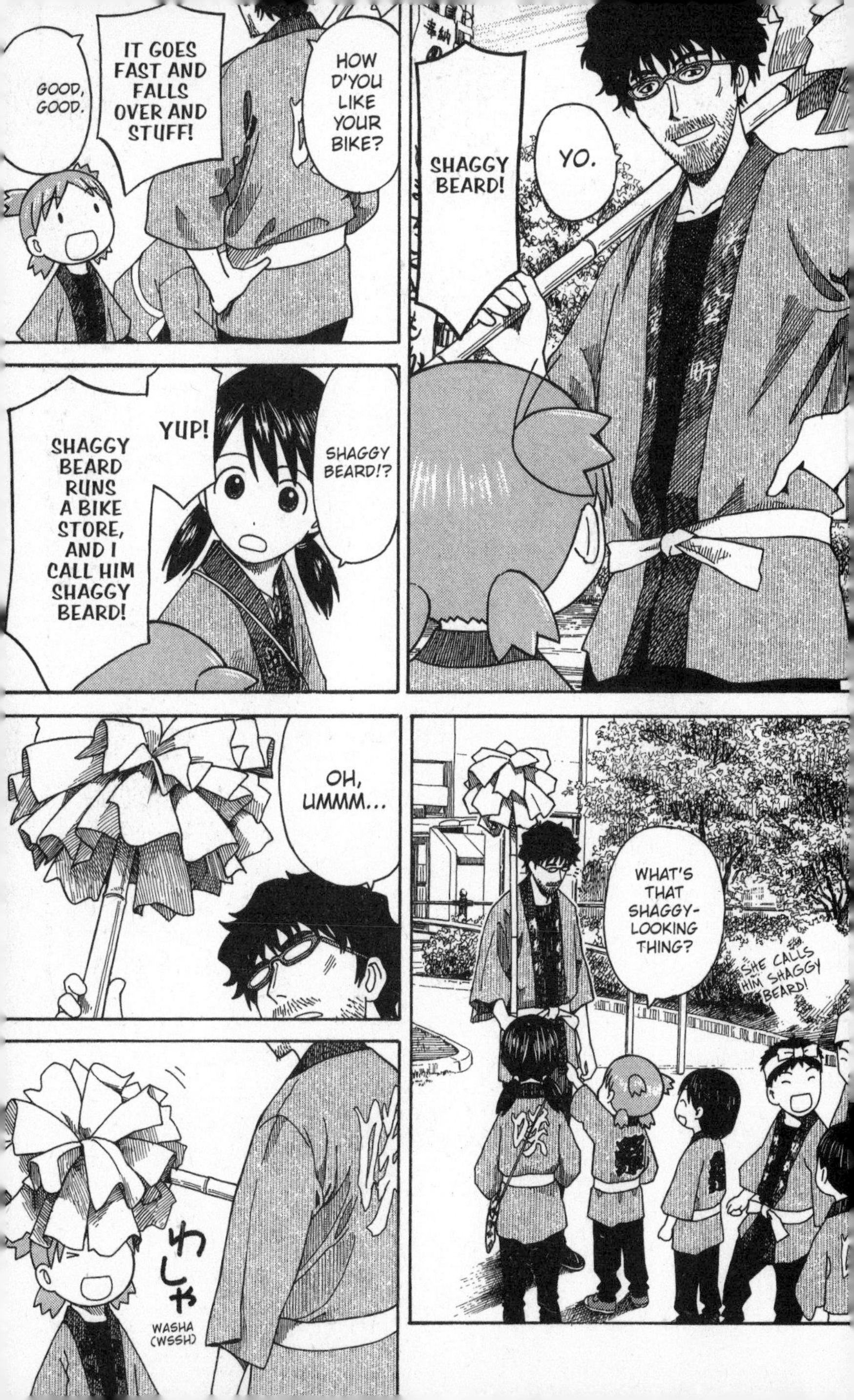
YO.
SHAGGY BEARD!
HOW D'YOU LIKE YOUR BIKE?
IT GOES FAST AND FALLS OVER AND STUFF!
GOOD, GOOD.
SHAGGY BEARD!?
YUP!
SHAGGY BEARD RUNS A BIKE STORE, AND I CALL HIM SHAGGY BEARD!
WHAT'S THAT SHAGGY-LOOKING THING?
SHE CALLS HIM SHAGGY BEARD!
OH, UMMM...
わしゃ
WASHA (WSSH)

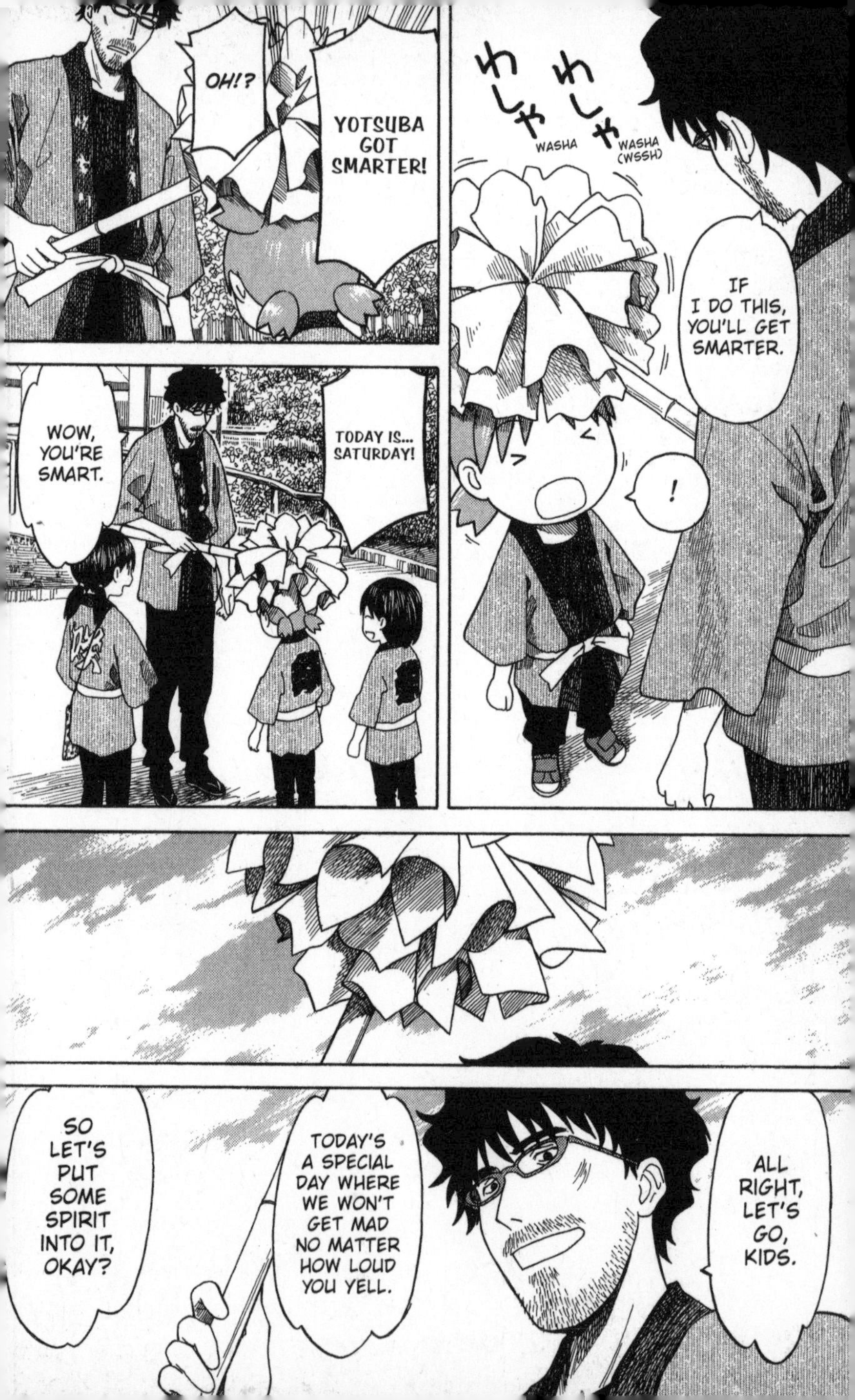
わしゃ
WASHA
わしゃ
WASHA (WSSH)
IF I DO THIS, YOU'LL GET SMARTER.
!
YOTSUBA GOT SMARTER!
OH!?
TODAY IS... SATURDAY!
WOW, YOU'RE SMART.
ALL RIGHT, LET'S GO, KIDS.
TODAY'S A SPECIAL DAY WHERE WE WON'T GET MAD NO MATTER HOW LOUD YOU YELL.
SO LET'S PUT SOME SPIRIT INTO IT, OKAY?

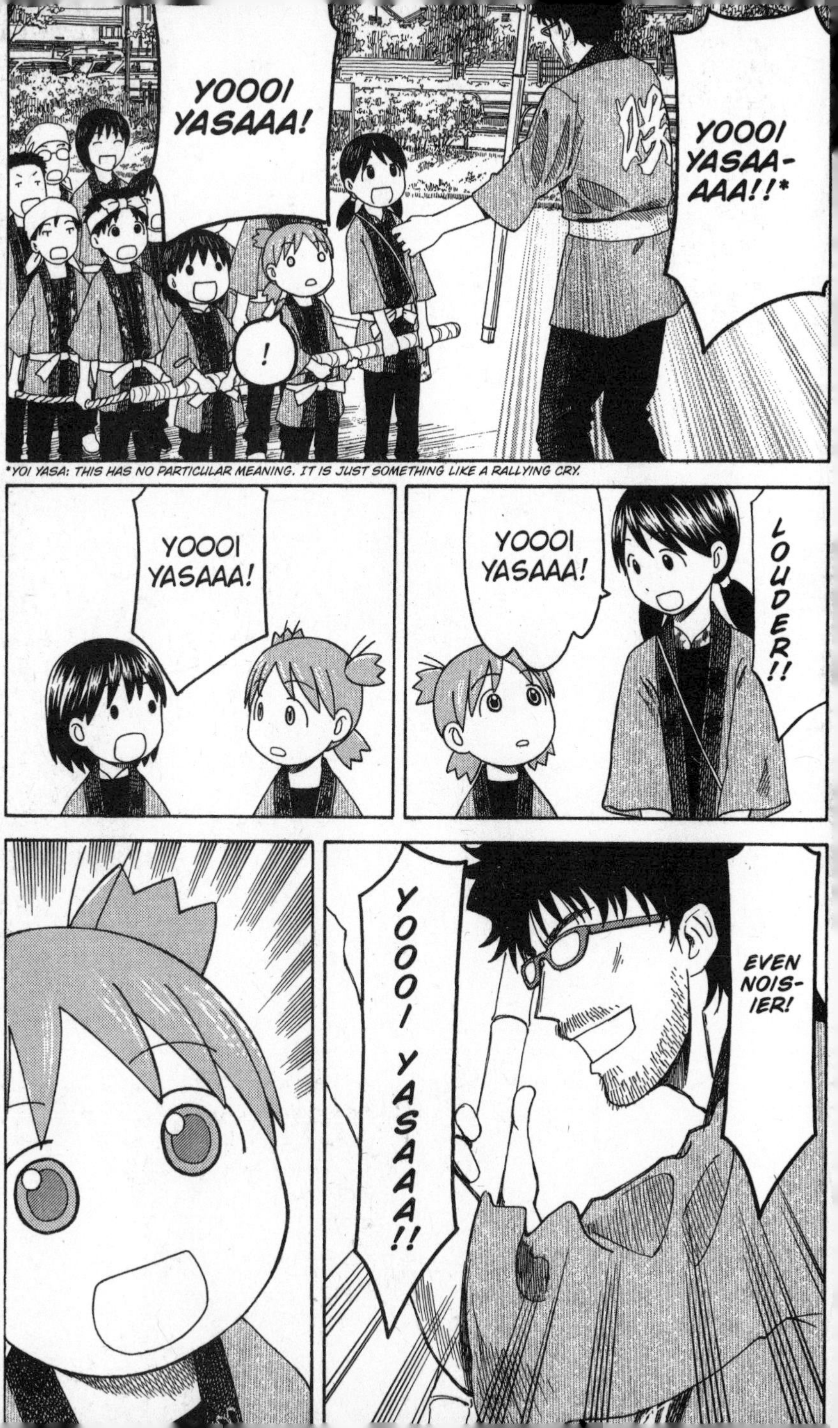
YOOOI YASAA-AAA!!*
YOOOI YASAAA!
!
LOUDER!!
YOOOI YASAAA!
YOOOI YASAAA!
EVEN NOISIER!
YOOOI YASAAAA!!
*YOI YASA: THIS HAS NO PARTICULAR MEANING. IT IS JUST SOMETHING LIKE A RALLYING CRY.

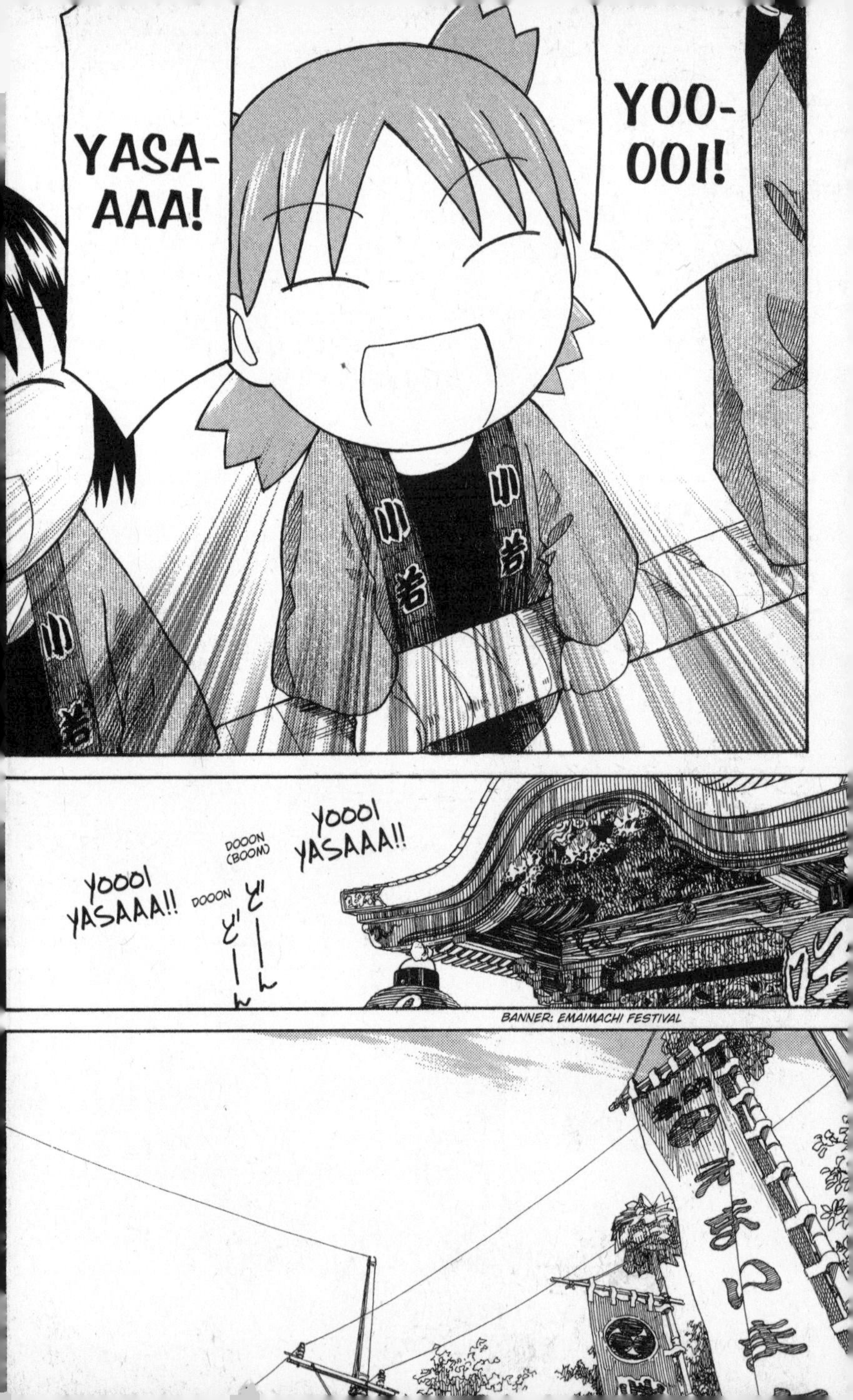
YOO-OOI!
YASA-AAA!
YOOOI YASAAA!!
DOOON (BOOM)
どーん
DOOON
どーん
YOOOI YASAAA!!
BANNER: EMAIMACHI FESTIVAL

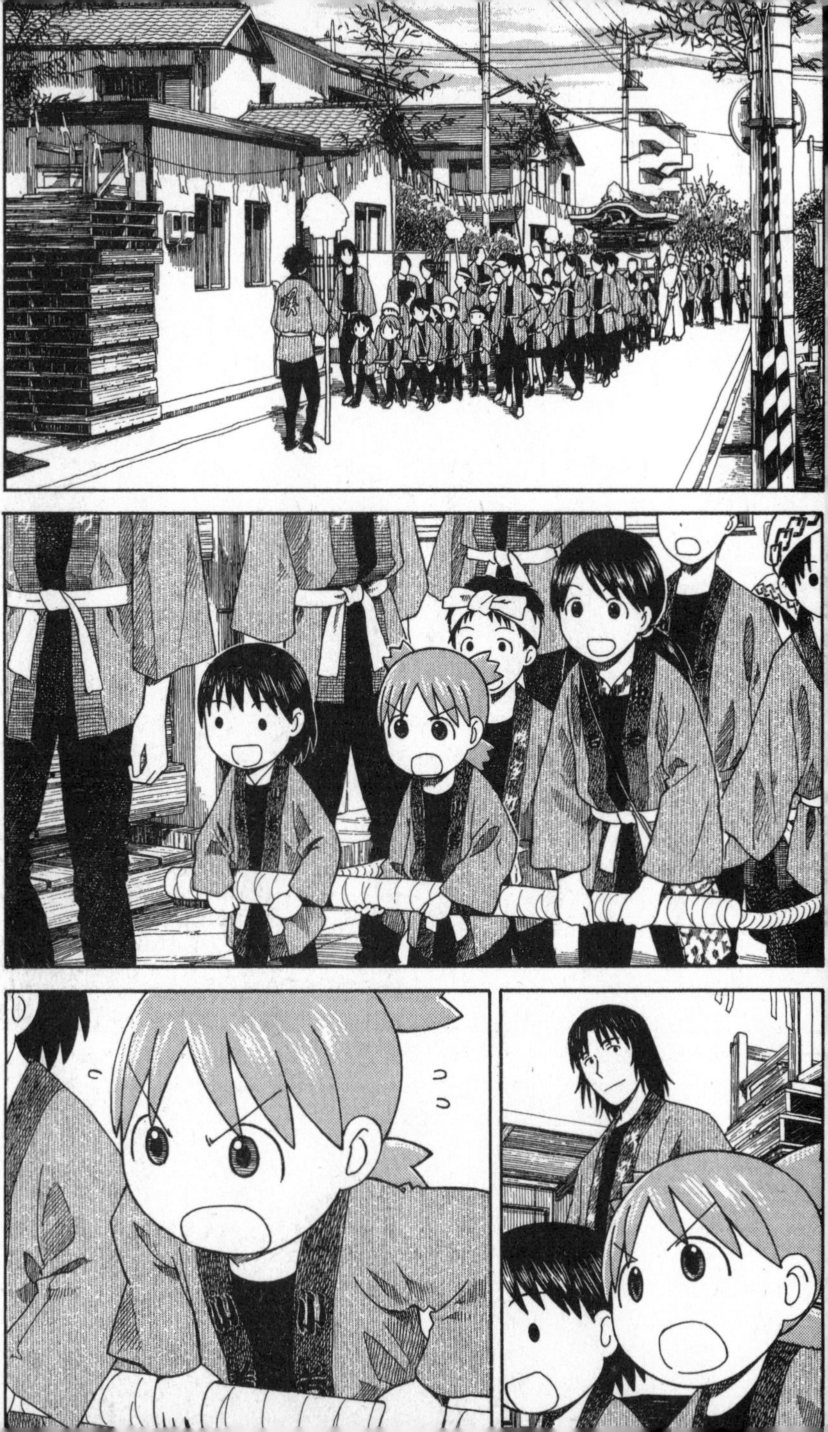

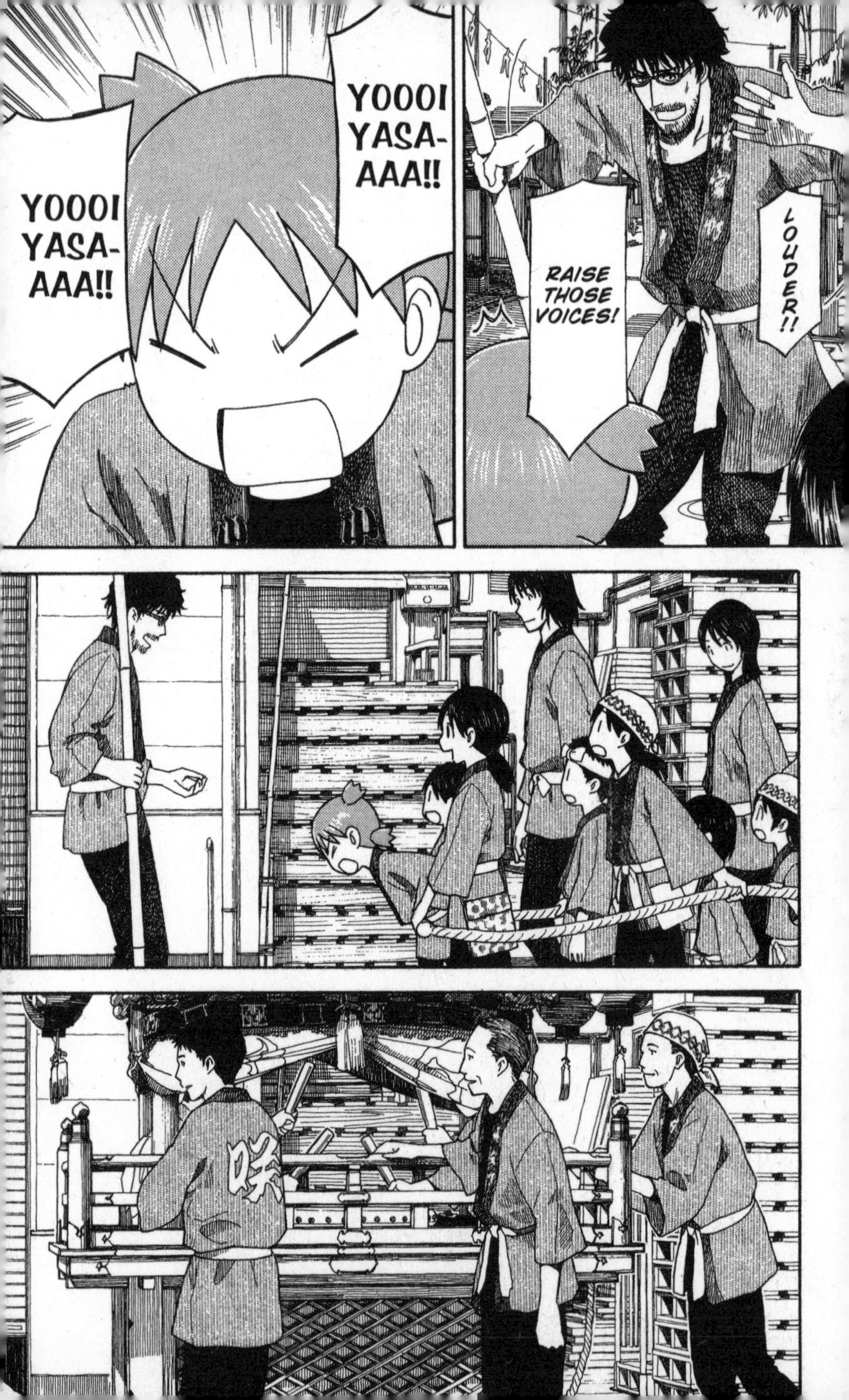
LOUDER!!
RAISE THOSE VOICES!
YOOOI YASA-AAA!!
YOOOI YASA-AAA!!
咲

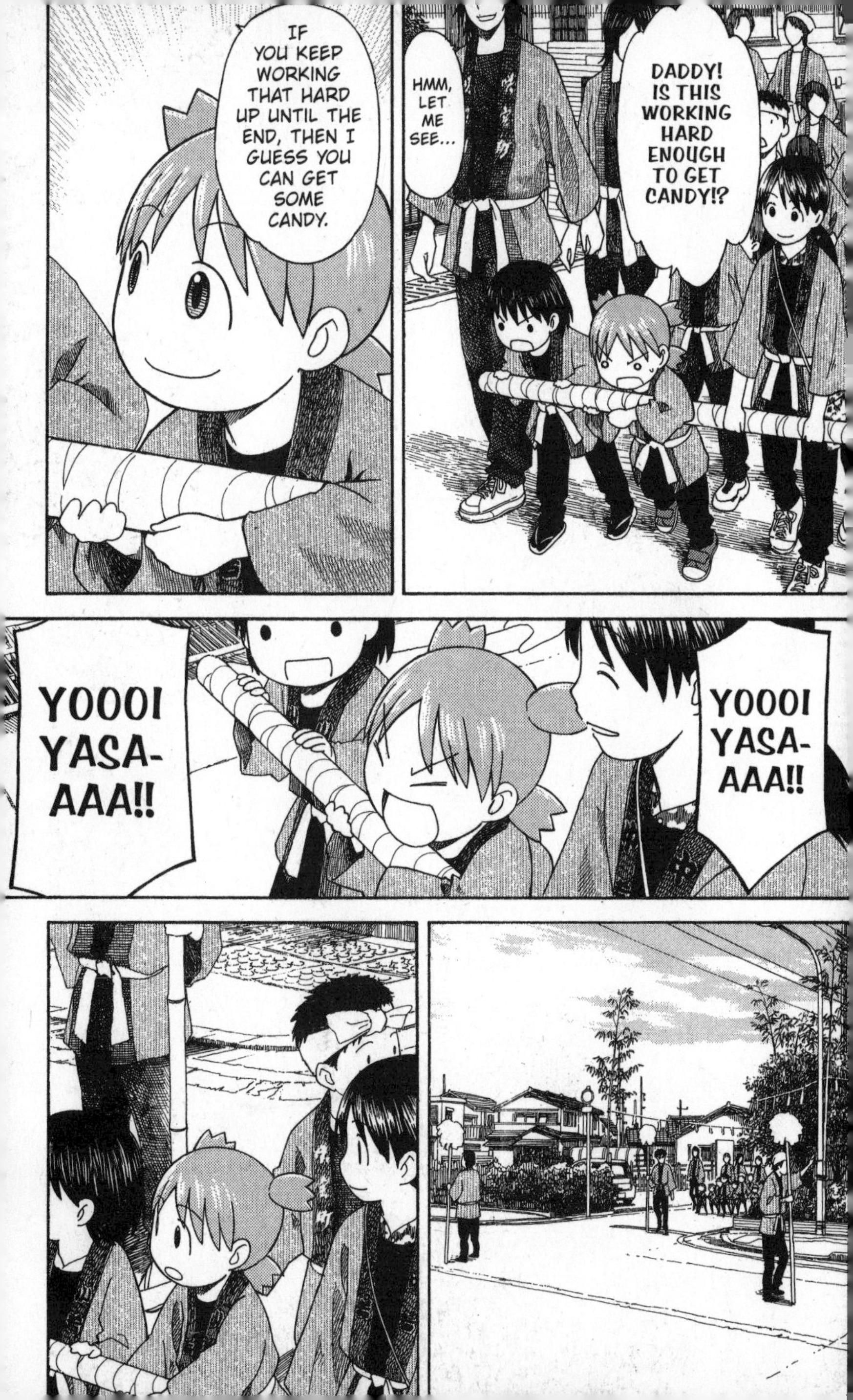
DADDY! IS THIS WORKING HARD ENOUGH TO GET CANDY!?
HMM, LET ME SEE...
IF YOU KEEP WORKING THAT HARD UP UNTIL THE END, THEN I GUESS YOU CAN GET SOME CANDY.
YOOOI YASA-AAA!!
YOOOI YASA-AAA!!

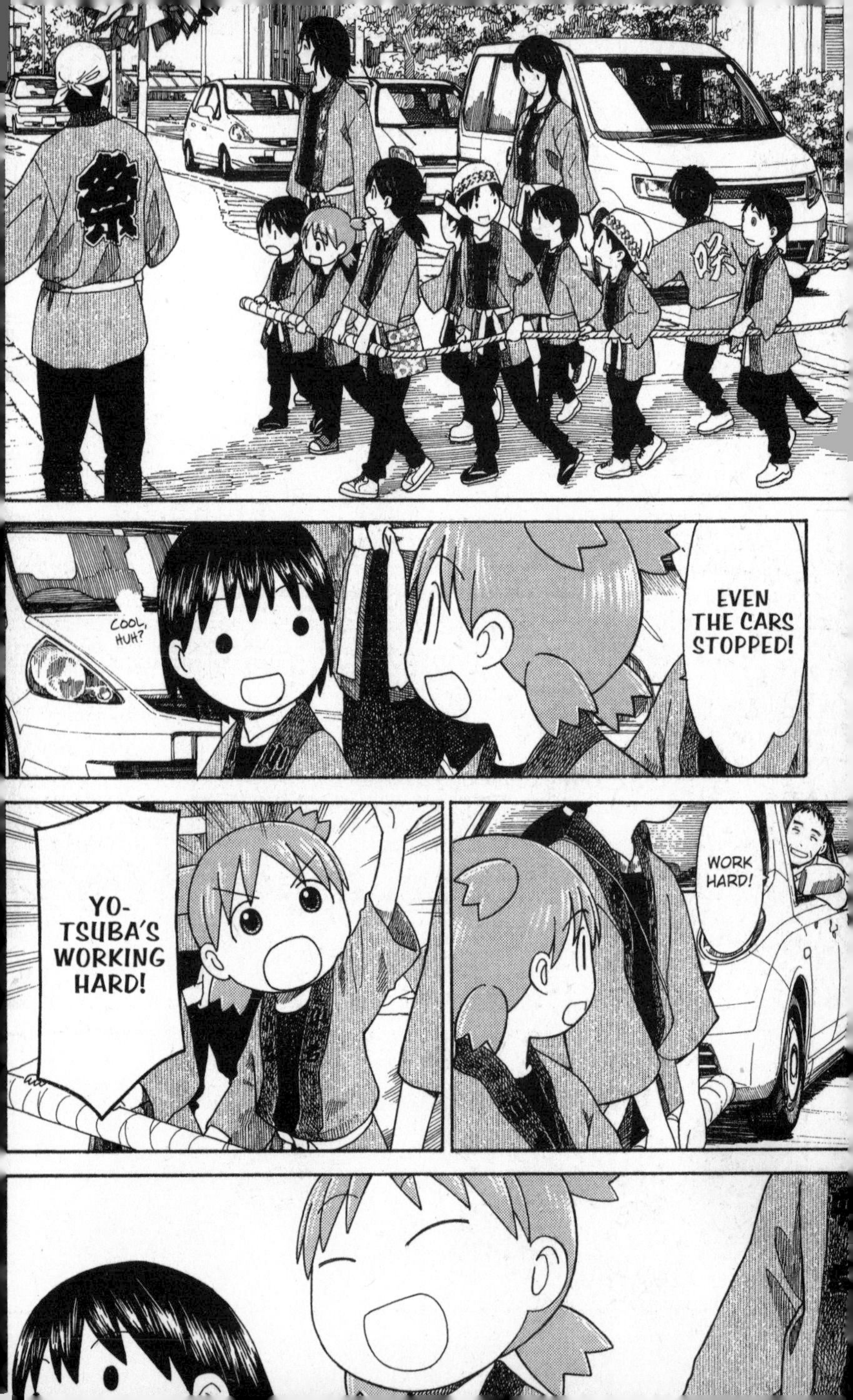
EVEN THE CARS STOPPED!
COOL, HUH?
WORK HARD!
YO-TSUBA'S WORKING HARD!

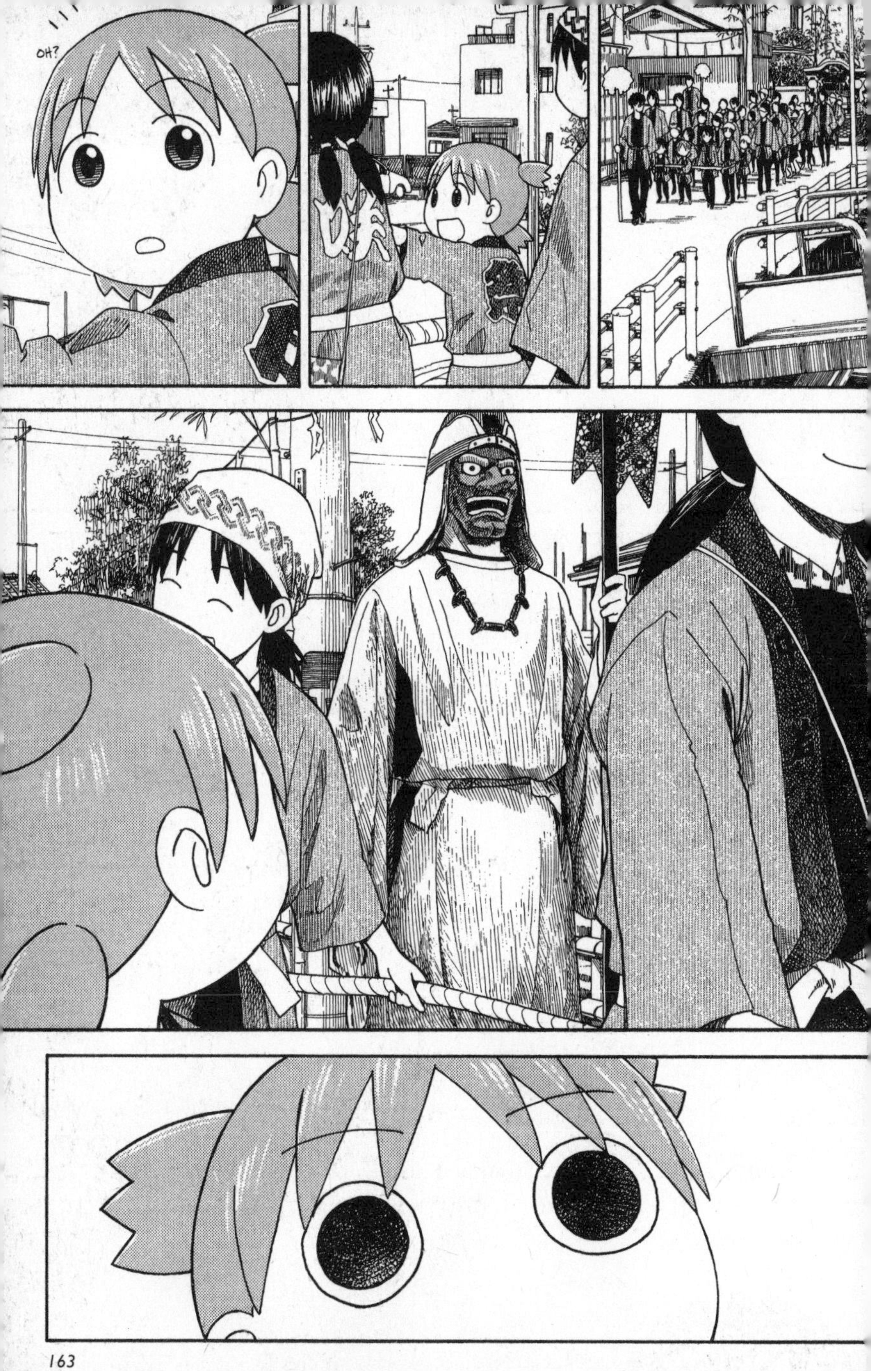
OH?

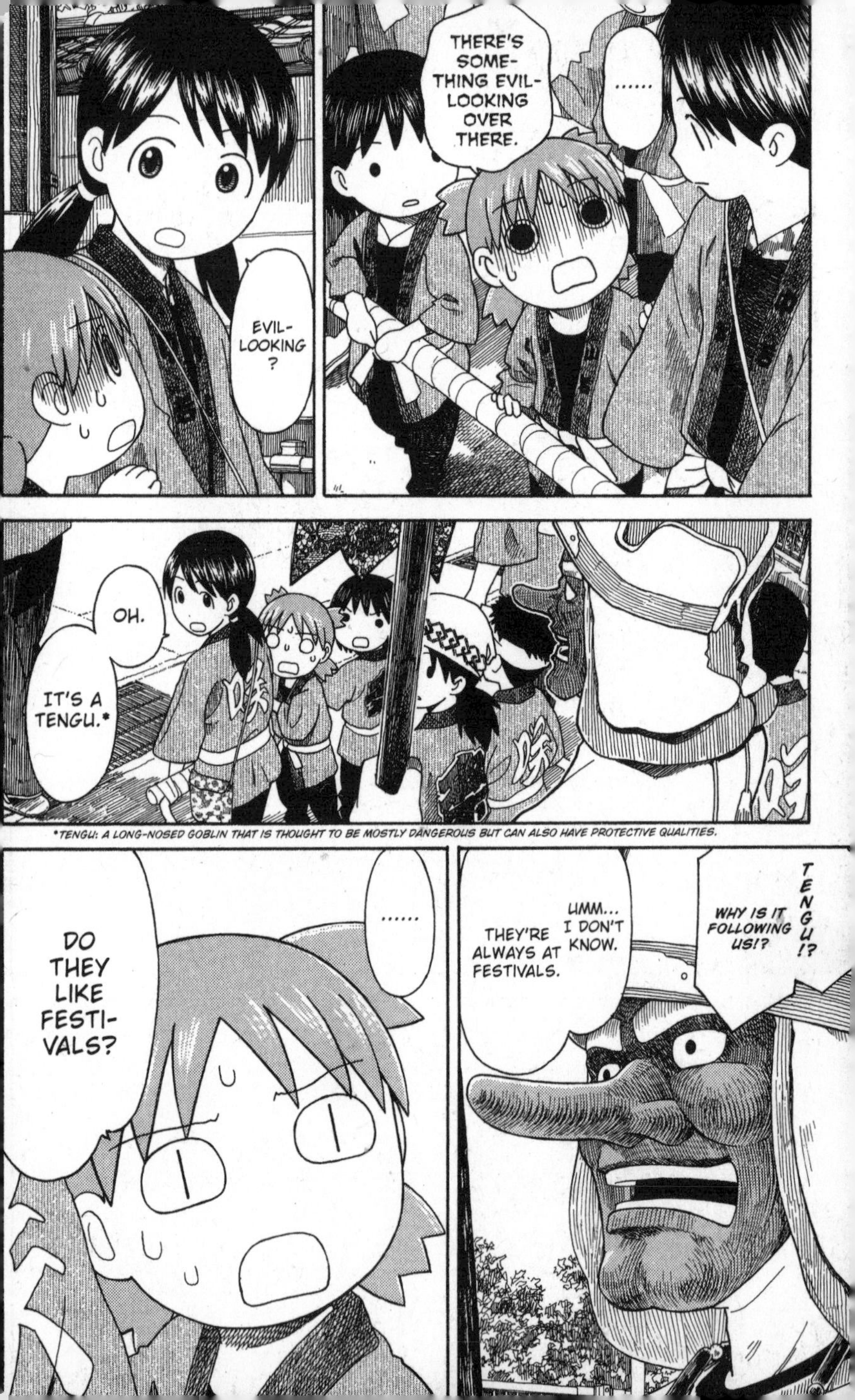
......
THERE'S SOME-THING EVIL-LOOKING OVER THERE.
EVIL-LOOKING?
OH.
IT'S A TENGU.*
TENGU!?
WHY IS IT FOLLOWING US!?
UMM... I DON'T KNOW.
THEY'RE ALWAYS AT FESTIVALS.
......
DO THEY LIKE FESTI-VALS?

*TENGU: A LONG-NOSED GOBLIN THAT IS THOUGHT TO BE MOSTLY DANGEROUS BUT CAN ALSO HAVE PROTECTIVE QUALITIES.

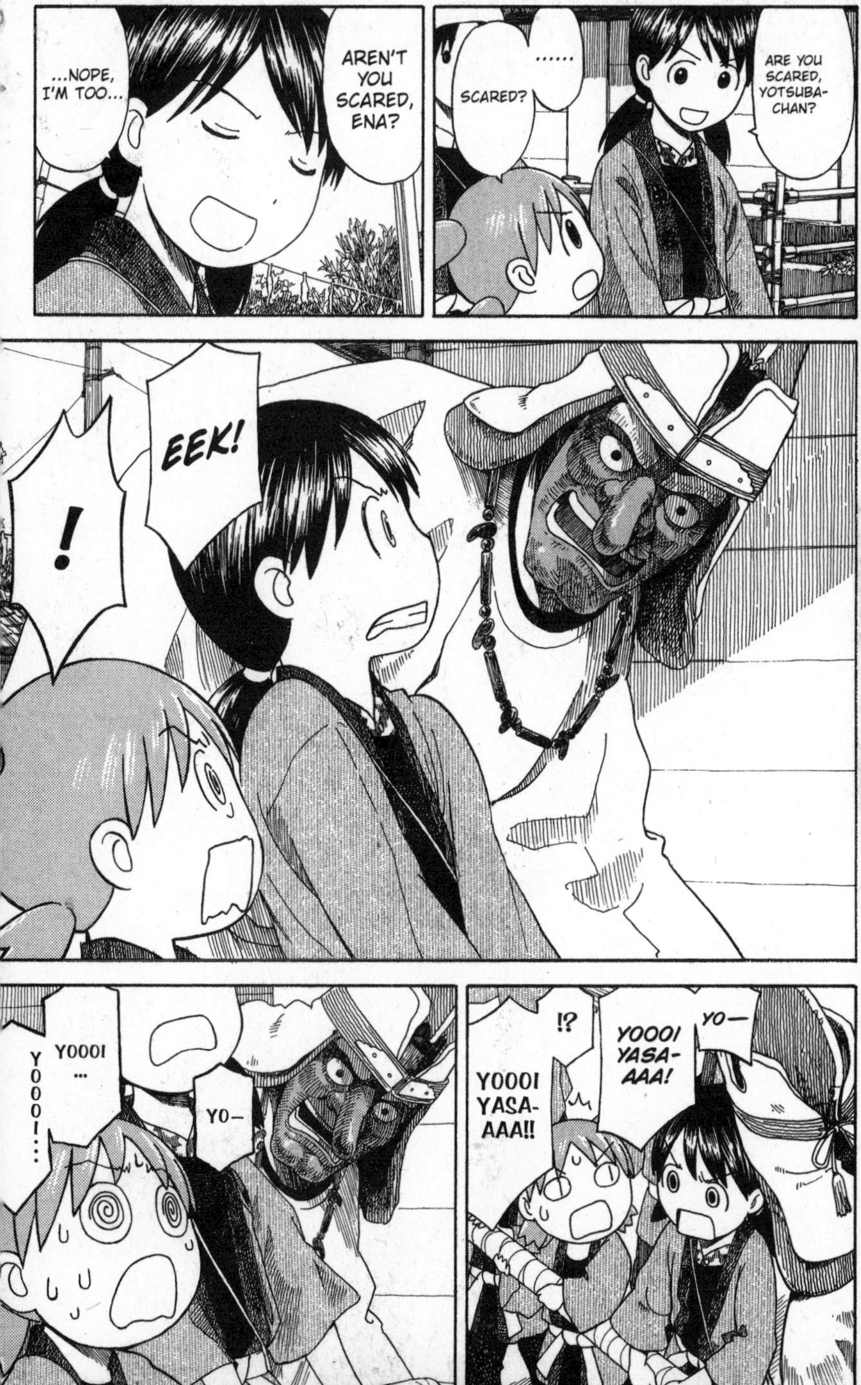

ARE YOU SCARED, YOTSUBA-CHAN?
......
SCARED?
AREN'T YOU SCARED, ENA?
...NOPE, I'M TOO...
EEK!
!
YO—
YOOOI YASA-AAA!
!?
YOOOI YASA-AAA!!
YO—
YOOOI ...
YOOOOI...

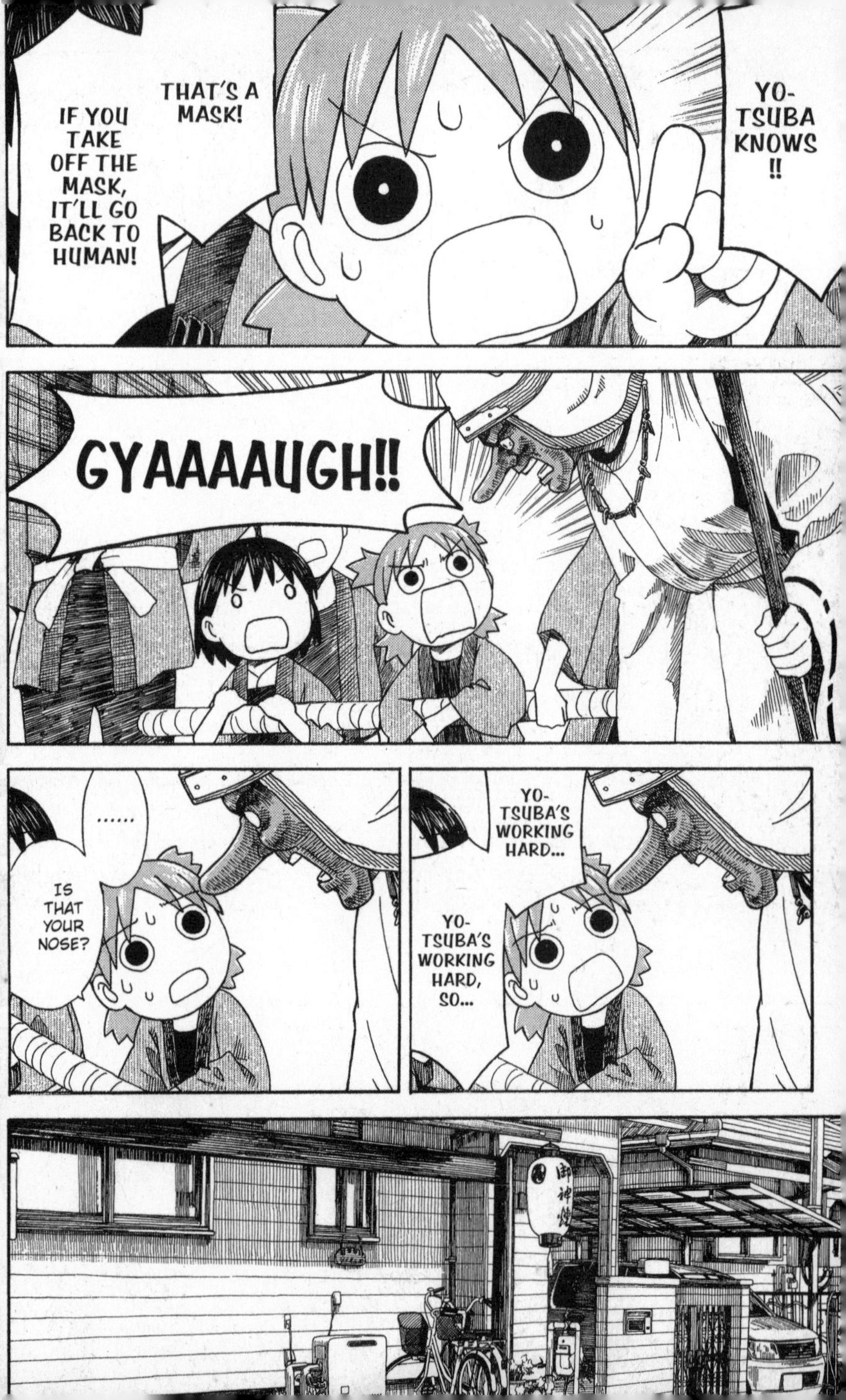
YO-TSUBA KNOWS!!
THAT'S A MASK!
IF YOU TAKE OFF THE MASK, IT'LL GO BACK TO HUMAN!
GYAAAAUGH!!
YO-TSUBA'S WORKING HARD...
YO-TSUBA'S WORKING HARD, SO...
......
IS THAT YOUR NOSE?

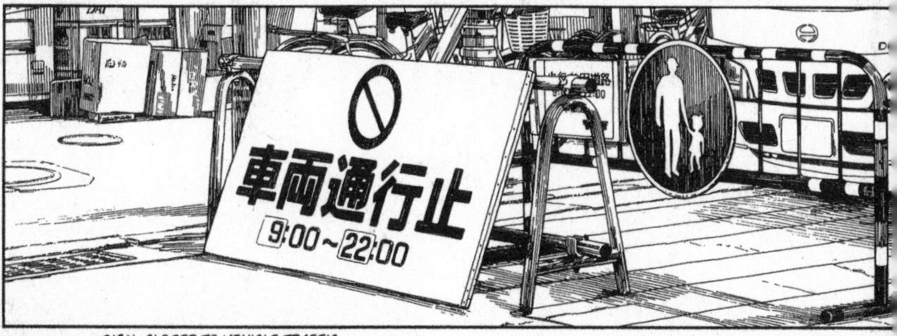
車両通行止
9:00~22:00
SIGN: CLOSED TO VEHICLE TRAFFIC

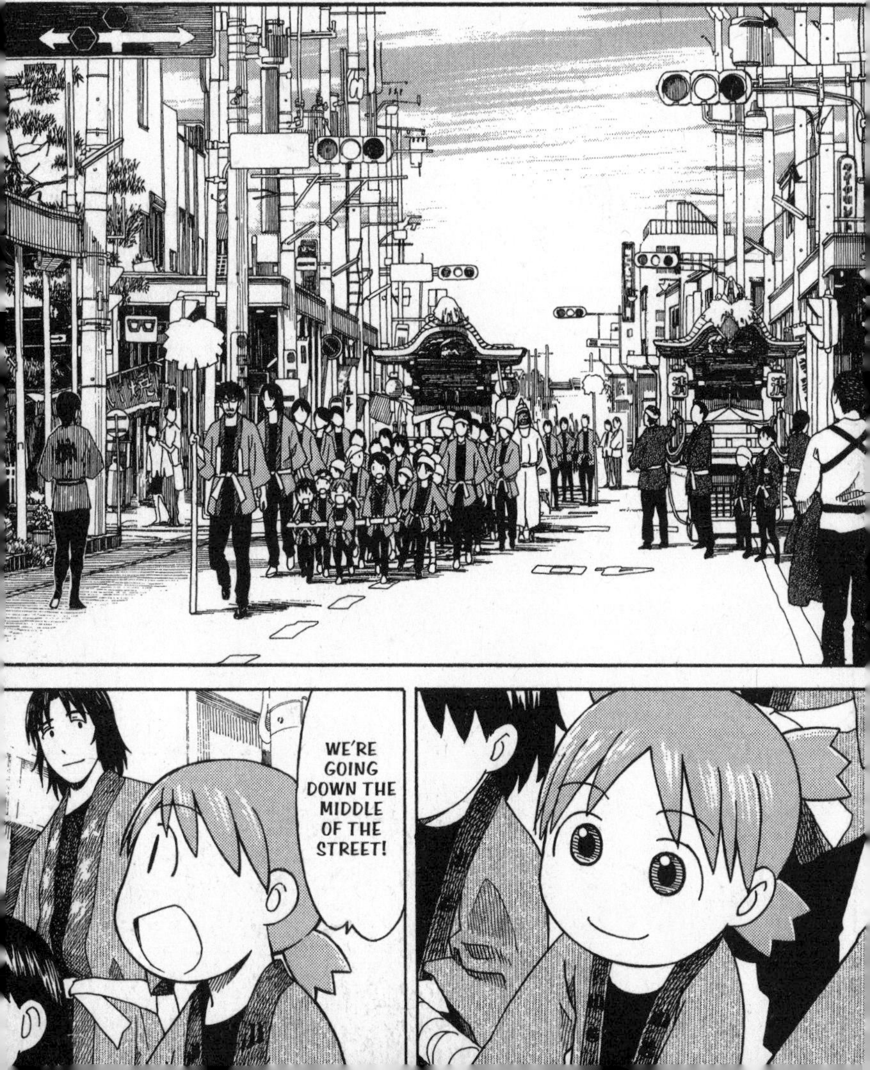
WE'RE GOING DOWN THE MIDDLE OF THE STREET!

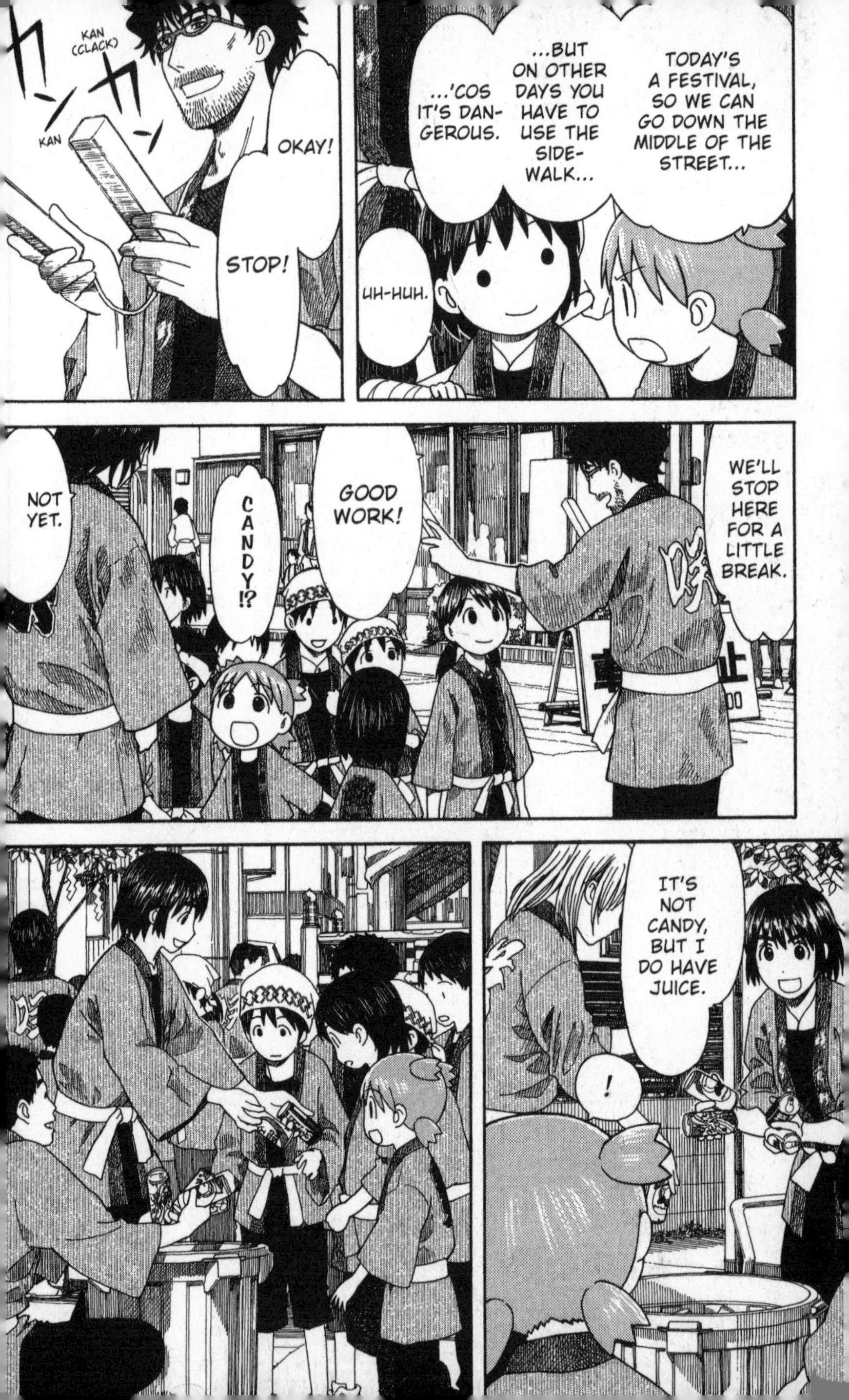
TODAY'S A FESTIVAL, SO WE CAN GO DOWN THE MIDDLE OF THE STREET...
...BUT ON OTHER DAYS YOU HAVE TO USE THE SIDE-WALK...
...'COS IT'S DAN-GEROUS.
UH-HUH.
OKAY!
STOP!
KAN (CLACK)
KAN
WE'LL STOP HERE FOR A LITTLE BREAK.
GOOD WORK!
CANDY!?
NOT YET.
IT'S NOT CANDY, BUT I DO HAVE JUICE.
!

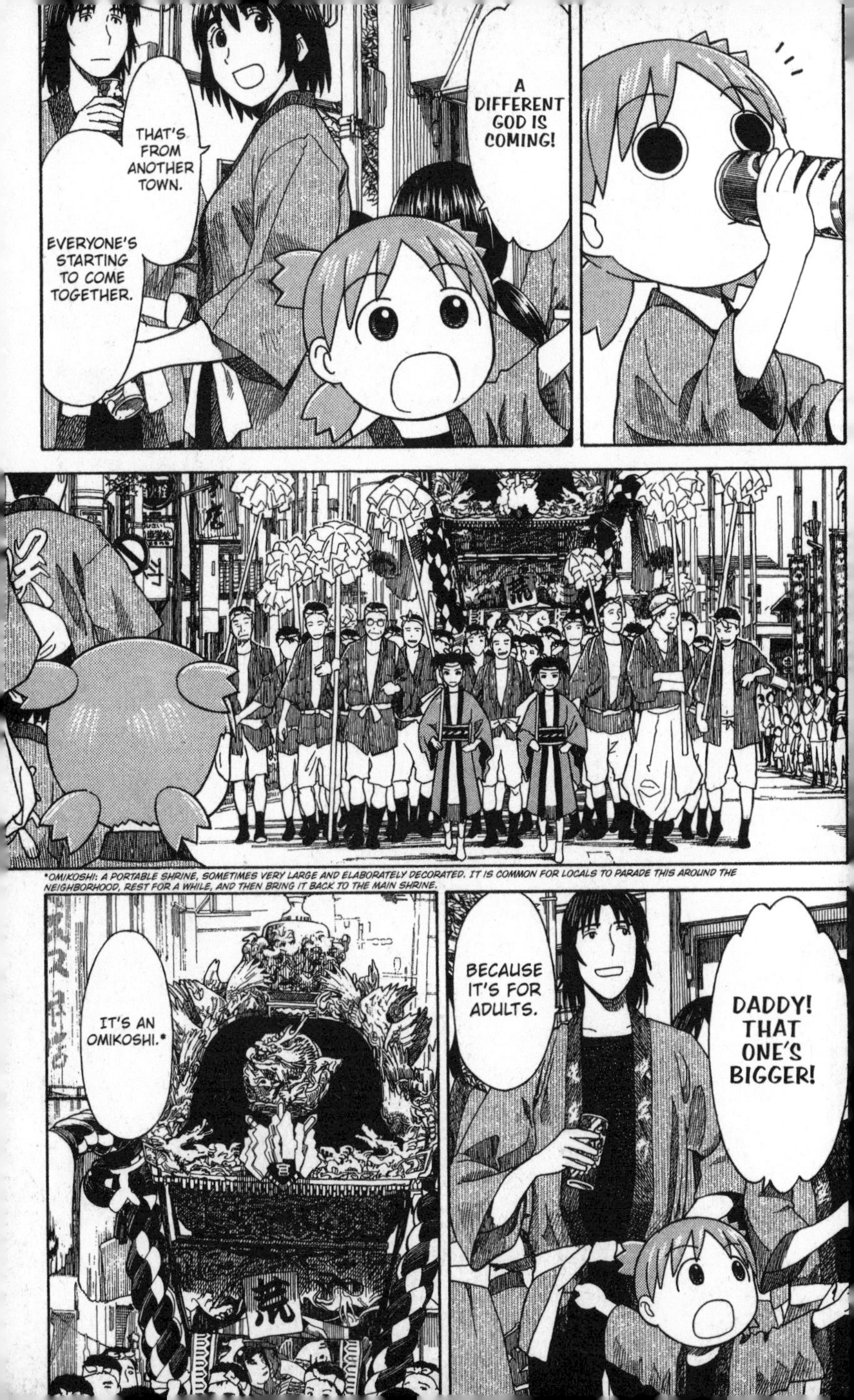
A DIFFERENT GOD IS COMING!
THAT'S FROM ANOTHER TOWN.
EVERYONE'S STARTING TO COME TOGETHER.
DADDY! THAT ONE'S BIGGER!
BECAUSE IT'S FOR ADULTS.
IT'S AN OMIKOSHI.*

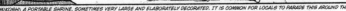

*OMIKOSHI: A PORTABLE SHRINE, SOMETIMES VERY LARGE AND ELABORATELY DECORATED. IT IS COMMON FOR LOCALS TO PARADE THIS AROUND THE NEIGHBORHOOD, REST FOR A WHILE, AND THEN BRING IT BACK TO THE MAIN SHRINE.

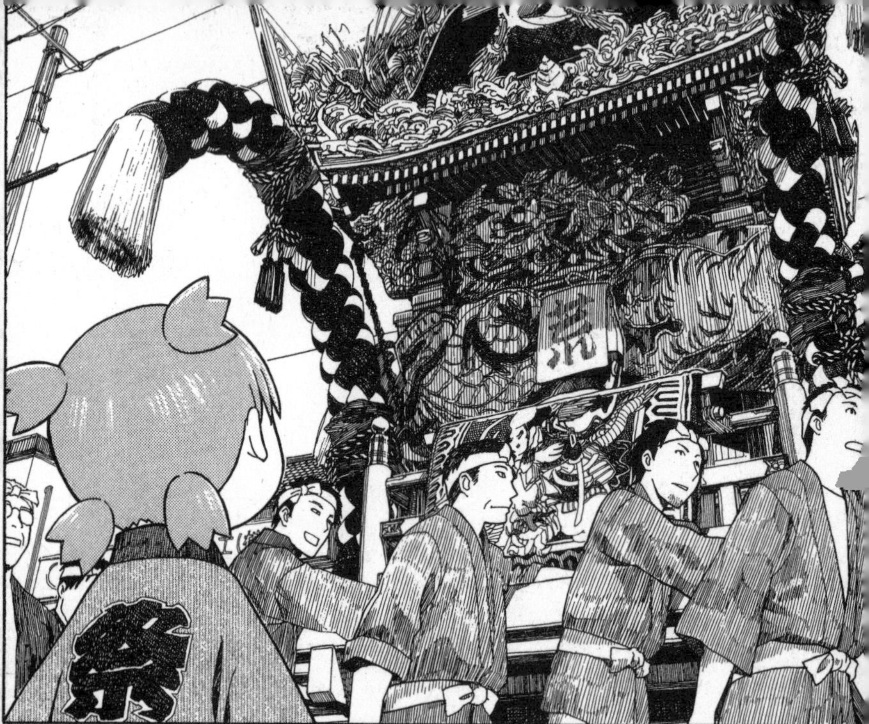
*THE CHARACTER SEEN ON THE OMIKOSHI IS TYPICALLY THE FIRST CHARACTER IN THE TOWN'S NAME.

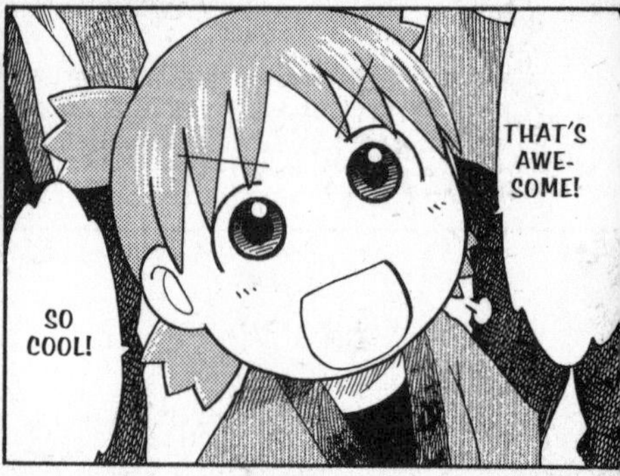
THAT'S AWE-SOME!
SO COOL!

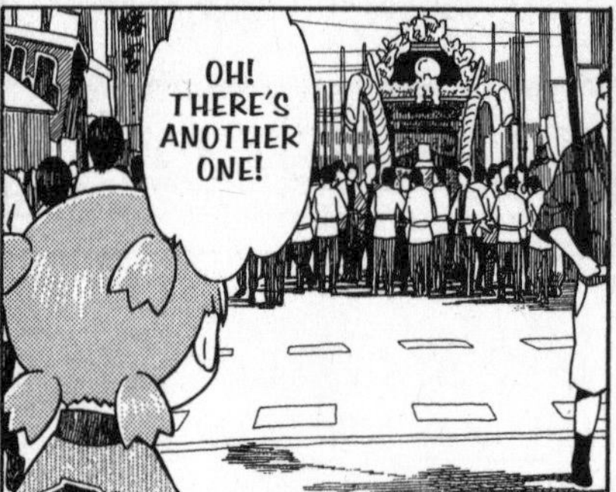
OH! THERE'S ANOTHER ONE!

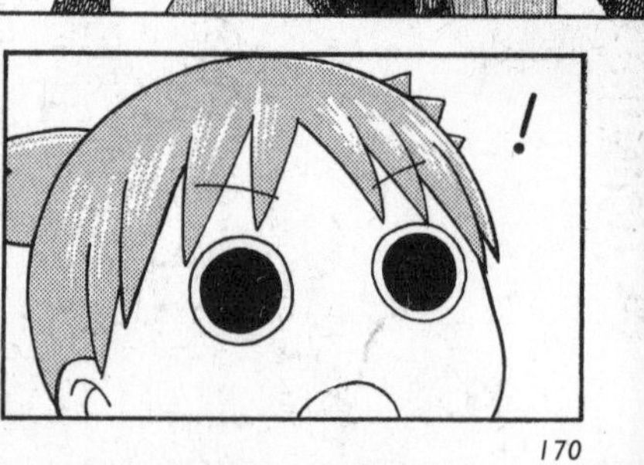
!

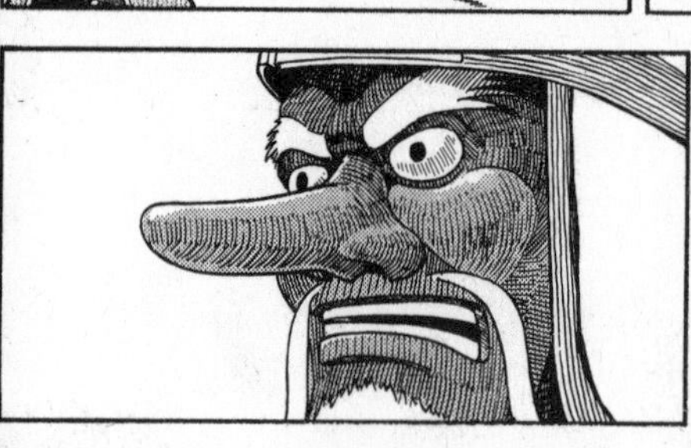

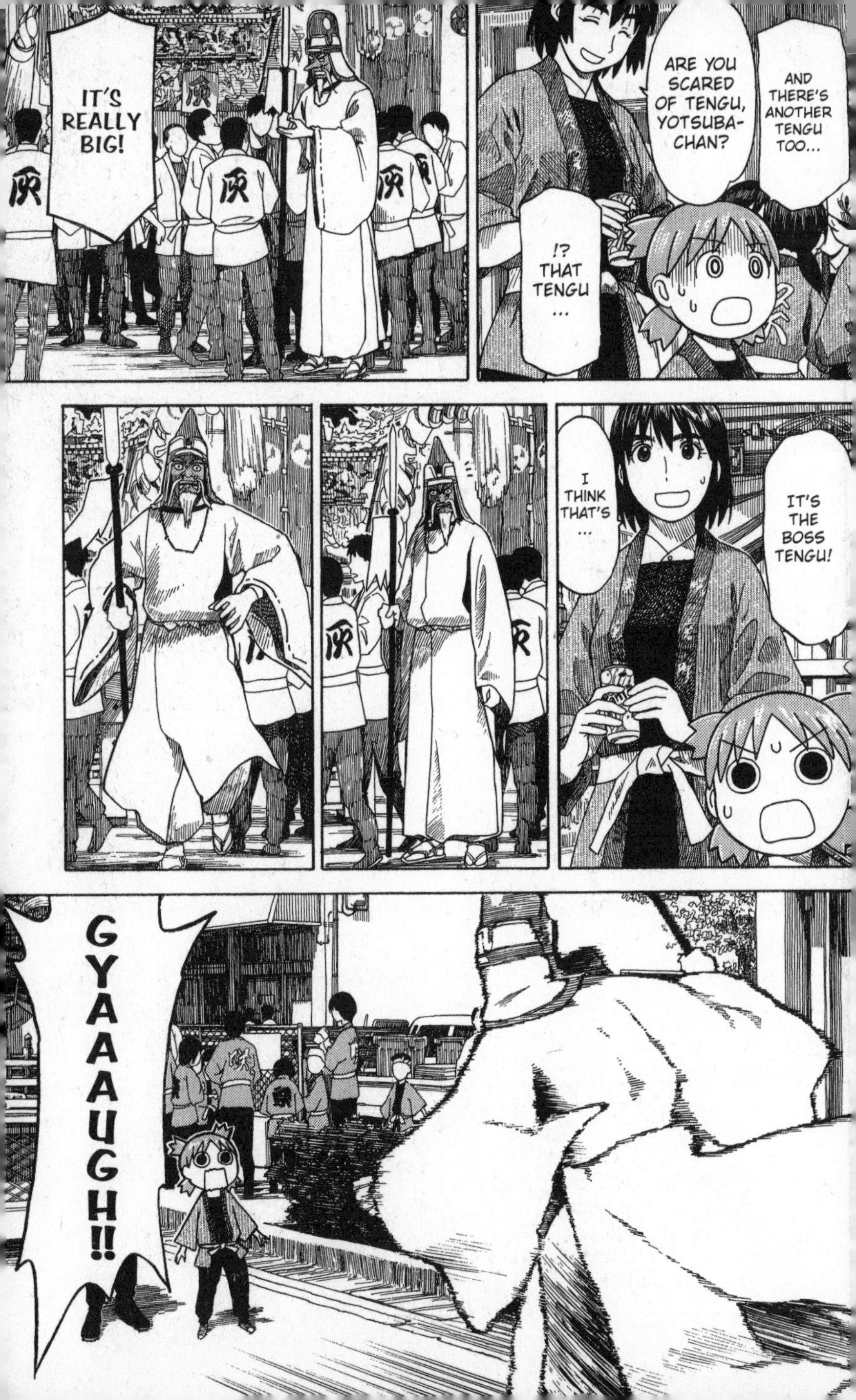
AND THERE'S ANOTHER TENGU TOO...
ARE YOU SCARED OF TENGU, YOTSUBA-CHAN?
!? THAT TENGU ...
IT'S REALLY BIG!
IT'S THE BOSS TENGU!
I THINK THAT'S ...
GYAAAUGH!!

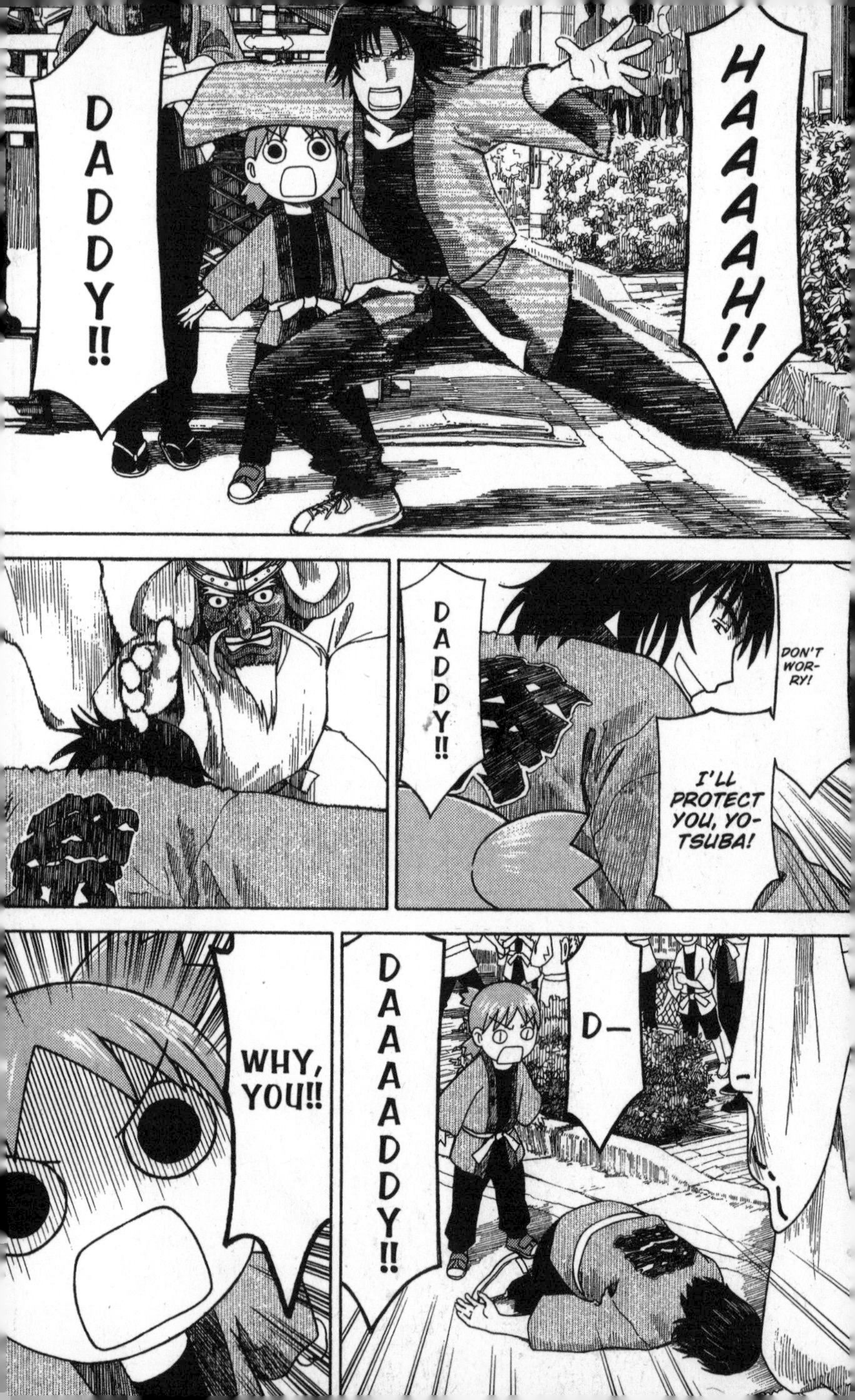
HAAAAAH!!
DADDY!!
DON'T WOR-RY!
I'LL PROTECT YOU, YO-TSUBA!
DADDDY!!
D—
DAAAAADDY!!
WHY, YOU!!

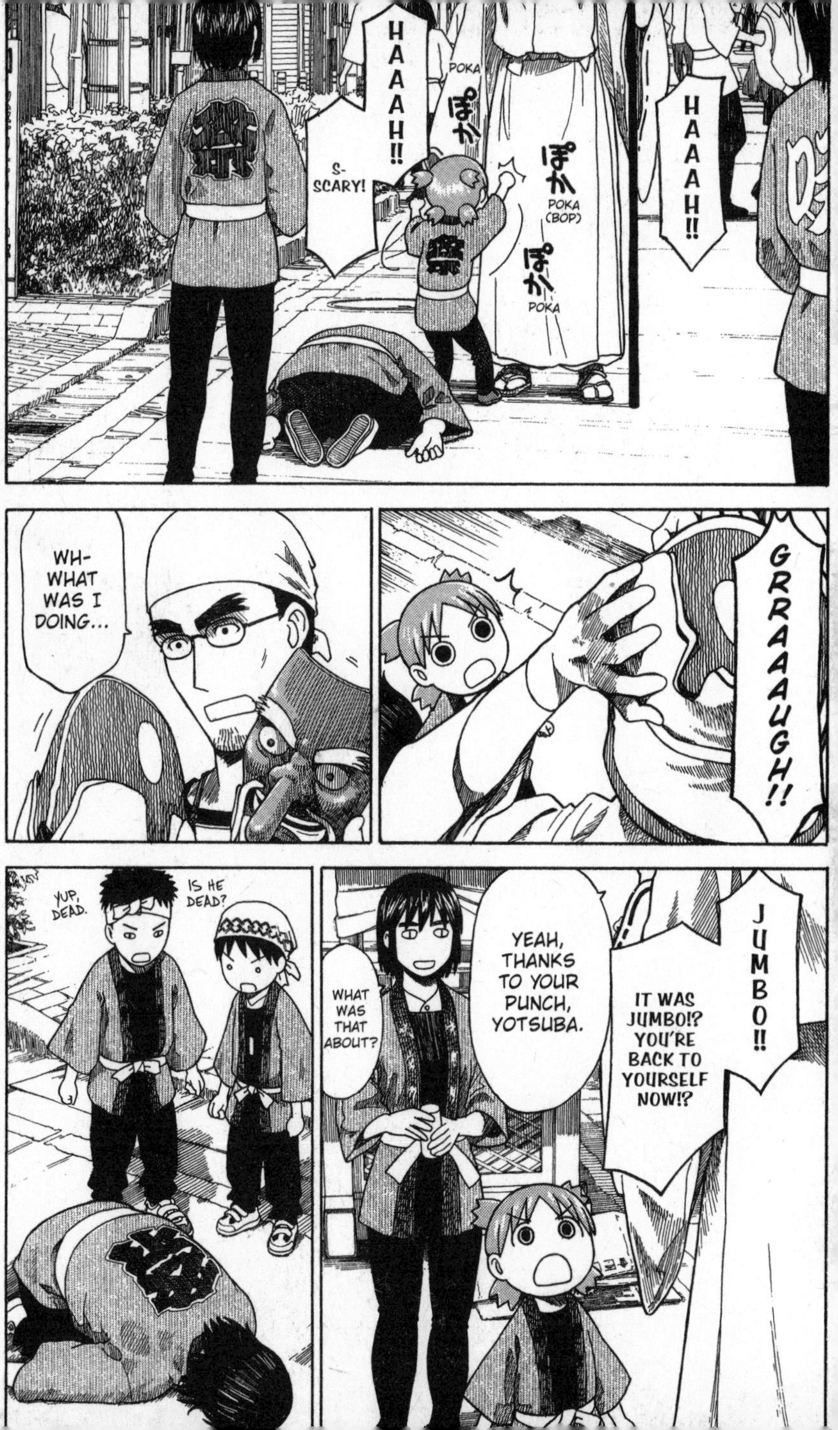
HAAAAH!!
ぽか
POKA (BOP)
ぽか
POKA
POKA
ぽか
HAAAAH!!
S-SCARY!
GRRAAAAUGH!!
WH-WHAT WAS I DOING...
JUMBO!!
IT WAS JUMBO!? YOU'RE BACK TO YOURSELF NOW!?
YEAH, THANKS TO YOUR PUNCH, YOTSUBA.
WHAT WAS THAT ABOUT?
IS HE DEAD?
YUP, DEAD.

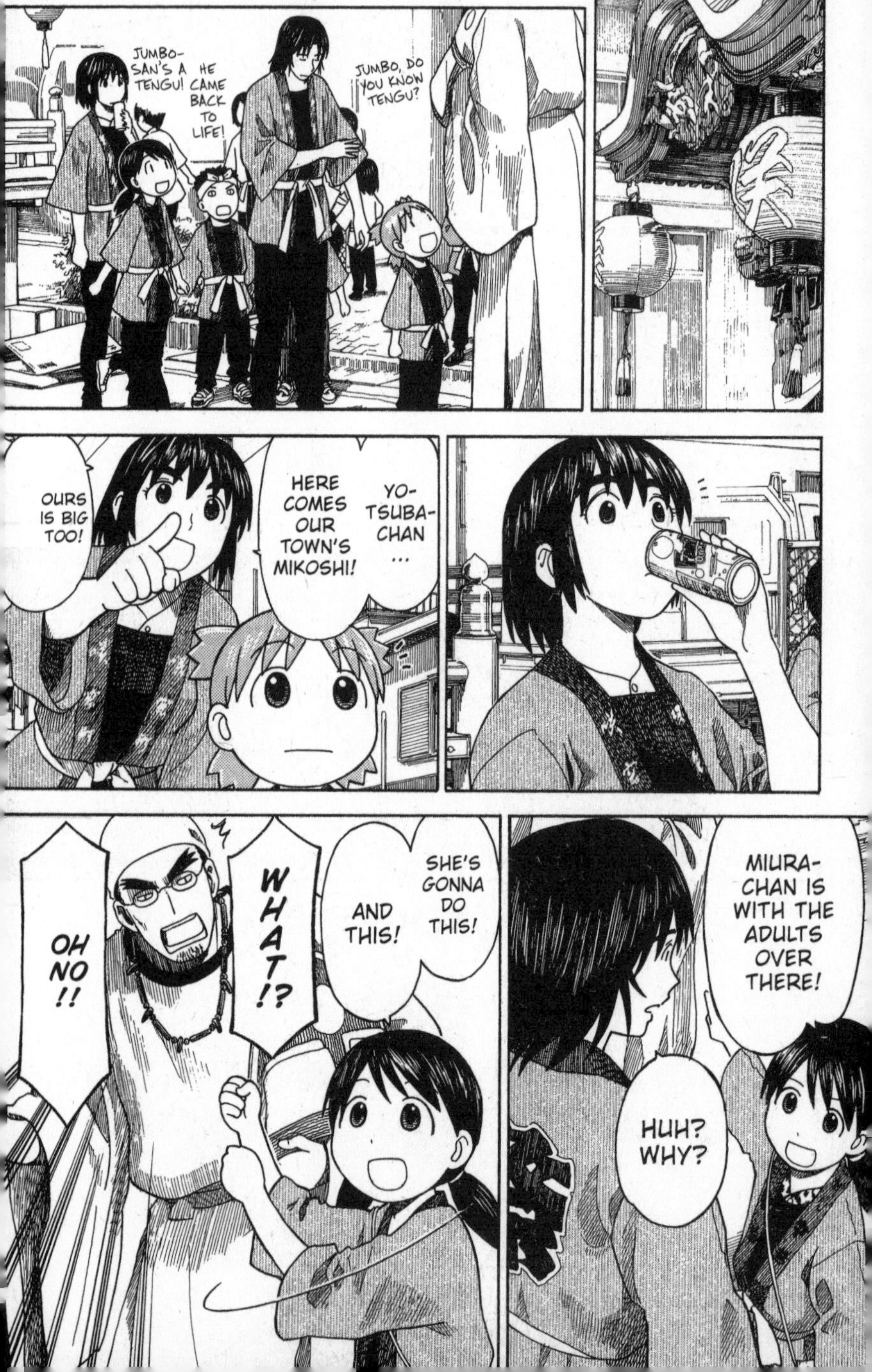
JUMBO, DO YOU KNOW TENGU?
JUMBO-SAN'S A TENGU!
HE CAME BACK TO LIFE!
YO-TSUBA-CHAN ...
HERE COMES OUR TOWN'S MIKOSHI!
OURS IS BIG TOO!
MIURA-CHAN IS WITH THE ADULTS OVER THERE!
HUH? WHY?
SHE'S GONNA DO THIS!
AND THIS!
WHAT!?
OH NO!!

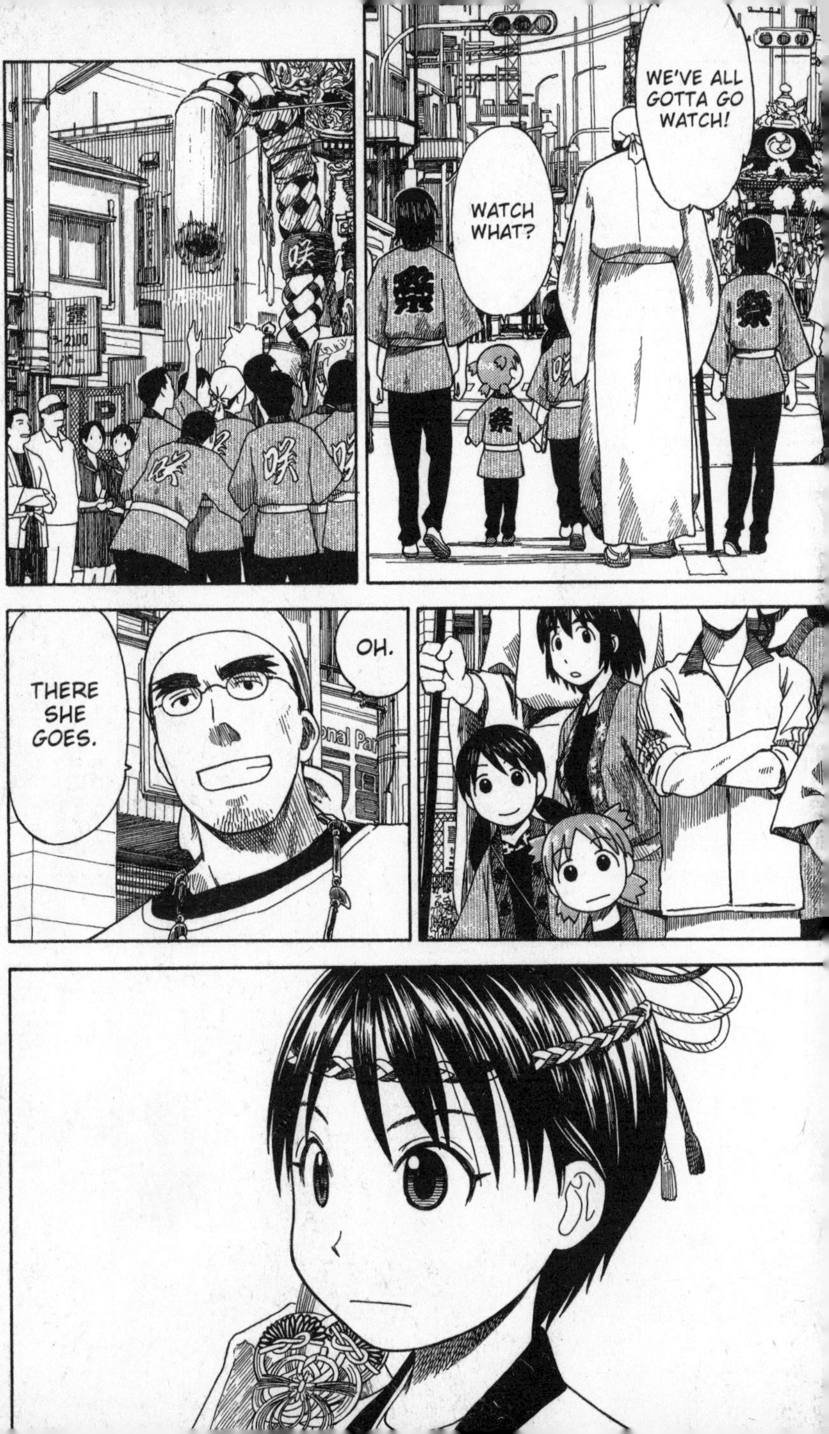
WE'VE ALL GOTTA GO WATCH!
WATCH WHAT?
OH.
THERE SHE GOES.

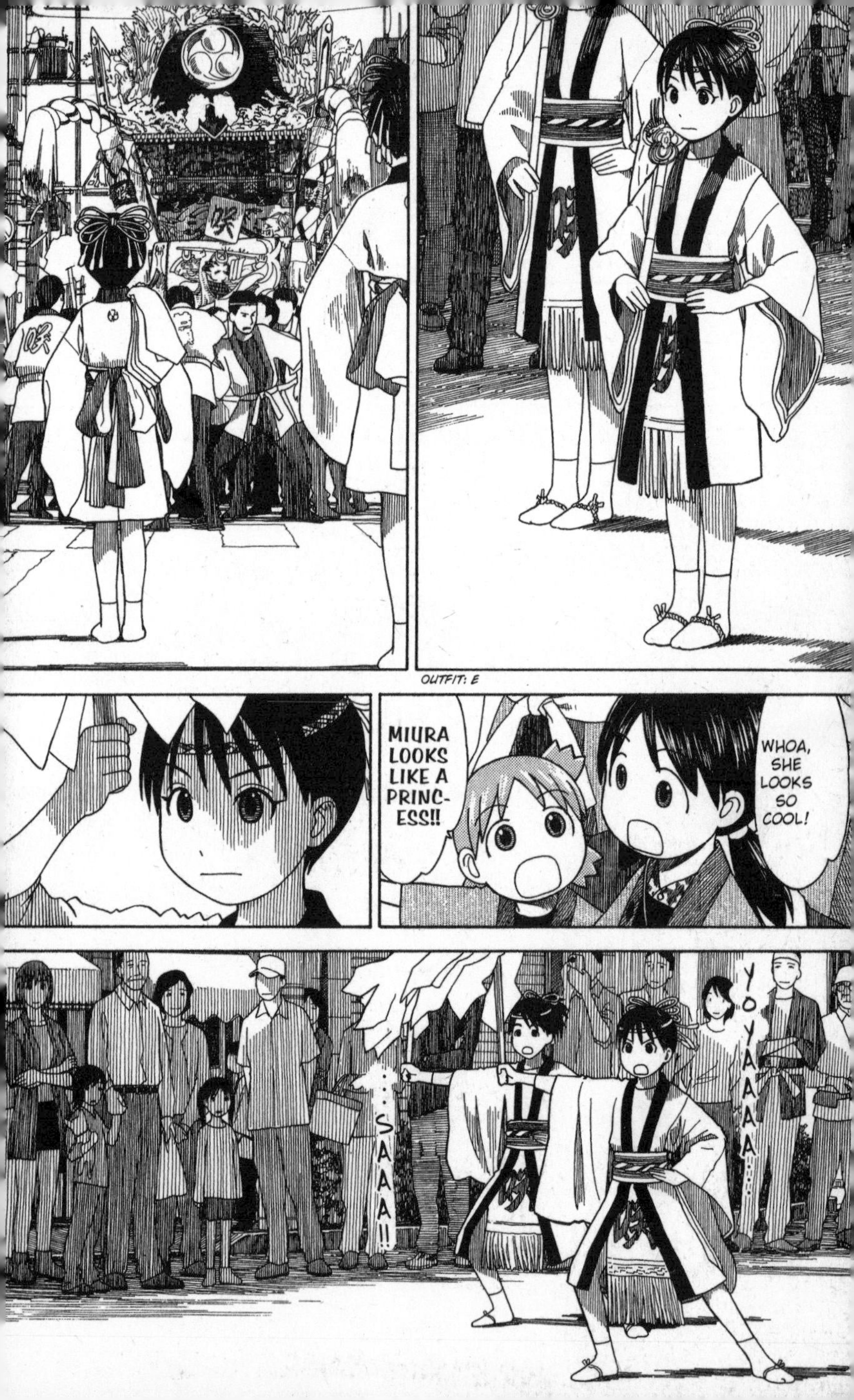
OUTFIT: E
WHOA, SHE LOOKS SO COOL!
MIURA LOOKS LIKE A PRINC-ESS!!
YOYAAAA...
...SAAAA!!

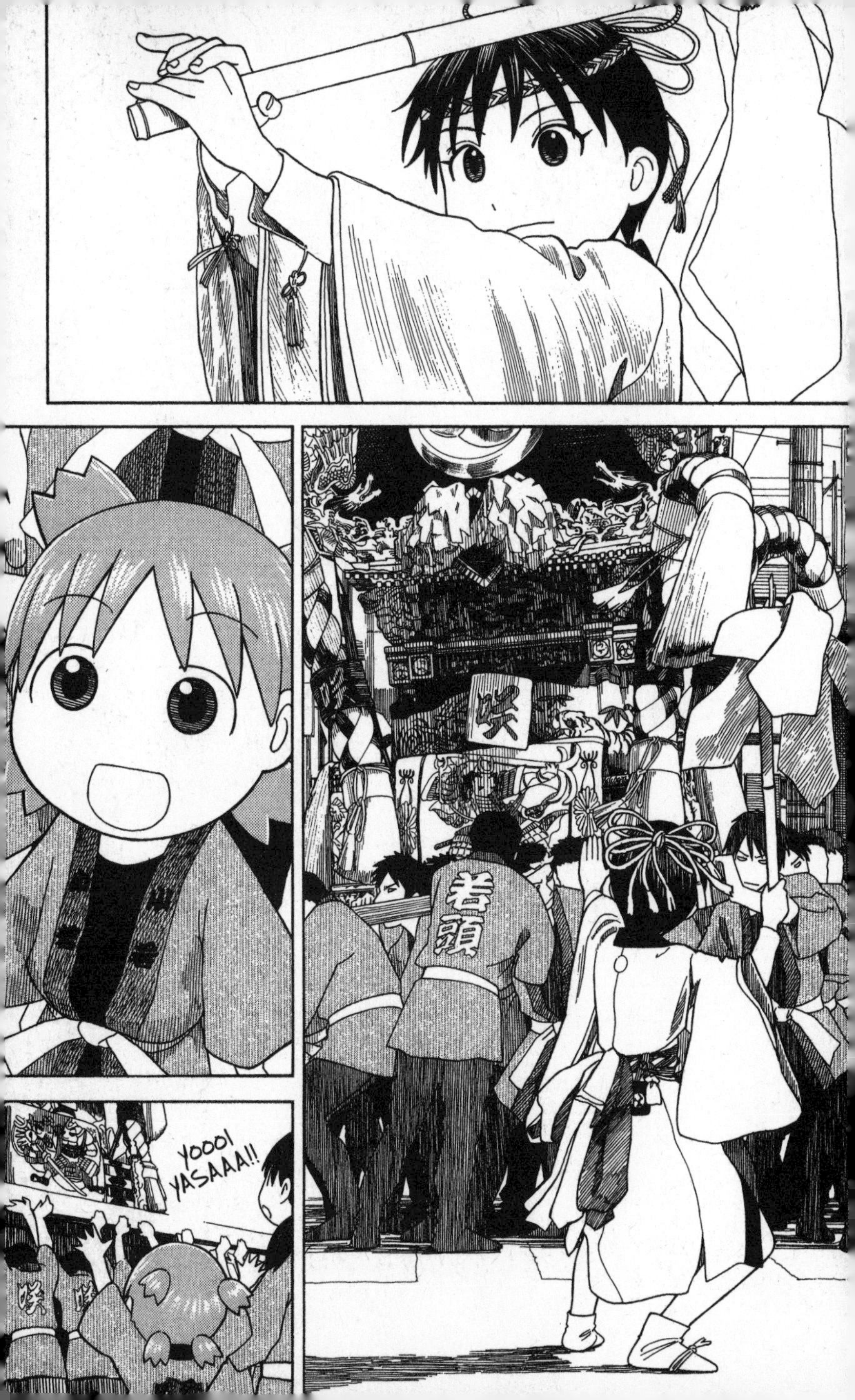
YOOOI YASAAA!!

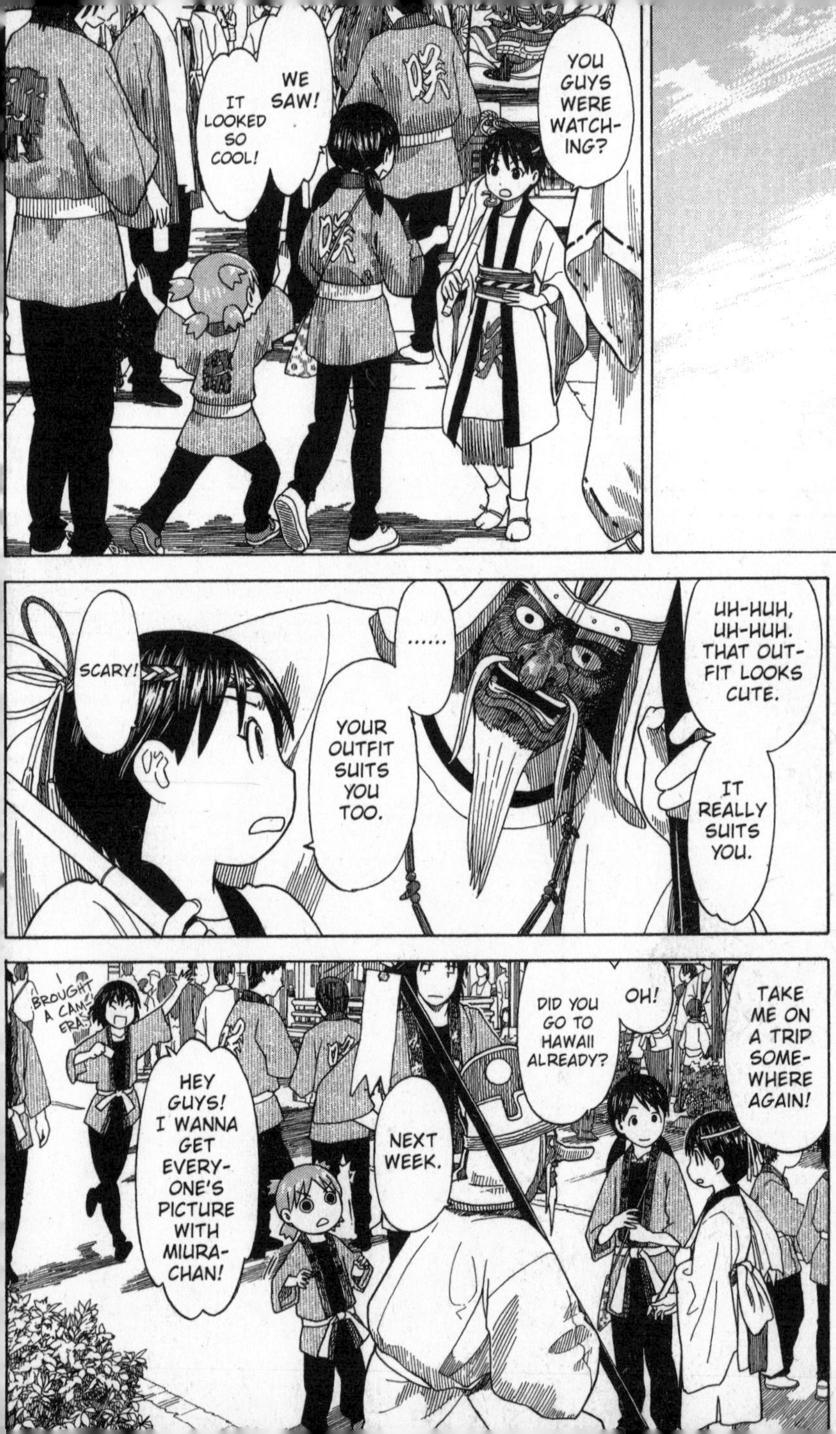
YOU GUYS WERE WATCHING?
WE SAW!
IT LOOKED SO COOL!
UH-HUH, UH-HUH. THAT OUTFIT LOOKS CUTE.
IT REALLY SUITS YOU.
......
YOUR OUTFIT SUITS YOU TOO.
SCARY!
TAKE ME ON A TRIP SOMEWHERE AGAIN!
OH!
DID YOU GO TO HAWAII ALREADY?
NEXT WEEK.
HEY GUYS! I WANNA GET EVERYONE'S PICTURE WITH MIURA-CHAN!
I BROUGHT A CAMERA!

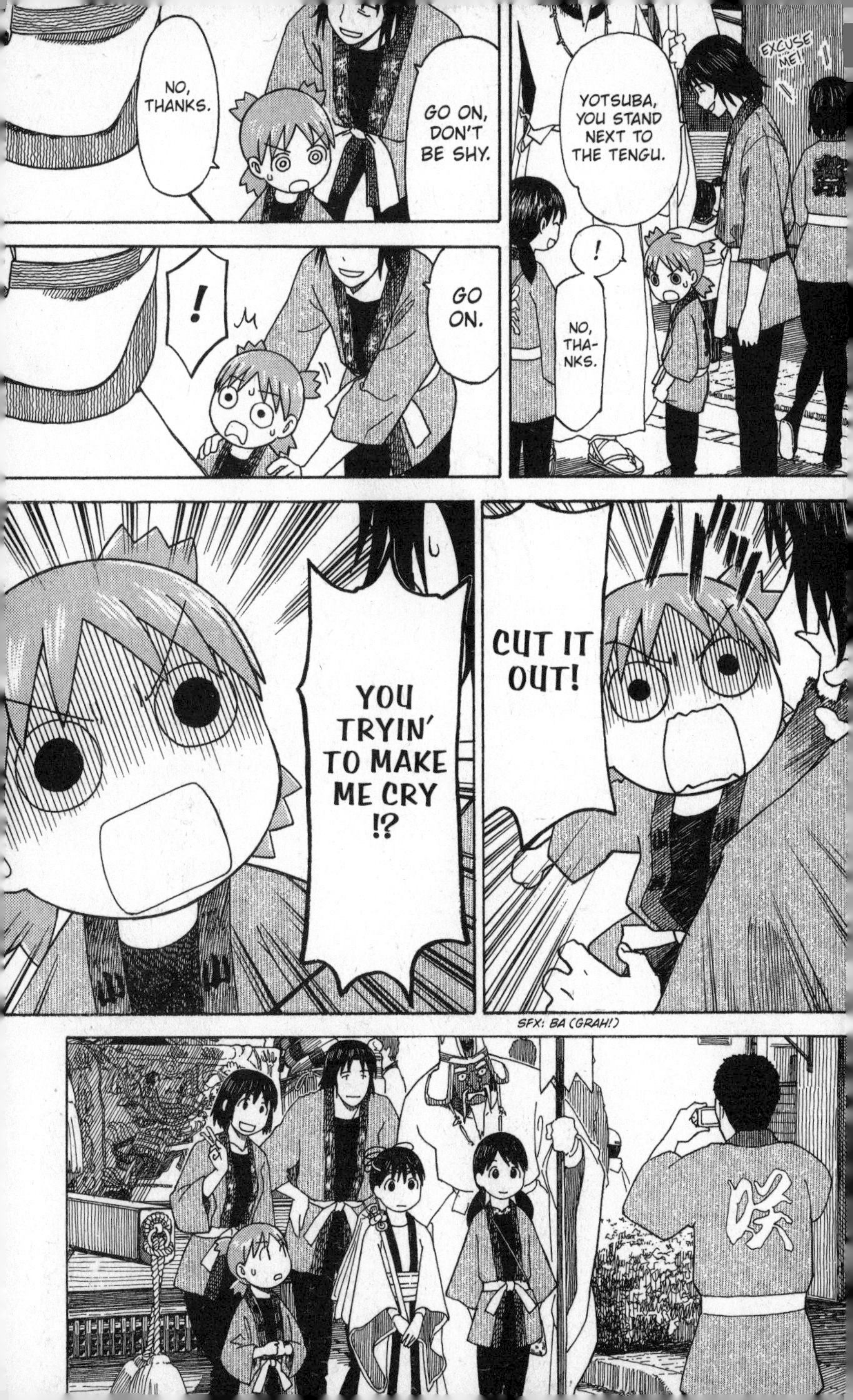
EXCUSE ME!
YOTSUBA, YOU STAND NEXT TO THE TENGU.
!
NO, THANKS.
GO ON, DON'T BE SHY.
NO, THANKS.
GO ON.
!
CUT IT OUT!
YOU TRYIN' TO MAKE ME CRY !?
SFX: BA (GRAH!)
咲

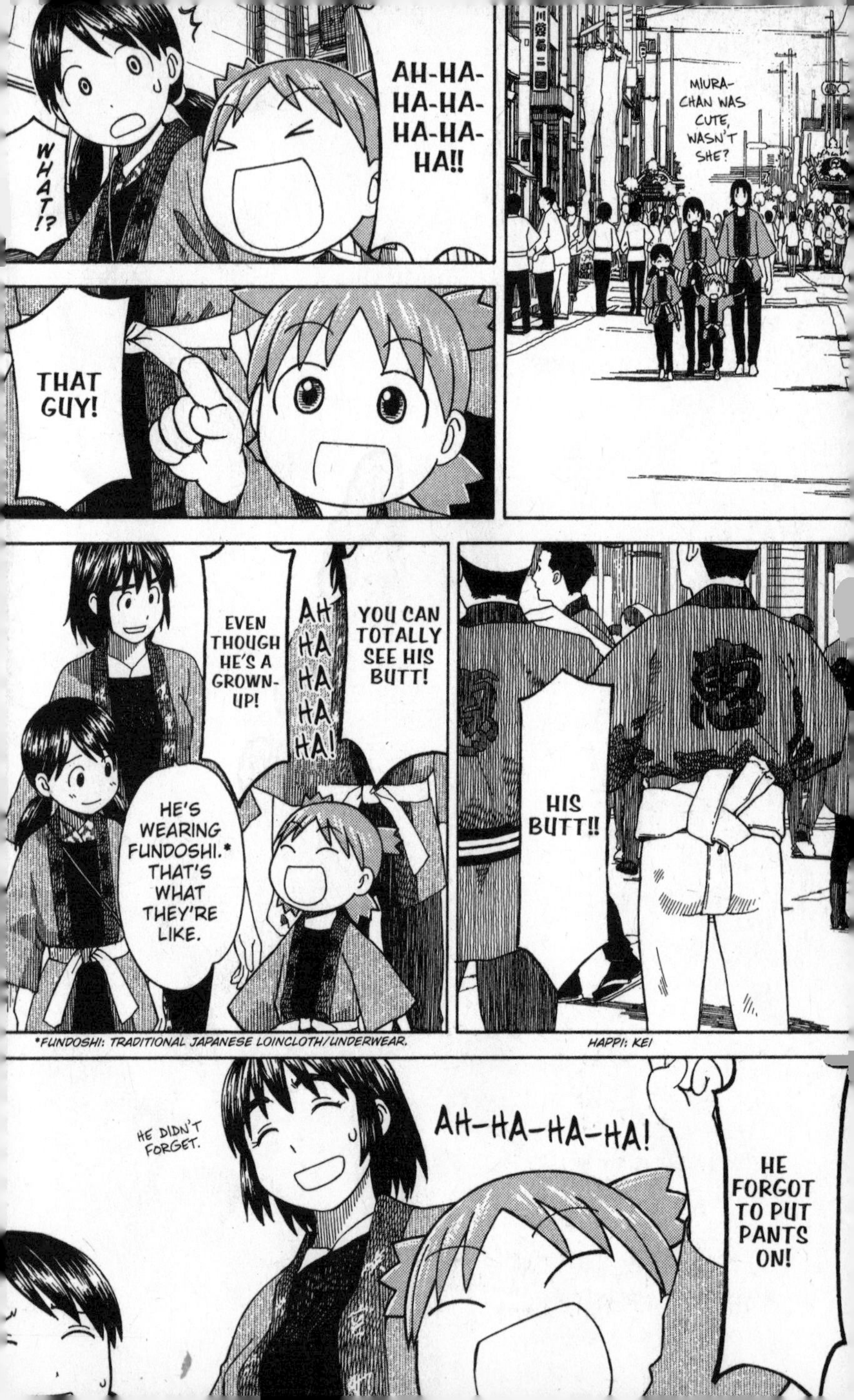
MIURA-CHAN WAS CUTE, WASN'T SHE?
AH-HA-HA-HA-HA-HA-HA!!
WHAT!?
THAT GUY!
HIS BUTT!!
YOU CAN TOTALLY SEE HIS BUTT!
AH HA HA HA HA!
EVEN THOUGH HE'S A GROWN-UP!
HE'S WEARING FUNDOSHI.* THAT'S WHAT THEY'RE LIKE.
HE FORGOT TO PUT PANTS ON!
AH-HA-HA-HA!
HE DIDN'T FORGET.

*FUNDOSHI: TRADITIONAL JAPANESE LOINCLOTH/UNDERWEAR.

HAPPI: KEI

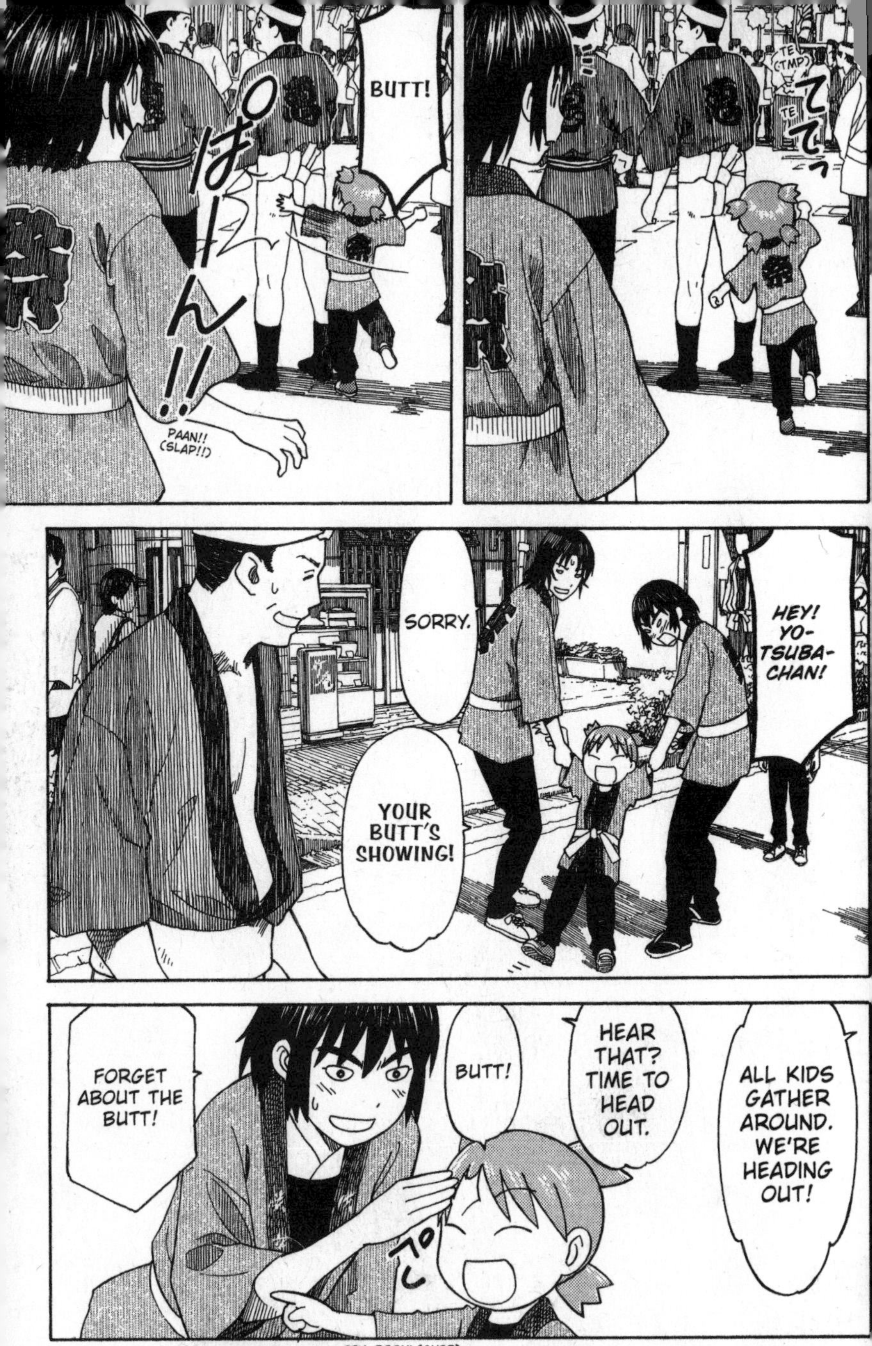
TE (TMP) TE TE
てて
BUTT!
ぱーん!!
PAAN!! (SLAP!!)
HEY! YO-TSUBA-CHAN!
SORRY.
YOUR BUTT'S SHOWING!
ALL KIDS GATHER AROUND. WE'RE HEADING OUT!
HEAR THAT? TIME TO HEAD OUT.
BUTT!
FORGET ABOUT THE BUTT!
ぺし
SFX: PESHI (CHOP)

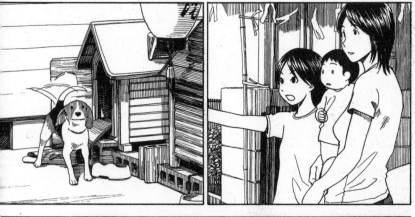

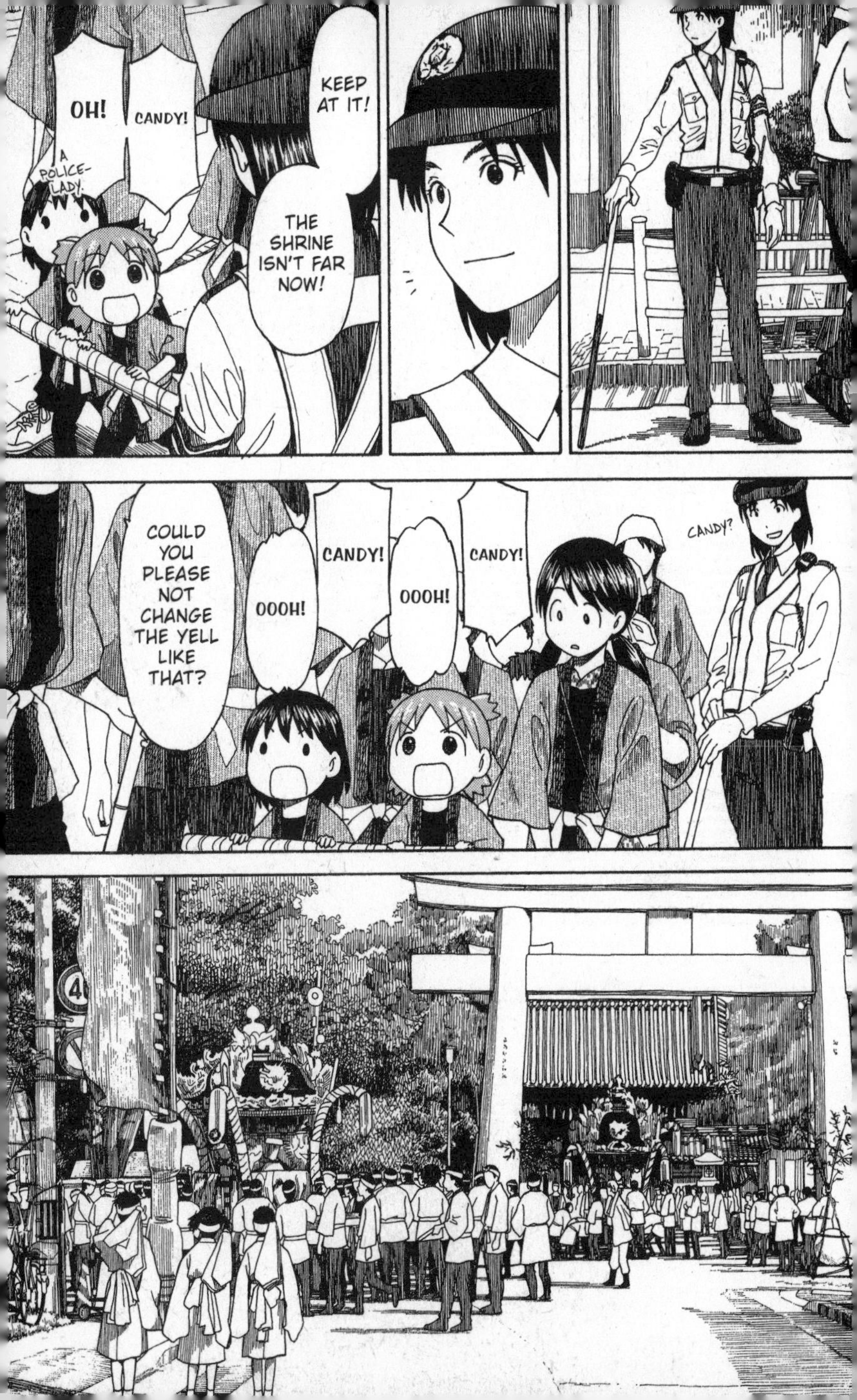
KEEP AT IT!
THE SHRINE ISN'T FAR NOW!
CANDY!
OH!
A POLICE-LADY.
CANDY?
CANDY!
OOOH!
CANDY!
OOOH!
COULD YOU PLEASE NOT CHANGE THE YELL LIKE THAT?

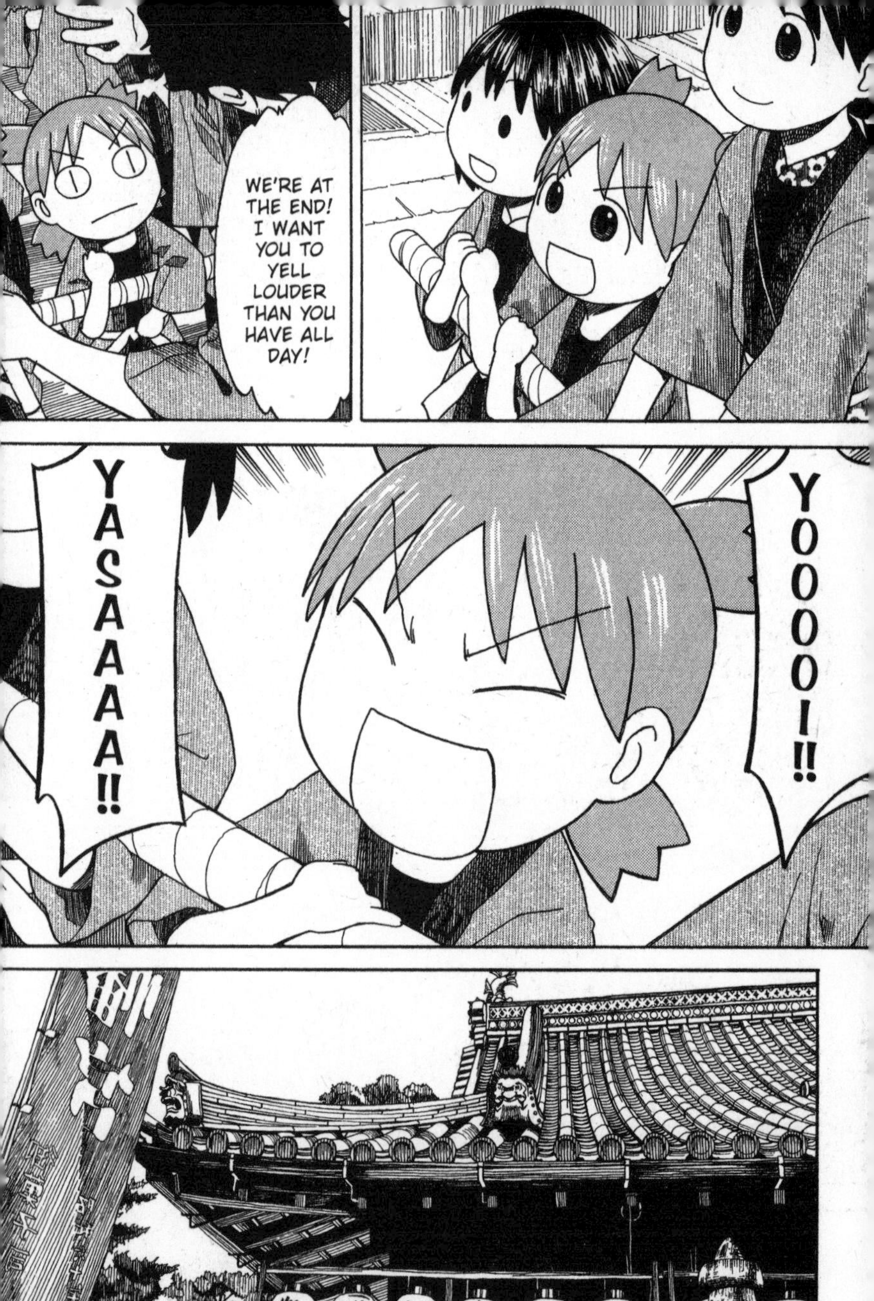
WE'RE AT THE END! I WANT YOU TO YELL LOUDER THAN YOU HAVE ALL DAY!
YOOOOOI!!
YASAAAAA!!

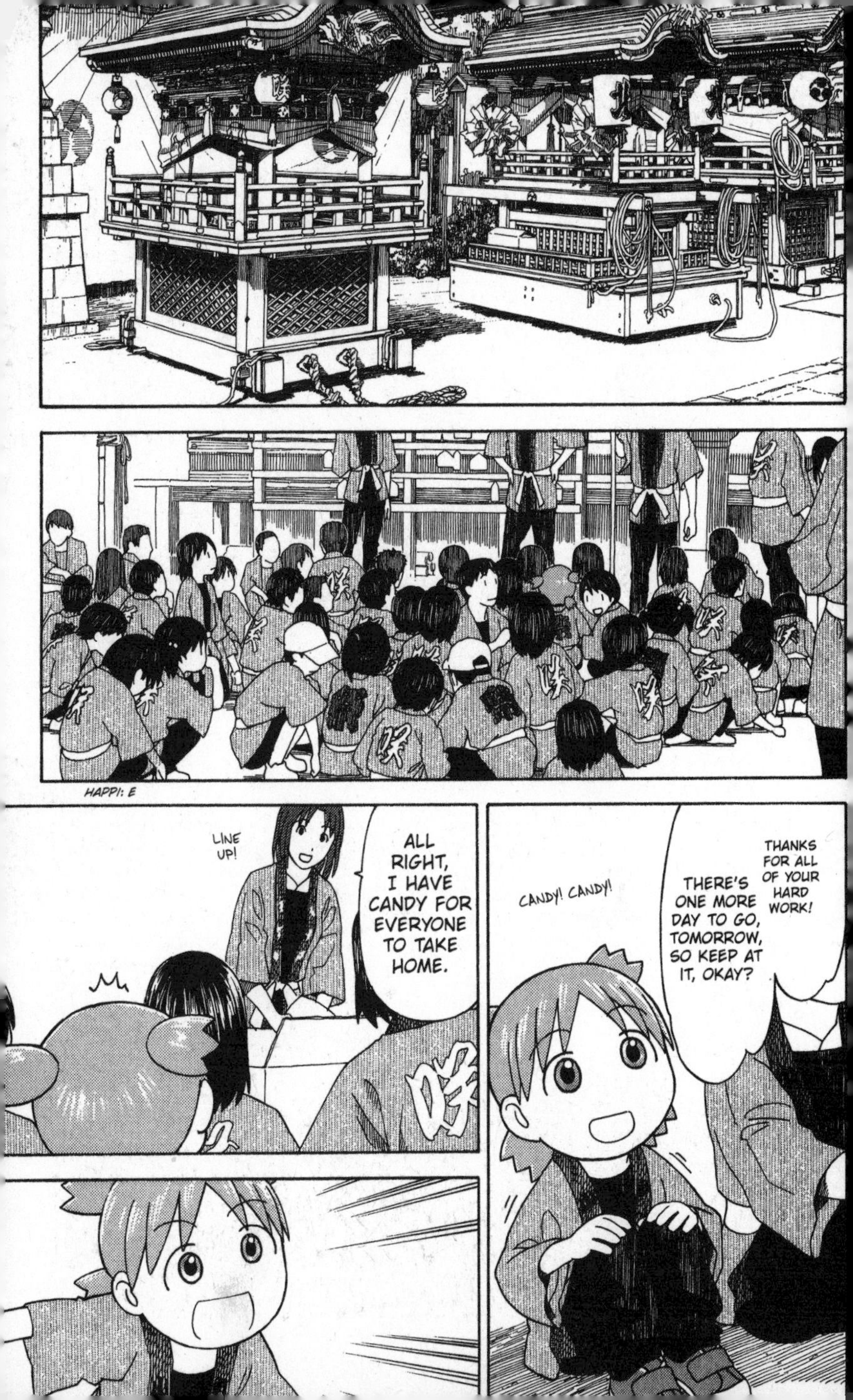
HAPPI: E
THANKS FOR ALL OF YOUR HARD WORK!
THERE'S ONE MORE DAY TO GO, TOMORROW, SO KEEP AT IT, OKAY?
CANDY! CANDY!
ALL RIGHT, I HAVE CANDY FOR EVERYONE TO TAKE HOME.
LINE UP!

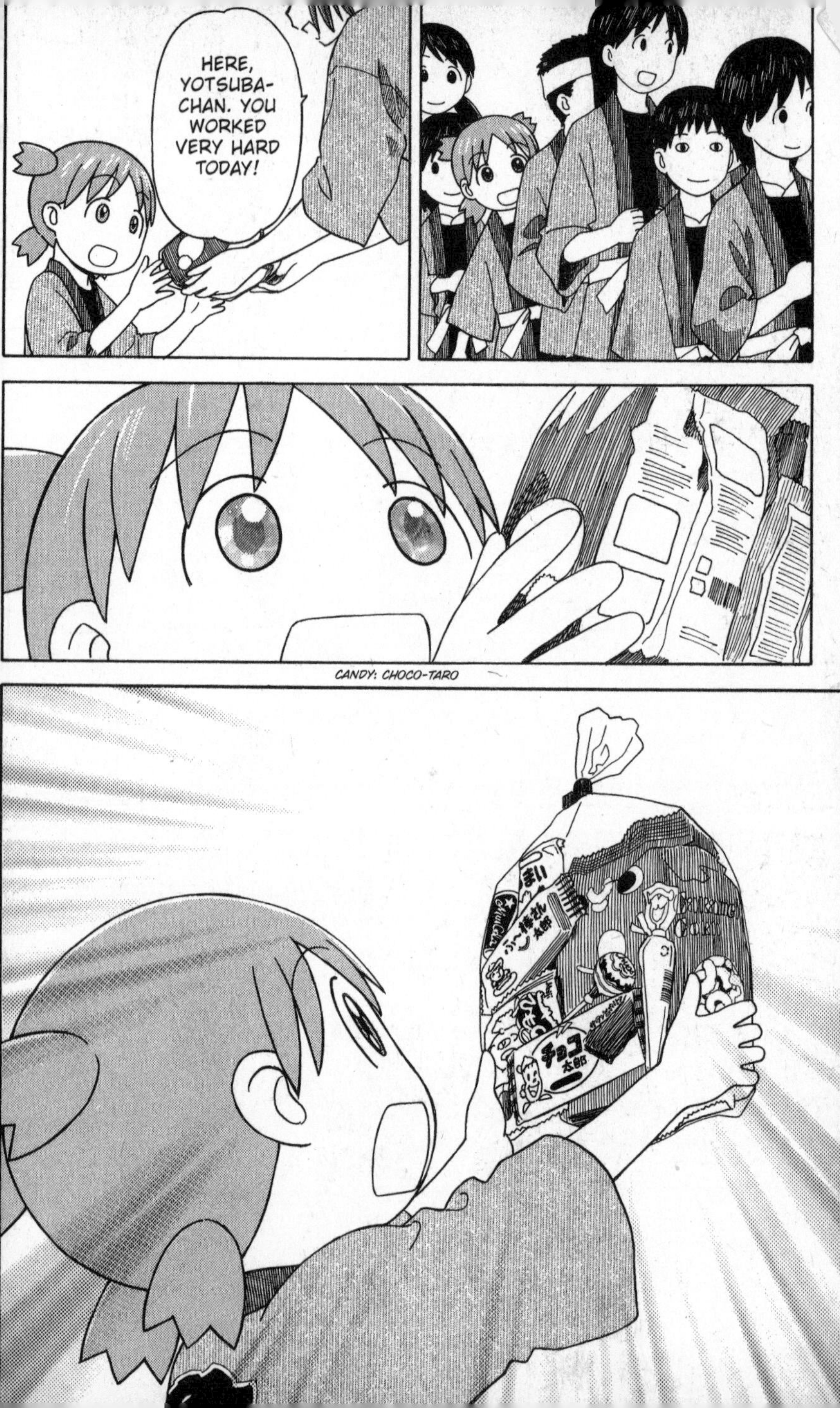
HERE, YOTSUBA-CHAN. YOU WORKED VERY HARD TODAY!
CANDY: CHOCO-TARO
チョコ 太郎

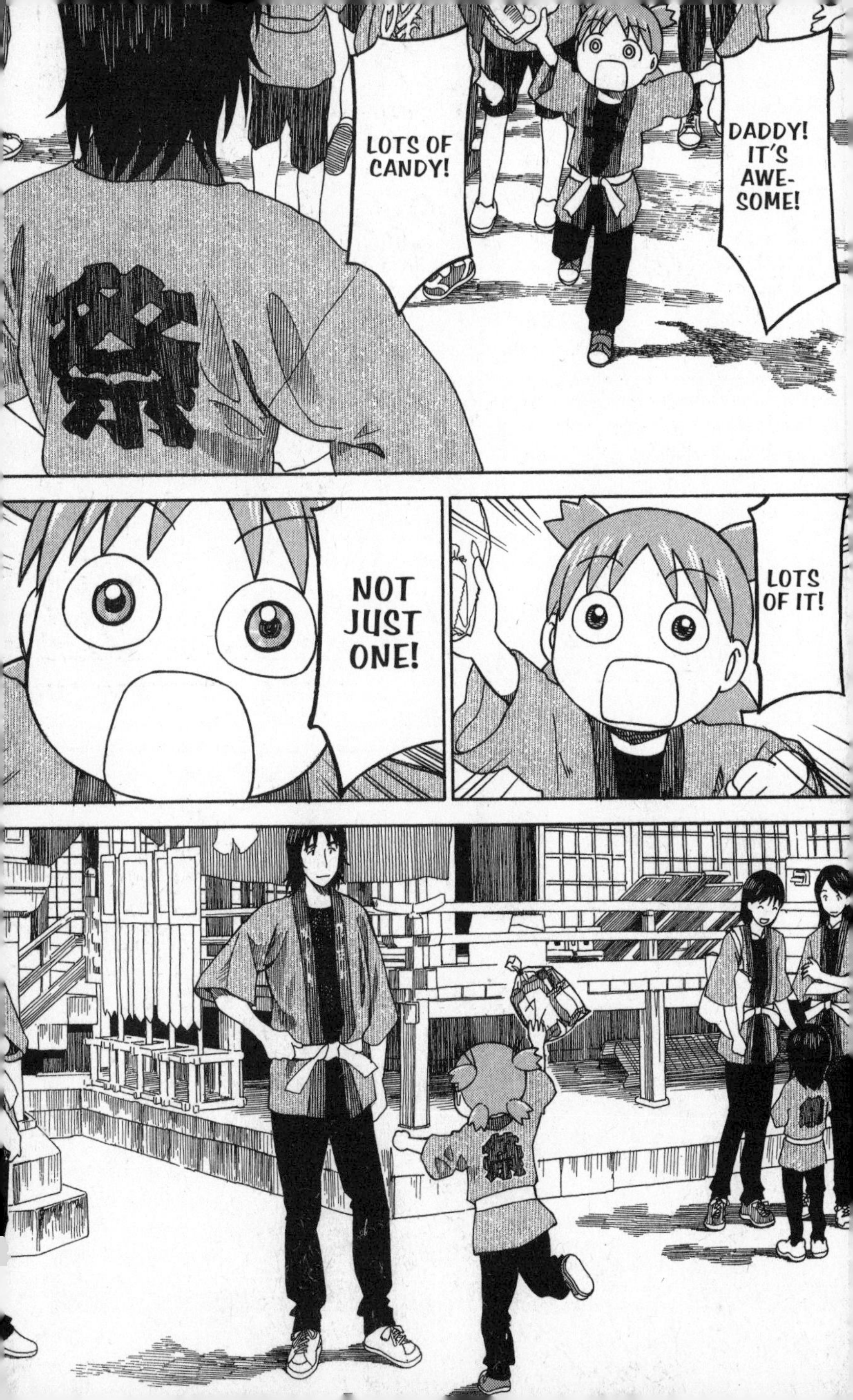
DADDY! IT'S AWE- SOME!
LOTS OF CANDY!
LOTS OF IT!
NOT JUST ONE!

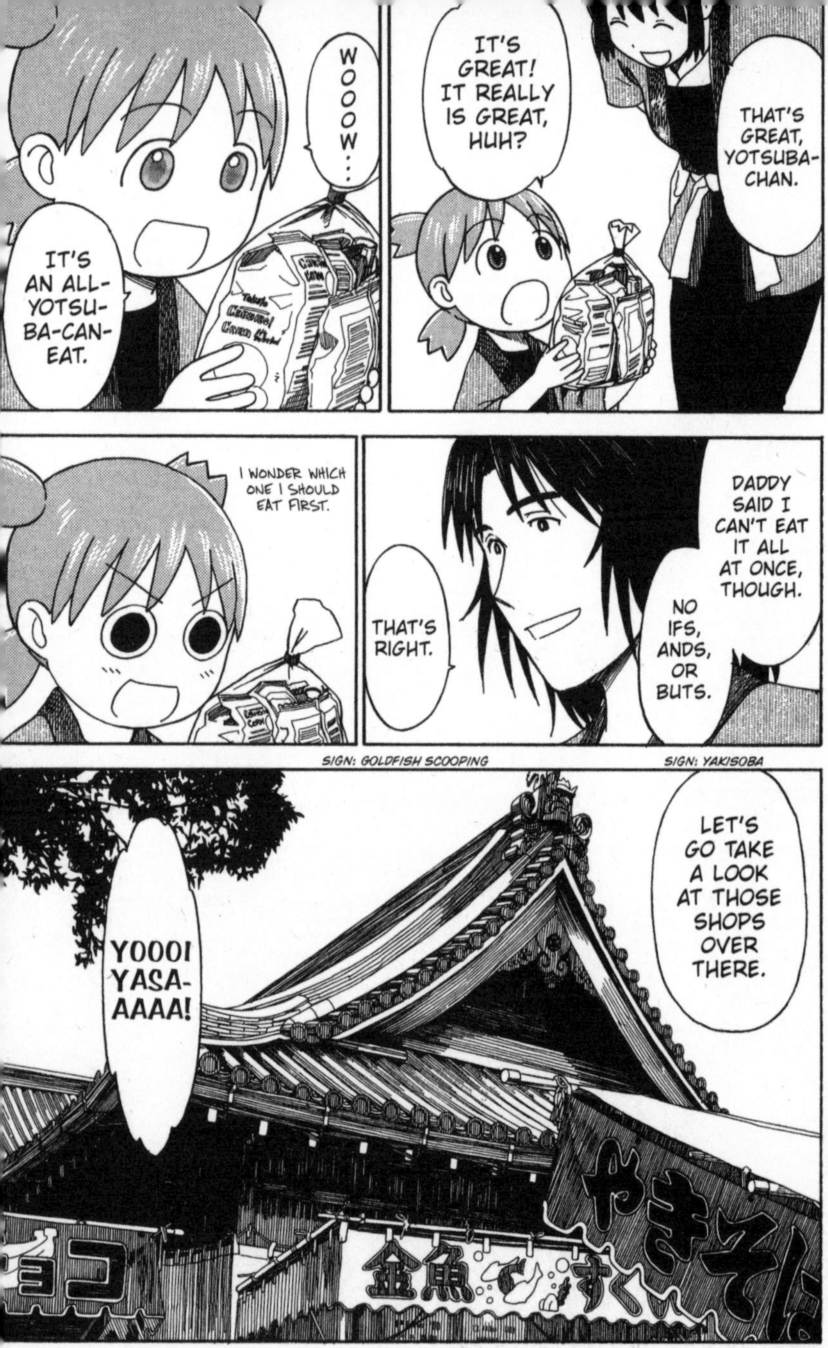
THAT'S GREAT, YOTSUBA-CHAN.
IT'S GREAT! IT REALLY IS GREAT, HUH?
WOOOOW...
IT'S AN ALL-YOTSUBA-CAN-EAT.
DADDY SAID I CAN'T EAT IT ALL AT ONCE, THOUGH.
NO IFS, ANDS, OR BUTS.
THAT'S RIGHT.
I WONDER WHICH ONE I SHOULD EAT FIRST.
SIGN: YAKISOBA
SIGN: GOLDFISH SCOOPING
LET'S GO TAKE A LOOK AT THOSE SHOPS OVER THERE.
YOOOI YASA-AAAA!

YOTSUBA&!

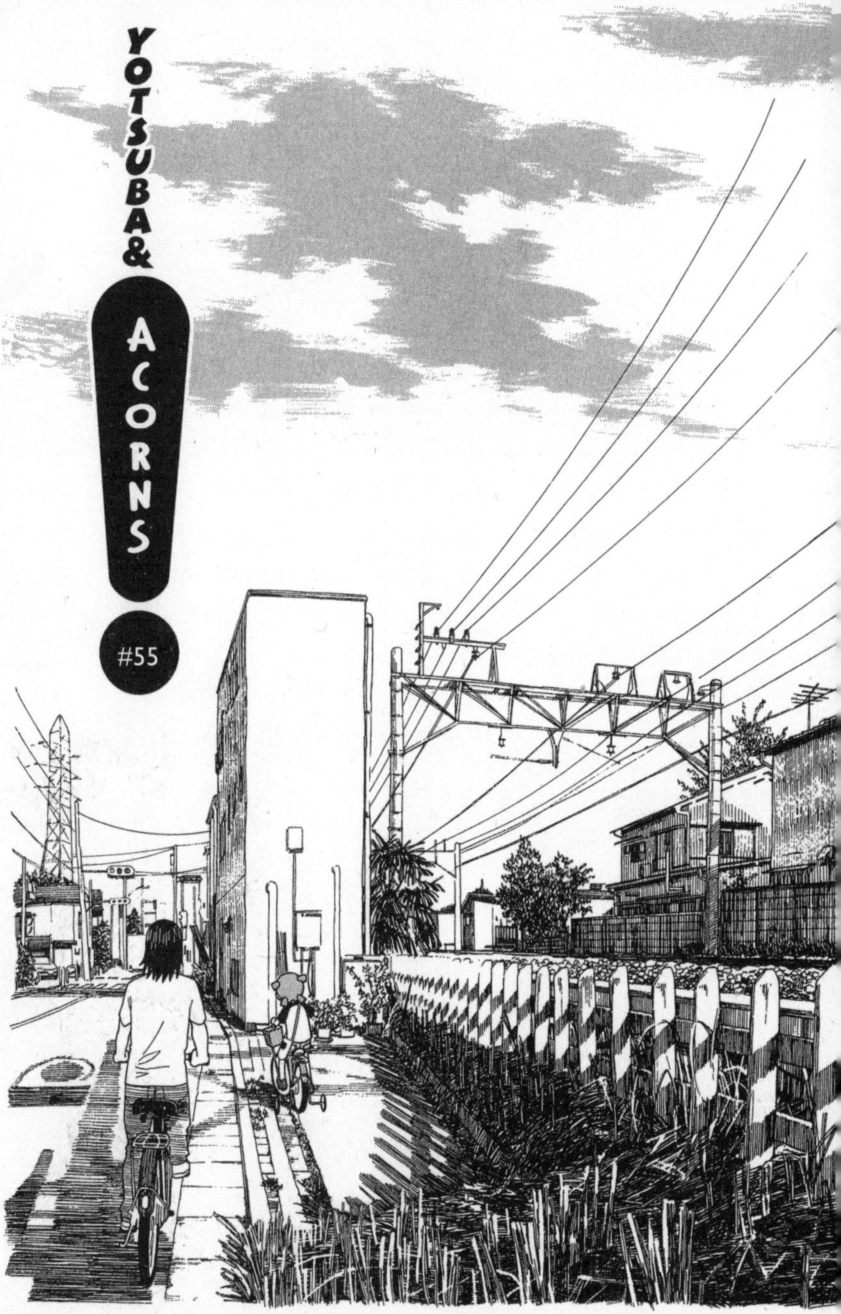
YOTSUBA&
ACORNS
#55

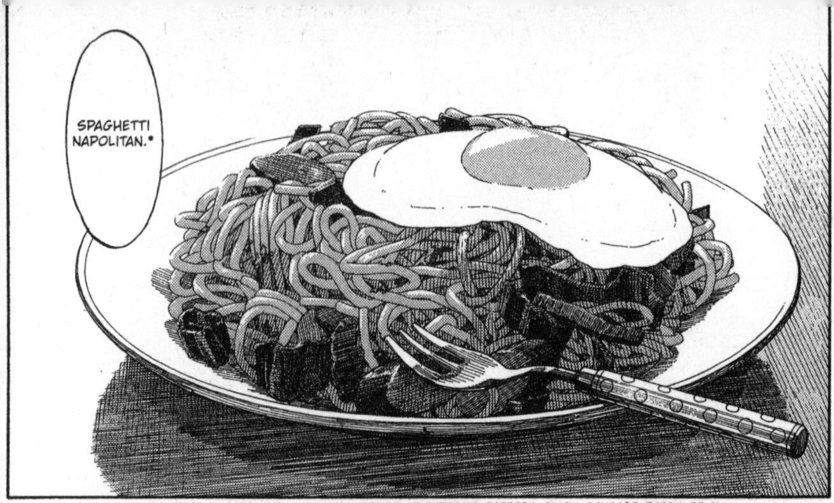
SPAGHETTI NAPOLITAN.*

*NAPOLITAN: A JAPANESE TAKE ON SPAGHETTI MADE WITH KETCHUP, MUSHROOMS, PEPPERS, ONION, SAUSAGE, BACON, ET. AL.

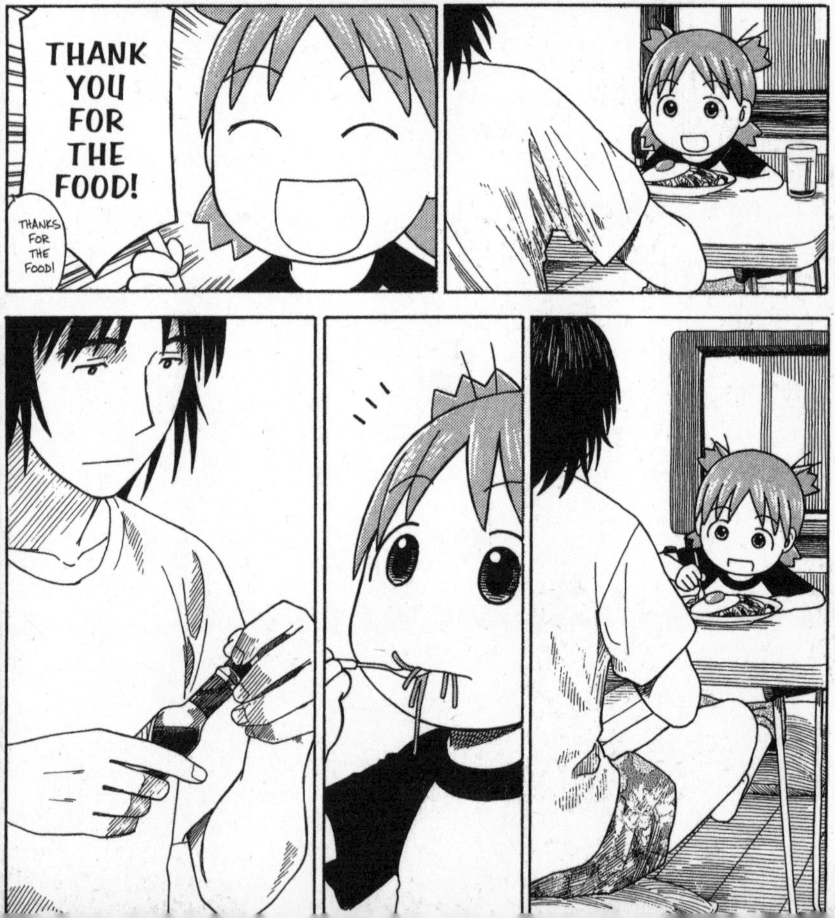
THANK YOU FOR THE FOOD!
THANKS FOR THE FOOD!

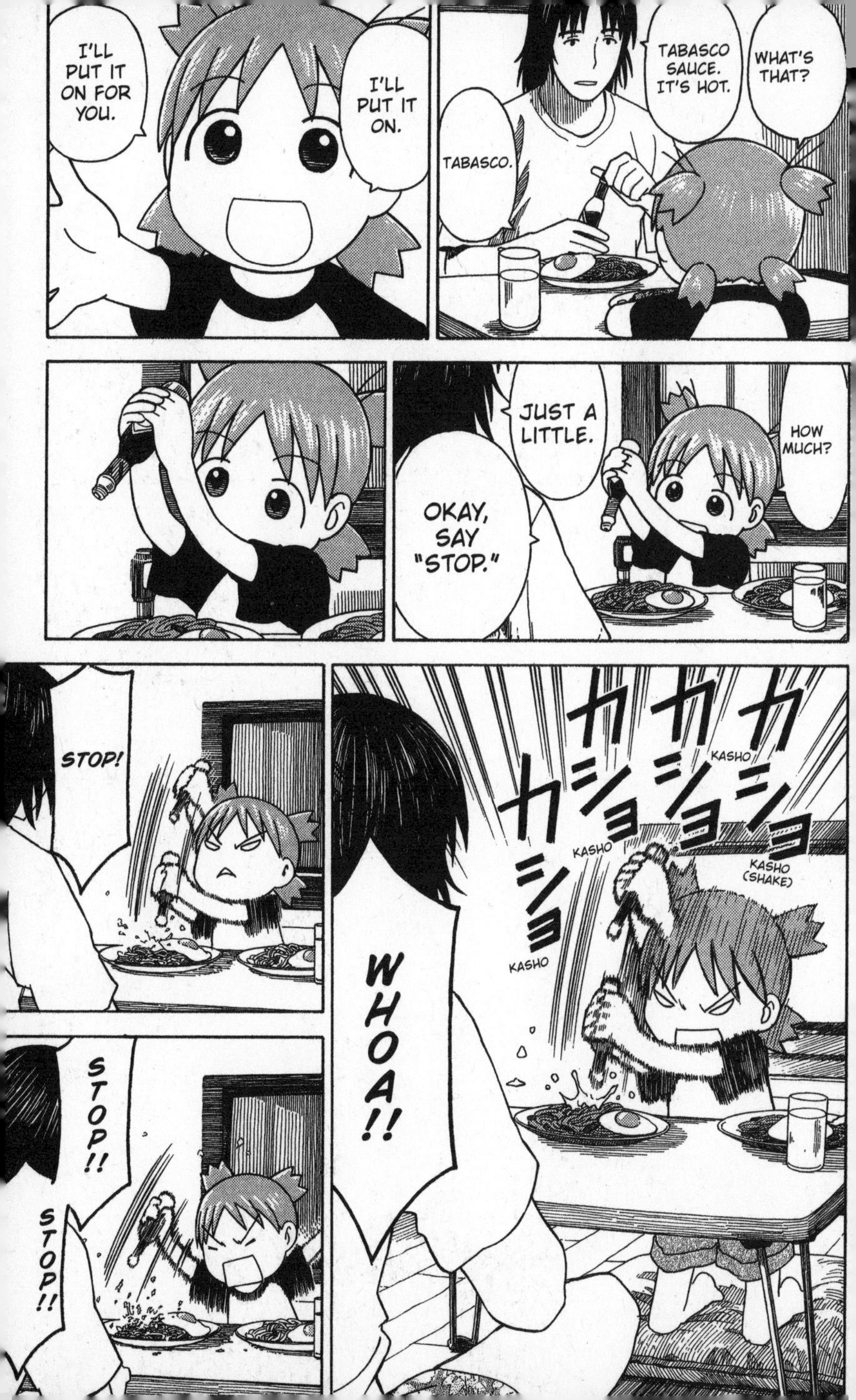
WHAT'S THAT?
TABASCO SAUCE. IT'S HOT.
TABASCO.
I'LL PUT IT ON.
I'LL PUT IT ON FOR YOU.
HOW MUCH?
JUST A LITTLE.
OKAY, SAY "STOP."
カショ
KASHO
カショ
KASHO (SHAKE)
カショ
KASHO
カショ
KASHO
WHOA!!
STOP!
STOP!!
STOP!!

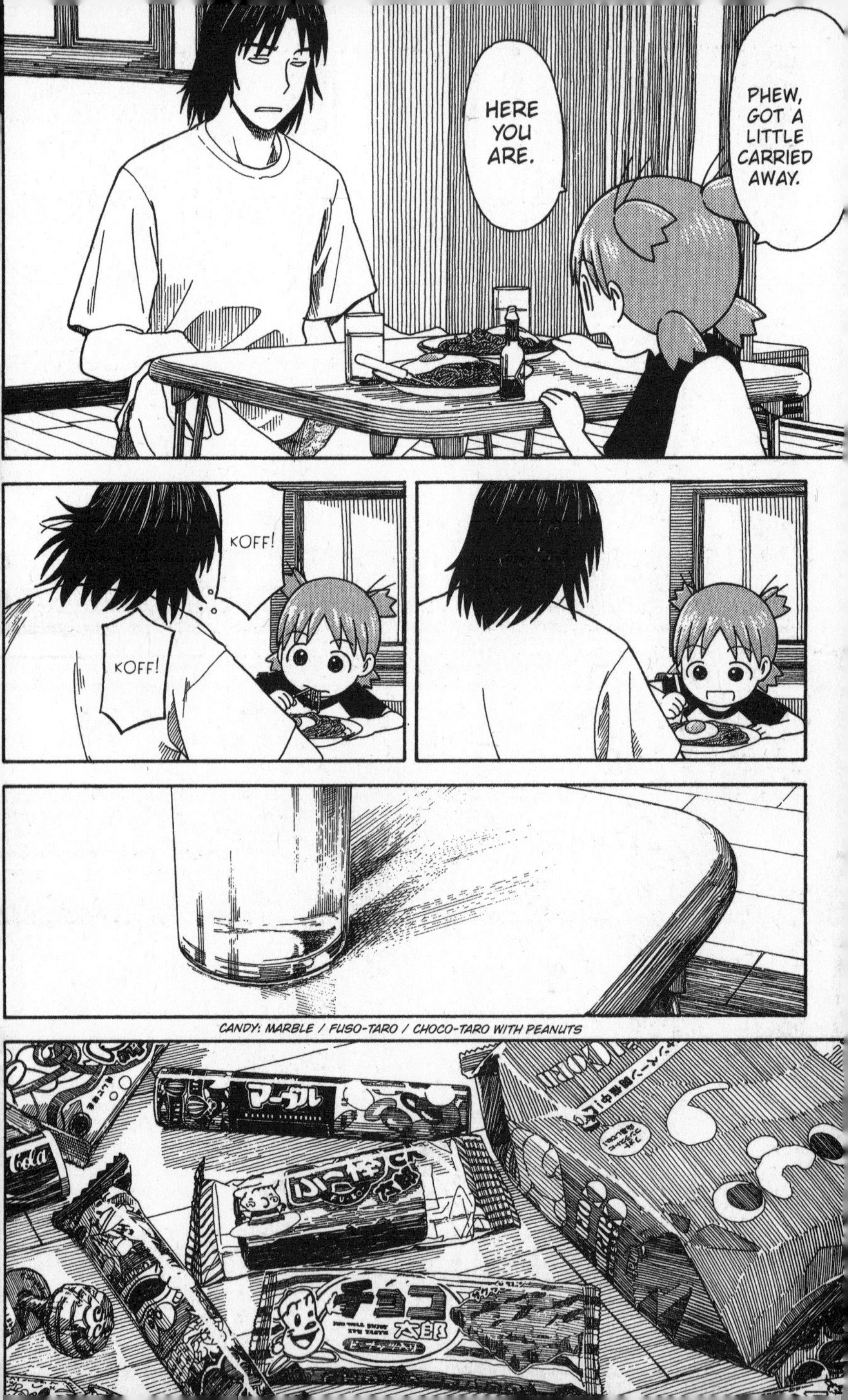
PHEW, GOT A LITTLE CARRIED AWAY.
HERE YOU ARE.
KOFF!
KOFF!
マーブル
チョコ太郎
CANDY: MARBLE / FUSO-TARO / CHOCO-TARO WITH PEANUTS

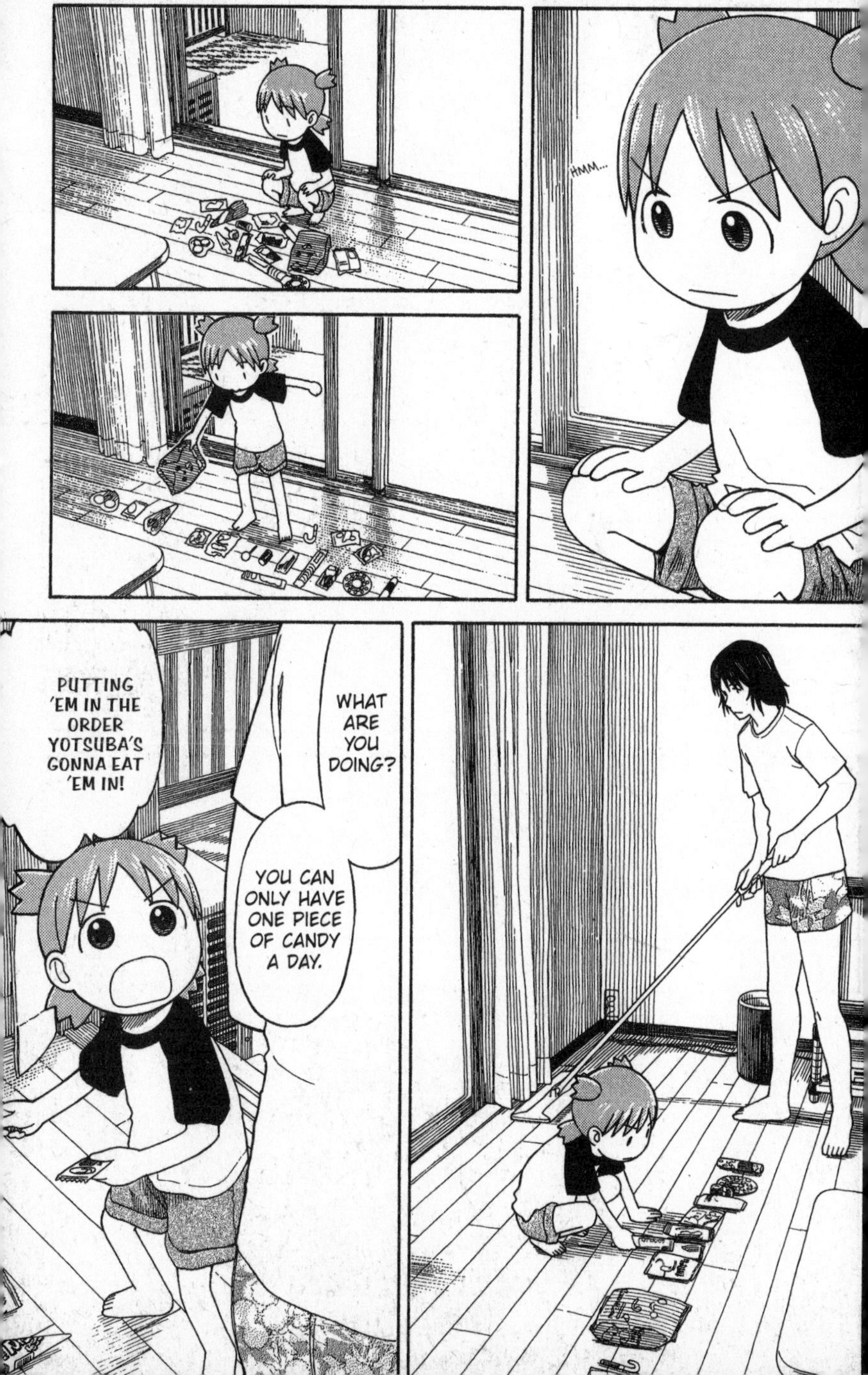
HMM...
WHAT ARE YOU DOING?
PUTTING 'EM IN THE ORDER YOTSUBA'S GONNA EAT 'EM IN!
YOU CAN ONLY HAVE ONE PIECE OF CANDY A DAY.

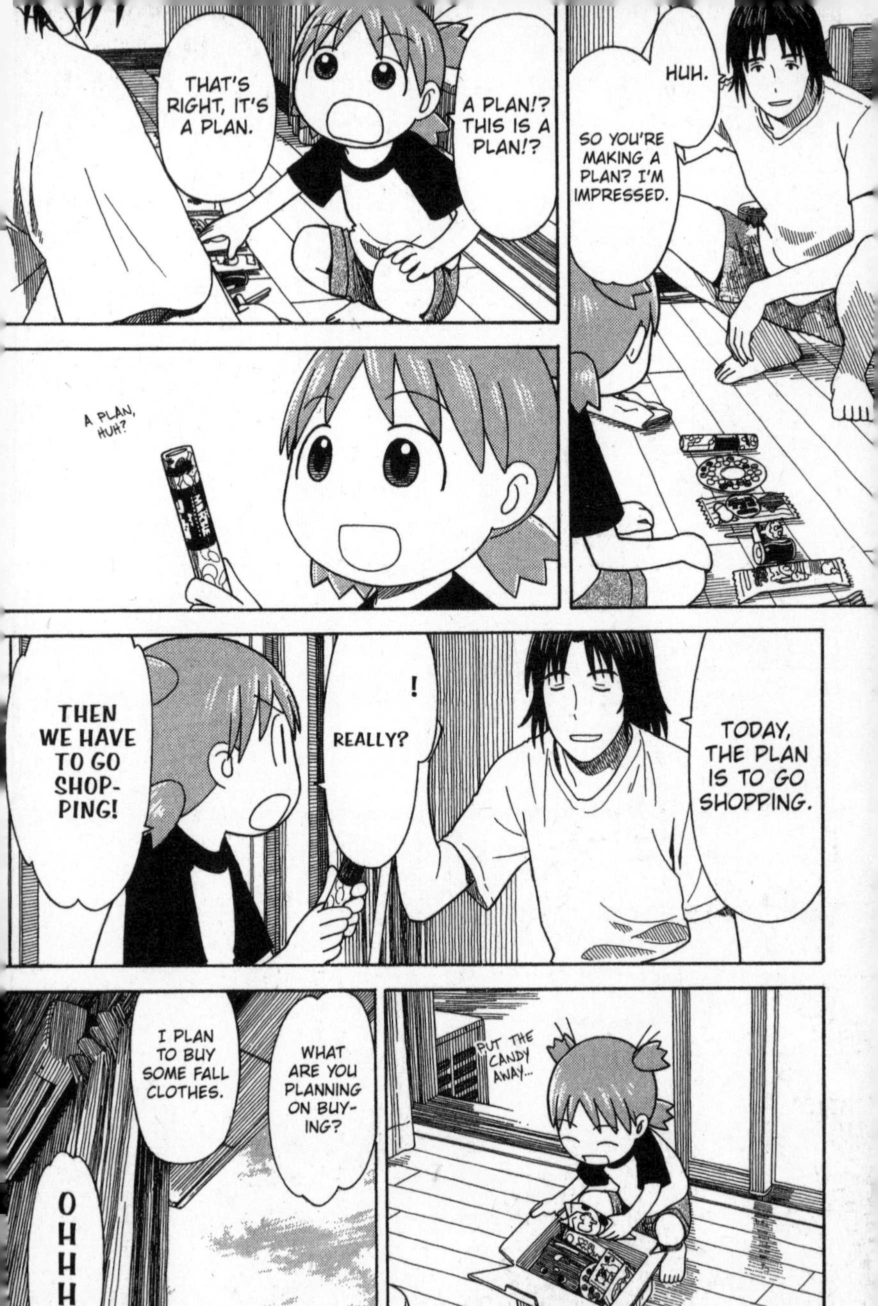
HUH.
SO YOU'RE MAKING A PLAN? I'M IMPRESSED.
A PLAN!? THIS IS A PLAN!?
THAT'S RIGHT, IT'S A PLAN.
A PLAN, HUH?
TODAY, THE PLAN IS TO GO SHOPPING.
!
REALLY?
THEN WE HAVE TO GO SHOP-PING!
PUT THE CANDY AWAY...
WHAT ARE YOU PLANNING ON BUY-ING?
I PLAN TO BUY SOME FALL CLOTHES.
OHHHH!!

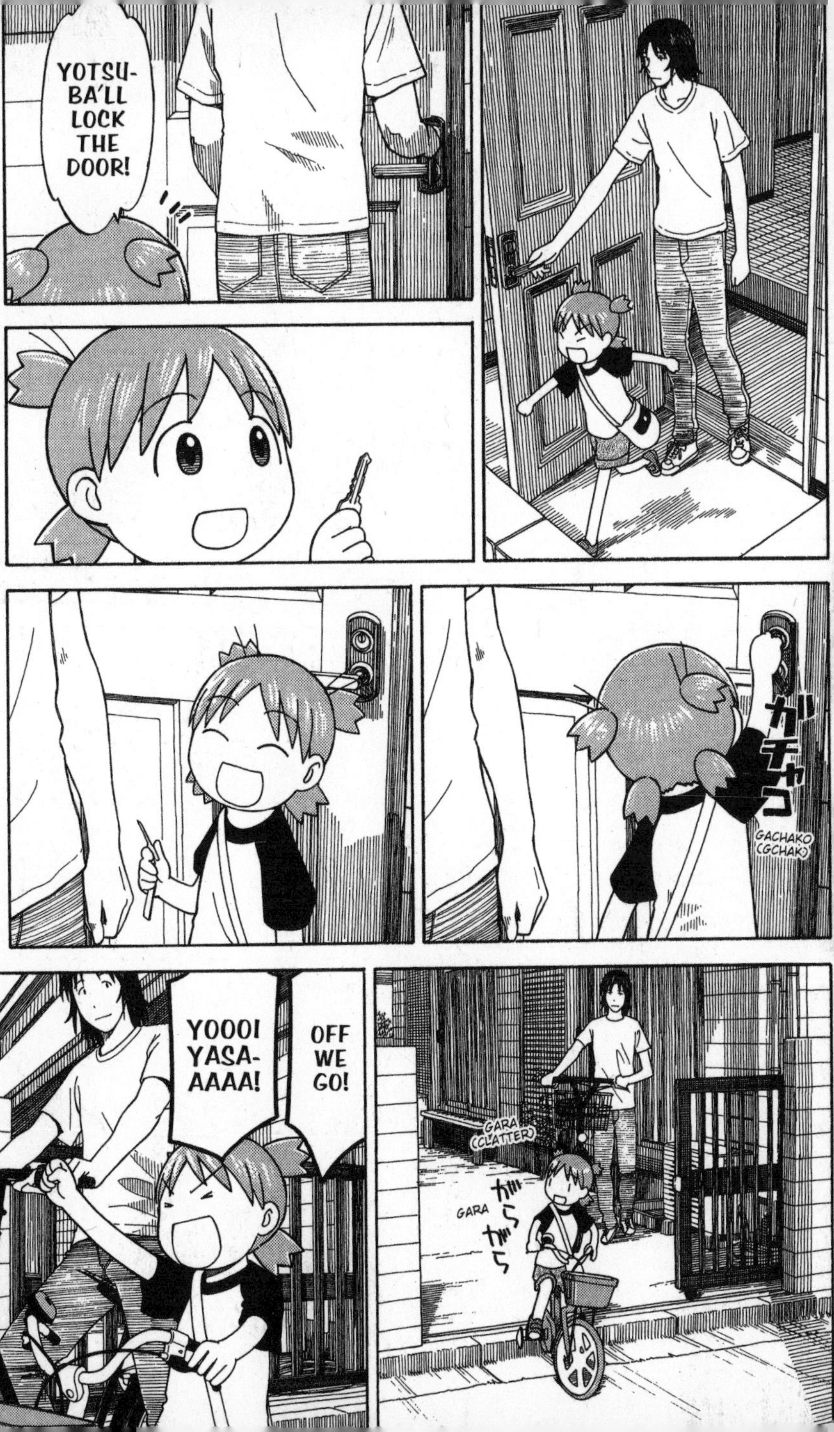
YOTSU-BA'LL LOCK THE DOOR!
ガチャコ
GACHAKO (GCHAK)
GARA (CLATTER)
がらがら
GARA
OFF WE GO!
YOOOI YASA-AAAA!

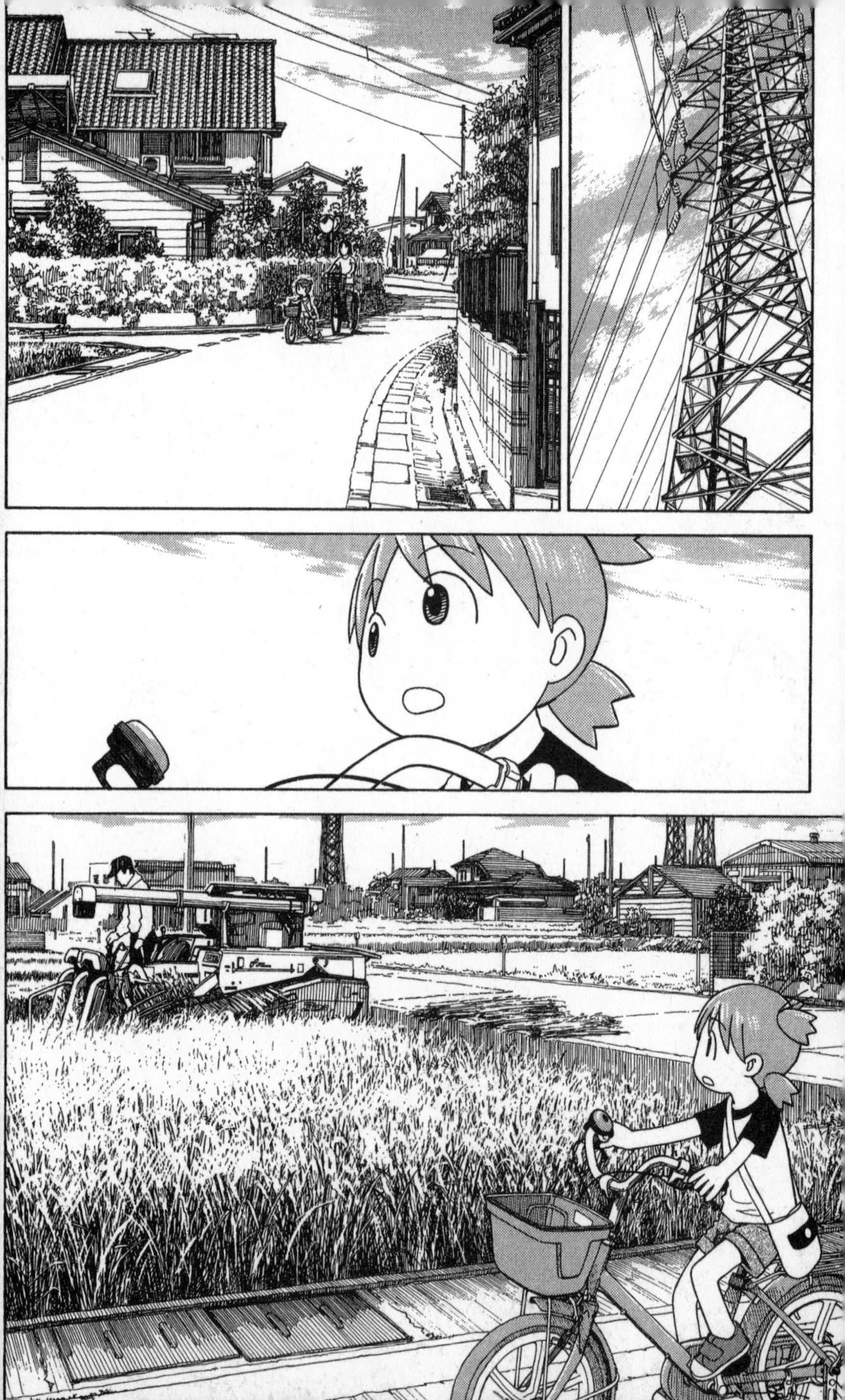

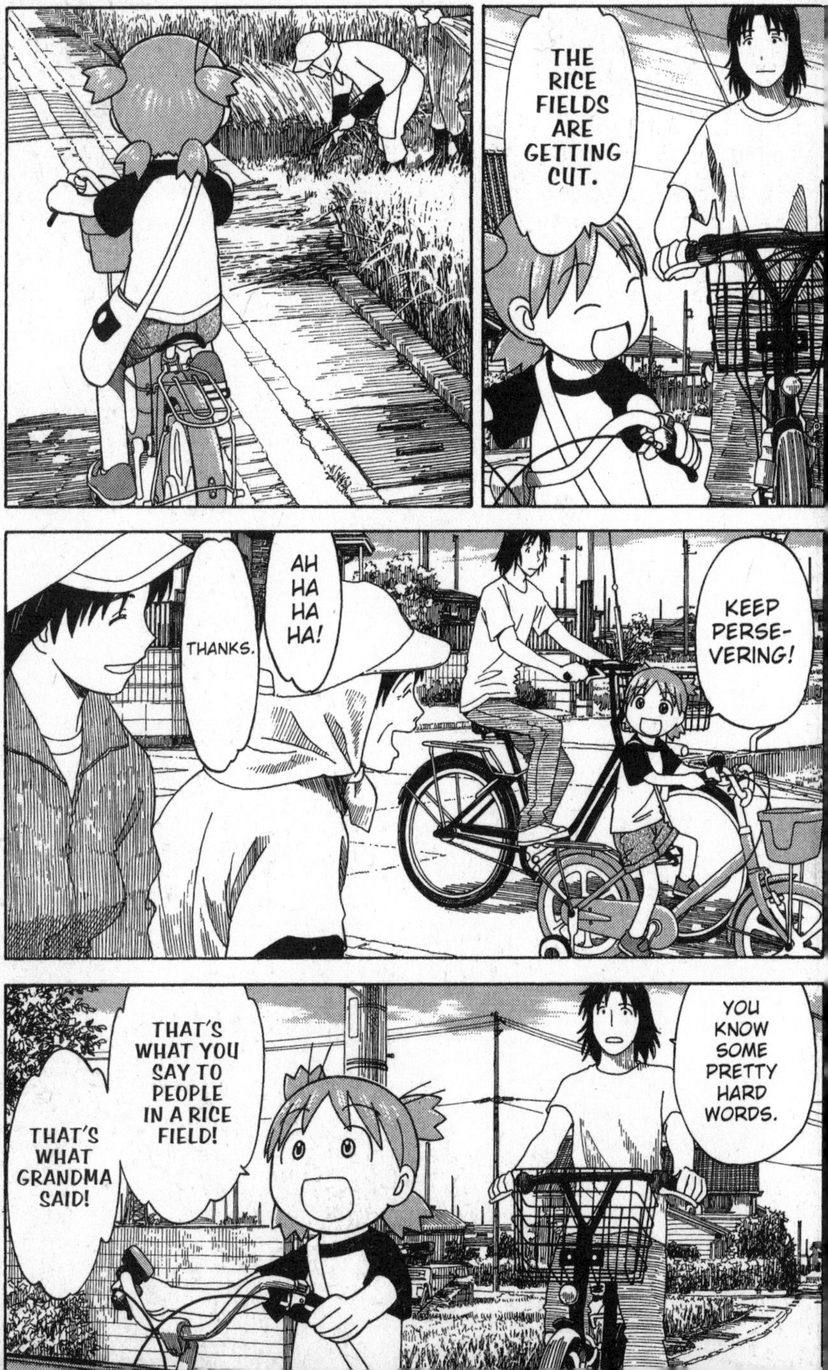
THE RICE FIELDS ARE GETTING CUT.
KEEP PERSE-VERING!
AH HA HA HA!
THANKS.
YOU KNOW SOME PRETTY HARD WORDS.
THAT'S WHAT YOU SAY TO PEOPLE IN A RICE FIELD!
THAT'S WHAT GRANDMA SAID!

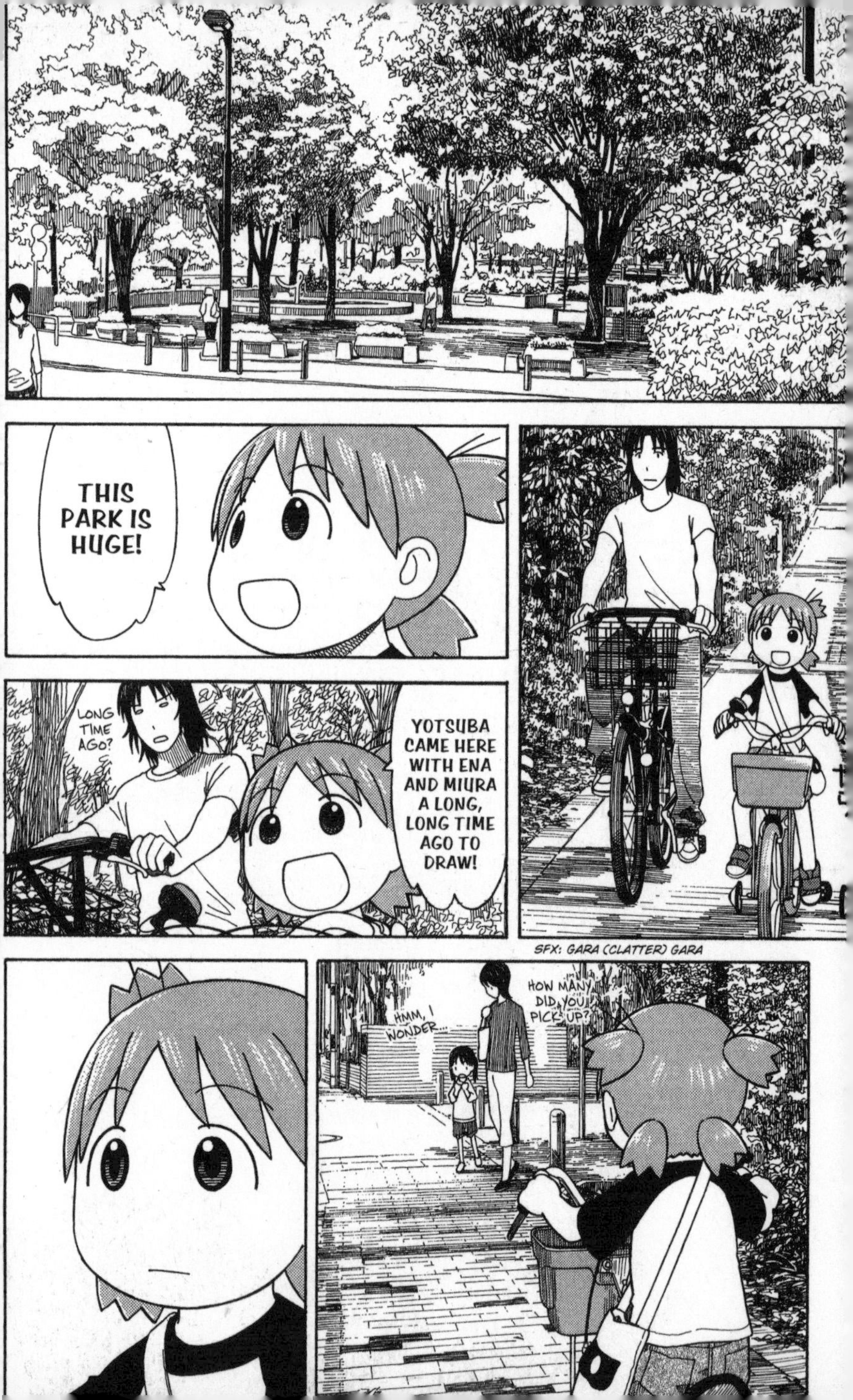
SFX: GARA (CLATTER) GARA
THIS PARK IS HUGE!
YOTSUBA CAME HERE WITH ENA AND MIURA A LONG, LONG TIME AGO TO DRAW!
LONG TIME AGO?
HOW MANY DID YOU PICK UP?
HMM, I WONDER...

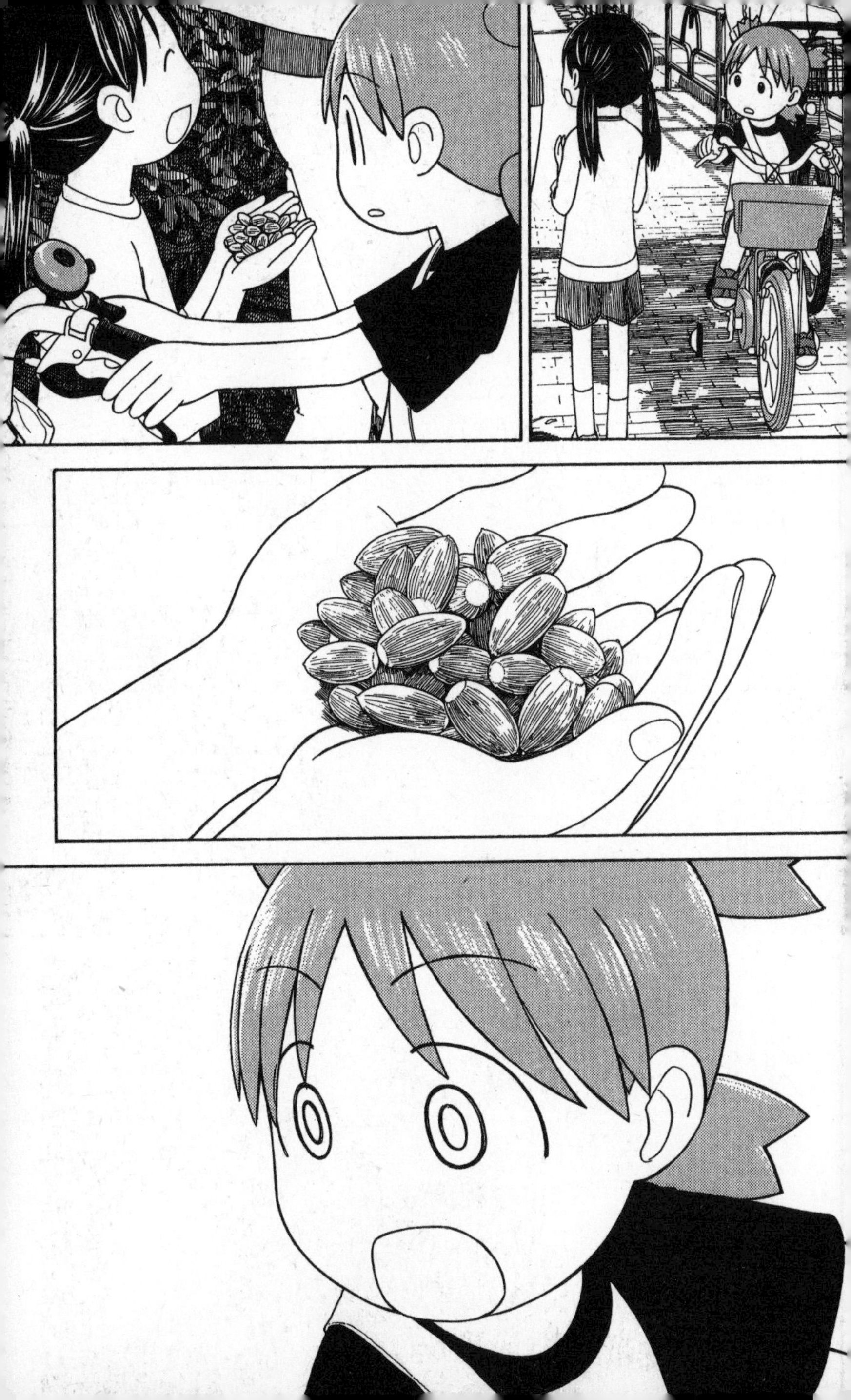

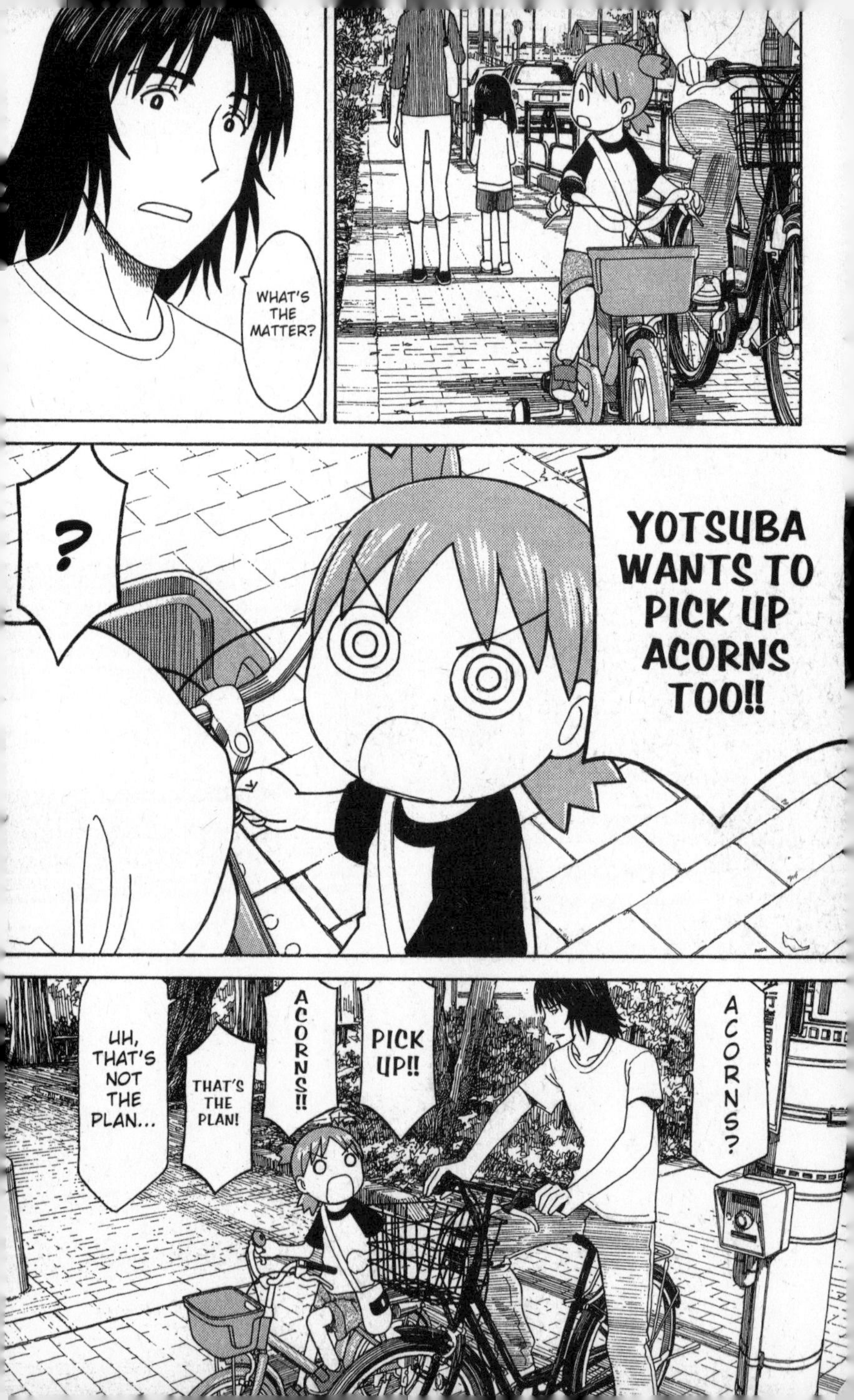
WHAT'S THE MATTER?
YOTSUBA WANTS TO PICK UP ACORNS TOO!!
?
ACORNS?
PICK UP!!
ACORNS!!
THAT'S THE PLAN!
UH, THAT'S NOT THE PLAN...

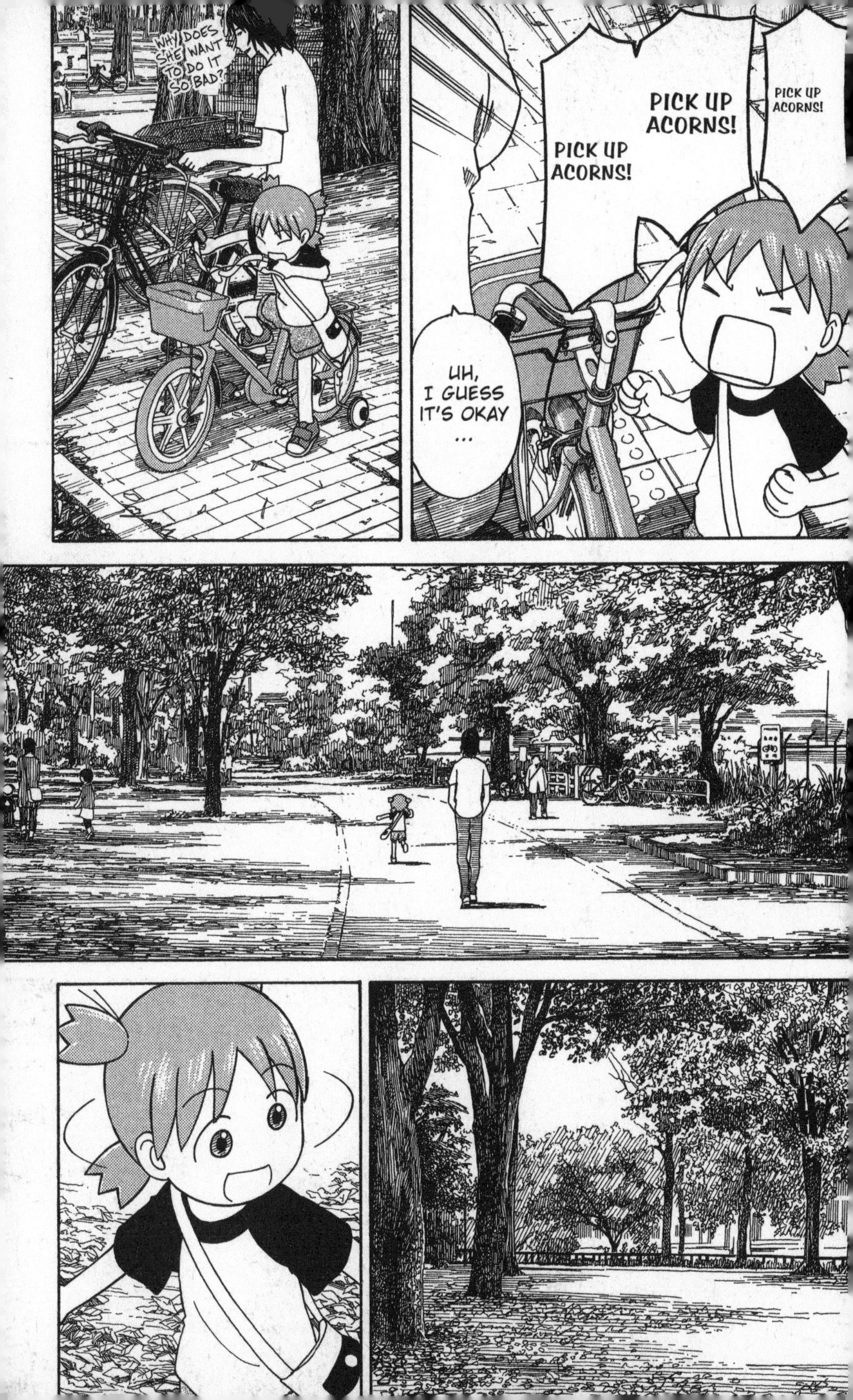
PICK UP ACORNS!
PICK UP ACORNS!
PICK UP ACORNS!
UH, I GUESS IT'S OKAY ...
WHY DOES SHE WANT TO DO IT SO BAD?

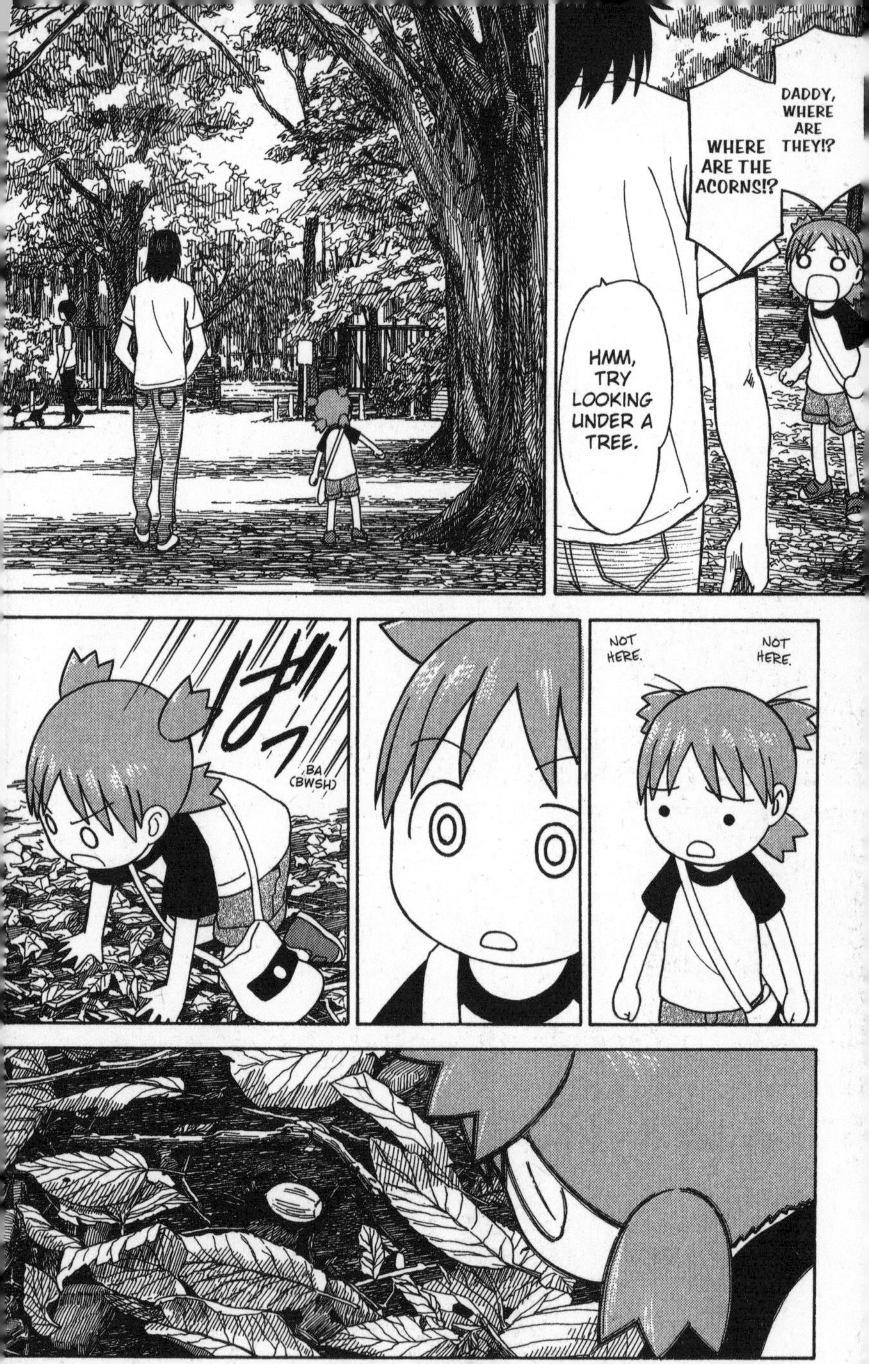
DADDY, WHERE ARE THEY!?
WHERE ARE THE ACORNS!?
HMM, TRY LOOKING UNDER A TREE.
NOT HERE.
NOT HERE.
ばっ
BA (BWSH)

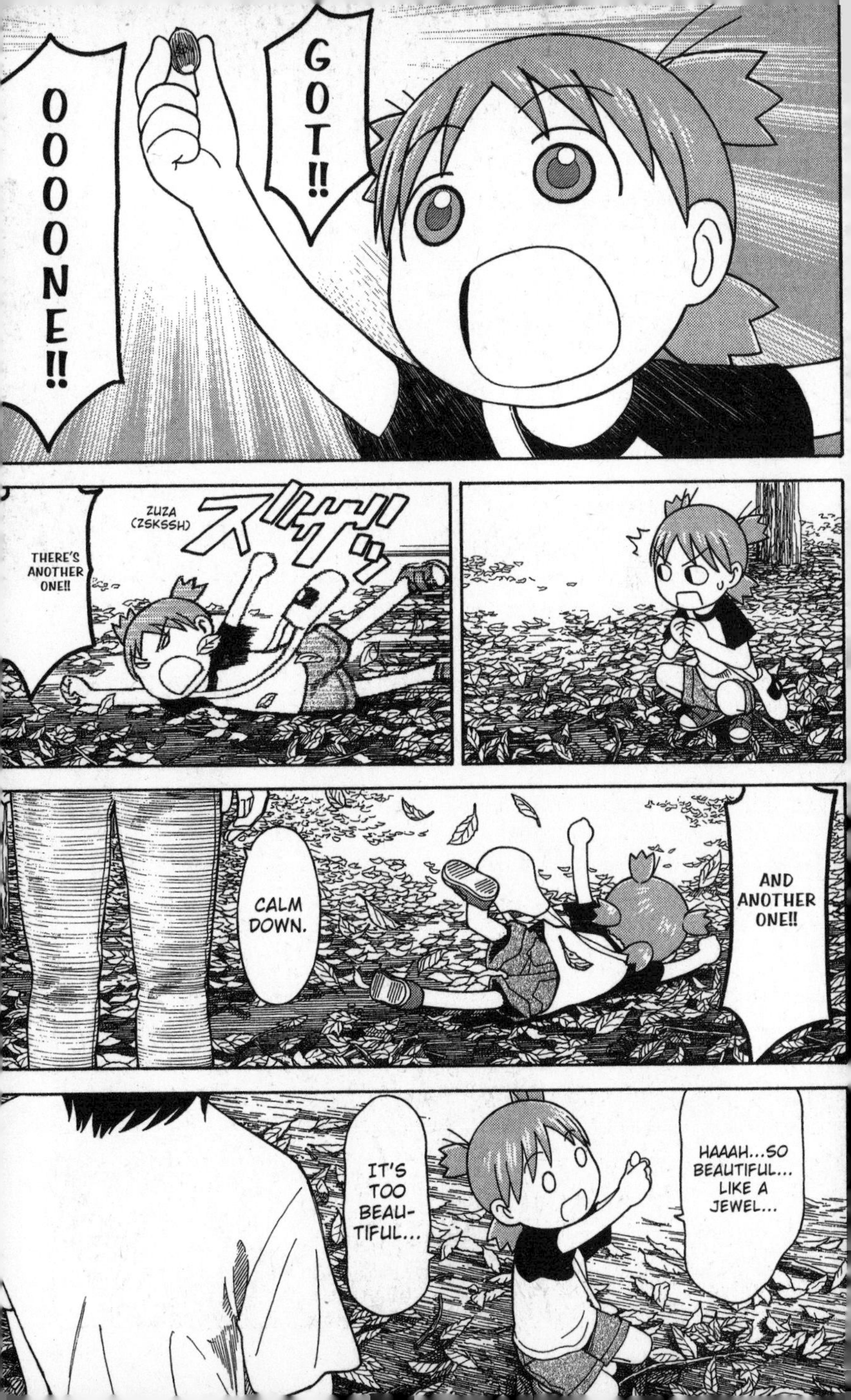
GOT!!
OOOOONE!!
ZUZA (ZSKSSH)
THERE'S ANOTHER ONE!!
AND ANOTHER ONE!!
CALM DOWN.
HAAAH...SO BEAUTIFUL... LIKE A JEWEL...
IT'S TOO BEAU-TIFUL...

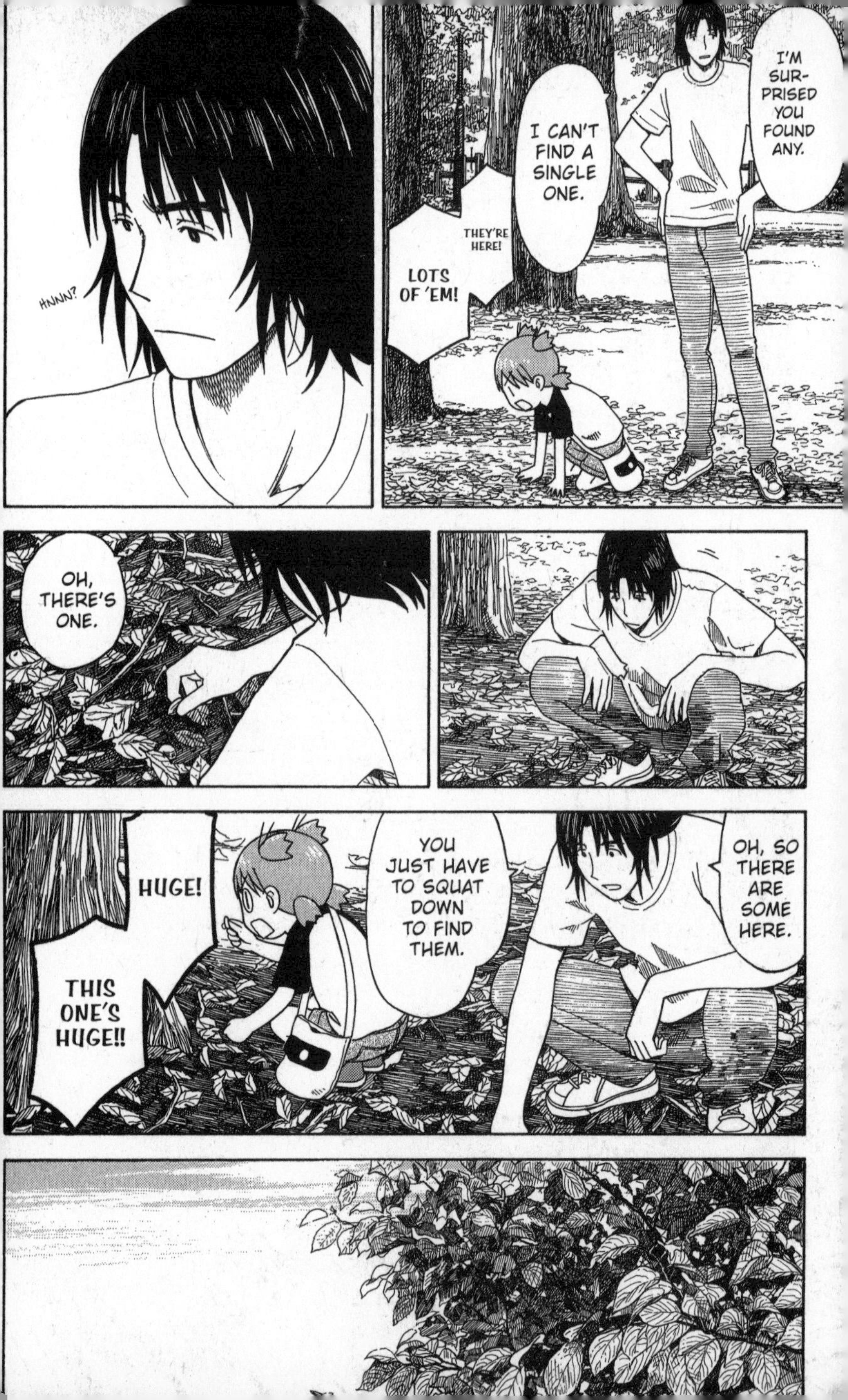
I'M SUR-PRISED YOU FOUND ANY.
I CAN'T FIND A SINGLE ONE.
THEY'RE HERE!
LOTS OF 'EM!
HNNN?
OH, THERE'S ONE.
OH, SO THERE ARE SOME HERE.
YOU JUST HAVE TO SQUAT DOWN TO FIND THEM.
HUGE!
THIS ONE'S HUGE!!

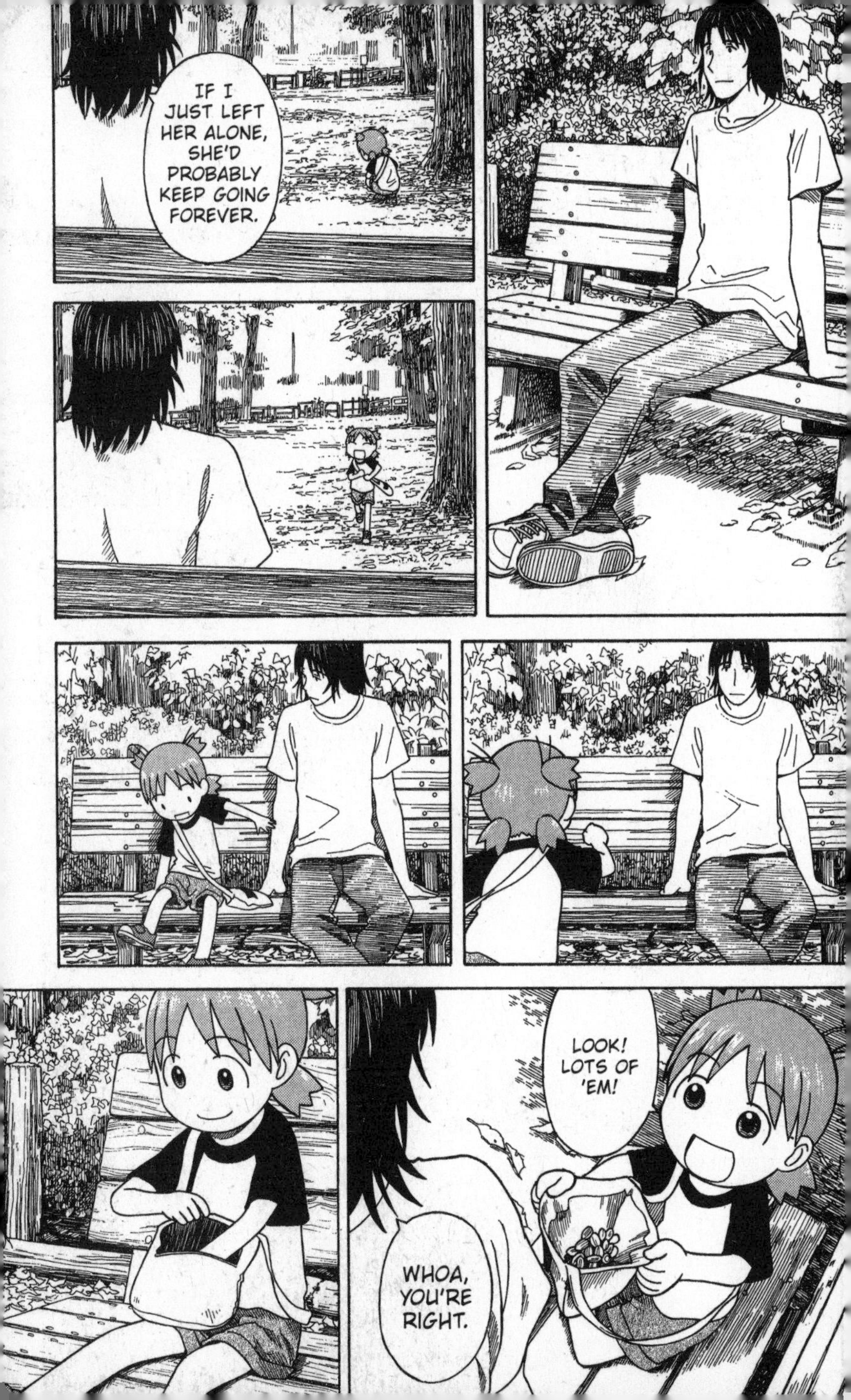
IF I JUST LEFT HER ALONE, SHE'D PROBABLY KEEP GOING FOREVER.
LOOK! LOTS OF 'EM!
WHOA, YOU'RE RIGHT.

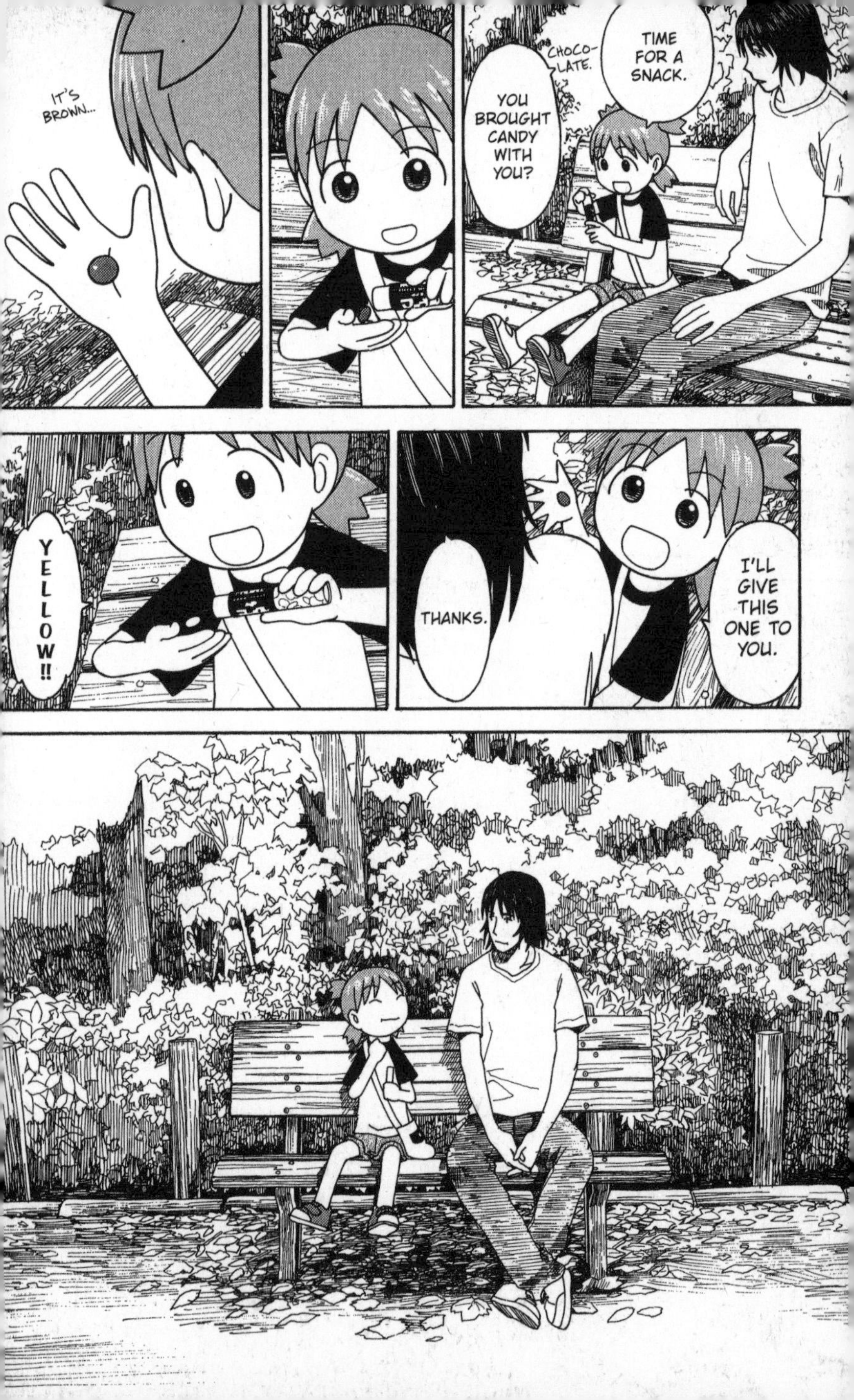
TIME FOR A SNACK.
YOU BROUGHT CANDY WITH YOU?
CHOCO-LATE.
IT'S BROWN...
I'LL GIVE THIS ONE TO YOU.
THANKS.
YELLOW!!

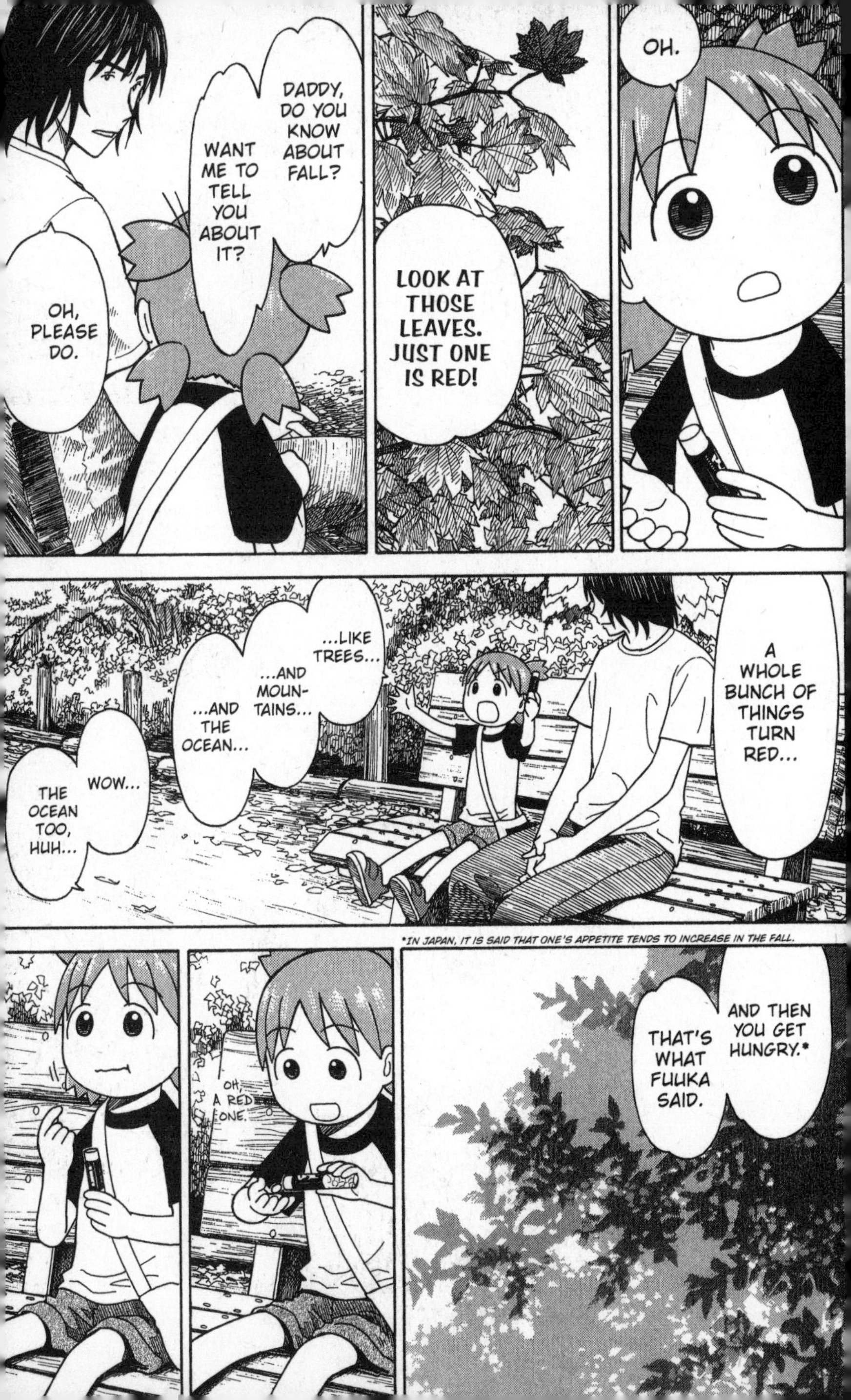
OH.
LOOK AT THOSE LEAVES. JUST ONE IS RED!
DADDY, DO YOU KNOW ABOUT FALL?
WANT ME TO TELL YOU ABOUT IT?
OH, PLEASE DO.
A WHOLE BUNCH OF THINGS TURN RED...
...LIKE TREES...
...AND MOUN-TAINS...
...AND THE OCEAN...
WOW...
THE OCEAN TOO, HUH...
AND THEN YOU GET HUNGRY.*
THAT'S WHAT FUUKA SAID.
OH, A RED ONE.

*IN JAPAN, IT IS SAID THAT ONE'S APPETITE TENDS TO INCREASE IN THE FALL.

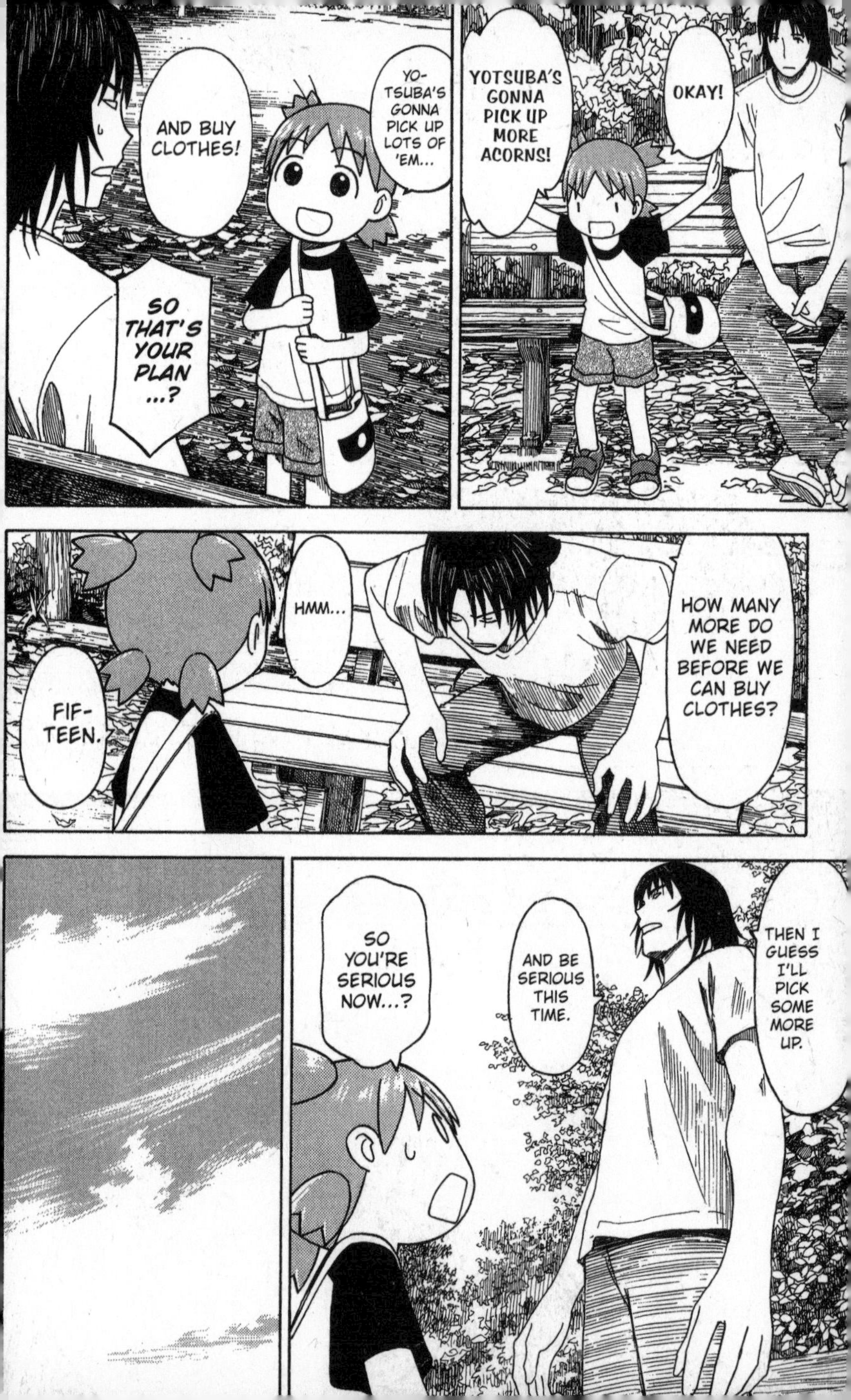
OKAY!
YOTSUBA'S GONNA PICK UP MORE ACORNS!
YO-TSUBA'S GONNA PICK UP LOTS OF 'EM...
AND BUY CLOTHES!
SO THAT'S YOUR PLAN ...?
HOW MANY MORE DO WE NEED BEFORE WE CAN BUY CLOTHES?
HMM...
FIF-TEEN.
THEN I GUESS I'LL PICK SOME MORE UP.
AND BE SERIOUS THIS TIME.
SO YOU'RE SERIOUS NOW...?

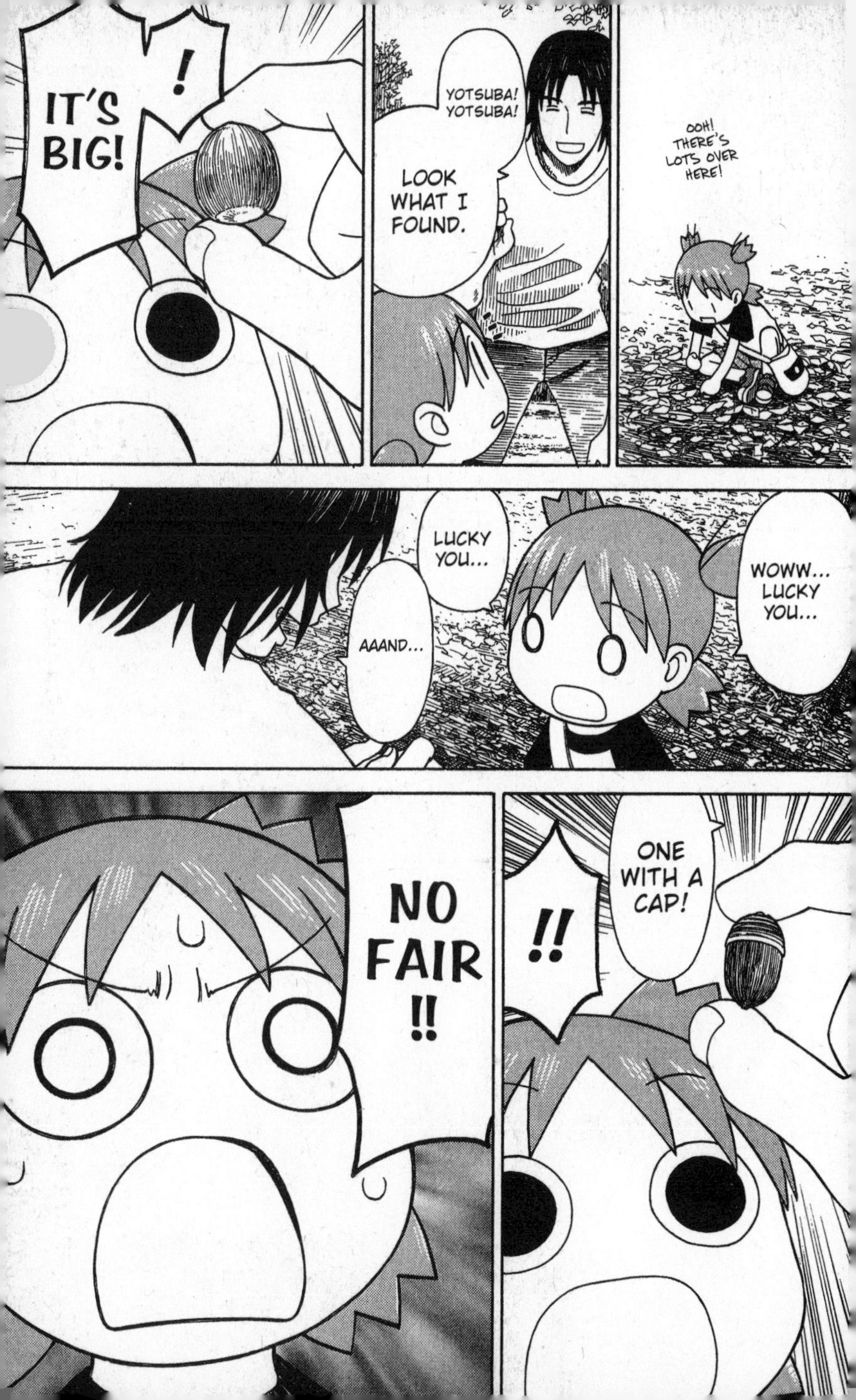
OOH! THERE'S LOTS OVER HERE!
YOTSUBA! YOTSUBA!
LOOK WHAT I FOUND.
!
IT'S BIG!
WOWW... LUCKY YOU...
LUCKY YOU...
AAAND...
ONE WITH A CAP!
!!
NO FAIR !!

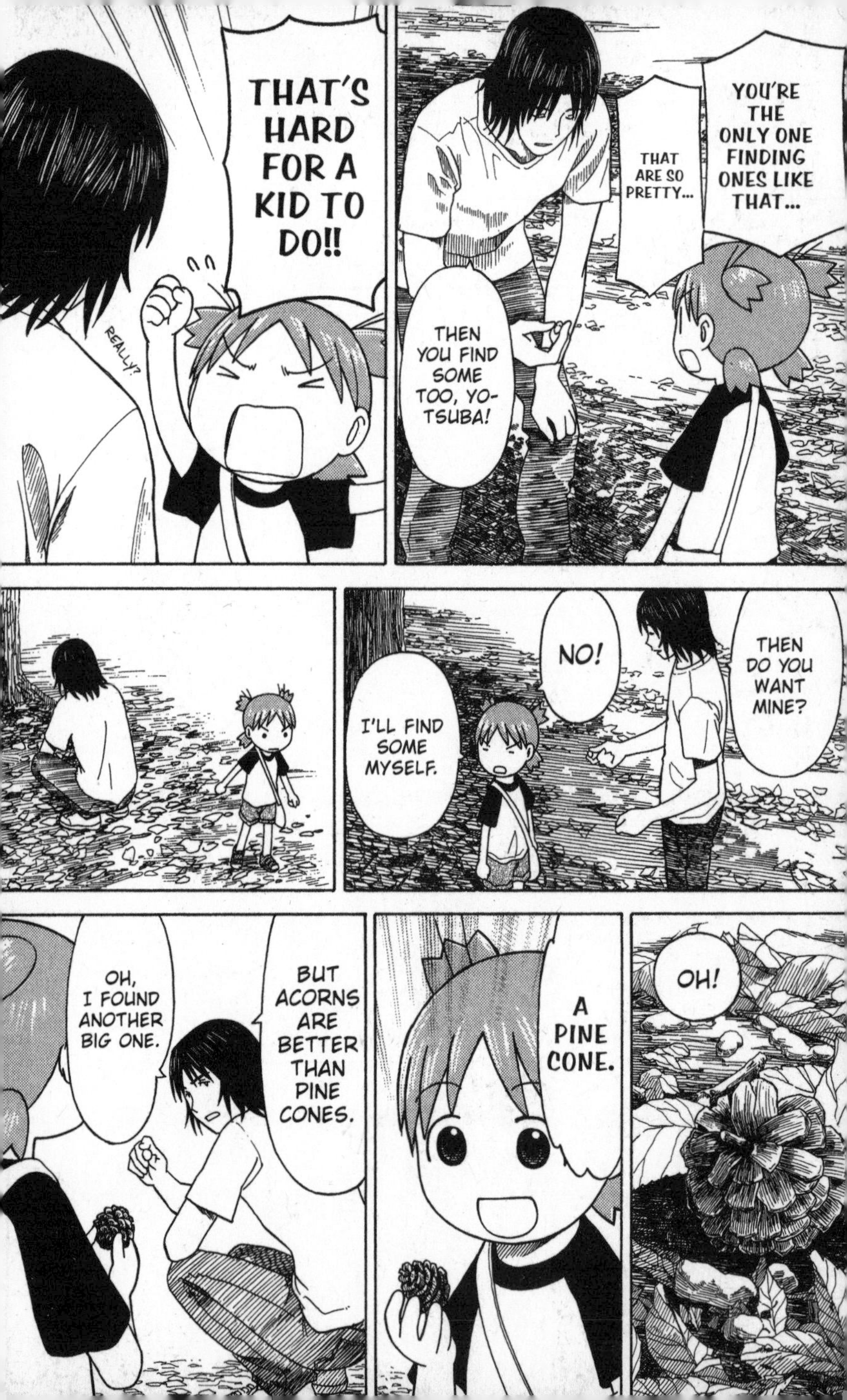
YOU'RE THE ONLY ONE FINDING ONES LIKE THAT...
THAT ARE SO PRETTY...
THEN YOU FIND SOME TOO, YO-TSUBA!
THAT'S HARD FOR A KID TO DO!!
REALLY?
THEN DO YOU WANT MINE?
NO!
I'LL FIND SOME MYSELF.
OH!
A PINE CONE.
BUT ACORNS ARE BETTER THAN PINE CONES.
OH, I FOUND ANOTHER BIG ONE.

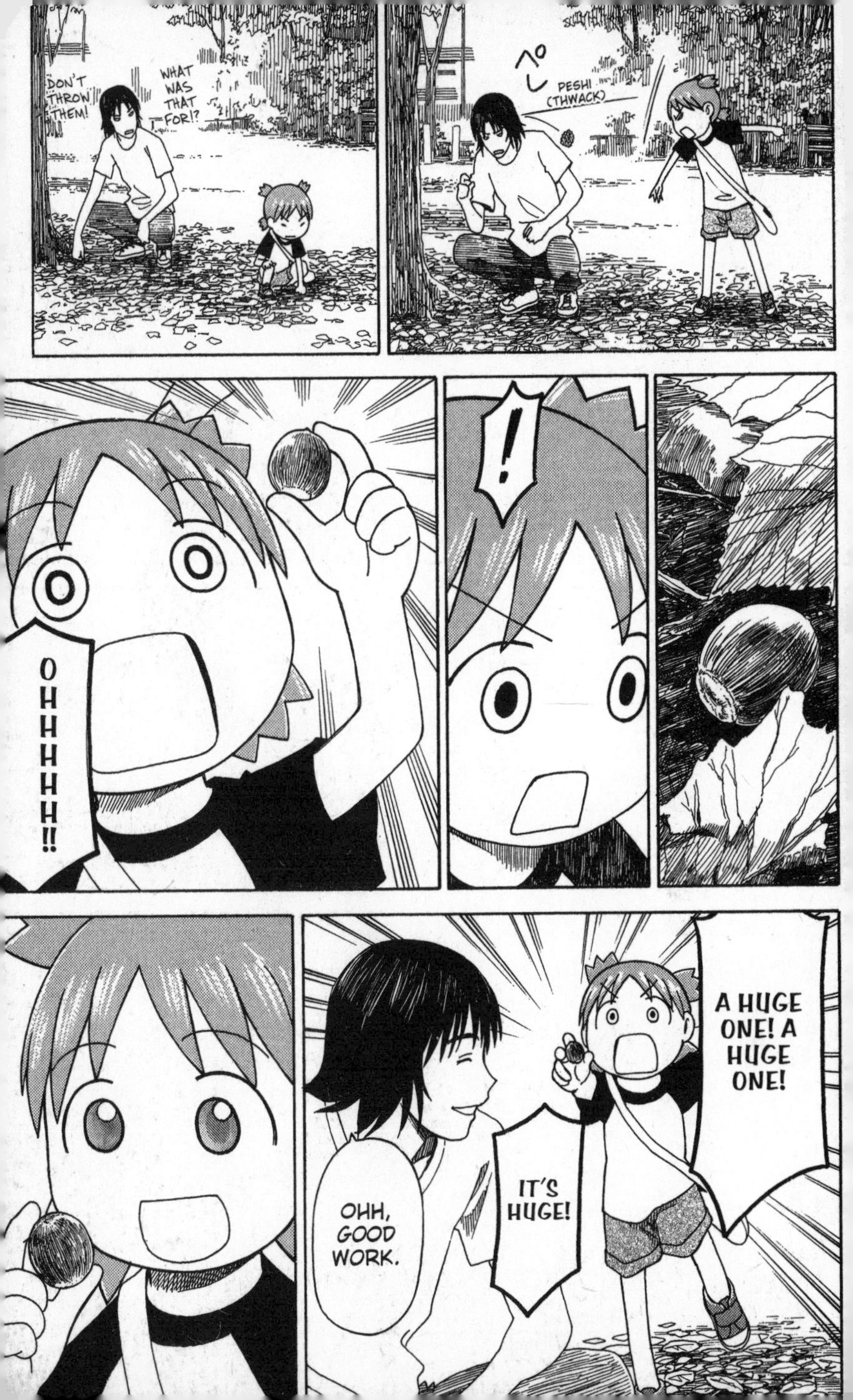
ぺし
PESHI (THWACK)
WHAT WAS THAT FOR!?
DON'T THROW THEM!
!
OHHHHHHH!!
A HUGE ONE! A HUGE ONE!
IT'S HUGE!
OHH, GOOD WORK.

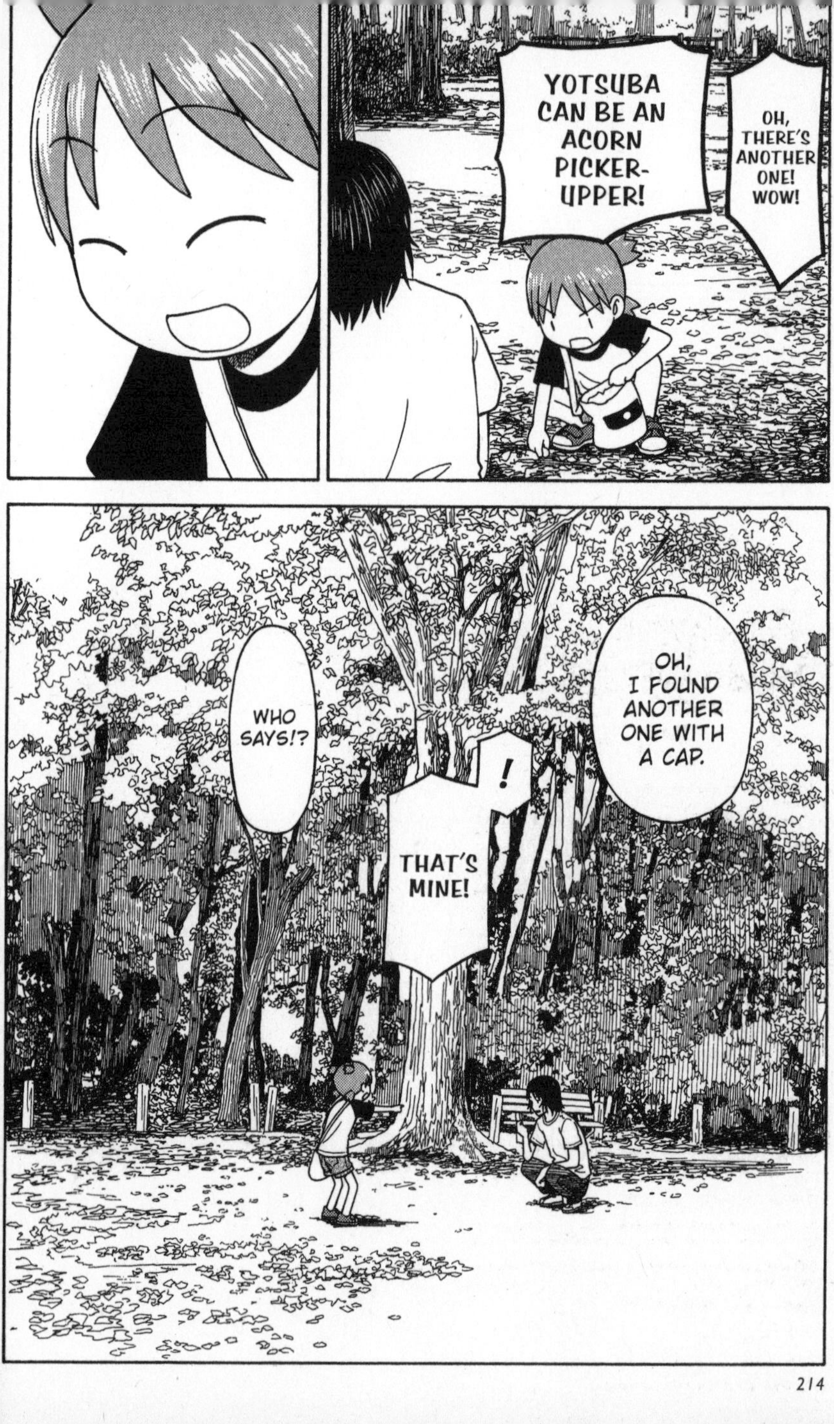
OH, THERE'S ANOTHER ONE! WOW!
YOTSUBA CAN BE AN ACORN PICKER-UPPER!
OH, I FOUND ANOTHER ONE WITH A CAP.
!
THAT'S MINE!
WHO SAYS!?

YOTSUBA&! 8

KIYOHIKO AZUMA

Translation: Amy Forsyth
Lettering: Terri Delgado

YOTSUBA&! Vol. 8 © KIYOHIKO AZUMA / YOTUBA SUTAZIO 2008. All rights reserved. First published in Japan in 2008 by ASCII MEDIA WORKS INC., Tokyo. English translation rights in USA, Canada, and UK arranged with ASCII MEDIA WORKS INC. through Tuttle-Mori Agency, Inc., Tokyo.

English translation © 2010 by Yen Press, LLC

Yen Press
1290 Avenue of the Americas
New York, NY 10104

Visit us at yenpress.com
facebook.com/yenpress
twitter.com/yenpress
yenpress.tumblr.com

First Yen Press Edition: April 2010

Yen Press is an imprint of Yen Press, LLC.
The Yen Press name and logo are trademarks of Yen Press, LLC.

The publisher is not responsible for websites (or their content) that are not owned by the publisher.

ISBN: 978-0-316-07327-1

20 19 18 17 16 15 14

WOR

Printed in the United States of America

YOTSUBA&!

ENJOY EVERYTHING.

TO BE CONTINUED!

YOTSUBA&!

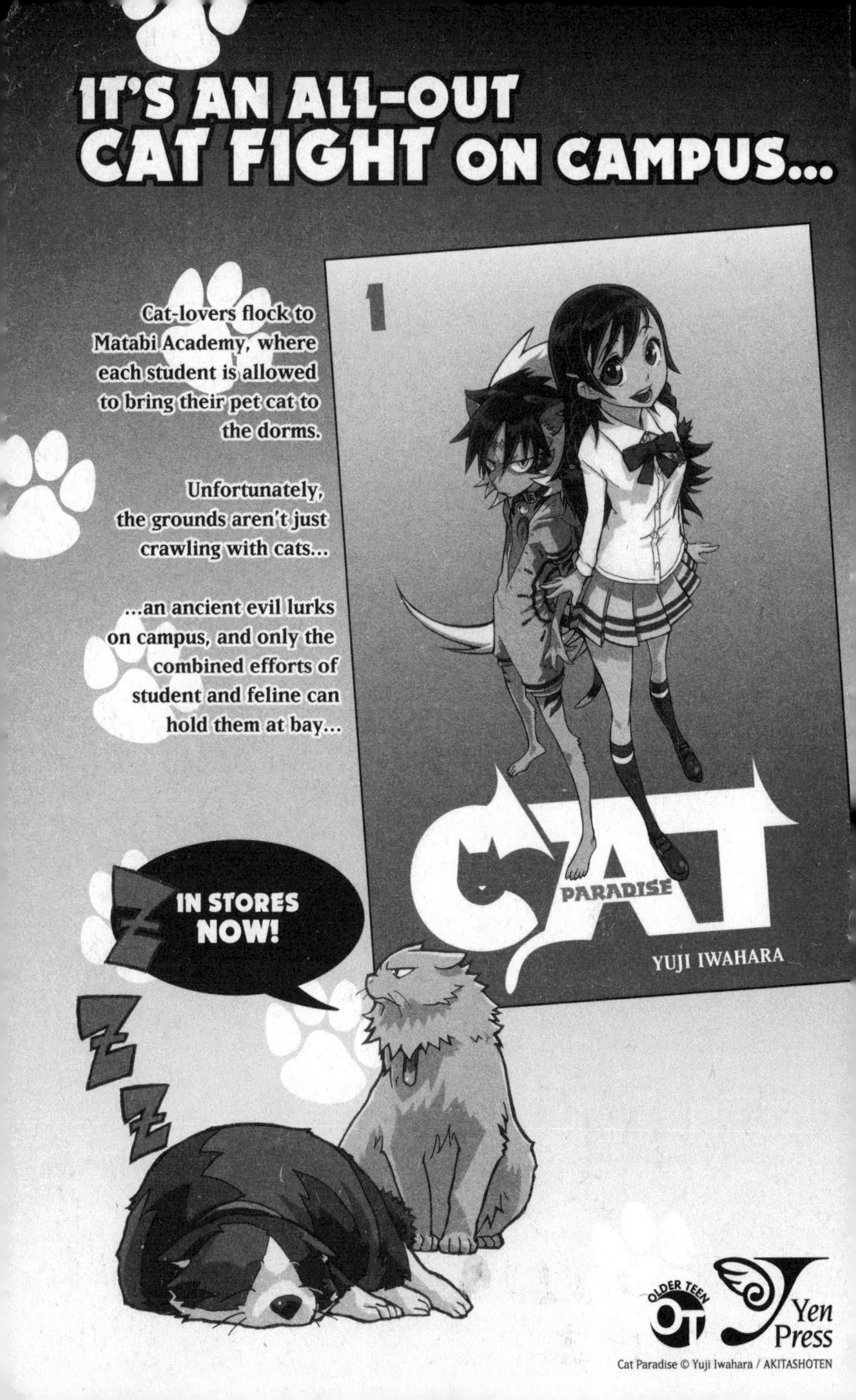
IT'S AN ALL-OUT CAT FIGHT ON CAMPUS...
Cat-lovers flock to Matabi Academy, where each student is allowed to bring their pet cat to the dorms.
Unfortunately, the grounds aren't just crawling with cats...
...an ancient evil lurks on campus, and only the combined efforts of student and feline can hold them at bay...
1
CAT PARADISE
YUJI IWAHARA
IN STORES NOW!
OLDER TEEN OT
Yen Press
Cat Paradise © Yuji Iwahara / AKITASHOTEN

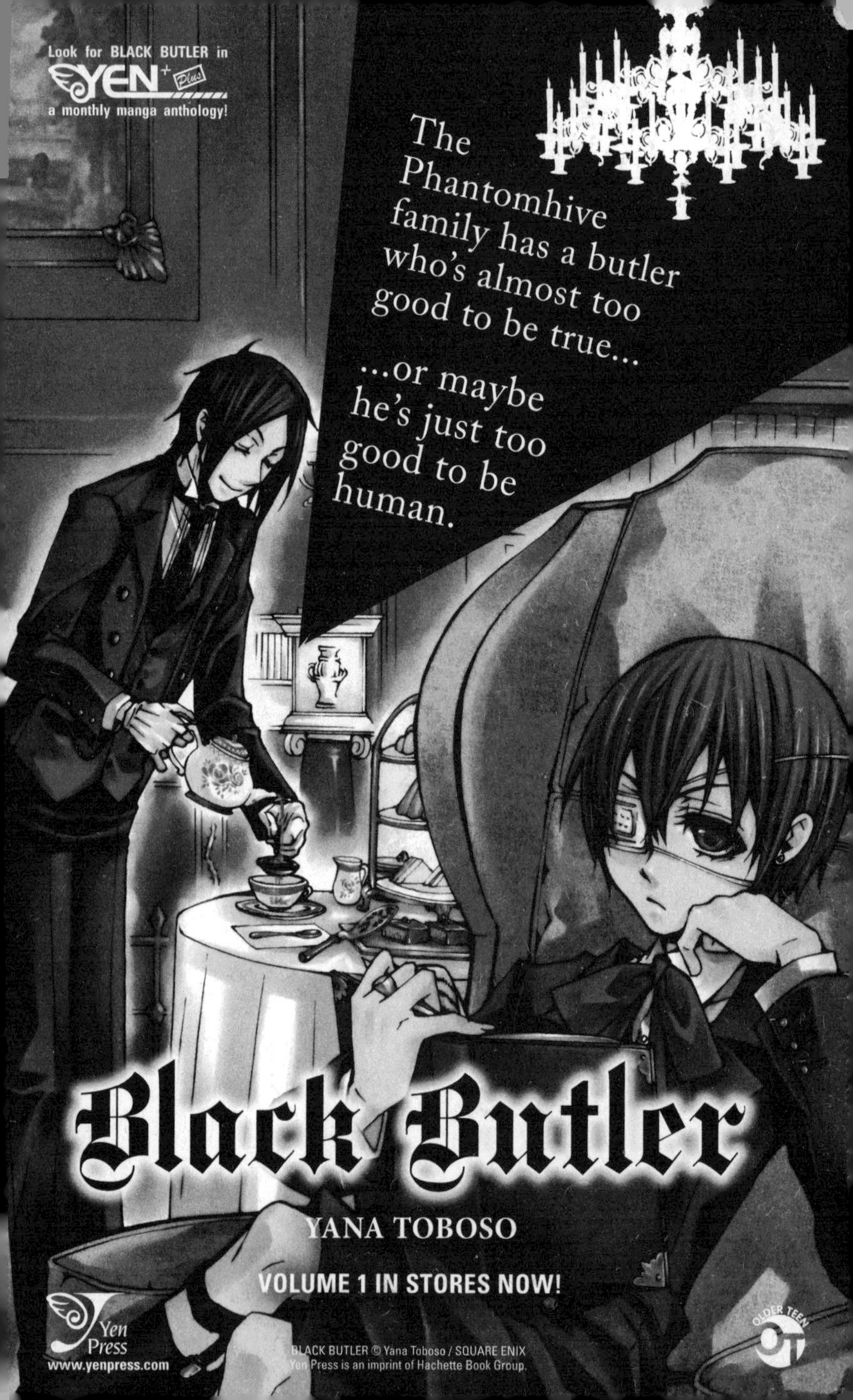
Look for BLACK BUTLER in
YEN+ Plus
a monthly manga anthology!
The Phantomhive family has a butler who's almost too good to be true...
...or maybe he's just too good to be human.
Black Butler
YANA TOBOSO
VOLUME 1 IN STORES NOW!
Yen Press
www.yenpress.com
BLACK BUTLER © Yana Toboso / SQUARE ENIX
Yen Press is an imprint of Hachette Book Group.
OLDER TEEN
OT

Kieli sees ghosts.

Harvey cannot die.

He will throw her world into chaos...

...and become her one true friend.

STORY BY **Yukako Kabei**

ART BY **Shiori Teshirogi**

KIELI

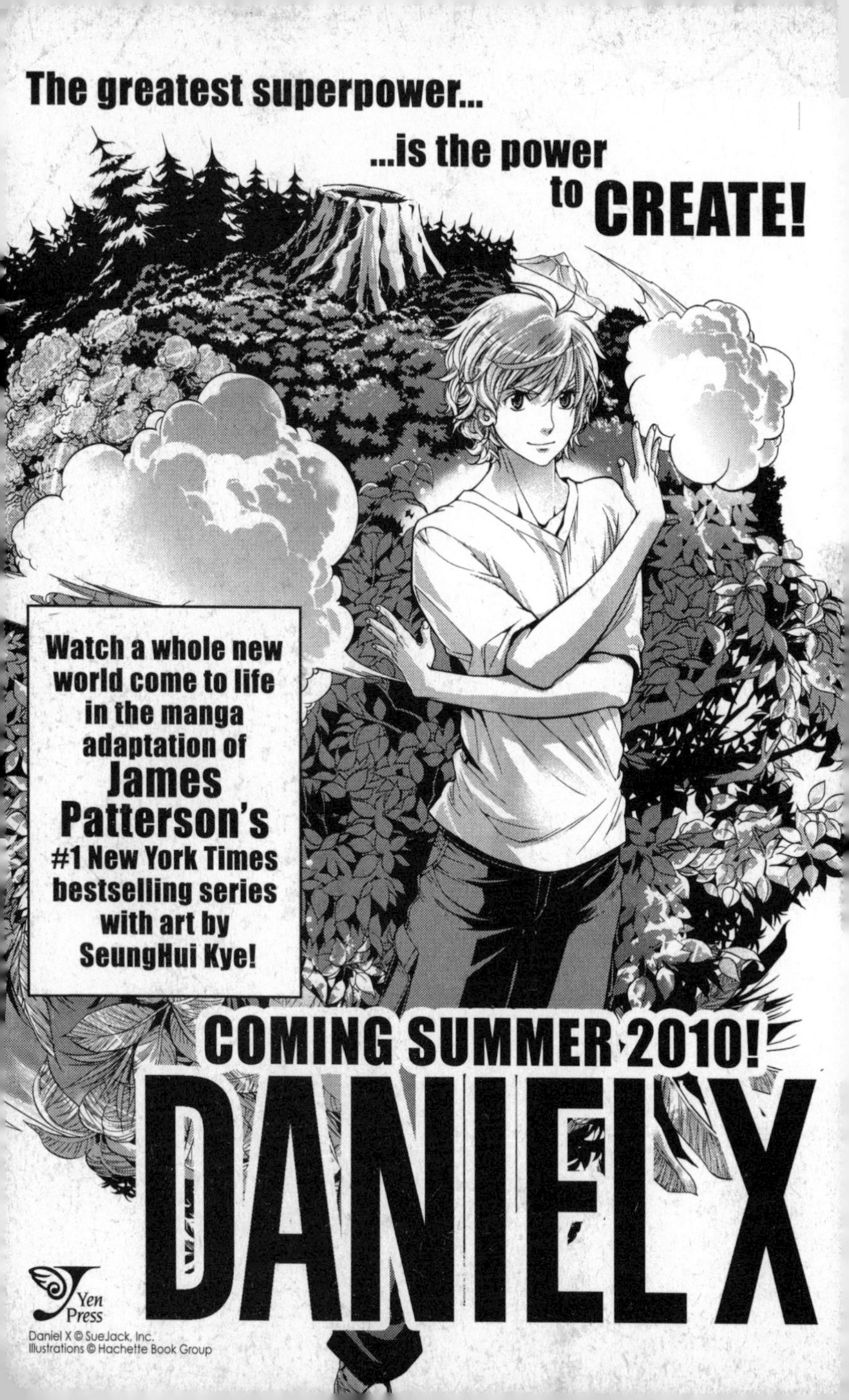
The greatest superpower...
...is the power to CREATE!
Watch a whole new world come to life in the manga adaptation of James Patterson's #1 New York Times bestselling series with art by SeungHui Kye!
COMING SUMMER 2010!
DANIEL X
Yen Press
Daniel X © SueJack, Inc.
Illustrations © Hachette Book Group

THE POWER
TO RULE THE
HIDDEN WORLD
OF SHINOBI...

THE POWER
COVETED BY
EVERY NINJA
CLAN...

...LIES WITHIN
THE MOST
APATHETIC,
DISINTERESTED
VESSEL
IMAGINABLE.

Nabari No Ou
Yuhki Kamatani

MANGA VOLUMES 1-3
NOW AVAILABLE